HOLY SOBRIETY IN MODERN RUSSIA

A volume in the
NIU Series in Slavic, East European, and Eurasian Studies
Edited by Christine D. Worobec

For a list of books in the series, visit our website at cornellpress.cornell.edu.

HOLY SOBRIETY IN MODERN RUSSIA

A FAITH HEALER AND HIS FOLLOWERS

PAGE HERRLINGER

NORTHERN ILLINOIS UNIVERSITY PRESS
AN IMPRINT OF
CORNELL UNIVERSITY PRESS
Ithaca and London

First published 2023 by Cornell University Press

Library of Congress Cataloging-in-Publication Data
Names: Herrlinger, Page, 1964– author.
Title: Holy sobriety in modern Russia : a faith healer
    and his followers / Page Herrlinger.
Description: Ithaca [New York] : Northern Illinois
    University Press, an imprint of Cornell University
    Press, 2023. | Series: NIU series in Slavic, East
    European, and Eurasian studies | Includes
    bibliographical references and index.
Identifiers: LCCN 2023003099 (print) |
    LCCN 2023003100 (ebook) | ISBN 9781501771149
    (hardcover) | ISBN 9781501771163 (pdf) |
    ISBN 9781501771156 (epub)
Subjects: LCSH: Ioann Samarskiĭ, Brother—
    Influence. | Russkaia pravoslavnaia tserkov'—
    Influence. | Spiritual healing—Russia—History—
    20th century.
Classification: LCC BT732.5 .H465 2023 (print) |
    LCC BT732.5 (ebook) | DDC 234/.1310947—
    dc23/eng/20230421
LC record available at https://lccn.loc.gov/2023003099
LC ebook record available at https://lccn.loc.
    gov/2023003100

This book is dedicated to all the people in Russia and around the world who have suffered from alcoholism or addiction, either their own or that of someone close to them

Contents

Illustrations

ACKNOWLEDGMENTS

The research for this book would not have been possible without the generous support of a Research Fellowship from the National Endowment for the Humanities, a Franklin Research Grant from the American Philosophical Society, and a grant from the Bowdoin College Fletcher Family Fund. I am also grateful to Bowdoin College for the gift of research time, and the Kemp Family Fund for supporting a 2017 symposium on women, faith, and revolution in Russia, at which I presented work related to this project. I also owe thanks and appreciation to the government of the Netherlands for sponsoring the working group "Orthodox Paradoxes" and to the organizers, Katja Tolstaja and Frank Bestebruertje. Any views, findings, conclusions, or recommendations expressed in this book do not necessarily reflect those of the National Endowment for the Humanities or other funders.

I would also like to express enormous gratitude to Sergei Iurevich Palamodov for sharing his knowledge and many materials that were essential to this project. I am also thankful for all the assistance I received from the librarians and archivists at the Russian National Library in St. Petersburg, the Russian State Historical Archive, the Historical Archive of the City of St. Petersburg, and the Archive of the State Museum for the History of Religion, especially Irina Viktorovna Tarasova. Photographs in this book have been reproduced courtesy of the Central State Archive of Documentary Films, Photographs, and Sound Recordings in St. Petersburg, where this project was born. I am also indebted to the wonderful librarians at Bowdoin College, especially Carmen Greenlee and Guy Saldanha, and to Rebecca Banks in the History Department, for helping me to keep my life together and for making our department such a fun place to show up every day.

Scholarship is never a solo project, and I am profoundly grateful to Catherine Wanner and one anonymous reviewer for reading a draft of the entire manuscript and giving me so many helpful and insightful comments. Thanks too to my editors, Amy Farranto and Christine Worobec, for all their support and feedback, and most of all, for believing in this project. Greg Freeze introduced me to the rich world of Russian Orthodoxy many years ago, and I never would have been able to pursue this project without the benefit of his prodigious archival work or his personal support. Bill Rosenberg's encouragement has also been much appreciated over the years. Thanks also to my Bowdoin students, who ask great questions and always keep me on my toes. I am profoundly grateful for my wonderful colleagues in History and Russian too.

This book has also benefited from comments and questions I received at conferences from Moscow to Los Angeles. I owe special thanks to many colleagues whose interests intersect most closely with mine, especially Alex Agadjanian, Eugene Clay, Scott Kenworthy, Nadia Kizenko, Irina Paert, Roy Robson, Stella Rock, Vera Shevzov, Francesca Silano, and Victoria Smolkin—you have all challenged, enlightened, and inspired me over the years, and every time I am with you, I know I'm with "my people." It is heartbreaking to know that Bill Wagner will never read the final version of this book; I was always grateful for his comments and congeniality, and after his untimely death in Fall 2021, I realized with profound sadness that I had been writing this with him in mind all along. I also deeply regret that my colleagues Sonja Luehrmann and Bob Greene are no longer with us, but their important contributions to the field have shaped this work in many ways, and I am immensely grateful to them. Reggie Zelnik left us all too soon and now almost two decades ago, but he is still a big presence in this book.

On a happier note, I'd also like to extend thanks to Kristen Ghodsee, whose example and encouragement have been hugely helpful in keeping me on track to finish this book. And to Dallas and Lorry, Kristin and Paul, and Arielle and Kavi, who have made the few evenings I took off from writing this book a lot of fun. Your friendship means a lot to me.

Last but never least, I want to thank the members of my family for all their support, patience, and love—especially my parents, my late grandmother Mimi, my brother David, and my amazing children, Alexander, Talia, Lily, and Laney, who were all much littler when I began this book! I know you didn't always understand my passion for this project, but I appreciate that you never questioned it. I also want to thank my husband, Paul, who still remains perplexed about why I chose to spend so much time with sober Russians rather than the more "fun" kind, but supported me nonetheless. I couldn't have done this without him, since writing a book while parenting four children and a big dog is always collaborative project, whether one wants to admit it or not. Most of all, I want to thank him for his patience and understanding. And finally, I want to express my gratitude for Mallomar and my (mostly) Bernese Mountain dog, Clover, the very best friends a human could ever have. They kept me smiling and walking when I needed it most, reminding me that spiritual support is essential and comes in lots of different forms.

A Note on Terms and Transliteration

Before 1917, the followers of Brother Ioann Churikov referred to themselves as "trezvenniki-pravoslavnye" (Orthodox teetotalers) to clarify the connection between their sobriety and their Orthodox identity. Nontrezvenniki tended to call them "Churikovtsy," to signify their common identification with Brother Ioann Churikov. This difference is meaningful, and it changes over time. I will refer to the group alternately as "trezvenniki," "Churikovtsy," "followers of Brother Ioann/Churikov," and whenever possible, by personal name.

"Bratets" (literally, "little brother") is an affectionate form of "brother," and "sestritsa/y" translates as "sister." "Trezvennik" is the singular male form, and "trezvennitsa" is the female. Members of Brother Ioann's commune, BICh, which existed from 1918 to 1929, will also sometimes be referred to as "kommunary" (plural) or, in the singular, as "kommunar/ka."

I have used the Library of Congress system of transliteration, except when referring to commonly known names, such as "Tolstoy" and "Maria." All translations are mine, unless otherwise indicated.

HOLY SOBRIETY IN MODERN RUSSIA

Introduction

In the 1990s, Aleksandr Zagoskin suffered from a dangerous addiction to alcohol; almost every workday on a collective farm ended in a drunken stupor so bad that he had to rely on a local truck driver to dump him in his yard at night. When she could, his wife Elena would drag him into the house; when she couldn't, he would sleep it off outside, even in the dead of winter. On his way to becoming a death statistic, Aleksandr decided at some point to seek help from a sober community in Vyritsa, a town not far from St. Petersburg, where, rumors held, even "incurable" alcoholics had been healed of their addiction.[1] Upon his arrival in Vyritsa, he was instructed to write a note to "Brother Ioann" Churikov, the preacher and faith healer who had founded the sober community there almost a century earlier. Aleksandr did as he was told, and before long, he too was able to put his addiction behind him. After his healing, his family committed themselves to the practice of "holy sobriety," Brother Ioann's prescription for a physically and spiritually disciplined life grounded in Scripture.

By the early 2000s, Aleksandr was making a good living in the lumber business, and his family was living peacefully in a small town in a remote corner of northern Russia. In the fall of 2008, however, their faith would be tested, when Aleksandr's sixteen-year-old daughter, Sveta, developed a life-threatening tumor on her ovaries. When school

1

doctors discovered the tumor and sent her to the hospital, Aleksandr and his wife brought her home before any treatment, believing, as Brother Ioann did, that her healing would come through prayer. The couple had witnessed how even individuals suffering from cancer and AIDS had been cured by prayers to Brother Ioann, and these healings in turn strengthened their faith. Thus, when Sveta's tumor was discovered, her father felt confident proclaiming in a television interview, "we believe that God will work a miracle with our daughter too."[2]

But Sveta's tumor continued to grow for the next two years, once again galvanizing state and medical authorities to take charge of her care. The case divided the local community, some of whom were Brother Ioann's followers as well, and Aleksandr and his family soon found themselves at the center of a minor media storm. Sveta wrote a letter rejecting surgery, but as public opinion leaned more heavily in the opposite direction, secular authorities were able to wear her down and convince her to have the procedure against her parents' wishes. While state medical authorities celebrated Sveta's quick recovery, others remained concerned that her siblings were still in danger on account of their parents' faith. After all, for the Zagoskin family as well as other followers of Brother Ioann, what proof had there been that the doctors' intervention—rather than their prayers—had saved her?

Belief in the power of prayer to heal has revealed equal amounts of faith and doubt in places throughout the modern world, especially when the lives of children have been at stake. While raising questions about the ambiguous boundaries between science and faith, as well as body, mind, and soul, cases like Sveta's almost inevitably provoke debates about the limits of parental rights, religious freedom, and state authority. But the story of the Zagoskin family also has deep roots in Russian history and culture. Although some of the details are specific to contemporary Russia, the dynamics of their case are part of a long-running story of faith, community, and controversy involving Brother Ioann and his followers since the end of the nineteenth century. Like the Zagoskins, hundreds of thousands of people believed themselves saved from addiction, illness, or misfortune because of Brother Ioann's prayers, and many went on to embrace his teachings. Similarly, generations of Brother Ioann's followers have encountered suspicion and persecution from state, medical, or religious authorities on account of their faith.[3]

Brother Ioann emerged as a preacher and healer in St. Petersburg in the 1890s, at the same time and on the same working-class streets that would produce the most impactful generation of Marxist revolutionaries the world had ever seen. These same neighborhoods lay at the heart of what historian Patricia Herlihy called the "Alcoholic Empire,"[4] a country existentially threatened by its collective drinking problem and also, consequently, obsessed with figuring out how to break free from its addiction. As the imperial capital and an important industrial city, St. Petersburg was the epicenter of a vast network of religious and secular temperance projects designed to save working-class people—and by extension, the quickly modernizing nation—from the disastrous consequences of their passion for vodka and other forms of drink. In spite of this competition for the hearts and minds of the local population, Brother Ioann's weekly preaching on scriptural themes and rumors of his "miraculous" healing abilities attracted a diverse and devoted following, which included many former alcoholics and some of the most spiritually and morally challenged individuals in the city. By 1916, a Petrograd journalist estimated Churikov's followers at one hundred thousand,[5] and by 1930 he was so well known that even Stalin wanted to meet him in person.

Both before and after the 1917 revolutions, Brother Ioann's followers, most commonly known as *trezvenniki* (literally, "teetotalers"),[6] found support for their lifestyle even among those who did not share their faith or vision. Churikov's ability to cultivate a productive community of sober, pious, and politically obedient workers seemed promising to Duma members and tsarist authorities searching for ways to promote a uniquely Russian path to modernity. He was lauded as a "spiritual elder" for the masses, a modern-day hero or bogatyr, and a miracle-worker in both the moral and spiritual sense, and he was praised for the orderly and prosperous colony he founded in the revolutionary year 1905 in Vyritsa. After 1917, and for some of the same reasons, the Bolsheviks considered the trezvenniki "useful" workers who shared dominant Bolshevik notions of the profane—that is, drunkenness, laziness, and excessive individualism. While militantly atheistic, the Bolsheviks thought it prudent to allow Brother Ioann and his pious followers to convert the colony into an agricultural commune.

Yet praise for Churikov and his followers has never been universal. On the contrary, the trezvenniki's extreme devotion to Brother Ioann and their pious and ascetic lifestyle kept them on the margins of mainstream culture for most of the twentieth century—first as devout followers of Brother Ioann suspected of deviance by the Orthodox Church, and then as religious believers living under a regime committed to atheistic socialism. Under both tsarist and Soviet rule Brother Ioann and his followers were subjected to varying degrees of persecution, from ridicule to official prohibitions or penalties to incarceration. They have endured no less than three eras of official intolerance, beginning in 1910–14, when long-simmering tensions between Brother Ioann and Orthodox Church authorities resulted in his excommunication in 1914. The second assault on the community began in 1927, during the early stages of Stalin's move toward collectivization, when religious believers who failed to trade in their faith for the militantly secular truth of socialist construction were imprisoned or exiled. One of Stalin's many victims, Brother Ioann died in a Soviet prison in 1933. A third period of increased surveillance and criticism came in the late 1950s and early 1960s under Khrushchev.

In response to these challenges, the trezvenniki have had to reinvent themselves in various ways, and at times they have divided over core issues, including their relationship to the Orthodox faith, the divinity of Brother Ioann, and the legitimacy of medical forms of healing. But holy sobriety has remained the defining core of their identity, and thus the root of their survival both as individuals and as a community. Today Brother Ioann's followers can justifiably claim to be part of the single oldest sobriety movement in Russia.

The evolution of Churikov's community of faith is the focus of this book. Written as a collective biography, it reconstructs and explores the experiences of Brother Ioann and his followers over the course of Russia's tumultuous twentieth century. A study of both "lived Orthodoxy" before 1917 and "lived socialism" after the revolution,[7] it examines Brother Ioann's identity as a charismatic spiritual leader and healer and analyzes the alternative community and culture the trezvenniki created on the basis of "holy sobriety," a simple yet powerful philosophy of life grounded in ascetic living, hard work, and Scripture. No less importantly, this book is concerned with the two societies and regimes that held the sober community at the margins, and both the logic and consequences of their repressive practices.

Many of the themes explored here—faith healing, addiction, and religious conversion especially—will be undoubtedly familiar to many readers, and my hope is that this book will serve as a basis for comparisons between Russians and individuals from different times and places. But the primary goal is to understand Brother Ioann and his followers as evolving moral, spiritual, and religious beings in the specific contexts of modernizing Russia, living in and engaging with the cultures of prerevolutionary Russian Orthodoxy and Soviet socialism. By providing a more intimate and multifaceted knowledge of my subjects and their experiences, my aim is also to cultivate a fuller and more meaningful awareness of the broader world in which they lived. For the historian, "the life story," Jill Lepore has observed, is "a means to an end—and that end is always explaining the culture."[8] While a case-study approach enables interpretive depth at different cultural and political moments, the longevity of Brother Ioann's sober movement opens up an unusually long view of modern Russian history and allows reflection upon shifting norms of identity, belief, and authority. In this way, the analysis also highlights previously unseen connections *between* "lived Orthodoxy" and "lived socialism."

What Sobriety Has to Offer

Until now Russia's drinking problem has understandably gotten far more attention from historians than sobriety. Excessive drinking has long been lamented as a national crisis and a persistent threat to public health, family life, gender relations, and work productivity. In addition to recreational drinkers, it was estimated as recently as 2015 that some ten million Russians were alcoholics, and Vladimir Putin has routinely reminded his people that each year in Russia "smoking, alcohol, and drug abuse [alone] claim 500,000 lives"—likely a conservative figure.[9] Before the 2020 pandemic at least, efforts to sober up the country appeared to be having positive, if uneven, results, with alcohol consumption down overall 43 percent between 2003 and 2016.[10] Nonetheless, an overwhelming majority of the Russian people have a keen and deeply personal awareness of the problem, and in a recent survey, 50 to 60 percent of Russian respondents pointed to alcohol and drug addiction as the country's single greatest challenge, over and above problems such as crime, terrorism, and national security.[11] And efforts to slay the notorious "green dragon" have been a consistent theme in Russia's modern history, involving a range of state and nongovernmental actors.[12]

As the tsarist regime took on the project of rapid industrialization and modernization in the late nineteenth century, new anxieties about Russian "backwardness" and the inability of a traditionally rural society to meet the demands of modernity forced state authorities, lay activists and philanthropic societies, and most of all, Orthodox priests to become more proactive with respect to solving the country's drinking problem. Of all these efforts to sober up the people, the most momentous came in August 1914 when Tsar Nicholas II declared the first ban on alcohol in history, in spite of the substantial loss of income this would mean for the state. Although not without positive impact, even the radical step of prohibition fell short, as alcoholics and entrepreneurial types quickly figured out ways around the state's dry law during World War I.

In spite of the continued ban on alcohol production into the early Soviet period, by 1922 one-third of Russian villages were engaged in illicit manufacturing.[13] Thus, like rulers before them, the proudly puritanical Bolsheviks found themselves the unhappy inheritors of Russia's drinking problem and struggling to answer the eternal question: What is to be done? In spite of the widely shared hope that the promises of socialism would mitigate the people's need to drink to excess, the Soviet record on the alcohol issue, long buried under false statistics and propaganda campaigns, would prove as dismal as the tsar's.[14] Just as widespread alcohol abuse had been both a symptom and cause of imperial Russia's problems, the same could be said of the Soviet Union—although not for a lack of trying. Mikhail Gorbachev's antialcohol campaign in the mid-1980s constituted yet another chapter in the long, often tragic story of Russian/Soviet temperance.

Many factors have contributed to the magnitude of Russia's drinking problem over time. While most historians agree on the importance of drinking as a deeply rooted cultural tendency tied to rituals of celebration and norms of masculinity,[15] others have highlighted the state's encouragement of alcohol consumption because of its profitability—at least in the short term.[16] The traditional tendency within Russian Orthodoxy to conceptualize excessive drinking as a sin rather than a disease has also prevented alcoholics from seeking effective treatment, in spite of the many temperance initiatives launched by the Church both in prerevolutionary and post-Soviet times. Another obstacle to abstinence or moderation stems from popular definitions of "alcoholism," since traditionally Russians have been reluctant to acknowledge someone has a drinking problem until they are at the end stage of chronic alcohol abuse, with their lives and bodies already all but destroyed.[17] Even among those who seek out treatment, the aim is often to get control of their drinking only so they can keep doing it.[18] But according to some experts, including Svetlana Moiseeva, formerly the director of the St. Petersburg branch of Alcoholics Anonymous, the single biggest obstacle to sobriety has been that many Russians cannot *imagine* a life without alcohol, so they cannot move beyond their drinking even when it threatens to destroy them and those they love.[19]

All this might reasonably lead one to conclude that Russians have as much of a problem with sobriety as with drinking. Yet this is not the case. On the contrary, many Russians do not drink and have never done so. This includes many religious believers, including the community of faith at the center of this study. While the factors encouraging sobriety are as varied as the reasons for drinking, it is no coincidence that religious faith is a common denominator. Like many believers, Brother Ioann understood that the tendency to indulge in alcohol (and related vices) is often a sign of a deeper spiritual problem, which in turn demands a spiritual cure. Seeing physical sobriety as merely the absence of a vice (not in and of itself a virtue), he taught that true sobriety was a matter of conscience and an ongoing spiritual project. The individual's successful liberation from a physical addiction to alcohol was thus only the first step in a longer journey of faith and self. "Holy sobriety" entailed a whole new way of being, grounded in ascetic living and hard work, the application of Scripture to all aspects of life, and the fullest possible integration of life and faith in the context of a supportive community. As such, it has appealed not only to alcoholics seeking to be free of their addiction, but to all kinds of people, men and women, rich and poor, looking to remake their lives.

As a collective biography of the trezvenniki, this study brings sobriety to the historical center and, in doing so, offers a new set of perspectives on Russian culture and society in the modern period. Drawing attention to sobriety rather than the usual suspects (drinking, war, poverty, or revolution) forces us to consider the flip side of almost every important issue—to focus on healing instead of illness or death, on personal agency and subjectivity instead of victimhood or victimization, on community and family instead of social disintegration, on productivity instead of destruction, and on faith and hope instead of despair. In short, when we explore the Russian past through the lens of sobriety— that is, the trezvenniki's lens—what emerges are stories not merely of tragedy, failure, or loss, but also of life, resilience, and salvation. For most observers of Russia in the twentieth century, dominated by epic stories of extreme violence and unrealized dreams, this is no minor shift in perspective. At the same time, focusing on Brother Ioann's community invites us to the local level, to the realm of everyday life, to the urban grass roots of Russia, where power was still personal, and family and community were key to survival. Given that most of Russia's twentieth-century history has been written with a focus on big ideas, major events, and massive institutions, this too is a productive shift in focus. Last but not least, the trezvenniki's faith-based perspective presents a meaningful complement to the secular questions and priorities that have continued to shape histories of Russia's modern period.

There have been other sober communities in Russia's past—among them, Tolstoyans, Baptists, Evangelical Christians, and many Old Believers and Muslims—and I would not want to suggest that their stories are any less worthy of our attention.[20] Nor do I want to argue that the trezvenniki's experience stands in some kind of metonymical relationship to Russian culture as a whole; on the contrary, I offer their story as one part of Russia's very diverse and fluid religious and spiritual landscape, the contours of which we are only beginning to appreciate in full. Drawing inspiration from Laura Engelstein's work on the self-castrating religious Skoptsy, I consider this study a kind of "folktale," in which the protagonists are believers "comprehensible in relation to the culture from which they emerged but of which they are not the ultimate expression."[21] However, unlike the Skoptsy, the Churikovtsy make a compelling case study not so much because they were eccentric but because in many ways they were not. As a community of predominately pious, sober, law-abiding workers, they were positioned, rather uncomfortably and precariously at times, on the very edge of both mainstream Orthodox and socialist culture. And while they were often pushed to the margins by those who did not understand or agree with their beliefs or way of life, they maintained their culturally liminal position intentionally, out of their conviction that the principles of holy sobriety were not only complementary but essential to the realization of true Orthodoxy in the modern world, and after 1917, to the success of the socialist project. Because the trezvenniki were at once insiders and outsiders, both exemplary and unique, their experiences can help us to interrogate the dominant beliefs, norms, practices, and values of the societies in which they lived, as well as to reflect in new ways on important issues and tensions in Russia's modern history.

Approach and Sources

I originally encountered Brother Ioann Churikov and his followers in connection with my first book, *Working Souls*,[22] which explores the changing religious landscape among the working population of revolutionary St. Petersburg before 1917. I was then, and remain now, interested in expanding upon what the historian Mark Steinberg has referred to as the "proletarian imagination," especially as it concerns thoughts on God and issues of the sacred.[23] But my decision to pursue further study of holy sobriety came about quite serendipitously—as if the project found me, rather than the other way around. A random encounter in a Petersburg archive in 2006 led within days to an introduction to a community of Churikov's followers. At the time, I must confess, I had no idea that any trezvenniki existed beyond the early years of the revolution, let alone a century later. In fact, I had never thought to ask. Like other scholars who had written on Churikov up to that point, I had fallen prey to the misguided assumption that they had not—could not—have survived decades of official atheism.[24] I was both stunned and thrilled to learn that I was wrong. During my first visit to one of their meetings, I felt as if I had been transported back in time. Although Churikov died in 1933, his followers were engaging in what I knew to be exactly the same practices that he had introduced over a century before. To be clear: the meeting in 2006 was not a recreation of a prerevolutionary experience in 1906; as I learned, communities of his followers had continued to practice much in the same way throughout the Soviet period. Again, I was intrigued: How could this be? What explains such resilience? How did their faith-based community survive communism? How did it survive Churikov's death? These are the main questions that informed my initial research, and ultimately this book.

At the end of that first meeting, I was invited to join members of the community for tea and conversation—another tradition started by Brother Ioann. As the only stranger at the table, I felt mildly uncomfortable. They were kind to me, but I could tell it was a tightly knitted group. Almost immediately, the community's leader, Vladimir Glinskii, turned to me and asked, "so why are you interested in Brother Ioann?" With all eyes at the table on me, I choked up the only answer I had, something along the lines, "Because he seemed so good and pious, and he helped so many people, and yet he was persecuted." Glinskii smiled and began nodding, and I knew I had said exactly the right thing. He then told me, "we'll have to introduce you to our archivist, Sergei Iurevich. He's running late, but he should be here soon." You have an *archivist*? I thought. Like I said, it's as if the topic found me. Sergei Iurevich Palamodov, the archivist, arrived a few minutes later, having been stopped for speeding on his way to the meeting (which proved to be a funny introduction to a prominent trezvennik, given the group's disciplined lifestyle). He invited me to speak with him a few days later, at which time he began sharing information and copious materials with me about Brother Ioann's life, including texts from the community's archive. I would later share with him what I had gathered from state and local archives and libraries. Our aims were different, but our collaboration was mutually beneficial, for which I am extremely grateful.

The promise of this case study stems in large part from the rich sources the trezvenniki and their detractors have left behind. As the target of ongoing official surveillance for almost a century, Churikov and his followers produced a wealth of institutional records, including official reports, clerical assessments, trezvennik petitions in defense of their faith, and secret polices files from the 1920s and 1930s. As the object of public scrutiny and debate, Brother Ioann and his followers were highly visible on the pages of the religious and secular press, especially between 1905 and 1917; Churikov's controversial status also made him the subject of biographical studies written by prerevolutionary religious scholars, "godless" journalists after 1917, and Soviet researchers from the 1920s to the 1960s. Due to the ongoing efforts of Ivan Tregubov, a Free Christian and Brother Ioann's close acquaintance, many of Churikov's spiritual conversations (*besedy*) and individual trezvennik testimonies were also recorded. In recent years, believers have published extensive correspondence between Brother Ioann and his followers and family, and compiled collections of photographs and key texts documenting the Church's persecution of the trezvenniki. With Palamodov's help, I have also been able to consult testimonies produced by trezvenniki in self-published (*samizdat*) form in the 1960s and 1970s, and seen up to this point by only a handful of people. Even more recently, a range of primary materials including personal testimonies, besedy, and newspaper accounts have been made available on websites maintained by the two main sober communities in existence today.[25]

Together, these sources have helped me to reconstruct the trezvenniki's experiences in detail, and to gain insight into their beliefs, fears, hopes, and motivations. As much as possible, I have tried to listen to their voices on their own terms and to figure out what mattered to them and why. What are the stories they told about themselves? What did Brother Ioann mean to them? How did they understand the world around them? Studying people of faith can be challenging, since so much of what matters to them as believers is expressed through silence, not words. But to the extent that it has been possible, my ability to make sense of the trezvenniki's perspectives on faith and self has been largely due to the extraordinary body of scholarship that has come out in recent years on Orthodox identity and subjectivity, and what has been called "lived Orthodoxy."[26]

As a term, "lived Orthodoxy" evolved in post-Soviet scholarship on Russian Orthodoxy in opposition to what was once characterized as "popular" (vs. elite) expressions of faith, and as distinct from "prescriptive" or "official" Orthodoxy.[27] The working definition has come to mean Orthodoxy as it is "encountered, understood, interpreted, and practiced" by believers,[28] and a central premise is that Orthodoxy should be approached as "a lived, adaptive, and flexible cultural system, rather than as a static set of rigidly applied rules and dictates."[29] This does not mean that church authorities have not attempted to shape the faith "from above," or that the laity has had full autonomy to believe or practice as they saw fit. Rather, as the religious historian Vera Shevzov has rightly cautioned, it suggests that instead of overdrawing the boundary between the "official" and the "popular," we should think more about lived Orthodoxy as Robert Orsi has done in the case of American religions—that is, as a conversation or ongoing dialogue between clergy and laity, in which each side shapes the other in various ways.[30] To be sure, the "conversation" could at times involve painful disputes and conflict over notions of the sacred, but importantly, the concept of lived Orthodoxy acknowledges and allows for a significant degree of lay agency, authority, and diversity.

As one reviewer has already asked me, "how Orthodox were the trezvenniki" anyway? This is a legitimate question, and one that remains very much alive today, given Brother Ioann's excommunication in 1914, the significant erosion of the relationship between Orthodox clergy and trezvennik communities during the Soviet period, and the belief among some (but not all) trezvenniki that Churikov was none other than Christ, the Second Coming. The simplest answer is that some of Brother Ioann's followers were and are more "Orthodox" than others in their beliefs and practices. The more complicated answer is one that animates much of the discussion in this book: their relationship to Orthodoxy has always been a subject of controversy, prompting debate over the nature of Orthodox identity. Indeed, at the heart of the Church's case against Churikov in the late tsarist era was not simply the question of "what does it mean to be Orthodox?" but also, "who gets to decide?" and "by what means?" Again, though, since my aim is to center the trezvennik perspective, it is important to start with the fact that many of them, including Brother Ioann himself, identified as Orthodox; more than this, they believed that because of the moral transformation he had inspired in them and their deep engagement with Scripture, they were *better* Orthodox.

Prior to 1917, Brother Ioann was understood by many of his contemporaries as a spiritual elder (starets) for the masses.[31] As recent scholarship has emphasized, *starchestvo* was a popular yet liminal institution within the Orthodox tradition, both diverse and evolving in nature.[32] Details about individual elders from the laity are often hard to come by, but the rich record of correspondence, petitions, and reports related to Brother Ioann offers valuable insight into the religious and cultural influences that enabled an otherwise ordinary individual to *become* extraordinary in this way. Given that a starets—much like the saint—is made not born, Churikov's reputation as "Brother Ioann" can also be seen as an expression of the needs, desires, and sensibilities of his followers. In this sense, his celebrity functions for us as a kind of mirror onto the religious, spiritual, and moral landscape of the Orthodox people as they navigated the same alienating and often unforgiving world that produced the 1917 revolutions.

The religious beliefs and spiritual sensibilities of Russia's working people can be a challenge to access as well, given that most workers did not leave personal accounts, and those that did either tended to be involved in revolutionary movements (and were often agnostic or atheistic), or they recorded their experiences with the help of people unknowledgeable about or even unsympathetic toward religious belief. But Churikov's followers (of all classes) were eager to testify to the transformative influence he had on them, and their testimonies thus offer us a unique (if not wholly transparent) window onto their understandings of self, sacredness, and spirituality. While pointing to gender differences within the sober community and in the construction of a trezvennik identity, sober testimonies reflect a widely shared need for the comfort, certainty, and hope provided by Scripture, and a desire for righteous living and personal dignity. To be sure, Brother Ioann's ability to work "miracles" was a powerful factor in his mass appeal, but his reputation for healing should be seen as both cause and effect of people's perception that he was a righteous person, close to God. Equally important were qualities such as compassion and accessibility, and the fact that he not only showed up for people in their moment of greatest need, but also worked to empower rather than control them. Although many of his followers became very dependent on him, the resilience of holy sobriety lay in the practical wisdom and spiritual consolation his followers found in his recorded scriptural interpretations, and in the memory of his compassionate approach toward all people; both would be embraced and shared by members of the sober community long after he was physically absent.

The Orthodox Church's struggle with Brother Ioann's popularity and spiritual influence reveals a disconnect between its concerns and priorities and the laity's needs in the final days of tsarism. Following the tsar's decision to grant the right to freedom of conscience and religious toleration in 1905, conservatives within the church hierarchy and professional missionaries were overwhelmed by evidence of "sectarianism" and a "kaleidoscope" of beliefs and behaviors among the Orthodox laity,[33] and they found in Brother Ioann an important test case for establishing the limits of lay religious authority. While the clergy had reasonable concerns about the nature of Churikov's influence on some of his more fervent followers, it is also clear that most trezvenniki cared a lot about the Church's teachings and approval, even as they passionately defended Brother Ioann. Together, the clergy's inability or unwillingness to acknowledge different perspectives among the *narod* (people), their tendency to judge and stereotype the faithful rather than nurture or guide them, and their decision to excommunicate Churikov pushed the trezvenniki further toward Brother Ioann and the certainty of Scripture, in effect solidifying their identity as a community apart. While exposing a profound lack of trust and respect between the laity and Orthodox authorities in the final years of the tsarist regime, the Churikov case also revealed a divide between the Orthodox Church and secular elites over the right of religious toleration, and highlighted competing priorities on the eve of the war.

For those deemed "sectarians" by the Church, including Brother Ioann and his followers, the 1917 revolutions offered a welcome (albeit temporary) liberation from fear of persecution, and a new opportunity to practice their faith openly, in spite of the Bolsheviks' commitment to secularism and atheism. As one of many diverse expressions of "the revolutionary imagination" in the 1920s,[34] Brother Ioann's colony-turned-commune became a rich experimental field on which the trezvenniki tried to bring their vison of holy sobriety into reality. At the same time, sober youth responded to the zeitgeist of this transitional era by approaching holy sobriety not simply as a set of Scripture-based principles for living, but as a movement with its own revolutionary potential. Although this period of relative autonomy was not to last, the trezvennik experience in the 1920s offers an interesting yet little-known chapter in the people's history of the revolution.

The various forms of state repression suffered by Brother Ioann's followers after 1927 will not seem unusual to anyone familiar with the persecution of religious groups under Stalin. But a microhistorical approach to the suppression of the sober community and commune in 1929 is revealing with respect to the practices of the emergent Stalinist state as well as the religious dimensions of popular protest during collectivization.[35] Trezvennik sources from the 1930s are thin, but samizdat testimonies and memoirs collected after the war make clear the trauma and disruption caused by the mass arrests and destruction of the commune in 1929, which scattered the sober population and forced it underground for decades. Yet they also show how Brother Ioann's followers were able to use the tools he had given them to make sense of their experience and move on. Long after his arrest in 1929, their practices and beliefs—which included a collective reimagining of him as a saintlike presence in their lives—would help them navigate the challenges of everyday life under atheistic rule and provide essential sources of hope, meaning, and community.

Continuing the theme of "lived socialism," the final two chapters of this book examine the trezvenniki's experiences after Brother Ioann's death in 1933, both as people of faith living under sometimes militant atheism, and as believers living and working in the Soviet socialist context. While sensitive to the repressive conditions of Soviet rule, the discussion moves beyond the "believer-citizen" dichotomy and narratives of victimhood that once dominated the field to emphasize the trezvenniki's agency and resilience as Soviet subjects. Mindful of the "permeability" of the boundary between the religious and secular in most believers' lives,[36] it also highlights the intersections and tensions that emerged between the trezvenniki's sober beliefs and practices on the one hand, and dominant Soviet social and cultural values and norms on the other. As Catherine Wanner has observed, the relationship between religious practice and the secularizing Soviet system was, after all, "mutually constituting,"[37] and the process of interaction inevitably shaped and changed both.

While the threat of persecution continued well into the 1960s, small but active communities of trezvenniki were reconstituted after the war. As Tamara Dragadze pointed out, the impact of Soviet repression was not only to force all religious life into the private sphere but also to empower new lay "specialists" (such as elders) in the domestic practice of faith, often with little training or oversight.[38] Importantly, and somewhat paradoxically, the "domestication" of religious life often meant that local communities of trezvenniki enjoyed more autonomy and individual elders more authority than they might otherwise have had. Thus, although sober communities proved remarkably resilient and continued to provide meaningful support to people suffering from addiction, illness, loneliness, and spiritual emptiness, the physical fracturing of the movement and the lack of coherent leadership led to distortions and differences in belief over time, especially over the question of Brother Ioann's divinity. At the end of the Soviet period, the trezvenniki would emerge strong in faith but irrevocably divided.

The more I learned about Brother Ioann and his followers in the course of my research, the more perplexed I became about their continued persecution by religious and state authorities. After all, it would be hard to find people less ostensibly threatening to any political or social order than the sober, hard-working, peace-loving trezvenniki. As I puzzled through the persecutory logic used by Orthodox missionaries before 1917 and godless critics and authorities after 1917, I came to appreciate multiple lines of (dis)continuity between Orthodox and Bolshevik approaches to religious belief and forms of deviance.[39] While sharing a tendency to think in Manichaean terms, Soviet atheists followed most closely in Orthodox missionary footsteps by othering Brother Ioann and his followers in an effort to solidify their own ideological and moral narratives. They also demonstrated a similar tendency to ignore the contradiction between their claims to be saving Churikov's followers from their false beliefs and the sometimes physically and spiritually violent means they used in the salvation process. Unlike the Orthodox Church, however, the godless made little effort to take the trezvenniki seriously or to understand their beliefs or perspectives, alternately writing them off as remnants of a backward religious past and distorting their beliefs and practices to their own ideological or political ends. They also seemed to care little about the (re)integration of the trezvenniki into socialist society; on the contrary, they targeted them primarily as a way to define Soviet norms and to integrate nonbelievers emotionally and spiritually into the broader atheistic collective.

Well into the 1960s, in fact, it seemed that the trezvenniki needed the Soviet system far less than Soviet atheists needed the trezvenniki as perpetual others, necessary both to their own self-definition and to the class struggle at its various stages. While some of Brother Ioann's followers continued to see sobriety as complementary to the socialist project, decades of "living socialism" would, for many, confirm the importance of faith and, more specifically, the saving power of holy sobriety. These conclusions were underscored by their success at drawing in new converts seeking a more meaningful life and a supportive community. For their part, Soviet atheists were frustrated in their attempts to explain the continued vitality of the sober movement and other sectarians through the 1950s and 1960s, and eventually would be forced to reconsider how they understood and approached issues of religious identity and spirituality. In this way, the resilience of faith-based communities contributed to the crisis of meaning experienced by proponents of atheism in the last decades of Soviet socialism.[40]

In their pursuit of hope and community outside the Soviet mainstream, the trezvenniki were far from alone, especially by the final decades of the socialist era; on the contrary, alternative communities of like-minded thinkers and believers, both religious and secular in orientation, had become an important source of support and meaning for many people by the 1960s–1970s.[41] Even in Moscow, the heart of the Soviet project, signs of religious life were becoming visible everywhere, forcing the godless "to concede that religion is not a marginal survival on the edges of modernity but rather a complex, living part of Soviet life."[42] At the same time, Aleksei Yurchak has observed, many people in the "last Soviet generation" were beginning to live *vne*—that is, outside the official socialist imaginary—and to pursue whatever "deep truths" or lifestyles (secular, aesthetic, and otherwise) that satisfied them personally, while remaining largely indifferent or agnostic to the official socialist regime.[43] In this context, the Soviet state—much like the Orthodox Church in the 1905 era—would be forced to confront the diverse spiritual needs of the people as well as the profound consequences of its inability to meet them.

The history of Brother Ioann and his followers over the course of the twentieth century serves above all as testimony to the enduring and transformative power of faith to heal, empower, and unite people; it also reflects a widely shared need among Russians to search for evidence of God at work in the world, and to work together toward building the kingdom of God on earth. At the same time, the trezvenniki's experience forces us to confront and appreciate the different paths taken by individuals in search of God, and in this way, contributes to a fuller sense of Russia's complicated religious past.

Unexpectedly, my desire to share the trezvenniki's story became even stronger on February 24, 2022, when Russia invaded Ukraine with the blessing of the Orthodox Patriarch Kirill (Guniaev) of Moscow. As the bloody conflict rages on, and people in Russia and around the world reflect on the meaning of the ideology known as *Russkii mir* (Russian World), the trezvenniki offer important perspective on what can often be an overly narrow understanding of Russia's religious traditions. Like many Russians in the early twentieth century, Brother Ioann and his followers loved the Orthodox faith and aspired to make the Church a more meaningful presence in people's lives and, by extension, in Russian society. But at the same time, their history as a persecuted yet enduring community of faith reminds us that Russia has never thrived because of an official insistence on religious or ideological conformity but rather in spite of it; the people's faith has taken many forms and inspired great hope, comfort, beauty, and strength, but it needs a culture of tolerance, freedom, and peace to reach its full potential.

CHAPTER 1

Becoming "Brother Ioann"

Belief, Behavior, and Image

In a widely circulated photograph taken around 1900, thirty-nine-year-old Ivan Alekseevich Churikov stands alone, with a neat beard and a half smile. Still youthful, he wears a long, plain tunic and a large pectoral cross; his posture is straight and calm as he rests one hand on the table beside him and holds up a copy of the New Testament with the other. Of the hundreds of photographs taken of Churikov over the next three decades, including some twenty-five portraits, it was this image of his younger self holding forth the Holy Book to the world that best captured his identity as "Brother Ioann."[1]

When pushed to talk about himself Brother Ioann would say he was a "simple" person, a phrase that conveyed his sense of humility, lack of formal education, and singularity of purpose: he identified above all as an Orthodox Christian, devoted to the Holy Mother Church, and to the spreading of the Word of God. His faith had not always been his priority, however; though raised in the Orthodox tradition like most Russian people, for the first thirty-three years of his life he was preoccupied with secular pursuits, including a young family and a string of businesses. After suffering a life crisis, he turned his back on his past and dedicated himself to Scripture, where he found the comfort and healing he needed to survive. In 1894 he moved to St. Petersburg, a quickly modernizing and deeply divided, unstable, and troubled city, where he threw himself into helping others find faith and healing through Scripture, just as he had. Within only a few years, he established a reputation as "Brother Ioann" and attracted a growing circle of followers, including many former alcoholics he had helped break free of addiction, and others he had "miraculously" healed of injury and disease.

As much as Churikov aspired to live simply, by and for the Word of God, he quickly discovered that his life as "Brother Ioann" was far from uncomplicated. With visibility came great vulnerability, and the more well-known he became, the more his identity would be shaped by others, most of all by the needs and hopes of those who loved and worshiped him. To his followers, he was an extraordinary individual endowed with great spiritual gifts and knowledge, and uniquely close to God, an identity that was prefigured and influenced in part by a broader cultural context of eldership among the laity. An important figure on the Russian Orthodox landscape, the "elder" has been characterized in different ways, most commonly as a kind of spiritual doctor or advisor, but also as a miracle worker or seer and sometimes a "living saint."[2] While typically a monk or priest, as in the case of the much beloved Amvrosii at Optina pustyn' (who died in 1891), recreated by Dostoevsky in the figure of Father Zosima, the elder could also be a charismatic layperson who took upon him- or herself the task of providing moral and spiritual leadership to ordinary believers. Although not all of Brother Ioann's behaviors fit the model of an elder, especially his choice of public preaching over more interior forms of communication such as letter writing,[3] the fact that many of Brother Ioann's followers seemed to see him as an elder shaped their expectations of him. In this sense, the identity was an important influence on his evolution as a spiritual figure and a critical source of the authority attributed to him.

Churikov's evolution as a preacher and healer was also shaped by his encounters with the clergy, both those he admired, such as the popular Father Ioann of Kronstadt and the ambitious Grigorii Petrov, as well as those who were suspicious of his intentions and growing spiritual authority among the laity. By 1900 he would endure two arrests and incarcerations as a result of clerical distrust, and these experiences profoundly affected him. Although Brother Ioann did not leave behind an autobiography or memoir as other famous individuals of his era often did, the controversy surrounding his identity forced him to speak about his beliefs and intentions on occasion, and thus produced a rich trail of documents, including his personal letters, occasional interviews, and petitions or statements directed toward authorities. These sources enable us to get an unusually close look at an unusual man, and to appreciate the factors and experiences that helped to shape him, his interactions with his followers, and his increasingly troubled relationship with the Orthodox Church. While highlighting how his followers inspired him and empowered his faith, they also show that clerical doubts about his preaching and intentions deeply grieved him. In the end the Church's persecutory tactics would have the opposite of their intended effect: the more church authorities went after him, the more Brother Ioann became determined to live and define himself by Scripture, and the greater his followers' devotion to him.

The Journey from Samara to St. Petersburg

When Ivan Churikov first arrived in St. Petersburg in 1894, little in his past suggested the role he was about to assume. He had been born far to the east, in a recently settled village, Aleksandrov-Gai, in the Novouzenskii district of Samara province, on January 12, 1861, just weeks before the tsar proclaimed the emancipation of the serfs. The region, which was relatively sparsely populated and far from the Orthodox centers of western Russia, was known for its religious pluralism, including communities of Old Believers and an assortment of non-Orthodox believers. Although Churikov's parents and sisters were extremely devout Orthodox and raised him to believe in God and the importance of faith, he had no formal religious training (aside from his elementary education at a parish school) and devoted his early adult years to starting a family and making money, primarily as a trader of fish, horses, cattle, and machinery. He had also owned a tavern at one point.[4] Life was good for the hardworking and prosperous merchant with a young family. But his fortune quickly turned. First, he was deeply shaken by the need to kill off many of his cattle during an outbreak of plague; he then suffered the death of his only child, a two-year-old daughter named Olga, and, shortly after, the complete mental breakdown of his wife, Evdokiia Grigor'evna.[5] In the wake of this series of tragic events, Churikov experienced a life-altering crisis.

The twenty-eight-year-old Churikov left behind everything he had known and turned toward God. In 1889, he gave away all his belongings to the poor and assumed a state of total poverty. Although some would later claim that he had lost his wealth in a fire, he told a journalist in 1914 that the choice to live in poverty was the result of his sudden realization that the pursuit of material wealth had corrupted him and that his wife's illness was punishment for his secular ways.[6] "My wife was suffering, and thus I had to suffer," he explained.[7]

Three years later, as his wife's health deteriorated, Churikov decided to seek out the spiritual counsel and prayers of Father Ioann of Kronstadt, by then the most popular priest in the empire widely known for his ability to heal, significant liturgical innovations, and unprecedented outreach to the poor.[8] Little evidence exists as to exactly what Churikov did while in Kronstadt or the extent of his contact with Father Ioann. Although Ivan Tregubov claimed that the two men had only one extended conversation in 1906,[9] it is likely that Churikov learned a lot by witnessing the charismatic Father Ioann tend to the spiritual needs of suffering people,[10] and the fact that Churikov carried the priest's image in his pocket suggests that at the very least he admired him very much.[11]

Father Ioann's prayers did not save Evdokiia, however, and Churikov interpreted his wife's untimely death as a sign that God was still punishing him for his dishonest past. As she lay in the asylum for the final years of her life, he dealt with his own prolonged state of grief by "wandering" through the countryside for two years, wearing heavy iron chains to intensify the experience of suffering and to test his own spiritual endurance. To what extent Churikov's renunciation of his former ways was an act of kenosis, the deliberate "emptying" of one's life, is hard to say.[12] But the decision for someone who had experienced a great loss to embrace a life of active piety and devotion was in line with the dominant cultural currents of the day. Indeed, the "charisma of renunciation," Laura Engelstein has observed, attracted many Russian believers from the Orthodox founding fathers and contemporary monks to those on the far margins of Russian religious life, including the extremely ascetic, self-mutilating, self-castrating Skoptsy.[13]

The Orthodox practice of "strannichestvo," or spiritual wandering, was especially widespread in the nineteenth century. Although generally associated with folk as opposed to institutionalized religiosity, it attracted people of all classes, including Tolstoy, who popularized the idea in many of his works. As the ethnographer Sergei Maksimov documented in the late 1870s, wanderers took to the road for many reasons (among them poverty or homelessness), but often as a form of penance, a way to walk off their pain and past sins and, for some, to please God by means of a "*podvig* [great spiritual feat]."[14] Distinct from the ritual of "pilgrimage," Pål Kolstø has explained, the point of wandering was the journey itself, "on being under way," and in this sense, an expression of the Christian's belief that he or she is but "a stranger on this earth, under way to his true home, which is the kingdom of God."[15]

With the explosion of printing in the last decades of the nineteenth century, religious practices like wandering were becoming more popularized than ever before, just as Churikov was struggling to make sense out of his future. Literary works extolled the renunciation of life's pleasures in the pursuit of faith, and of the self to live for others, as in the case of Nekrasov's Vlas, the repentant peasant who found God and was reborn to a life of wandering, suffering, and collecting alms to build a church. Late nineteenth-century religious literature also regularly encouraged believers to follow the model of the saints in their own lives. For instance, an 1895 series entitled "Lessons from the Lives of the Saints" offered readers accessible instructions on how to lead an ideal Orthodox life, while the popular *Troitskie listki* (1884–1917), published by the Trinity-St. Sergius monastery, highlighted heroic tales of holy fools and wanderers as alternative models of identity for individuals from all walks of life.[16] As one author put it: "being like the saint did not mean copying the outward actions of the saints, but rather their *spirit*—their firmness of faith, their passionate love for God, their obedience to the will of God, their meekness and endurance, their zeal for salvation, or, as the Apostle succinctly says: [we] *must imitate their faith* (Hebrews 13:7)."[17]

Churikov's two years of wandering effected a personal transformation so complete that he would forever see them as a breaking point in his life. Although he would not speak of having been "born again," he made a conscious decision never to look back on his former life—a piece of advice he would offer many other people over the coming years. As revealed in a series of letters written in the late 1890s, he found the experience of grief—or more precisely, the act of suffering and conscious renunciation—to be an excellent teacher of faith. While instructing him in God's mercy, it had opened his heart to Scripture as a source of healing and knowledge.[18] But with time, he came to reject the otherworldliness associated with wandering and decided to settle down both physically and spiritually. Instead of a life of contemplation and service in a monastery, he took the opposite path into the very heart of secular modernity.

In 1894, after two years on the road, thirty-three-year-old Churikov arrived in St. Petersburg determined to begin his life anew, with nothing but a Gospel in his pocket. Even after settling down there he retained the ascetic habits of the wanderer, embracing his poverty and committed to regular fasting and prayer. For the rest of his life, he dressed in simple clothing, including a silk peasant-style shirt, high black boots, and an oversized cross around his neck. While picking up jobs as a carpenter to support himself, he devoted his free time to visiting the local parish church and reading the Gospel to anyone willing to listen, including people who lived on the streets. Scripture, which more than anything else appears to have saved him from anger and deep despair, became the foundation stone of his new self.

Churikov lived in local flophouses for some time but eventually found a more decent living situation on Vasil'evskii Island with a shoemaker, Vasilii Antonovich, his wife, and their children. The couple took him in, and he helped both of them recover their lives; Vasilii conquered a severe drinking problem, and his grateful wife Vera believed that Churikov's prayers had cured her of scarlet fever. He soon grew very close to the couple and came to think of them as his "son and daughter," comparing them to the early Christian missionary couple Aquila and Priscilla because of their critical role in support of his preaching.[19] Three days a week, Vasilii allowed him to hold readings in his shop, and on other days he visited private apartments in order to read and discuss the Gospel.[20] As he would explain, his intent was to make the Word more "religiously and morally" available to ordinary people (the *narod*), and thereby make himself useful to the Holy Church.[21]

It was around this time that Churikov began to introduce himself as Brother Ioann. Although the reason for this varies by source,[22] one convincing explanation points out that the title *bratets*, an affectionate form of "brother," was quite common in the region where Churikov had been raised, particularly among the so-called *besedniki*, a grass-roots current within Orthodoxy that began to spread in the 1830s and 1840s. Founded by a peasant, Shchlegov, the movement's adherents were devout Orthodox who were skeptical about the spiritual integrity of the clergy and organized regular prayer meetings (*besedy*) to discuss Scripture on their own, even as they continued to observe all the rituals of the faith. Like Churikov, they practiced an ascetic lifestyle, giving up drink and meat, along with all forms of secular pleasure such as dancing and singing.[23] Although Brother Ioann did not identify as a *besednik*, his new behavior had much in common with their traditions and likely resulted in part from exposure during his youth.

Churikov's Critique of Modern Life and the Origins of Holy Sobriety

As Churikov settled into St. Petersburg in the mid-1890s, he found a city undergoing a profound transition, coinciding with the death of Tsar

Aleksandr III and the reign of the last Romanov, Tsar Nicholas II (1894–1917). As a center of power and industry in the rapidly modernizing empire, the capital city was developing quickly and unevenly, giving rise to serious concerns about the moral and spiritual health of the urban working classes, as well as their political volatility. With thousands of peasants migrating to work in the factories each year, the streets where Churikov lived and preached were flooded with poverty, violence, and despair; indeed, they were the same neighborhoods that would give rise to not one but three revolutions in the next twenty-five years.

Living in one of the capital's most impoverished neighborhoods, Churikov encountered a great deal of suffering, equal to if not greater than his own. In the factory districts especially, the air was so saturated with dust, soot, and nasty fumes that it was almost impossible to breathe. Workers' housing was cramped and filthy, as well as loud, foul-smelling, and often very dangerous, especially for young women. And those who had roofs over their heads were the lucky ones; the city's bridges and streets served as home for some ten thousand people, and the flophouses took in even more, if only temporarily.

In these conditions, life was as psychologically challenging as it was physically unhealthy. Wages were low, hours were long, and the unpredictability of the job market was matched by the certainty of everyday *katastrofy*, including every kind of misfortune from workplace and traffic accidents to rabid dogs and building collapses.[24] Illness (especially typhus and cholera) was everywhere, as was violence in its many forms. Many people drank to escape. Seeking out vodka or some other distilled spirit, they took temporary refuge in taverns.[25] But drunkenness in turn led to extreme and destructive behaviors—not only the more mundane vices such as smoking, swearing, fist fighting, or gambling, but also morally heavier crimes like sexual assault, theft, domestic violence, and even murder. Indeed, contemporary estimates held that as many as 90 percent of crimes were committed by people who were intoxicated.[26]

To be sure, there were signs of hope as the new century approached. Temperance activists, including local clergy and lay philanthropists, were working hard to provide the urban population with opportunities to educate themselves and healthier ways to spend their free time, away from the tavern. Since the 1880s, the capital's clergy had set up a large network of temperance tearooms throughout the city, the most popular of which were associated with the Aleksandr Nevskii Society, under the direction of much beloved Father Aleksandr Rozhdestvenskii.[27] The most well-known lay activist in St. Petersburg was Countess

Sofia Panina, who founded the very successful Narodnyi Dom ("people's house") on Ligovskii Prospekt in the heart of the city.[28] More efforts would soon emerge as well, including Father Georgii Gapon's Assembly of Russian Mill and Factory Workers, which helped organize workers in the interest of self-help and mutual aid.

But the city's problems were bigger than the solutions, and despair outweighed hope. While the revolution of 1905, which began with a petition of grievances from Father Gapon's workers, has rightly been seen as the most visible manifestation of the people's discontent, another equally powerful sign was St. Petersburg's tragic reputation in the first decade of the twentieth century as the suicide capital of the world, with the highest rates among young members of the working classes. Poverty—or more specifically, the hopelessness of an individual overwhelmed by need—was cited as the most frequent cause of suicide, followed closely by shame, typically associated with sexual transgressions.[29] Indeed, one of the first people Brother Ioann met after arriving in St. Petersburg was a man about to jump off a bridge, a memory that haunted him for the rest of his life.[30]

The extent to which Churikov arrived in the Petersburg slums with any kind of coherent vision, philosophy, or sense of the role he should play there is unclear. Of course, his own perspective on the urban eco-system was that of an outsider; he was new to the city, had never worked a factory job, and had consciously chosen to live in poverty rather than wealth. But the more he stayed and observed the habits and hardships of the working people of the capital, the more he became convinced of their desperate need for spiritual guidance and comfort, especially in the form of Scripture and prayer.

With his own religious sensibilities heightened by the experience of loss, Brother Ioann understood the massive poverty of Petersburg's working-class slums as far more spiritual than material in nature. For him, the capital was less an industrial hell, in which workers struggled against powerful forces of exploitation and dehumanization, than a modern-day Sodom, in which the masses lost themselves in sin and vice and chose to remain distant from God.[31] Piety, he observed, was no longer "in fashion" on the urban streets: "we are ashamed to profess [our faith in] Christ and to talk about Him, because we will be called stupid . . . but [when] we talk about debauchery they say to us: 'that's so great!'" Even those who considered themselves Christians routinely went to taverns, seeking out the false promises of spectacle and the cheap pleasures of the city rather than turning to God. But in the taverns, "longing does not leave us," he would warn: on the contrary, intoxication invariably serves as a gateway to other sins and vices, and in turn, to despair and even suicide.[32]

In many ways, Churikov's perspective echoed that of local Orthodox clergy, who were increasingly vocal about the decline or absence of faith among urban workers, especially the factory youth. Yet, as much as he remained a stern critic of modern life, he refused to accept the Church's pessimistic conclusion that the world was beyond hope because of man's inevitable inclination to sin. At the same time, he rejected the secular revolutionary's agenda of violent protest and apocalyptic change. On the contrary, Brother Ioann believed deeply in the possibility of redemption for every individual through peaceful means. Unlike many clergy who doubted that ordinary people had the willpower to resist the temptations of the secular city, and unlike revolutionaries who questioned the ability of individuals to effect meaningful change on their own, he believed unconditionally in each individual's "worthiness before God" (*bogopodobie*), in their capacity for self-improvement and desire for dignity, and in their ability to choose good over evil.[33]

The key to salvation, Brother Ioann would insist, was the Word of God. In contrast to the traditional peasant conception of the Bible as "a sacred object in the narrowest sense of the term—taboo in everyday life and used in strictly defined cases: for divination, protection, treatment,"[34] Churikov took a far more expansive view. While never dismissing the importance of the Holy Sacraments as a channel of divine grace, he saw Scripture as the essential tool with which to cultivate the individual's natural inclination to be good. "It is not enough for a man to be born from his mother, he must also be warmed by the Word of God, and only then will he be a child of God," he preached. "Just as a living [bird] cannot turn out from an unheated egg and can easily break from the slightest shock, so a person who is not warmed by the Word of God cannot be a heavenly bird, that is, a spiritual person, and he is easily broken by an insignificant push."[35] Likewise, scriptural guidance was needed to repress bad inclinations, for "in whom there is the Word of God, [there] is also the fear of God, which keeps him from vices and crimes." "No one wants to be a drunk or a thief," he continued, "but in reality they exist . . . because [people] don't embrace the teachings of Christ. Without the teachings of Christ and the apostles no one can be good, honest, and just. But if we embrace Christ's words, then they will cleanse us."[36] While serving as a shield against temptation and an inoculation against illness, the Word of God provided essential nourishment for the human soul, since "whoever feeds on the words of Christ has neither longing, nor need, nor sorrow, nor sighing, nor illness, but an endless life, which is always good and cheerful."[37] For these same reasons, Churikov believed, Scripture was the source of salvation not just for each individual, but for society as a whole.

Churikov's views on the condition of the modern individual were perhaps best captured in his interpretation of John 5:1, the story of the paralytic who had been completely immobilized for thirty-eight years. Lying just steps away from the healing pool (*kupal'nia*) that would have given him a full life, he had never been able to dive in since no one had offered to help him get there. When Jesus arrived at the pool, however, he asked the paralytic if he wanted to be healed. When he replied yes, Jesus did not lift him up, but rather commanded him to pick up his mat and to walk. On hope alone, the man did as Jesus instructed, and he was healed.

The pool, in Churikov's interpretation, was the Word itself—which was there for each and every individual who wanted to be healed, no matter how long they had suffered. His role, or so he believed, was to bring people to the pool, especially those who believed it beyond their reach. Going door to door with Bible in hand, he would ask them if they wanted to live, teach them about Scripture, and reassure them that God was on their side, no matter who they were or what sins they had committed.[38] By reassuring them that God exists for those who seek him out, he sought not only to comfort people but to empower them with the courage to choose a new life, founded in faith and the Word of God.

Early Healing and Preaching

In his early days as a preacher, Churikov's spiritual conversations (besedy) attracted only five or six people at a time.[39] But word about Brother Ioann's unusual healing abilities spread quickly, and this more than anything else drew people to him. Among them was the working-class couple Maria Vasil'evna Kuz'mina and her husband Evlampii Kuz'mich Kuz'min, who first approached him in the winter of 1895. Maria was just thirty at the time, but her lived experiences made her seem much older. Like many urban migrants, the couple had lived for years in a cycle of hard work, poverty, and ill health, made all the more difficult by their own poor decisions, bad behaviors, and tragic circumstances beyond their control. Their prolonged suffering bleeds through their attempts at a straightforward narrative of their lives, and the power of Brother Ioann's simple message of faith and compassion comes through as well.[40]

When the couple married in 1888, Evlampii was employed as a porter, but his severe drinking problem was already compromising his work and his relationships. Raised in a foundling home, he had started drinking at age fourteen. Over the years, he failed at a string of positions, including a stint as a conductor, and often drank his way through both his own wages and his wife's. Maria worked as a laundress and maid to support them. Although she lived apart from her husband, she gave birth at least eight times but lost five of her children in infancy. The cause of their deaths is not clear, but Maria claimed to have suffered from serious "female problems," which sent her to the hospital twice. The couple did not speak of their grief directly, but Maria admitted that after they lost their fourth child, she suffered from serious anguish (*toska*) and soon betrayed her husband with another man. When she confessed to him, he kicked her out. Although the couple reconciled, the marriage remained in trouble. Evlampii admitted to being deeply ashamed of his drinking, which he knew kept the family in poverty, and in 1894 he tried in vain to be cured of his addiction at the hospital in Obukhovo. But after Maria's adultery, he remained distraught and refused her pleas to seek out Brother Ioann, claiming "it'll be worse for you, since if I stop drinking, I won't be able to look at you." Still tormented by her adultery as well as his own demons, he exercised what little patriarchal authority he still had and ordered her to repent her sin.

One year later, in the winter of 1896, Brother Ioann responded to a request from Maria to visit her husband, who was suffering from chronic pains in his arm and finding it difficult to work. Although still reticent, Evlampii agreed to the meeting out of desperation. "Change your way of life," Brother Ioann advised firmly. "Pledge to the Lord that you will not do what you have been doing, and the Lord will heal your arm."[41] Then, in what the couple would recall as a strikingly intimate moment, Brother Ioann knelt down before their icons. They joined him as he prayed for Evlampii's healing. He then stood up and offered Evlampii a piece of the communion wafer he'd brought from church, along with the instructions to pledge to God that he would never drink again. In spite of his lingering skepticism, Evlampii did exactly as he was told, and within several days the pain in his arm had disappeared, as had his urge to drink. Evlampii remained sober from then on, his family life improved, and he and Maria became more active in their local parish.

A strikingly similar pattern of events would be told by many others in the years to come, and by 1896–97, Brother Ioann found himself inundated by people hoping to be healed of a physical illness or freed from addiction. They were a diverse crowd of men and women of all ages and classes, including peasants and townspeople, actors and widows, merchants and landowners, colonels and generals.[42] But the majority appear to have been artisans or skilled workers—blacksmiths, saddle and harness makers, plasterers, plumbers, shoemakers, tailors, house painters, yardmen—as well as small traders or shopkeepers.[43] Whatever their background or occupation, however, the addicts arrived at Churikov's doorstep in a shared condition of shame and desperation that cut across the class lines that typically divided the city's population. Brother Ioann never refused anyone, even those commonly ignored or reviled, including homeless drunks, prostitutes, thieves, hooligans, and murderers.

Unlike Maria and Evlampii, many seeking Brother Ioann's help openly admitted to lacking belief in God—not so much because they were consciously atheist or agnostic, but because they had never truly engaged with faith or developed a religious consciousness of any significance.[44] Among them was Sergei Ermolov, a thirty-year-old shoemaker with four children and a severe drinking problem, whose relationship to the Orthodox Church was rooted in habit alone. He made a confession every year, but "only to brag about [his] sins," and then went right back to drinking. After a single meeting with Brother Ioann, however, Ermolov not only became sober, but also began to attend church regularly.[45]

In spite of success stories like Ermolov's, clerical responses to Churikov were mixed. Given long-standing concerns about the spiritual health of the urban population, especially those recently migrated from the village, some clergy welcomed Brother Ioann's efforts to sober up workers, spread scriptural values, and send long-lost Orthodox back to church. This was especially true of those who got to know him personally, including his own parish priest, Father Vasilii Lebedev at the Spaso-Preobrazhenskaia Church.[46] Others included Father Dmitrii at the Church of the Sign (Znamenie), who soon became beloved among Brother Ioann's followers, and Father Ioann Al'bov at John the Baptist (Ioann Krestitel') on the Vyborg side, who had educated him in Zakon Bozhii.[47] Churikov was also in contact with Father Grigorii Petrov, a young and enthusiastic graduate of the St. Petersburg Spiritual Academy, active in the church's internal mission, the Society for Religious and Moral Enlightenment, and a big presence in working-class neighborhoods. Petrov served as a kind of tutor to Brother Ioann and was so impressed by his success at bringing Scripture to life for ordinary people that he dedicated a section of his 1904 short novel *Zateinik* to him.[48]

However, not all parish clergy were receptive to Churikov's efforts. While some temperance activists saw him as competition,[49] others openly questioned his knowledge of the Orthodox faith and expressed concern about the nature and scope of his influence among the laity. In 1897, for example, when Churikov tried to send thirty-two of his followers to Father Ioann Labutin for confession and communion, the priest apparently turned them away, instructing them to stay sober for a month or two and return after Maslenitsa (the last week before Lent). He scolded them for not fasting properly before communicating, adding, "Don't you know the rules? Aren't you Orthodox? Could it be that you are sectarian?"[50] Undeterred, Churikov's followers found another priest, a Father Megorskii at the Church of the Sign, who let them make a confession and then (after they had fasted properly) welcomed them back a few days later to receive communion. Clearly wary of Churikov's growing authority, Father Labutin continued to lash out at the trez-venniki both orally and in print.[51] As time would tell, he was not the only local priest to harbor such suspicions.[52]

Churikov also found himself at odds with Orthodox authorities early on, primarily because he was a layman preaching Scripture without proper oversight.[53] As Irina Paert has discussed, the Church's concern about the emergence of charismatic lay preachers was especially acute by the late nineteenth century, just as Brother Ioann was beginning to develop a following.[54] It stemmed from the challenge to church discipline and hierarchy that lay preachers posed, as well as unease about their influence on ordinary believers. This concern had deepened with the increasing accessibility of Russian translations of the Bible. As Ekaterina Mel'nikova has observed, lay engagement with the Bible was still relatively new among the Orthodox laity, but by the late nineteenth century, interest in "the book of books" was high.[55] Although most clergy agreed that Orthodox believers should be educated in Scripture, they remained suspicious of the laity's curiosity with respect to the acquisition of religious knowledge. Without close oversight, they feared, lay Orthodox might evolve their own interpretations of Scripture and challenge clerical authority as in the case of Western Protestantism; the spread of the evangelical movement known as *shtundizm* among the Orthodox in Ukraine in the 1870s–1880s had heightened these concerns.[56] At the same time, the Church was wary that devotion to any given lay preacher—their beliefs and their person—could become either excessive or dangerous.

In the summer of 1897, Churikov was deported from St. Petersburg to his native village in the Samara region. While questions about his activities had been circulating for some time, the immediate catalyst was a report from Father Sorokin, the bishop (*blagochinnyi*) of Novouzensk, that Churikov was spreading "incorrect" ideas among the local Orthodox population. These included claims that there was no John the Baptist, that anyone can preach the Gospel, and that in light of his ability to heal alcoholics and the chronically ill, he was a "special emissary of God."[57] In response to Sorokin's report, the Spiritual Consistory directed the governor of Samara to look into Churikov's mental state. Local religious authorities, under the careful watch of the staunchly conservative procurator of the Holy Synod, Konstantin Pobedonostsev, immediately took note of the case, but secular officials moved less enthusiastically; even the police who were supposed to break up his meetings felt little incentive to act, given the fact that Churikov was making their job easier by turning around the lives of local thieves and hooligans. Nonetheless, in early 1898, Churikov was sent to the psychiatric ward of a zemstvo hospital (in Tomashev Kolok, near Samara), accused of being "infected with sectarianism" and "turning the *narod* away from the clergy."[58] As Daniel Beer has demonstrated, at the time the understanding of sectarianism (and religious deviance more generally) as a "highly contagious epidemic originating in the psychopathologies of its diseased leaders" was widespread among the Orthodox clergy; so too was the preference for a prophylactic rather than therapeutic response.[59] Thus church authorities decided to "quarantine" Brother Ioann in a mental institution, while they checked him out.

Brother Ioann's forced exile from St. Petersburg and subsequent incarceration deeply pained him and his followers. On the day of his departure, crowds rushed into the street to send him off and express their love and gratitude, their tears "flow[ing] like a river."[60] One young follower, Anna Grigor'eva, whose mother had recently been healed of a life-threatening illness, threw herself at his feet and kissed his hands; she was so overwhelmed by the thought of losing him that she fainted "dead" at his feet. Other followers shared her love for him, and out of their distress a community began to form.

The treatment Churikov received at the other end of his long journey lacked even the pretense of respect. The hospital's director greeted him roughly and stripped him of his beloved cross, his manuscripts and letters, and even his chains; one of the doctors branded him a "complete rogue and charlatan."[61] He received friendlier treatment from the rest of the hospital staff, however. This included the director's assistant, Dr. M. D. Lion, who praised Churikov's mind as "deep and bright" in spite of his lack of education and confessed that as much as he wanted to find some kind of mercenary motives or contradiction in his teachings, he could not—indeed, the more he got to know him, the more he respected his beliefs and efforts to reform alcoholics.[62] The two would continue their relationship after Churikov's release; in fact, Dr. Lion would later admit to sending his alcoholic patients to Brother Ioann on occasion.

Though unsettled by the harsh welcome,[63] Brother Ioann resisted the challenges to his dignity and identity by continuing the ascetic habits that had helped him endure suffering in the past—fasting, praying, and singing hymns. His time in the asylum was made more bearable by donations sent to him by his followers in St. Petersburg and by his relationship with one of most devoted among them, seventeen-year-old Agrippina Smirnova (known as "Grusha"), the daughter of a shoemaker who had taken him in. Grusha traveled to Samara to be near him, and throughout his confinement served as his closest confidante and primary link to the outside world. In doing so, she revealed herself as a person of extreme faith, courage, and self-abnegation, with a seemingly unlimited capacity to give of herself to those in need.[64] Although many Orthodox women, including those who were barely literate, were able to recite passages from the Gospels from memory,[65] Grusha's profound knowledge of Scripture at such a young age impressed many people, including Churikov. The two quickly became spiritual interlocutors, and the devotion they exhibited toward each other was at times so intense that they were sometimes mistaken for lovers.[66] Yet their deep connection was a platonic love, based on mutal respect, admiration, gratitude, trust, and most of all, faith. And while at first, when Grusha was young, their relationship mimicked that between an elder and disciple (or parent–child), over time it evolved into a kind of spiritual marriage. They would live together and work side by side for the next thirty years.

With Grusha's help Churikov kept up an active correspondence with his followers in St. Petersburg while in the asylum, and he continued to write after his release, as he waited in Novouzensk for official permission to return to the capital. Much of his writing was an exercise in scriptural exegesis, a practice traditionally associated with elders and encouraged by the Church.[67] The letters also served as an epistolary form of preaching and counseling, reflective of Churikov's active desire to stay closely engaged with those who had grown dependent on his counsel. Intended to console and guide, they implored his friends and followers not to fear but rather to embrace hope, practice patience, and have faith that he would return to them. And indeed, in the absence of convincing evidence that he was mentally ill, he was released after several months.[68]

Nonetheless, Brother Ioann's experience in the insane asylum had a profound and lasting impact on him. He described living among the insane and under strict surveillance as a kind of purgatory, a confused state of being "among neither the living nor the dead."[69] The ordeal also changed his relationship to the Church. In an 1898 message (poslanie) to his "Petersburg brothers," Churikov elaborated on his growing disillusionment with spiritual authorities, especially after the decision by Bishop Gurii to seek his excommunication. At one point, the Novouzensk inspector of people's schools, I. P. Babin, who had himself been educated at the Spiritual Academy, publicly contradicted the bishop's assessment of Brother Ioann's teachings, claiming that he found nothing un-Orthodox about them.[70] Babin's endorsement lifted Churikov's spirits, but it did not change the position of diocesan authorities. In fact, during a visit to Novouzensk, the bishop did not even bother to meet with Brother Ioann personally, preferring instead to gather information from local clergy to support his case that Churikov was some kind of "sectarian, or a khlyst [flagellant], or a Baptist."[71] While alluding to the doggedness and desperation with which authorities had been pursuing him, Churikov emphasized how Bishop Gurii had proceeded without even questioning him, as if to suggest his actions were an exercise of naked power rather than an expression of sincere concern for anyone's spiritual welfare.[72] True or not, it is clear that Brother Ioann felt the full weight of the church's authority, since the simple fact of the accusation that he was insane caused even ordinary people to treat him as such. Suspicion, he sadly discovered, was a formidable foe, against which he was almost completely powerless.

Confused and disheartened, Churikov observed that the distance between "Evangelical truth [pravda]" and the "falsehood [krivda]" of the world was becoming more apparent to him than ever; he found it nothing less than an "abomination" that in Orthodox Russia no one wanted to preach God's Truth, and that those who did were declared insane or imprisoned, and questioned as to their "authority" to speak about Jesus Christ.[73] Why, he would ask in a letter to the missionary N. I. Bulgakov, did no one bother to question him about his behavior when he was a businessman, devoting all his time to money and secular pursuits? Why only now that he followed a path of faith was he the target of so much ill will?[74] That church authorities found Brother Ioann's influence on the laity worthy of investigation, even censure, is not surprising; after all, even ordained priests as visible and influential as Father Ioann of Kronstadt had been scrutinized because of their innovations and charisma. But Churikov clearly considered the clergy's treatment of him both excessive and unwarranted.

While offering solace, strength, and guidance during his ordeal, Scripture provided Brother Ioann with a malleable and powerful framework for understanding and justifying his experiences. In order to make sense of the clergy's opposition to his preaching, for example, Churikov turned to Matthew 10:32, in which Jesus sends his disciples off to preach but warns them of the possibility of rejection and persecution.[75] In a similar way, in a letter written after his release from the asylum he relied on the Apostle Paul's first letter to Timothy to defend his mission: "until I come, devote yourself to the public reading of Scripture, to exhortation, to teaching" (4:13) and "Persist in this, for by so doing you will save both yourself and your hearers" (4:16).[76] With respect to his persecutors' harsh treatment of him, he pointed to Matthew 18:15: "If your brother or sister sins, go and point out their fault, just between the two of you. If they listen to you, you have won them over."[77] More defiantly, he drew connections between his own experience and King Saul's pursuit of David and referenced Romans 8 in his defense.[78] Though he had suffered greatly, Brother Ioann's experience in the asylum had not broken his spirit; on the contrary, he emerged more determined to endure the lies and wounds of those who sought to silence him.[79]

Persecution Redux

Churikov returned to St. Petersburg after his arrest and exile in 1897–98 to find that several of his followers had broken with him completely for fear of damaging their reputations. As difficult as this was, he discovered that others had had the opposite reaction and now hailed him as a "sufferer for the faith."[80] Indeed, his "brothers and sisters" were bereft in his absence and more devoted to him than ever. The active sense of community among them also continued to evolve, in part because of the exigent need to stand up to the church authorities that refused to acknowledge his goodness. In a testimony dated November 2, 1899, fifty-two people testified that Brother Ioann had saved them, including a drunkard who became sober, a blind man who had regained his sight, and an adulterer who had returned to his marriage.[81] Their pleas were echoed by the local priest Father Lebedev, who claimed that as many as a thousand people had become "peaceful and meek like angels of Christ" as a direct result of his spiritual guidance.[82]

For all the support he received, however, Brother Ioann remained acutely aware of his continuing vulnerability before church authorities. In an effort to avoid further persecution, he submitted a petition to the newly appointed metropolitan Antonii (Vadkovskii) of St. Petersburg in early March 1900.[83] He confessed that he had been guilty of acting with "*samovol'naia* [unauthorized, and literally, self-willed] audacity" in that he had been preaching without permission from state or secular authorities.[84] But he also stressed the integrity of his intentions and, even more emphatically, the success and "usefulness" of his efforts to heal alcoholics of their addictions and to bring them back to church. By his own count, he had already saved some two hundred people. He thus begged the metropolitan to clear him of the charges that he was some kind of "sectarian" and to offer his blessing so that he could continue his work. In this same appeal to the metropolitan, as well as in a "tearful" letter to Father Grigorii Petrov dated April 11, 1900, Churikov referred to himself as an "Evangelical widow," a phrase he used repeatedly to describe the state of his faith—in his grief, he had given up everything and surrendered himself to his trust in God.[85] And like the widow he needed help defending himself against the "flying bullets" that were coming his way.

At least in the short run, Churikov's pleas for protection went nowhere, and on April 8, 1900, less than two years after his release from the asylum, he was arrested on the instigation of Bishop Gurii of Samara. On April 28, he was sent to prison in the Spaso-Evfimiev Monastery in Suzdal' for spreading "nonsense" among the people and "teachings contrary to the Orthodox Church." Once again he was stripped of all his things—his books, pencil, papers, sheets, and clothes, as well as his Psalter and copy of the Gospels. Four days later he met with Archimandrite Serafim (Chichagov), who allowed him to have his copy of the Gospels back, but also claimed it was a "pashkovite" (or "sectarian") version because passages had been underlined.[86]

Return to Preaching, 1900–1904

Even more than his first incarceration, Brother Ioann's second arrest galvanized his followers into action on his behalf, both individually and as a community.[87] Within a week of his arrest, a group of his followers expressed their grief and outrage in a passionately worded petition to the Holy Synod. Like Churikov, they relied on Scripture to make their case, drawing a parallel between the Church's campaign against Brother Ioann and High Priest Caiaphas's case against Jesus. They demanded a fairer "trial" and proclaimed their right to testify on Brother Ioann's behalf, supporting these claims with the Gospel passage John 7:51: "Does our law condemn anyone without first hearing him to find out what he is doing?"[88] In addition to a full review of his file, they asked the Church to consider appointing him a missionary upon his release, since, they pointed out, he had great faith but no income or permanent place to live.[89]

Although the biblical references could be (and often were) read by clerical authorities as a blasphemous attempt to compare Brother Ioann with Christ, the rest of the petition clearly portrayed him as a faithful servant of the Church. His followers understood the importance of proving his "usefulness" as much as his innocence. Most of all, they emphasized how he had inspired them to repent their sins, while making Scripture more accessible and meaningful to them. While careful not to criticize the clergy directly, they pointed out how much they benefited from the more intimate settings in which Churikov preached (such as an apartment), explaining that it was hard for poor people like themselves to get close to local priests and missionaries, since many churches were crowded and noisy, with shouting and children crying.

Although initially reluctant to get involved, Metropolitan Antonii of St. Petersburg soon secured Churikov's release from the Suzdal' prison. On September 28, 1900, he wrote to the metropolitan thanking him and appealing to him not to "abandon" the trezvenniki in the future, since his recent visit had raised their spirits and given them hope and strength.[90] The letter was signed, simply, "Ivan Alekseevich Churikov, Christian."

Churikov returned to the capital, now, more visibly than ever, "wearing a martyr's crown."[91] Indeed, he emerged from prison in 1900 like a celebrity, as rumors circulated among the local population that Churikov had been "persecuted for truth [pravda]" and that the missionaries had gone after him because the people (narod) "considered him a priest."[92] While some interpreted Brother Ioann's incarceration as a "divine calamity," undertaken to the delight of the "enemies of humankind," others saw it as a fulfillment of the Savior's Word, namely that "others would be persecuted in My name." Comparing him to Joseph, Job the righteous, John the Baptist, and his sufferings to those "of Jesus Christ Himself," his followers considered him to be an "innocent sufferer 'for the Word of God,'" hunted by priests and enemies (both secular and religious authorities), whom they predicted would someday be "covered with shame."[93]

A journalist estimated that when Brother Ioann returned from prison in 1900, his followers numbered as many as ten thousand,[94] although he himself estimated only 150–200. The discrepancy is most likely explained by the distinction between the wide circle of people whose lives he had touched in some way, and the emergent community of followers he knew and saw regularly. While the Church's persecution had divided those who opposed Brother Ioann, it had strengthened the bonds between his followers.

In early May 1901, 142 trezvenniki, mostly skilled workers, artisans, and small traders, successfully petitioned Metropolitan Antonii to grant them permission to hold meetings with Brother Ioann again.[95] Aware of accusations that Churikov was leading them away from the Orthodox Church, the trezvenniki insisted that the opposite was true: "before we knew our dear Brother, the entire Church was foreign to us, and if we went a few times a year, it was only out of a sense of ritual obligation and without any faith in the Gospel."[96] Many confessed to having failed to receive communion for many years, or to doing so only reluctantly or even hypocritically. Others admitted that they had been afraid to go to services or participate in sacramental life because of their drinking. But because of Brother Ioann, they were now "close to the entire Holy Church" and got up with "delight" to go to early Mass. And whereas they used to receive communion annually (if at all), they now went four times a year, and some even more often. As further evidence of his positive influence, they appended testimonies by fifteen people whom Churikov had healed; many were illiterate and suffered chronic illnesses (including cancer).[97] Evidently persuaded by their defense, the metropolitan agreed to allow Brother Ioann to resume preaching as of spring 1901. He would continue uninterrupted until 1904, when concerns about his influence would once again crescendo.[98]

Like many public figures, Bother Ioann found his increasing visibility as a preacher and healer both a blessing and a curse. Everyone, it seemed, wanted to define (or distort) him to their own ends, and the distance between his fans and his critics was wide. Among his followers, he was characterized as "righteous" and declared a prophet, and sometimes an apostle, a saint, or even "God." Among his critics, he was an "exploiter" or a "charlatan," and sometimes the "Antichrist," since in their view, his teachings led people away from God.

Churikov was deeply wounded by clerical questioning of his intentions and his devotion to the faith, although he learned to endure both. For all his suffering at the hands of religious authorities, he continued to profess his undying devotion to the Orthodox Church. In spite of clerical suspicions to the contrary,[99] at no time did Brother Ioann ever conceive of breaking with the faith or founding a new church. On the contrary, he was careful to stress his humility before the Orthodox Church, and often spoke of his willingness to suffer for it. He could maintain this belief in the face of clerical objections because he refused to accept the idea that a layperson reading and interpreting Scripture was in any way contrary to the Church's mission.

As much as he embraced the Church's teachings and prescription for living a good Orthodox life, however, Churikov resisted the suggestion that he solve his problematic relationship with the hierarchy by joining the clergy. When a bishop once suggested he consider the priesthood, he allegedly refused on the grounds that "those long priestly clothes would get in my way—I'd get lost in them."[100] He would explain that he was not worthy, and that he did not seek a status higher than other laypeople, but rather lived to serve them, not as a father or even as a teacher, but simply as a "brother." Exactly why he resisted remains a source of speculation. Perhaps he believed that his identity as a lay preacher kept him closer to his followers, as a model of someone both largely self-taught and confident in his own ability to interpret Scripture. As he once explained, "if one does not climb to the high mountain of a clerical position, then one has nowhere to fall."[101] Or perhaps he understood that his secular origins and lack of formal education would always keep him from earning the full respect of other clergy. As Laurie Manchester has pointed out, although priests were emerging from secular families at the time (including Grigorii Petrov and Georgii Gapon), those born into the sacred estate tended to believe in their own moral superiority due to the circumstances of their birth.[102] Perhaps his resistance stemmed from his own experience at the hands of the clergy, causing him to fear becoming one of them—that is, being not only subjected to, but also responsible for, the kinds of clerical control he had witnessed.

Whatever the case, Brother Ioann's trust in church authorities had clearly been broken by his incarcerations, although perhaps not irreparably so. Aside from the few individuals he knew he could trust, Brother Ioann kept his distance from the clergy as a whole. Over the coming years, there would be times when he would agree to submit to clerical instruction and questioning, but only out of respect for the Church and a fear that it would shut him down unless he complied. Even with clerical oversight, his words and actions suggested that he was intent on carving out his own niche, responsible only to God.

As in the years of his wife's illness, Churikov had found suffering productive and instructive. Although traumatized by his two incarcerations, he had learned to cope by reframing his experiences in a meaningful way. As he observed in a letter dated August 21, 1902, the many trials he had endured—the "thorny path" of his life—had all begun to make sense to him for the first time; he came to the conclusion that everything had been for a reason, because he had gained invaluable insight into the many different types of people who would come to him for help. From the peasant to the prisoner, the widow to the wanderer, the trader to the publican—he could now relate to the troubles and trials of each and every one.[103]

Periods of forced solitude in the mental hospital and prison had also inspired Brother Ioann toward an even more intimate relationship with God's Word. As he expanded his mission in the future, Scripture would remain both his comfort and his cure, his weapon and his shield. At some point, he would even begin to add scriptural passages to his favorite portrait, including the passage from John 8:20: "'You do not know me or my Father,' Jesus replied. 'If you knew me, you would know my Father also.' He spoke these words while teaching in the temple area near the place where the offerings were put. Yet no one seized him, because his time had not yet come." Whether this reference would be interpreted as an invitation to faith and hope or a blasphemous threat depended entirely on the reader and their assumptions about who he was and what he was trying to do.

CHAPTER 2

An Extraordinary Man on a Sober Mission

In the spring of 1901, Brother Ioann received official permission to resume his preaching. His two incarcerations by Orthodox authorities had not lessened his desire to bring Scripture to the capital's spiritually needy; on the contrary, he remained more determined than ever. He immediately threw himself into his work, and a clear sign of the growing demand for his preaching was the need for a bigger meeting space to accommodate those who regularly came to listen to him. In 1901, with help from his followers he secured the rental of a two-room meeting space in Petrovskii Park, located in a complex housing charitable and educational programs for the working population.[1] The main hall, which held up to five hundred people, was set up as a dedicated space for prayer, the singing of hymns, and spiritual-moral discussions; in the tradition of chapel building in more rural areas, his followers funded and maintained the space and adorned it with icons and pictures of the tsar and his family, as well as Father Ioann of Kronstadt.[2] It was intended—like Brother Ioann's mission itself—to complement (not replace) local churches. The hall would serve as the center of the trezvennik community for almost a decade, until it too would be outgrown.

In spite of lingering clerical doubt, Brother Ioann's mission underwent a period of impressive growth from 1901 to 1910, expanding in both nature and scope. Central to his outreach were his weekly besedy, and the acquisition of a permanent space for his preaching led to more regular contact with his followers, as well as a greater sense of community among them. Although much of his time was still spent meeting petitioners, visiting the seriously ill, and tending to new pledges to sobriety, his mission to spread "holy sobriety" was becoming associated with a distinct set of rituals as well as a new way of life. As of 1905, it would also become associated with the town of Vyritsa, where Churikov established a successful colony to help his followers carve out space for their spiritual lives, and to live and work in a sober community.

Brother Ioann's unfaltering devotion to his followers and seemingly endless reserve of energy had a lot to do with the success of his efforts, as did the willingness of the trezvenniki to testify publicly and enthusiastically to his healing abilities and positive influence on their lives. But the shape and impact of his mission would also be determined by the continuing concerns and demands of the clergy about his spiritual authority, as well as by the broader context of revolution in 1905. Unlike Fathers Georgii Gapon and Grigorii Petrov, both of whom were known for their efforts to promote social justice among workers in St. Petersburg, Churikov consciously avoided any form of social or political activism and explicitly counseled his followers to stay away from revolutionary unrest. While silence was itself a political choice, he made it clear that he believed only in the use of spiritual tools to fix what was broken in the world. Nonetheless, the political turmoil, violence, and social dislocation that dominated the city's streets in 1905 would impact how his efforts to promote holy sobriety among the city's working-class population would by understood by state authorities as well as the broader public.

Besedy: The Application of Scripture to Life

The centerpiece of Churikov's mission to promote holy sobriety were his weekly besedy. Every Sunday afternoon, people would arrive from throughout St. Petersburg to gather in the large hall at Petrovskii Park. Although the besedy were scheduled in the afternoon so as not to interfere with morning church services, it was not uncommon for trezvenniki to arrive hours early with the hope of meeting Brother Ioann for a personal blessing or advice. Anyone was welcome to attend, as long as they were sober; anyone showing signs of inebriation was turned away. As the size of his regular audience grew, he had to rely on his closest followers, especially the women known as his *sestritsy* (sisters), to help organize and manage the crowds. By official order, children were also barred from the meetings, although in the summer months, many could be found in the courtyard listening through the open windows.[3]

An attending priest would open the beseda with a blessing, and then Brother Ioann would preach for up to three hours, beginning with the liturgically scheduled scriptural passage of the day. With the "application of Scripture to life" as his main goal,[4] he approached Scripture metaphorically, as a resource for how to live and how not to live as well as for moral guidance. His most common themes included, in order of emphasis, the importance of actively embracing the Word of God, living soberly, and the pursuit of honest work and family life. To connect with his audience, he spoke in a conversational, some said "feminine," tone and used words and examples that would be familiar to his largely working-class audience.

While some more educated observers found Brother Ioann's besedy overly mundane, many people found "holy meaning" in his words.[5] His followers described his preaching as a "life buoy" for those caught in a "drunken and depraved whirlpool,"[6] and his words "a stream of living water" from which they could drink again and again to quench their souls.[7] According to the religious scholar A. S. Prugavin, the simplicity of Churikov's demeanor and language was precisely what enabled him to connect with his listeners so effectively: "a lowly man with a tender voice, gentle gestures, and long hair speaks of Christ's science of life, a pot of porridge, a sick horse, a tattered coat. And simple crude examples become symbols of life, symbols of the fall and suffering of man, symbols of salvation and joy."[8]

In part to satisfy clerical demands, Ivan Tregubov began publishing Churikov's besedy in abridged form from June 1909 to April 1910, in the newspaper *Novaia Rus*. After it closed, he published them as separate sheets in "more or less complete form," and then gathered the leaflets into a bound collection. Given that they were collected after Brother Ioann had been preaching for the better part of a decade, they unfortunately do not tell us much about the content or format of the conversations as they evolved in the early years. Nonetheless, the accuracy of Tregubov's collection is good, since Brother Ioann checked over the transcripts himself.[9]

Like the charismatic Father Ioann of Kronstadt, whom he had observed in practice and clearly admired, Churikov threw a lot of himself into his preaching, and in the course of two to three hours he could cover a lot of scriptural ground. On October 30, 1911, for example, his beseda began with a passage from Luke 16, the parable of the shrewd manager and the impossibility of serving both "God and money"; it was followed by a discussion on the theme of marriage and adultery. The final Gospel passage was the parable of Lazarus, which tells of the confrontation between a beggar oozing visibly with the sores of poverty and an extraordinarily wealthy man who is condemned to eternal torment for ignoring him. The story was often told by clergy to the poor as a way to condemn the love of money and greed, and to emphasize and extol the virtue of spiritual (as opposed to material) wealth.[10] An extended excerpt offers a sense of Brother Ioann's style, rhythm, and tone, as well as his "take":

> If people see a rich person, they say to him: "Give us bread, we are poor," but they do not ask him for spiritual bread. And the rich, while feeding them their earthly bread, do not feed them the bread of heaven, and they remain poor and hungry. Why? Because if you nourish a hungry man with earthly bread alone, and do not nourish him with heavenly bread, he will not get rid of his defects, disease, poverty, and tatters and will remain forever sick and poor. Therefore it is necessary for people to share not only earthly bread, but also spiritual bread, that is, the righteousness of God. With God's Truth, the poor do not cry, but without God's Truth even the rich cry. Why? Because only the body is nourished, but the soul remains hungry and suffers from hunger.[11]

To make himself absolutely clear, Brother Ioann then circled back to the healing power of Scripture: "This is our wealth—the testament of Christ, which is left to everyone—both rich and poor, and kings and slaves, and if we live according to all this, then we will have neither need nor sickness." He would never get tired of repeating this theme; it was his single most important message.

Although Brother Ioann spoke for most of the beseda, he would pause occasionally for celebratory hymns. His words were also punctuated by the audience's shouts, cheers, and even weeping. Quick interjections from his listeners, such as "have mercy, Dear Brother," or a simple "thank you!" were common; although they had an air of spontaneity, they came at regular intervals. Periodically, Brother Ioann would invite his audience to renounce their vices together, conducting them to an emotional crescendo. With intentional theatricality, he would raise his soft voice in stages, and then suddenly and boisterously call upon everyone to "repent!" According to recorded transcripts and eye-witnesses, this practice provoked wild rejoicing. While some observers likened the beseda to a mass confession,[12] others found the frequent audience participation more appropriate to an evangelical revival than an Orthodox prayer service.[13]

In terms of subject matter and format, Brother Ioann's besedy over-lapped with the extraliturgical discussions regularly offered by Ortho-dox clergy to the working-class population. Using the same texts as Churikov—Scripture and the lives of the saints—the clergy also encour-aged ordinary believers to meditate on their lives and on their sins.[14] Like Brother Ioann, the clergy engaged in this work understood the impor-tance of using simple language and illustrative examples. As one reflected somewhat condescendingly, "Our *narod* is not accustomed to theory or to any kind of abstract thinking, and has difficulty grasping the sim-plest truths. They are children in their understanding of everything that falls outside the sphere of their everyday, earthly needs."[15] Like Churikov, the clergy often addressed issues of specific interest to workers, like the evils of drinking, family issues, and the moral dangers of gossip, excessive materialism, and theft.[16] Importantly, however, their project of enlight-enment also meant teaching the laity about Orthodox doctrine and the importance of a proper ritual life, as well as explanations of common liturgical prayers or the Ten Commandments. The Orthodox under-standing of salvation, sinfulness, atonement, suffering, and resurrection were also regular themes.[17] Brother Ioann was neither permitted to touch nor interested in touching on any of these issues.

For Churikov, each beseda was a call to critique the modern world and to help his audience imagine a new way of seeing and acting. This involved appealing to the heart, spirit, and mind. In line with the practice of what theologian Walter Brueggemann has called the "pro-phetic imagination,"[18] Brother Ioann tried to strike a balance between judgment and hope as he helped his listeners navigate from a sinful past to a more aspirational future, grounded in Scripture and faith in God. As passionate as he could be when projecting a sense of hope and possibility, however, he could be equally brutal in his words and delivery as he warned against the temptations of secular life and the wages of sin. As his followers appreciated, his sermons were intended as a wake-up call, a call to prayer and faith: "[His] sermon serves as the thunder, thanks to which a person has a desire for prayer," the trez-venniki Davydov and Frolov explained, "Until the sermon touches our hearts, until the thunder strikes, we will not cross ourselves"—a play on the Russian proverb, "If the thunder is not loud, the peasant will not cross himself."[19]

Repeatedly, Brother Ioann would point out the contradiction—and hypocrisy—that many of those who called themselves Orthodox Christians structured their lives in ways that led them far away from God. "Today people are used to justifying themselves by saying 'there's a time for prayer, and time for fun,'" Churikov observed in his beseda on December 11, 1911, "but one cannot serve two masters. It is impossible to pray to God and play the balalaika [at the same time]." Again, tailoring the metaphor for the benefit of his audience, he continued: "If a worker works at his job while the owner is around, but plays the balalaika when he isn't, would the owner pay him his wage?" In the same way, "the Lord will not heal or give wealth or health to those who only hypocritically go to church to pray but then leave to play the balalaika."[20]

Among the many visitors who came to hear Churikov preach was Father Grigorii Petrov, who led his own spiritual-moral conversations in working-class neighborhoods. He too was struck by the emotional intensity of Churikov's beseda, especially when Brother Ioann called his listeners to account for their sins. Petrov later tried to capture what he had witnessed in a section of his novel *Zateinik*, entitled "The Priest at the Brother's Beseda." As Brother Ioann elaborated on the "festering wounds" caused by leprosy, commonly likened to the spiritual scars caused by sin, his words "rang out abruptly, like gun shots, sweeping [through] the room like a whistling whip, [as if] not only striking the listeners' souls, but ripping pieces from them." People in the audience "forgot about each other," convinced that "Brother Ioann was speaking only to him or her," to their sins, to their pain. Many people exhausted themselves with tears, as if Churikov was tearing the bandages off their sores and then washing them with "caustic medicine." Eventually, though, the listeners reached a state of peace, of healing: their "gloomy and concentrated faces" softened, and "their hearts were like earth in the spring under the bright sun, thawed and softened after a warm rain."[21] The beseda, Father Grigorii appreciated, was about more than scriptural enlightenment or meditation; it was also intended as an exercise in moral and spiritual reconciliation. Not unlike the method promoted by Alcoholics Anonymous decades later, the trezvenniki were encouraged to confront their weaknesses as part of the process of becoming someone new.

After preaching, Brother Ioann would take time to pray before the icons and then greet all of his followers for as long it would take.

In another scene reminiscent of Father Ioann,[22] crowds of women would rush to kiss his hand and ask for his blessing, as if to draw spiritual strength from him. According to Ivan Tregubov, a frequent observer of the besedy and Churikov's friend, Brother Ioann did not like these overt displays of physical affection and adoration, but he tolerated them because they seemed to be very important to his followers.[23] Indeed, he rarely turned anyone away, even when the lines stretched into the thousands, as they often did on Easter.

At the end of his beseda, Churikov would routinely invite his closest followers to join him for tea and conversation on scriptural themes—another event that had no defined timetable and often lasted well into the night. Not unlike the regular conversations led by spiritual elders in the village,[24] these "sober" evenings offered Brother Ioann the opportunity to elaborate on the beseda in a smaller setting and to engage more intimately with his followers. Photographs show Brother Ioann seated at the head of the table, his female followers mostly on one side and men on the other, arranged in a set order. In spite of this formality,

FIGURE 1. Brother Ioann and his followers at tea in Vyritsa. Reprinted with permission from TsGAKFFD SPb.

the evenings were as much about community as enlightenment, and when Tolstoy's son visited in 1914, he found the mood "friendly, loving, and happy."[25] While giving Brother Ioann the opportunity to step down from the pulpit and sit among his followers, the teas also gave the trezvenniki—especially former addicts and women—a safe space in which to socialize and support one another. In stark contrast to the high emotionality and performative nature of the mass meetings beforehand—not to mention the rowdiness of the tavern—the intimate setting was the site of a different kind of sociability or *obshchenie*, defined by anthropologist Aleksei Yurchak as "a space of affect and togetherness," not just for conversing, but also for "nonverbal interaction" and "exchanging human warmth."[26]

In addition to the Sunday beseda, Brother Ioann set aside one day each week to meet and counsel alcoholics ready to take a pledge to renounce drinking. He reserved yet another day for receiving petitioners seeking his prayers and advice. As time permitted, he continued to visit individuals in crisis, especially the desperately ill. But as word of

FIGURE 2. People waiting in line to petition Brother Ioann, Obukhovo, ul. Troitskaia, d. 60A, photograph by K. K. Bulla, winter 1914. Reprinted with permission from TsGAKFFD SPb.

his healings spread, the vast number of people seeking him out forced him to regularize his receptions. On any given day, he would spend long hours receiving hundreds of people, some of whom had made difficult pilgrimages to his door and then waited hours in the snow and biting wind for a few precious minutes of his attention. Many were very sick or desperate for prayers on behalf of someone they loved. Although it was common for people to petition spiritual elders in this way, the expectations placed on him were extraordinary in scale.

Meeting petitioners was exhausting work, both physically and spiritually. In addition to the energy and patience the receptions required, they demanded no small degree of faith and courage as well. In St. Petersburg, where violence was everywhere and trust in strangers almost nonexistent, petitioners came with all kinds of troubles and disorders, and the crowds could sometimes get rowdy and noisy.[27] In fact, on at least one occasion Brother Ioann was approached by a man with a knife and the intent to kill him on the spot.[28] Nonetheless, he kept the door open to anyone seeking his help and for as long as necessary. This kind of extreme generosity is perhaps best understood as an exercise of "kenosis," by which an individual follows Christ by humbly and voluntarily "emptying" themselves out on the behalf of others, even to the point of suffering.[29]

Judging from hundreds of petitions that have survived, people appreciated Brother Ioann's accessibility and took great advantage of it. Although the majority of notes were submitted anonymously, the wording makes it clear they were written both by his regular followers as well as by people who knew him only by reputation. Typically short and to the point, the requests ranged from the familiar and mundane (as in "Pray for me, Brother, I am going bald," or "my nose hurts and I have a cold") to the tragic and hopeless; desperate pleas for help from abused children, the chronically ill, and the unemployed and unhoused were common.[30]

Whatever the nature or magnitude of the request, Brother Ioann's response was clear and consistent: read Scripture and have faith, and God will take care of you. To a petitioner complaining of melancholy (*toska*), he advised simply to "look to the Word of God and you will find comfort." To another claiming memory loss, his answer was much the same: make yourself accountable for the Word of God, and the Lord will give you memory.[31] The biggest variation on this theme was reserved for those who needed to practice self-discipline. Free yourself from your sins, he would tell them, and you will no longer be punished because of them; become better yourself and everything around will become better. To a man who confessed that his lustful desires had turned him into a "dog," Churikov promised that if he struggled against his urges, the Lord would make him stronger.[32] To a woman complaining about her husband's anxiety, he reassured her that if she stopped "annoying" him, he would calm down; and to a man with a difficult horse, he counseled, "reform yourself and then your horses won't be ill."[33]

When responding to the many people who came to him with health issues, Brother Ioann would first pray for them, and then send them off to fast, pray, and meditate on Scripture—a remedy rooted in the widely held belief that illness was the result of sin and therefore the best cure lay in turning to God. "Whoever can heal the soul can also heal the body. But if someone cannot calm the soul, then can he heal the body?" he asked in a beseda on March 20, 1911. "It is necessary to begin with the heart [in order] to heal the body of a sick person."[34] Although the Orthodox Church's position was that it was prudent to pursue both medical and religious means (neither one exclusively), Brother Ioann resisted medical forms of healing in part because of his deep mistrust of "godless" medical doctors, whom he associated with the Antichrist.[35] This position was still common, especially among peasants. Medical doctors "were by definition outside the camp of God," Leonid Heretz has explained, "and since godlessness was not a neutral category, it meant that they had to be active servants of evil." As such, "their function was inverted. Claiming to cure the sick, they in fact spread disease and hasten death."[36]

In his so-called "Antichrist letter" written to his sestritsa Grusha upon his release from the mental asylum in 1898, Brother Ioann labelled medicine a "dark science" and faulted doctors for privileging only what they could see and understand; while rejecting what they could not see as impossible or irrational, they assumed the power of the material over the spiritual, and of the human over the divine. "[Doctors teach] us to be afraid of microbes in the water, which can scarcely be seen with a microscope," Churikov wrote, "yet they don't want to see the Lord's miracles."[37] And surgeons "waged war" against the teachings of Christ but used their limited knowledge and imperfect skills to exert "excruciating torture, and often excruciating death" on their patients. In short, he asserted, faith in medical science led to immoral acts of violence and unnecessary suffering instead of healing.[38] And when medical efforts appeared to result in success, medical practitioners glorified themselves (or science) rather than God.

Religious Authorities Weigh In (Again)

As Brother Ioann's reputation as a preacher and "miraculous" healer became more widespread, the level of clerical attention given toward him naturally increased. Some clergy openly—even enthusiastically—supported his efforts to bring Scripture alive for ordinary people, as well as his success with alcoholics. In addition to the praise he received from Father Grigorii Petrov, for example, Churikov enjoyed the support of Father Vasilii Lebedev, at the Spaso-Preobrazhenskaia (Koltovskaia) Church in a very poor working-class district on the Petersburg Storona; their collaboration had led not only to the sobering up of many local believers, but also the invigoration of parish life.[39] And in a noteworthy reversal of opinion, the ultraconservative Bishop Gurii, who had led the investigation of Churikov in the 1890s, declared himself "deeply conscience-stricken" and recanted his position on *besedniki* in 1902: "it seems to me more and more that we have incorrectly understood them, and we ourselves have alienated them from the life of God by suspecting them of sectarianism."[40]

Tolerance—let alone admiration—for Brother Ioann remained far from universal, however. One of his biggest critics was Bishop Gurii's assistant in the 1890s investigation, the missionary priest Evgenii Vasil'evich Kesarev. In a highly unsympathetic profile published in 1905, Father Evgenii fueled doubts about Brother Ioann's identity by claiming that he was a fraud and a hypocrite who pretended to be a spiritual ascetic but actually got up late, slept on a soft pillow, drank fancy tea, and wore an expensive hat. More damningly, the priest portrayed him as a predator, both exploiting his followers to support his expensive habits and taking advantage of his young female admirers in inappropriate (sexual) ways.[41] Tapping into fears of sectarianism as a form of spiritual infection, Kesarev cast Brother Ioann's religiosity as the perverse product of a delusional and psychologically unstable mind. While acknowledging that he possessed a certain religious "mood," the priest made it clear that he found Churikov's deep distrust of medical healing extreme and unhealthy. Brother Ioann's "fanaticism," he surmised, was the result of two traumas that had scarred him permanently—his wife's insanity, and the killing off of all of his plague-ridden cattle by official order.[42] The danger that Churikov's beliefs might pose to the health of the Orthodox population was further magnified by Father Evgenii's portrayal of his followers as "weak" and spiritually vulnerable. Although based largely on innuendo and stereotypes, Kesarev's account successfully played into a range of contemporary fears, and it articulated themes that would be recycled by Brother Ioann's critics well into the Soviet era.

Churikov's image in the secular press was also mixed, and some of the same charges circulated. While he was sometimes praised as a man of deep faith, intuitively in touch with the struggles and needs of ordinary people,[43] Brother Ioann's lack of clerical status and the extreme devotion his followers exhibited toward him made him the target of suspicion, criticism, and sometime ridicule. Dismissing him as a hypocrite and charlatan, the well-known columnist Vlas Doroshevich reduced Churikov's influence to a function of "ignorance," and accused him of "exploit[ing] the people's darkness and superstition."[44] In a similar key, a journalist for the popular daily *Petersburgskii listok*, Liubomirov, mocked Brother Ioann for his pseudo-clerical dress and characterized his spiritual powers as "hypnosis."[45]

Brother Ioann was sensitive to and frustrated by his critics, especially those who doubted his sincerity, but he was reluctant to engage the press or to respond publicly, and for the most part left it to others to defend him. Still in Churikov's corner, Metropolitan Antonii met with him in early 1904 to point out that some clergy had been "grumbling and complaining" about him. Although no names were mentioned, Brother Ioann was well aware that the high profile antisectarian missionary N. I. Bulgakov, who had once been friendly to him in a personal encounter, had accused him of seeking "worldly glory" and characterized his unauthorized teachings as not "from God."[46] When he defended himself to the metropolitan by pointing out that he had repeatedly sent his followers to church for the sacraments, Antonii responded, "yes, true. You send people for sobering up to church [to partake of] the Holy Sacraments, and the Holy Sacraments heal them of drunkenness and illness, but the *narod* attributes glory to you."[47] While offering reassurance that he did not consider Churikov a "sectarian," the metropolitan clearly felt under pressure from those who did. He further reiterated the need for Brother Ioann's followers—as Orthodox—to submit to clerical authority.[48]

On February 1, 1904, Churikov's besedy were again shut down, and Antonii advised Brother Ioann to cease his personal receptions with his followers. The decision to ban all physical contact had several possible sources, including an awareness that the quality known as "charisma" had to be reinforced and reaffirmed through interaction.[49] Another possible explanation related to the tendency of the Orthodox to place enormous importance on "tangibility and proximity in their devotions."[50]

In other words, if Brother Ioann could not get physically close to those petitioning him (or vice versa), his chances of healing them would be lower. Yet another stemmed from the belief that the best way to stop the spread of a spiritual infection was to quarantine the source and prevent mass gatherings. As Daniel Beer has discussed, concerns about the spread of moral contagion were magnified by contemporary theories of crowd psychology.[51]

Whatever the exact reasoning, the ban on his besedy did not prevent Brother Ioann from healing people or attracting a sizeable number of new followers. Nonetheless, it would be repeated multiple times over the coming years, forcing him to receive petitioners by note only, with the help of his sestritsy. Frustrated and discouraged by the decision, he stopped sending his followers to church for the sacraments, and instead handed out three pieces of sugar as a "symbol of the transition from a bitter to a sweet life." He would later blame the clergy for disrupting the flow of his followers to church in this way.[52] His besedy would not resume again for almost two years.

FIGURE 3.   Petitioners waiting at the door of Brother Ioann's office at Obukhovo, ul. Troitskaia, d. 60A, photograph by K. K. Bulla, winter 1914. Reprinted with permission from TsGAKFFD SPb.

Rather than lessening his popularity, attempts to silence Brother Ioann again motivated his followers to speak out on his behalf, primarily through appeals to the Synod and spirited editorials.[53] Although outraged at the lies and disrespect shown toward Brother Ioann—as when Liubomirov referred to him pejoratively as "Brother Ivanushka," as if he were a "five year boy or a half-wit"—their biggest concern was reopening the weekly besedy.[54] A petition to the tsar dated April 12, 1904, and written by two of his more well-connected followers, officers from the imperial guard, Matvei Pavlov Sergachev and Aleskei Egorov Andreev, brought together the various strands of the trezvenniki's defense.[55] The petition began by praising Brother Ioann for halting "the fatal course of their lives" and exposing them to the Word of God. In addition to sharing their own stories and evidence of his ability to heal the chronically ill, they highlighted his successful conversion of "foreigners" to Orthodoxy (including Tatars, Jews, Catholics, and Lutherans), and his transformation of immoral and lazy individuals into "chaste" and "industrious" workers. In these ways, they implied, Churikov was the best cure for what ailed not only the individual addict, but the modernizing empire as a whole.

Given the increasing social and political instability in the empire in 1904, heightened by strike waves and war with Japan, it is difficult not to see the trezvenniki's emphasis on the more secular effects of Brother Ioann's preaching and prayers as strategic. It also suggests their awareness of the utility in appealing to the specific concerns of secular authorities as a way to protect Brother Ioann against the clergy who found his influence problematic. Although Churikov did not endorse this strategy himself, the trezvenniki's approach appears to have worked. On December 25, 1905, at the end of a bloody year of revolutionary unrest, Brother Ioann was given permission to reopen his besedy.[56] Although spiritual authorities did not contest the decision, they added the stipulation that he preach only those parts of the Gospels and Acts of the Apostles that had been read during Liturgy on that day. Brother Ioann agreed to the condition, and his public besedy resumed in the meeting space in Petrovskii Park without interruption until 1910.[57]

To Vyritsa

At some point during his enforced silence in 1904–5, Brother Ioann made the decision to move away from St. Petersburg. After months of searching, he purchased unwanted marshland from brothers named Korneev on the banks of the Oredezh River, about six to seven minutes from the train station in Vyritsa, some fifty versts on a direct line to the south of St. Petersburg. There he would found a sober colony with some of his closest followers, many of whom were recovering alcoholics. A world apart, the colony was a refuge from the city he repeatedly compared to both Sodom and Egypt—that is, a place dominated by immorality, excess, and oppression in various forms, including clerical suspicion and secular temptation. By contrast, Vyritsa promised an environment where his followers could work and live together peacefully. While still allowing him access to his Petersburg followers by train and by telephone, the new site also afforded him some welcome distance from both his critics and his overly adoring crowds.

Churikov's retreat was likely in part a reaction against the increasingly politicized and socially unstable atmosphere of the capital in 1904–5. "Simple and conservative," the journalist Zhivotovskii observed, the trezvenniki wanted to settle in peaceful Vyritsa where they could live according to their slogan "sobriety and labor."[58] Averse to political activism and violence of any kind, Brother Ioann consciously avoided engaging in the unrest that dominated the capital in 1905. In the days leading up to January 9, as thousands of Petersburg workers prepared to accompany the progressive Orthodox priest Georgii Gapon with a petition of grievances to the tsar, Brother Ioann counseled his followers not to join in.[59] And even when the march ended in the "Bloody Sunday" massacre of unarmed workers and their families, sparking a year of revolutionary unrest, Brother Ioann urged respect for civil authorities, firm in his belief that prayer not protest was the best path forward. "The Word of God was written so as to construct peaceful (forms of) government," he preached; "it is not possible to introduce peace on earth by any means other than the Word of God."[60]

Firm in this conviction, Brother Ioann stayed away from revolutionary unrest throughout 1905, even as mass strikes and demonstrations drew in many members of the worker population he had come to know so well. In this respect he differed greatly from his clerical mentor, Father Grigorii Petrov. The two had bonded through their mutual commitment to improving the spiritual lives of the urban poor through Scripture, and they shared an equally strong sense that most Orthodox clergy had been failing the faithful in this respect. But in the wake of Bloody Sunday they parted ways as Petrov became politicized and engaged directly in reform of both society and the Church. Far more of a social architect and political animal than Churikov, Petrov came to believe that the clergy's true mission was to lead the people in building the kingdom of God on earth. "The essence of the Church is Christ," Petrov argued, "and the realization of scriptural truth in life," by which he meant public and state institutions, as well as in personal life.[61] Rejecting state control of the Church and embracing a new model of pastoral leadership, Petrov called upon his fellow parish clergy to advocate for the poor before the institutions that oppressed them.[62] He even ran as a candidate to the new Duma with the hope of effecting substantial reform—an ambition that would ultimately get him defrocked in 1908.[63]

For Churikov too, building the kingdom of God on earth was a sacred project of the highest priority, but it was not a collective one; rather, it entailed the work of each individual soul striving toward God, each day, one day at a time. Lacking any hint of the apocalyptic thinking that animated some religious sectarians and revolutionaries at the time, he rejected any promise of radical social or political change, even urging workers not to act out against their employers.[64] When asked directly to explain his own political point of view, he replied, "I have only one 'political view' [politika]: believe in God and the Holy Church, don't drink and don't smoke."[65]

Even the democratic gains of 1905, which included the tsar's granting of civil rights and a State Duma, did little to impress Churikov. In a beseda recorded in 1911, he elaborated on his political perspective: "Without the Word of God, revolutions occur and people kill each other, because civil law means nothing to those who are not enlightened by the Word of God." Referring nostalgically to the early Christians, who lived in peace and bowed down to one another out of love, he observed that conflict between people grew only after they stopped looking to heaven and started relying on government. "When Christ grows dim in people's hearts and souls," he continued, "civil law can do nothing with those people who are not enlightened by the Word of God," because they are neither afraid of God nor ashamed.[66] It was in this same spirit that a group of trezvenniki in Moscow later sent a Bible directly to the Duma in an effort to cut down on the "partisanship [partiinost'], arguments, and hatred" that dominated their discussions.[67]

Part of Brother Ioann's reluctance to engage in any form of political or social activism stemmed from his understanding of poverty and class. Although he had embraced a simple life by choice, his years among the urban poor had acquainted him with the violence of poverty and the devastating effects of rapid industrialization. For him, far more than even the most progressive urban priest, the "people" were not an abstraction, and the more he knew of their misery, the more he was convinced that their poverty was fundamentally spiritual, not material. To be sure, he acknowledged the importance of meeting people's material needs, observing that "people can only look at heaven when on earth they are warm and satisfied and not enslaved by excessive work."[68] But the redistribution of material wealth was far from enough: "it is easy to escape poverty," he reassured his followers; "one only needs to penetrate [*proniknyt'*] Christ's teachings, and then you will never be poor."[69] As many clergy taught, Churikov believed that the misery of the poor was not a function of social class, but of their choice of a life far from God and his teachings.

To the extent that Brother Ioann had a social vision to offer, it would be realized in the sober colony he and his followers built in Vyritsa. Far enough removed from the "deadly bustle of the world" and the many "temptations of urban bourgeois life,"[70] the colony represented both a return to the land and a kind of internal migration project designed to reclaim some sober space from the predominant culture of drink and sin that had caused his followers so much suffering in the past. According to Nina Grigor'evna Maslova, one of Brother Ioann's sestritsy in the 1920s, what the trezvenniki built in Vyritsa was nothing less than an "earthly paradise," modeled on the biblical "land of milk and honey," where they could live freely and joyfully. Smoking and drinking and swearing were forbidden, and in the summer one could hear the singing of prayer and psalms through the open windows. Where holy sobriety reigned, so too did peace and prosperity. "Just as the Lord Himself showed Moses the promised land for all those who fulfilled his commandments," Maslova claimed, "so now it is repeated in our life also according to Scripture: To those who are sober and observe all that is commanded by God Himself and Brother Ioann, everything will [come] [*prilozhitsia*]."[71]

Maslova's romanticized recollections aside, "paradise" in fact took a lot of hard work, imagination, and faith. The quality of the land was very poor when Churikov first acquired it. Previously uncultivated and covered with moss, shrubs, and forest, it was supposedly so worthless that local residents labeled him as an "idiot" for buying it. He responded to their ridicule with characteristic equanimity and self-assurance, pointing out that a person does not deserve merit for making something good out of something already good, but rather from turning bad into good.[72] One of his first projects was therefore to improve the land by clearing away the evergreens and replacing them with fruit trees and berry bushes; as the trezvenniki would explain, he did not like trees that did not promise to bear fruit. In spite of their initial doubts, the trees flourished and miraculously delivered fruit within a year. The sudden fertility of the soil so amazed people that it was interpreted as another sign of Brother Ioann's unique gifts.[73]

Churikov's vision and the trezvenniki's determination eventually paid off. The colony grew quickly and was soon transformed into an "idyllic" community, with some sixty-five clean and colorful houses dotting the landscape and banked by lush garden plots.[74] Like many visitors from St. Petersburg, I. V. Nikanorov was surprised by what he saw. Instead of the small, wretched little huts conjured by his bourgeois imagination, he found pretty, solidly constructed, single-family homes like those in the suburbs of the capital. With an equal measure of astonishment and approval, he described the environment as extremely "orderly" with an air of "prosperity and contentment."[75] Multiple photographs commissioned by Churikov confirm this impression and reflect the trezvenniki's pride in the colony they had built with their own hands.

Mirroring the composition of the trezvennik population as a whole, the colonists included a few wealthy people and a majority of working people and their families. Among the original members were several recovering alcoholics, including Stepan Ivanovich Ermolov, a shoemaker from St. Petersburg. Born in 1853, Ermolov had a large family, with four children ages three to eighteen. Although the oldest colonist, he joked that he was much younger; "I can't even account for those lost, drunken years. I have lived on this earth as a person for only seventeen years. Before I lived on earth as a beast. And I try to forget about those beastly years."[76] Another cobbler and former alcoholic, Dmitrii Grigor'evich Sergeev, confessed that Brother Ioann had practically dragged him to the colony. But in contrast to the desperation he and his family had experienced when he was an addict, life on the colony was like "heaven." They owned a house worth three to four thousand rubles with land and a horse, and they grew plenty of food in their kitchen garden.[77]

By the standards of the day, the Ermolov and Sergeev families were doing very well for themselves, and some of the colonists were wealthy enough to buy up extra parcels of land. At least twenty of them were well-off enough to contribute to the colony's mutual insurance (or firemen's) fund in amounts ranging from ₽1,500 to ₽6,000, depending on the value of their property.[78] Among the wealthiest was a widow, Elizaveta Arsen'eva Cherpukhovskaia, known among the trezvenniki as "Mary the Egyptian," a nickname she chose in order to highlight her former state of sinfulness. Rather than joining a convent, she was drawn to the colony from Kherson province in 1907 after hearing about Brother Ioann's reputation as a deeply pious person. There she built her own modest two-story wooden house, and a sewing workshop for women and children.[79]

As a whole, the colony's inhabitants aspired to be literate, independent, and self-sufficient workers; they also prized collaboration and consciously worked together to create an environment free from the social disharmony that governed the capital at the time. When the journalist A. T. Mikhailov expressed his amazement at the "fairytale town," he was referring as much to the social atmosphere as the built environment. Everyone was nice to each other and smiled as they worked. As the colonist Sergeev recalled, they were generous too, living in a state of "brotherly love and accord." Once upon a time, he confessed, he wouldn't have given his own brother a piece of bread, even if he had had plenty to spare, but after meeting Brother Ioann and sobering up, he had managed to keep his entire family well fed while also helping others less fortunate. Having observed the Sergeev brothers during his visit, the journalist Zhivotovskii declared it nothing short of a "miracle" that the formerly broken family had learned to live together in peace.[80]

Honest work was another foundation stone of the colony. Whatever their financial status, all members of the colony had some form of occupation, in line with Churikov's belief that earning a living helped raise the individual toward God.[81] Cobblers as well as other artisans worked on site, but the majority commuted to St. Petersburg, including many factory workers and at least one policeman. Brother Ioann offered prayers and references for those seeking jobs, especially those who had struggled with alcoholism. Second only to bringing Scripture into their lives, Brother Ioann believed that the best way to help people was to give them the practical tools they needed to be self-supporting and to engage in honest labor. To this end, he set up a range of opportunities through which they could learn new skills and perform useful work on the colony, including an extensive series of workshops dedicated to everything from shoemaking and sewing to metalworking, mechanics, and brickmaking. There was also a bakery and kitchen, a commercial shop, a barnyard, and an apiary.

FIGURE 4. Brother Ioann and his followers making bricks at the colony in Vyritsa. Photograph by the Bulla studio, 1911. Reprinted with permission from TsGAKFFD SPb.

Given the emphasis on prayer and Scripture, the promotion of agricultural labor and artisanal occupations, and the rejection of urban culture, it would be tempting to see the colony as an attempt to escape modern life and, in effect, reverse history. But Churikov's relationship to modernity was somewhat more complicated. True, he rejected early twentieth-century notions of "progress" and understood history to be a process of devolution, from the perfect communities of the ancient Christians to the highly imperfect. But he also embraced hope for positive social change through the widespread practice of holy sobriety. What bothered him most was secular knowledge in the absence of faith.[82] Thus he insisted on Scripture as the only true source of knowledge but could still indulge his fascination in the mechanical sciences. In fact, he loved innovation, especially when it came to useful technologies that could enrich people's lives or make their work easier. He read widely on myriad subjects and had a creative impulse that led him to experiment a lot; he also enjoyed being thrifty and clever, always making the most out every last scrap of material.

Churikov's familiarity with technology was a useful remnant of his old life in Samara, where he had worked a large farm with a steam thresher and other forms of mechanization. But his willingness to embrace both science and faith was also "in harmony with the spirit of the times."[83] The much revered nineteenth-century bishop-turned-contemplative monk Feofan (Govorov) was also a "believer in science and scholarship," with a microscope and telescope in his cell.[84] Another precedent might be found in the utopian socialists St. Simon and Pecqueur who not only saw faith and science as complementary, but looked to technology as a means by which to bring about greater equality and to lessen exploitation through labor. According to the journalist Mikhailov, while many religious-searching intelligentsia in the late nineteenth century "took up arms against science above all," and assumed that salvation could only be attained by adopting the "simple life," religious thinking among the *narod* (a category in which he placed Brother Ioann and his followers) "acknowledged science and knowledge [*nauka*]."[85]

In this spirit, the Vyritsa colony evolved as a place of faith and industry, of prayer and technological innovation. In addition to embracing new inventions such as cameras and telephones, the colonists constructed a sophisticated irrigation system and kerosene-powered artesian well, which they dug and built under Churikov's direction. They also designed a fuel-conserving stove, which they hoped to install in each home, and they set up a fire brigade, which was both practical and useful for fostering good will within the local community. Plans for the future included an electrical lighting system and a new school.[86]

Intentionally groundbreaking, the colony set forth a new, and some said "exemplary," model of working-class life, which straddled the cultural poles of modern life between the village and city, religion and science, poverty and wealth, the past and the future. Both present-minded and goal-oriented, Churikov's followers devoted themselves to realizing a highly moral, peaceful, and sober environment that was off the grid both culturally and socially. And while the colonists aspired to be bourgeois in their emphasis on cleanliness, personal responsibility, abstinence, family, and faith, they embodied values that were welcome in even the most radical worker circles, including hard work, mutual aid, resourcefulness, and most of all, intolerance for any kind of exploitation.

With his superior knowledge on so many topics, and his reputation as a healer, Churikov commanded enormous authority on the colony, far greater than anyone else. "We listen to Brother about everything," Ermolov confessed; "he is our head in everything."[87] To be clear,

Brother Ioann did not support this kind of thinking; on the contrary, even as he gave all he had to them, he encouraged his followers to be self-sufficient and to develop their talents, as long as they lived soberly and by the Word of God. Even independent striving was valued, as long as generosity was too. In fact, when the journalist Mikhailov engaged him in a discussion about forming an egalitarian *obshchina* (community) along the lines of the ancient Christians, Churikov rejected the idea on the grounds that "in an *obshchina*, the weak crush the strong." He much preferred to keep the colony as it was, that is, with everyone living "in freedom," according to his or her own strengths and inclinations.[88] Thus, although there was a sense of order and spiritual life was ritualized on the colony, everyday life was not as highly regulated as with some of the other intentional communities founded by the intelligentsia. The goal was to promote personal dignity and mutual respect, not full equality or conformity.

The colony's success brought both praise and condemnation from outsiders. Hailing it as a model of prosperity, moral living, and a healthy balance between work and faith, the state councilor M. M. Kovalevskii went so far as to express cautious optimism that the example might spark the imagination of people throughout Russia, and inspire them to live soberly as well.[89] At the very least, he suggested, the living example of the colonists in Vyritsa was likely to have a far greater social impact than a dry pamphlet or sermon on the evils of drinking. At the same time, however, the colony's culture of sobriety made it a target for those who did not understand it, including many of the locals in Vyritsa.[90] In an effort to live on good terms with the local population, the trezvenniki had carried out a series of high-profile projects in the town, including a new bridge, a well, and plans for a new school (which included not only the land but also the construction materials). Local inhabitants were also beneficiaries of the colony's fire brigade. But relations with the nonsober community living around the colony remained less than ideal.

Several factors might help to explain the locals' hostility, including the uncertainty about Brother Ioann's relationship to the Orthodox faith. Although at least some of the Vyritsa trezvenniki attended mass at the nearby church (Sv. Apostoly Petr i Pavel) and Brother Ioann supported it with donations,[91] the local priest was suspicious of them and worked with church authorities to shut Churikov down.[92] At the same time, accusations circulating in the press to the effect the trezvenniki were "sectarians" led to confusion about their identity among the local population.[93] Some associated them with the radical followers of Father Ioann of Kronstadt ("Ioannity"), others with the evangelicals known as *pashkovtsy*.[94] Their sober lifestyle might also have been taken by some as an implicit criticism of those who did not share it. The colonists' prosperous lifestyle created confusion too, especially given that so many of them had once been so very poor. Although the Ermolov and Sergeev families could legitimately point to their sobriety and hard work as the reasons behind their success, the negative rumors persisted.

The colony's prosperity also raised questions about Churikov's finances, especially in light of rumors in the press that he was exploiting his followers. It is true that Brother Ioann was largely dependent on gifts from the trezvenniki. Most were poor and left gifts in kind (especially sugar and kerosene) in the collection boxes set out at the besedy. But he also benefited from the generosity of a few wealthy patrons, including a state advisor's wife, Maria Pavlovna Spiridonova, who gifted him a nice carriage and horse so that he could ride back and forth into St. Petersburg from Vyritsa without using public transportation.

According to those who knew him well, Brother Ioann lived as he taught others—modestly, soberly, and piously. He ate well on occasion and was known to lay out a spread of tea, honey, fruit, and cookies upon the arrival of guests, but he also fasted often and rigorously.[95] Already forty-five when the colony was founded, he remained a tireless worker, living not for his own comfort or pleasure but in constant service to others, especially to God. In fact, even as he traversed the expanse of St. Petersburg to tend to his followers or helped the colonists in their workshops, he always found several hours to spend in prayer and to read and engage with Scripture, orally or in writing. Nonetheless, Brother Ioann remained the target of rumors to the effect that he lived in luxury, engaged in land speculation, and refused credit to the poor.[96]

The fact that in Vyritsa Brother Ioann lived in a large, uniquely colorful two-story house with a turret also contributed to questions about his financial status. Whenever anyone came to the colony, they would ask about the impressive house. The trezvenniki would respond proudly that it belonged "to Brother," and he would always claim that it was theirs.[97] Both were technically correct, since the trezvenniki had donated their labor (and money) to build it for him. On the ground floor, there was a large hall for besedy, as well as a small room for treating the sick. The second floor housed the living quarters for Brother Ioann, including his office and bedroom, as well as three other rooms for his female assistants. The house's grandeur nonetheless provoked suspicion about Brother Ioann's image as a man of God; as one non-trezvennik commented, "Christ did not live in a dacha."[98]

A Friend to Animals

On January 3, 1910, in celebration of the new year, Brother Ioann added one more image to his repertoire of identities. Calling upon his followers to renounce the eating of meat, he distinguished himself as a "friend to animals."[99] In a series of meetings with trezvenniki in private settings over several weeks, and later in a published pamphlet, he outlined his main points on the issue and answered questions. Drawing on scriptural passages that suggested the virtues of a vegetarian diet and the sinfulness of eating meat (for example, the Gospel according to Mark, and Romans 14:21),[100] he explained that meat-eating was an unnecessary and unjust form of violence against animals, many of whom provided useful service to mankind. Meat-eating also led to health problems, including cholera epidemics, Brother Ioann reasoned, but abstinence from meat, like abstinence from alcohol, was most of all an important step toward moral self-improvement. Although he dared not cite the excommunicated Tolstoy, Churikov similarly observed that meat-eating corrupted a person's soul by suppressing the natural inclination to protect life, and thus only by renouncing meat could an individual aspire to be "wise or gentle" like the Holy Fathers.[101] While achieving peace with the animal world would bring one closer to God,[102] it would also bring one closer to one's fellow men, since after renouncing violence against animals, the individual would experience a new sense of shame when treating fellow humans badly. Implicit in Brother Ioann's argument for vegetarianism was another critique of institutionalized Orthodoxy: the fact that the Church allowed the eating of meat on certain days was, he suggested, a sign of its willingness to cater to popular desire, rather than a function of its appreciation of Scripture. In this way, it also had something in common with the Church's tolerant stance on alcohol consumption.

Brother Ioann's call to renounce meat was intentionally spectacular; it was also very successful, resulting in the conversion of many thousands of people to a vegetarian diet. He made clear that the pledge should be made by each individual voluntarily, since God did not sanction the use of force, especially when it came to matters of conscience. Rather than a diversion from his work to promote sobriety, the campaign to renounce meat should be understood as a reflection of his commitment to the moral development of his followers, as well as his growing confidence in his vision of a sober Russia founded on the Word of God. And by calling on his followers to proclaim their vegetarianism to others, he encouraged a movement that expanded his vision of the kingdom by promoting peace over violence.

The success of Brother Ioann's vegetarian campaign was also a reflection of his growing spiritual authority. Although it is difficult to gauge the scale of Churikov's following at any point in time, more reliable sources estimate fifty thousand by 1910.[103] Others similarly estimated that the Petersburg region had about sixty thousand trezvenniki by 1913, while Moscow had another forty thousand.[104] Exact numbers are difficult to come by not only because no one was actually counting, but also because the fluid nature of labor migration took Churikov's reputation and teachings out into the countryside.[105]

Mass movements are difficult to quantify even with official membership rolls, but questions of definition further complicate efforts to count the trezvenniki. When trying to determine who exactly deserves to be considered a follower, however, several observations can be made. First, Brother Ioann had a relatively small, inner core of followers who were among the most visibly devoted to him. This included individuals such as the sestritsy, who worked by Churikov's side and embraced his teachings and way of life completely, and Ermolov, who was among his earliest followers and highly dependent on him. Second, at the center of the broader community of trezvenniki was a bigger population of several thousand active followers, who attended Brother Ioann's besedy regularly and petitioned him whenever in need of prayer or advice. Judging from the space constraints at his besedy, this number was growing steadily between 1900 and 1904, and even more quickly between 1905 and 1914. After his move to Vyritsa, Churikov traveled regularly into St. Petersburg on Saturdays to preach at his usual meeting place in Petrovskii Park. By 1910 or so, however, it became clear that the rented space was no longer sufficient to meet the needs of his growing number of followers. With funding and labor donated by trezvenniki, a new two- to three-story prayer house big enough to accommodate about four thousand people in a single room was built near the Obukhovo railroad station on the outskirts of St. Petersburg.[106]

Finally, the outer ring of Churikov's following consisted of individuals who had at one point petitioned him and/or were attracted to the idea of holy sobriety. Significantly, by 1906 or so, Brother Ioann's work in the Petersburg region had given rise to a similar movement in Moscow, under the leadership of two of his former followers, the former alcoholics and Petersburg workers Ivan Koloskov and Dmitrii Grigor'ev. Both had been inspired through their own personal experience to take up Brother Ioann's mission and began preaching Scripture and praying for the healing of Moscow's working population. Within the space of several years after 1905, the so-called "Moscow *brattsy*" had attracted a devoted following numbering in the tens of thousands. On the one hand, the success of Koloskov and Grigor'ev demonstrated the power of Churikov's message of holy sobriety and the laity's desire for the kind of spiritual guidance and healing that he offered. On the other hand, as chapter 5 will discuss further, their success also posed new challenges for Brother Ioann, since from that point on church authorities would judge him not only according to his own words and actions, but also theirs.

A Hero of His Time?

In the years following the revolution of 1905, Brother Ioann's mission to promote holy sobriety received approval from educated secular observers in a variety of fields, including journalists, lawyers, scholars, medical doctors, and representatives in the new imperial Duma. While the urban landscape was full of good intentioned people trying to lift workers up in a moral and cultural sense, the prevailing mood after 1905 was a dark one, marked by widespread skepticism, immorality, and despair, especially in St. Petersburg's working-class districts. For all the explosive violence and enthusiastic talk of reform that had marked the revolutionary year, little had improved in the everyday lives of working people; on the contrary, a lack of hope weighed even more heavily, reflected most tragically in the uptick in St. Petersburg's suicide rates. As many educated elites expressed a complete lack of confidence in the tsarist regime to repair the broken social order, the historian Mark Steinberg has observed, some journalists and public activists latched onto optimistic narratives that hinged on "belief in the power of positive emotions" or the "heroism of will [*volia*]" as a potential starting point for social transformation.[107] In this context, Brother Ioann's ability to inspire people to embrace faith and improve their lives though sobriety and hard work offered a much-needed source of hope.

Praise from secular corners was frequent and often hyperbolic. As the "people's soul" struggled against the challenges of modernity, the journalist A. T. Mikhailov observed, Brother Ioann was like Nekrasov's Uncle

Vlas, who set out to build a temple to God. Instead of a church, Brother Ioann had roused a community of believers, revealing the religious spirit within even the most "brutalized [and] impoverished people," and reminding all of the "Herculean strength and perseverance of the great Russian soul."[108] Taking a slightly different but no less laudatory approach, Professor L. E. Vladimirov observed Churikov's ability to produce "moral miracles," by which "the fallen are immediately reborn to a true, working life."[109] In effect sidelining the clergy's concerns that Brother Ioann was a source of spiritual infection or moral contagion threatening the health of an already weakened part of the Orthodox population, Vladimirov emphasized how, on the contrary, his preaching had strengthened the people's "moral self-defense." Against a background of "ethical anarchy [and] complete moral disintegration," he claimed, Churikov had revealed in the working people a healthy "instinct for self-preservation." For similar reasons, the prominent lawyer N. M. Zhdanov praised Brother Ioann as a hero of his time, performing "great spiritual feats [*podvigi*]" on behalf of all of Russian society.[110]

At a time when many secular elites seemed caught between their belief in the people (*narod*) as the bearer of an authentic faith and Russian identity and a concern about their debilitating "backwardness," some saw Churikov as a positive force precisely because he cultivated values and behaviors in his followers that might not otherwise emerge. Against the backdrop of revolutionary chaos, a prominent group of Octobrists in the Duma, nicknamed "Churikov's Apostles,"[111] hailed Brother Ioann as unique and praiseworthy because of his ability to act in "traditional" ways to "modern" ends. Pointing to the colony in Vyritsa, they highlighted his success at using Scripture and prayer to transform a morally disordered and politically unstable sector of the population into sober, hardworking, devout, nonpolitical, and nonviolent citizens of the empire. To them, the historian Arthur McKee observed, the trezvenniki embodied the ideal of the tsarist imagination and the highest potential of the Russian people liberated from its traditional vices.[112] Thus they celebrated Churikov as the unwitting hero in a social and political drama in which the Russian people were saved from themselves—and by extension, Russia was saved too.

Brother Ioann no doubt benefited from such arguments, and as clerical criticisms intensified after 1910, he would learn to speak strategically of his own "usefulness" to nation and state. In fact, at some point he commissioned famous Petersburg photographer Karl Bulla to make visible the work that he and the colonists were doing in Vyritsa:

at his desk surrounded by scriptural passages, tending to farm animals, or laboring beside his sober followers in the colony's various artisanal shops.[113] He also freely welcomed journalists and Duma members to the colony to show off its accomplishments, even granting rare interviews. Yet, even as Brother Ioann demonstrated his deference to the interests of secular and political authorities, his daily priority was still to show up for the many ordinary people who asked for his prayers and advice. He approached them not as members of the cultural and political abstraction known as "the people" (narod) in need of reform, but as individual souls desperately struggling to overcome a life broken by sin and pain, and striving to become better for their families and friends and, most of all, closer to God. Everything he did, he did for them, as their brother; he did not condescend to "lift" them up, but prayed for them, on his knees, with the singular aim of supporting them by the same means that had saved him—the Word of God.

CHAPTER 3

Sober Brothers

Male Trezvenniki Tell Their Stories

In 1903, forty-four-year-old E. V. Frolov, a former smoker and drinker of tragic proportions, mustered the courage to share the story of his troubled life with the Russian public. In a letter to the editor of the popular daily *Peterburgskii listok*, he confessed to sins so great in number and magnitude that he could not account for them all. In addition to (and likely because of) his bad behaviors, he suffered chronic pains in his hands and legs. But the real problem was the state of his soul. Raised as Orthodox, he had regularly fulfilled his sacramental duties, but only "like Judas," full of deceit. Wallowing in shame, he had contemplated suicide—a sign that Satan was at work in his soul. Then, on August 11, 1902, he met Brother Ioann, and everything in his life changed within a matter of minutes: "only he was able to lift from me that stone that had oppressed me my entire life, and to rouse my sinful heart."[1] After following Brother Ioann's instructions to seek out a local priest to confess and communicate, he was relieved of his pain and found the will to stop drinking and smoking after twenty-five years. Rejecting the suggestion that he had been cured by hypnosis, he insisted that he had been healed because of Brother Ioann's prayers.

Several years later, after a second healing, Frolov felt the need to testify again. In the spring of 1905 he found himself in revolutionary St. Petersburg, laid up in bed with pneumonia. His illness, he believed, was God's way of protecting him from a simmering desire to give into his old sins and temptations. After numerous doctors advised him to leave the city for cleaner air, Brother Ioann told him to stay put, insisting that even the filthy urban air was "from the Lord." "Stay in Petersburg so that the Lord can show you how strong and powerful He is," he told him; "put your hope in God, believe in His Words, and you will get healthy again, and you will be even better than before."[2] Frolov trusted his advice and soon recovered.

As Brother Ioann's reputation for healing spread, so too did the visibility of his followers, largely through similar efforts to share their stories. Indeed, as in the case of Russian Baptists, the early twentieth century was a time of active "storytelling" for trezvenniki, a trend that evolved in line with the Orthodox tradition of "making saints" and with a newer, more distinctly modern desire to give voice to individual needs and experiences.[3] Testimonies took many forms, both oral and written, and were addressed to multiple audiences. In addition to letters to editors, trezvenniki penned petitions to secular and religious authorities, granted interviews to journalists, and shared their stories with individuals sympathetic to the sober movement, especially Ivan Tregubov, a Free Christian and Brother Ioann's intimate acquaintance. They also routinely testified to each other during besedy and in private spaces, especially in Brother Ioann's absence, both after his excommunication in 1914 and after his death in 1933.

Trezvenniki tended to craft their testimonies in one or more of three distinct modes—the confessional, the defensive, and the didactic. The confessional mode was motivated by the individual's desire to lay bare their souls and to reveal their shame; they told the ugly truths of their lives as an act of self-criticism, a tool of self-fashioning, and a means of belonging. Rather than hiding their sins, they offered them up boldly, proudly even, as evidence of Brother Ioann's ability to transform and to heal, as well as a sign that they had left their former selves behind. In this mode, the individual spoke to multiple audiences at the same time. The first was God, in an act of humility and faith. Drawing on the example of the bleeding woman in the Gospel according to Luke, Churikov emphasized the need to testify to God's power to heal, even in the face of possible ridicule or alienation.[4] But testifying in the confessional mode was also a kind of witnessing intended for the individual self but performed within the context of a community.

As in Frolov's case, another mode of testifying stemmed from a need to defend and protect Churikov, and by extension the trezvennik community, against false interpretations of his behavior or accusations of wrongdoing. Brother Ioann first solicited testimonies in 1898 when he was incarcerated; indeed, he went so far as to offer instructions on how to compose them.[5] But encouragement was scarcely necessary, as the trezvenniki eagerly took it upon themselves, in Frolov's words, "to testify to the truth [*pravda*] and in defense of the truth [*istina*]." Paradoxically, the church's mission to silence Brother Ioann and weaken his relationship with his followers served only to intensify their need to testify on his behalf. Time and again, the Church's decision to forbid physical contact would result in a flurry of written petitions.

Finally, some testimonies had a didactic quality and were directed primarily toward those outside the community, including potential converts. In 1914, for example, the trezvennik Dmitrii Losev published his personal story in order to share the lessons he had learned from thirty-six years of drunkenness. He recounted how his own drinking had begun at age seventeen and with time destroyed his life and those around him, including his wife and children. On the brink of suicide, he petitioned Brother Ioann, and on April 30, 1912, his life was saved. Concerned that many other people were on the same destructive path, he shared his story as both a warning and a message of hope; indeed his account reads much like a contemporary miracle story.[6] Yet, as much as Losev's testimony was about converting others to sobriety, it was also an exercise in confession and thus central to his own conversion and the process of renewing his commitment to his sober self.

As texts of self-representation, testimonies—even when faithfully recorded by the individual or a highly responsible interviewer—can be challenging texts to interpret, shaped as much by language, audience, and memory as by experience or belief. By their very nature, all testimonies are performative and shaped with an intended audience in mind; they often rely on common tropes as well.[7] As one medical doctor familiar with the trezvenniki warned, their testimonies were especially prone to exaggeration, since passion often leads to distortion.[8] Working-class testimonies can also be frustrating in their brevity; even when recounting moments of spiritual crisis, they tend to focus far more on narrating than discussing motivation or intent, and they often resist engaging in self-reflection to any meaningful extent. Thus the fact that some trezvennik testimonies only hinted at the spiritual crisis that led them to Brother Ioann is perhaps not surprising; as Nadieszda Kizenko has noted with respect to written confessions to Father Ioann of Kronstadt, less educated believers tended to "concentrate less on their inner lives and more on their actions."[9]

The public nature of testifying naturally resulted in the repetition of certain shared elements from one testimony to the other, as well as a common narrative structure. While varying in terms of length and level of detail, many trezvennik stories unfold as if according to a script, beginning with the individual's struggles (with alcohol or poor health), followed by a description of their first encounter with Brother Ioann, and then a brief account of their transformation. Sometimes even the same phrases are repeated from one to another. That familiar patterns would emerge is to be expected, given that testifying took place in the context of community; as Laura Engelstein and Stephanie Sandler have remarked, "People tell stories not only to communicate but also to discover who they are as distinctive beings, bound by relations of sameness and difference to the others whose cultural and emotional fields they share."[10]

Trezvennik testimonies are nonetheless rich exercises in subjectivity and can reveal a lot about the individual's needs, struggles, and ideas about self and God. They provide a unique window onto Brother Ioann's influence, and they can also help us to understand how converts thought of themselves in relation to other people and institutions— to their families, to other trezvenniki, and to the broader Orthodox culture in which they were raised. In order to highlight gender differences, this chapter focuses on male narratives and the next will consider women's stories.

The following discussion centers on two individual stories of addiction and recovery, which are analyzed in the context of a bigger pool of testimonies. The first was told by a young tailor, Aleksei Semenovich Krylov, and the second by Vasilii Arsen'evich Guliaev, a former thief who became a skilled worker and a minor preacher in his own right after becoming sober. Given that their testimonies were crafted against the context of doubt and persecution levied by the Orthodox Church, they can also be seen as part of a contemporary conversation about popular Orthodox norms.

The Testimony of Aleksei Semenovich Krylov

Aleksei Semenovich Krylov wrote his testimony in a tortured scribble, at some point around the turn of the twentieth century.[11] This makes his account one of the earliest on record, and relatively free from the imprint of other trezvennik stories. It begins with his birth in 1875 in Pskov province to "Orthodox and sober parents," and then quickly moves on to detail his descent into alcoholism shortly after his arrival in St. Petersburg in 1889 to apprentice as a tailor. Like many young workers, he picked up the habit of excessive drinking from his coworkers. But before long what began as a form of recreation, social bonding, and an exercise of youthful masculinity evolved into a toxic addiction that would cost him everything he had once valued—his job, his home, and his wife and children. He slept on the streets and sold everything he had (including his last pair of pants) to buy alcohol, and when he had nothing left to pawn, he started to steal from others almost as poor as himself. He was chased by the police, despised by those he had robbed, and forced to live on the run.

In what might have been an act of catharsis, Krylov wrote in vivid terms about his physically and emotionally violent existence, reflecting an awareness that he was not only a longtime victim of addiction but also, in turn, a victimizer of others. His story exudes feelings of shame and regret. Like many trezvenniki, he wrote in a humble and self-deprecating tone and dwelt extensively on his sins to reveal the full extent of his degradation.

Rather than being motivated by shame to seek help or change, drinking initially made Krylov myopic and unable to contemplate the past or future in any meaningful way. This too was a common theme in alcoholic narratives. Even as he flailed about in a "maelstrom and mire" of sin, another trezvennik recalled, "I did not admit my guilt or my sinfulness. I left everything up to chance and to fate, and no one could open my eyes to the fact that [leaving my life to] chance was nothing other than my sin."[12] Many alcoholics also avoided church and their Orthodox duties, which only doubled the weight of their sins and made them afraid to confront them.[13] In this sense, as Tolstoy once observed, their addiction to drink was in part motivated by the need to avoid facing sin: "It is not because of taste, pleasure, or amusement that a person consumes hashish, opium, liquor, tobacco, but because of a desire to suffocate the demands of conscience."[14]

Given his long history of running from his problems, exactly why Krylov eventually sought out help remains unclear. At one point he suggested that he would have kept drinking forever but could not afford to. He also claimed that he missed his family. Perhaps he feared being arrested again. After all, for a migrant like Krylov the prospect of losing one's passport and being sent back to (a potentially unwelcoming) village was likely great. What we do know is that at some point, Krylov turned to the highly sought-after priest, Father Ioann of Kronstadt, whose reputation for helping the poor and the addicted was widespread at the time. But with little if any faith in his heart, he left disappointed by the advice he received: "Ask God, and the Lord will help you."[15]

Having failed to find meaningful help in Kronstadt, he returned to the home of his "Orthodox and sober" parents in St. Petersburg. This was neither the first nor last time he would turn to family out of desperation. As they had in the past, his parents welcomed him back and offered him money, food, and a place to sleep. As much as he feared disappointing them once more, he repeatedly put his addiction first and refused their help: "I can't stay, I want vodka, and you don't have any. I can't do anything without vodka."[16] While not entirely alone, his debilitating sense of frustration and powerlessness left him alienated from everyone—and this, in turn, made his shame all the greater.

In the end, Krylov's love of vodka was no match for his parents' love and concern for him. His mother was relentless in helping him to overcome his addiction, and in this way she was not unique; mothers and wives repeatedly show up in trezvennik testimonies suffering in proportion to their loved one as they endlessly searched for a way to help them. Although Krylov does not explain why his mother's pleas to meet with Brother Ioann eventually worked,[17] it seems clear that he sought out Churikov only as a last resort, at the lowest point of his life—that is, less out of a conscious faith in Brother Ioann's healing abilities than in the complete absence of good alternatives. This too is a common theme.

Both skeptical and fearful of rejection, Krylov found his initial encounter with Churikov awkward at first. In a room full of strangers, Brother Ioann turned directly toward him and asked point blank, "What do you want from God?" "I want to not drink," he responded. "I want to live with my family, which I lost a long time ago because of drinking. I have suffered greatly because of wine, but I cannot not drink." Brother Ioann instantly reassured him that—on the contrary—it was possible for him to stop, because "everything is possible for the believer." He then asked if he believed in God, although his first question had assumed he did. Krylov admitted that he did not, and that he often took the Lord's name in vain. Unsurprised, Churikov again reassured him with virtually the same advice that Father Ioann had offered him: it was only necessary to believe and then God would help him. Churikov then asked, "and what do you expect from me?" Turning to the crowd, he continued, "I have nothing, except this: I believe that if you ask God [to help you], the Lord will grant you[r wish] because of your faith."[18]

Brother Ioann then offered Krylov and the others bread and water (instead of wine), which, he explained, was meant to symbolize their pledge to work for the Lord (and not Satan). He compared it to the drinking of the *magarich* when a contract is being signed: "Now you have been hired to work for the Lord. You drank the *magarich* [to seal the deal] as a sign of the strength of your pledge. And don't break your pledge, or you will be given over to judgment." Making clear that the pledge was final and irrevocable, he added a clear warning: "Don't work for the Devil and don't look back, or you'll become like Lot's wife," who looked back toward Sodom (that is, sin) after leaving it and turned into a pillar of salt.[19] By the end of the meeting, Krylov felt like a completely different person, a statement that he linked to a sudden physical aversion to drinking and smoking: "I didn't want to drink, and I wasn't drawn to it; I didn't want to smoke, and through prayer I had become a completely sober person."[20]

The suddenness of Krylov's transformation to physical sobriety was not uncommon. On the contrary, the majority of trezvenniki described instantaneous moments of liberation from their addictions. As in Krylov's case, their narratives begin with a sense of hopelessness, skepticism, and even fatalism before meeting Brother Ioann, but they end with the sudden lifting of their urge to drink. Although belief in miraculous healings was widespread among the Orthodox at the time,[21] many people came to Brother Ioann without any faith at all—in his words, like "dead stone," devoid of life and spirit. As he saw it, his goal was to act on them like flint, so that a spark of God would appear.[22] In this way, Churikov would explain, "I help them to believe. Without faith it is impossible to be strong. And when there is faith, everything is possible." He would then send them off to the local church to confess and communicate, in order to "give them life."[23] But this explanation begs the question: How did he spark faith in them when, by their own admission, they didn't have any hope whatsoever (in God, or themselves, or anyone else)? Where did the "oxygen" come from, and in what form? More importantly, how did the trezvenniki understand what had happened to them?

For some trezvenniki, the sudden transformation they experienced with Brother Ioann's help simply defied explanation, or so they were content to believe. The former alcoholic Semen Beliaev, for example, had signed the pledge of sobriety in various church temperance societies *twenty-eight times* before Brother Ioann cured him, and when asked to explain, he replied simply, "I cannot."[24] Another trezvennik, Nikolai

Aleksandrovich Zhigachev, testified that "inexplicable forces" had held his feet in place when he met with Brother Ioann for the first time, even as his mind was telling him to run away; the same forces kept him from heading straight to the tavern on the way home.[25] Perhaps this willingness to leave their experiences shrouded in mystery was intentional; the less they could explain, the more powerful Brother Ioann seemed. Or perhaps it resulted from a lack of vocabulary to express adequately what had transpired.

Fortunately, most testimonies were more forthcoming as to how individuals made sense of Brother Ioann's influence on them. That they present a range of explanations and understanding is indicative of the fluidity in the broader culture of belief and unbelief, where both rational and irrational forces were thought to be at work. Of course, some testimonies were written long after the fact, so their explanatory framework probably tells us less about what the individual was thinking at the moment of their encounter with Brother Ioann than it does about how they understood it later—or, possibly, how they wanted their intended audience to think about it. Untangling these various explanatory strands completely is impossible. However, the high level of detail in Krylov's testimony suggests a concerted effort to remember and record exactly what he had experienced. Memories of his visceral reactions seem especially revealing in terms of what mattered most to him and, to a certain extent, why.

Krylov recalled how he was physically drawn toward Brother right away and felt safe enough to move closer to him in spite of his initial doubts and trepidation. Other testimonies suggest that this feeling was not uncommon. Even those who met Churikov only briefly—including some clergy troubled by his teaching—appear to have been softened by his serene presence and charmed by his warm yet powerful demeanor. "What a look of love he had!" one woman remembered after meeting Brother Ioann as a young girl. "His face was radiant [*svetloe-svetloe*]."[26] Others remarked on his "tender, quiet, endearing, and softly feminine voice,"[27] and his unique eyes, which were not only "translucent, clear, deeply thoughtful and so simple," but strikingly penetrating as if "focused on inner experiences and on the understanding of other people's lives."[28]

While some people raised in the Orthodox tradition attributed Brother Ioann with the spiritual quality known as "grace," others suggested as much without using the term. The writer A. Smol'ianikov, for example, described Brother Ioann as a "spiritual giant," whose entire being was in "complete harmony," and whose "sweet, kind face reflected an extraordinary peace of mind [and] joy."[29] Whatever terms they used, according to A. S. Prugavin, a religious scholar who had interviewed a lot of trezvenniki, the majority of people who met Brother Ioann face-to-face found him to be a person of "complete sincerity and conviction" and were "won over" by his "unusually gentle and loving attitude toward all of those around him."[30] This warmth and openness to others, Irina Paert has noted, were defining qualities of spiritual elders.[31]

As Ivan Tregubov observed, a surprising number of the trezvenniki he interviewed spoke about being deeply moved by the way Brother Ioann prayed. While in itself witnessing someone praying was not unusual—after all, the Orthodox prayed in public places all the time, not only in churches or at home but also on the street—the first time they observed Brother Ioann in the act they had found it extraordinary. "Brother prayed like no one in my family had ever seen," one trezven-nitsa recalled, "fervently, with faith [and] perseverance. By the time he was done, even the walls were crying."[32] For some, his style of prayer was a sign of his deep piety; for others, it reflected a special relation-ship with God or an "unearthly" form of spiritual power.[33] For his part, Krylov focused more on the intimacy of the moment and the powerful visceral impression it had on him. He recounted in detail how Brother Ioann began to sing a hymn and then, instead of kneeling, dove down to the floor with his entire body, as if he were praying to God for the whole world. He began to cry as he prayed, causing everyone else to cry as well. When Brother Ioann asked for the Lord's mercy, Krylov recalled, "I began to cry out against my will, and I began to feel so light, so nice [*priatno*], that I stood praying for a long time."[34]

The former alcoholic Lobanov recalled a similar experience at his first beseda. On that day, Brother Ioann's rendering of the parable of the prodigal son—the classic story of a loving father who joyfully and unre-servedly welcomes home his wayward, broken son—resonated so deeply that he was convinced it had been intended just for him: "in the life of the prodigal son, I saw myself—there was no use denying it, and it had such an influence on me that I just stood there and cried." Lobanov made it clear that it was not simply the message of paternal acceptance and forgiveness that moved him, but the fact that Brother Ioann seemed to know how desperately he needed to hear it. Even in a room full of peo-ple, Brother Ioann appeared to be speaking only to him: "no one had ever gotten that close to me, or showed such warmth toward me in my life. At the end of the besedy I left with such joy in my heart, such lightness, as if a great weight had been lifted from me."[35] Like the prodigal son who had been lost in the wilderness of sin, far from God, Lobanov had been welcomed home. His "return," his testimony suggested, was eased by Brother Ioann's ability to know what was in his heart—a gift known as *kardiognosis*, and associated with successful spiritual elders.[36]

The fact that Krylov recounted Churikov's beseda almost verbatim suggests that his epiphany occurred at least in part because he found in it a meaningful new framework for making sense of his life. The theme that evening—the *magarich*—contained many of the rhetorical elements common to Brother Ioann's popular sermons, and it was phrased in terms that ordinary workers could understand: When one pledges to labor for a lord and drinks the *magarich* to seal the deal, then everyone knows that one is bound to do that labor, or that person will be taken to court; the same is true of the Lord. More importantly, the parable offered Krylov a simple logic that was hard to escape, as in "work for the Lord," since "you used to work for the Devil and look where it got you." "[The Devil] beat you . . . [and] dressed you in worn-out shoes and a torn coat, took away your wife and children, chased you from your apartment, you slept under fences, and they chased you from there. Why did you work for such suffering, for such a tyrant?" "Work for the Lord," he instructed, and "the Lord will send [you] happiness and health."[37]

Here, as in all of Churikov's teaching, was the kind of binary thinking common to Orthodoxy, tailored for the benefit of individuals like Krylov, who had long branded themselves as "bad" and beyond redemption. There are only two kinds of people in the world: those who work for the Devil (and drink and sin), and those who work for the Lord (and are sober and hardworking). Similarly, there were only two kinds of lives: those passed in a state of hell (that is, drunkenness and the poverty and shame it brings), and those passed in a state of heaven (sobriety and the peace it promises). There was no middle path, but each individual had the power as well as the responsibility to decide what kind of life they would choose. In this way, the absolute terms of the "contract" became in themselves a source of motivation for those seeking change and empowered them to take control of their lives. It not only allowed for individual agency but mandated it. In addition to its moral clarity, the transactional nature of Brother Ioann's "contract" analogy likely resonated with the Orthodox who had been brought up to believe that relationships with the saints were founded on reciprocity: if one asked a saint for help, it was expected that one would pledge something in return.

Significantly, the force of logic in Churikov's preaching was further complemented by a fear of divine retribution. Testimonies suggest that even those who claimed to have no faith in God still believed in the threat of God's wrath—in other words, their image of God was often singularly negative. Thus, even as Brother Ioann helped them to reimagine the divine as a positive force in their lives, he was able to tap into an existing fear of hell. As Zhigachev admitted, "although I did not believe in anything at that time, I felt fear, especially when [Churikov] said: 'drunkards and fornicators do not inherit the kingdom of God.' It affected me a lot, as if I never knew it."[38] Likewise, after Churikov's preaching led the alcoholic V. Kolobov to count himself among the "children of the Devil," just "like Cain," he experienced an extreme and unfamiliar form of anxiety when Brother Ioann called him to account for his sins—as if he was already "in the other world, at the Final Judgment."[39] This fear, he wanted others to know, had motivated him to change his ways for good.

Moreover, by calling people out on their bad choices and behaviors, Churikov exhibited not just an abstract awareness of their capacity for evil, but a very clear, informed understanding of their sins and anxieties. In this way, he acknowledged that he understood and saw them, and at the same time encouraged them to make an active choice about how they were going to live from that day forward. The finality of the sobriety pledge, especially when it was sealed with the solemn ritual of taking holy water and bread, was for many of them, including Krylov, the moment of truth. He recalled that he instantly felt as if something "heavy" (tiazheloe) had been lifted from him and was then overcome with a "light, pleasant, and joyous" feeling, even as his body began to shake nervously and he started crying.[40]

Many alcoholic testimonies end, almost triumphantly, with the moment that Brother Ioann helped them to break free from their addiction. This is not surprising, given that most were written by those who had overcome their addictions and wanted to provide evidence of Brother Ioann's healing power. Yet, as Churikov would have been the first to acknowledge, true sobriety was not achieved simply by conquering the urge to drink, as momentous as this was. "Real trezvost' [sobriety] is only when a person undergoes a deep spiritual transformation," he told a reporter in 1913. "Trezvost' is [a matter] of the conscience."[41] Sobriety was also a matter of consciousness, of opening up a new perspective on life and self that one developed first and foremost through an active engagement with Scripture. Physical sobriety was a difficult challenge, but it was only the first step toward spiritual sobriety and the development of a new moral self.

Krylov's testimony is relatively unique in that it speaks at length about this second transformation—a process that turned out to be neither sudden nor linear. On the contrary, his first encounter with Brother Ioann was followed by a prolonged liminal state. Although he would never drink again, the journey from "hell" to "heaven" was one of trial and error, hope and doubt; his moral framework remained in disarray for years, and he continued to struggle with shame and hide from his sins, especially those of a sexual nature. "The Lord sent me work, but I was ashamed to confide in him that my lust tormented me. And I didn't hold out, I broke the seventh commandment." He soon contracted syphilis, which left an ugly sore on his lip as a visible sign of his "sin." He had no doubt that his illness was a form of punishment for his adultery, or that his infidelity was a symptom of weak faith (rather than a failure of willpower): "as Brother said, for each offense [narushenie] there is a punishment, and so it happened."[42]

On the subject of recidivism, Brother Ioann was clear: "if we sin after we have been healed, then God will punish us again with illness," a statement he supported with multiple passages from the New Testament.[43] This was both an essential part of his explanatory model and in line with both Orthodox teachings and popular norms. Yet, while never suggesting that humans would be immune from the cycle of sin and punishment, he offered his followers a clear path of redemption; those suffering from illness need only repent and live by the "science of Christ" (nauka Khristova) in order to return to good health. "We are not holy people," one female follower explained; "we sin willingly and unwillingly, and for this we receive punishment, but Brother Ioann wants to see us as good, and therefore helps us to improve ourselves."[44] His compassion and open-door policy made him an important resource for those in need of forgiveness. Thus, in spite of his shame, Krylov eventually returned to Brother Ioann for guidance.

Brother Ioann responded to Krylov's latest petition with his standard prescription to cleanse and discipline the soul: "Fast for two days, don't drink, don't eat, repent your sin and the Lord will forgive you and you will be healed." To Krylov's surprise, he added a few specific conditions. "You will need to try to live with your wife afterward. After all, the Lord sent you wages not only for you, but also for your family. You must not act in this way [ne nado, ne nado tak]."[45] While taking the instructions to fast in stride, the second command caught him off guard. Although Krylov had long desired to return to his wife and family, the fact that Churikov had been able to diagnose the cause of his illness (that is, his sexual infidelity) heightened his sense of shame; it also terrified him to realize that Churikov "knew everything"—including all of his "escapades." Clearly, Krylov had become accustomed to hiding from the consequences of his own behaviors—a habit that was easier in the big city, where one could live on the run or exist anonymously within the culture as a whole. Nonetheless, his moral conscience had evidently begun to evolve through his relationship with Brother Ioann, fragile though it still was, and thus his sinful ways became harder to hide, most of all from himself.

Once again, Krylov made the choice to run away. Vowing never to consult Churikov again, he decided to handle his health crisis by praying and reading the Gospels on his own—both actions revealing an implicit acceptance of Churikov's teachings, even as he distanced himself. His health deteriorated rapidly, yet he still refused to seek out Churikov and consulted a local doctor instead—in itself another sign of his alienation from Brother Ioann. He was sent to the hospital, and as the doctors prepared to give him an injection, he surrendered his body to their care but warned them, "don't touch my soul. I'm being punished for breaking the seventh commandment." He recalled the date exactly: December 12, 1899.[46]

The contradiction between Krylov's actions and his words on that day would seem to suggest a deeply divided self, and the fact that he remembered the exact day indicates that he saw it as an important milestone in his life. It turned out to be the beginning of another downward spiral. Krylov avoided Brother Ioann completely for two more years, and during that time, his body rotted to the point where he could no longer walk. He was literally falling apart. Only when doctors prepared to transfer him to a leper colony did he send his mother to seek out Churikov again. As if expecting him, Brother Ioann welcomed him back and repeated his message: if he believed, he would be healed. He then recounted the popular story of Lazarus, whose body was already rotting when Christ brought him back to life, and reassured Krylov that "for God these things are minor." In addition to hope, Brother Ioann offered him a small bottle of healing oil, which was intended to awaken in him a "healing faith" (tselebnaia vera).[47]

Convinced this was his last chance to avoid death, Krylov undertook three days of prescribed fasting. Then, in a description that mimicked the tale of the healing pool in John 5:1, he narrated how he was taken to the bath to be washed, and as his body entered the water, his sores stopped hurting.[48] For Krylov, as for many trezvenniki, the fact that his instantaneous healing had no obvious medical explanation was interpreted as evidence of Brother Ioann's spiritual power. His testimony ended with a reprimand from Brother Ioann to the effect that pride was "contrary to God." In other words, salvation would come only with humility and full surrender to God's will.

However long or short the process of conversion, many trezvenniki associated the experience of meeting Brother Ioann with a kind of temporal break. Some spoke of their life as broken in two (before and after Brother Ioann), while others thought of themselves as born again.[49] Another compared himself to a discarded flower shoot that Churikov had rescued from the gutter and brought back to life.[50]

As we have seen, however, Krylov's embrace of holy sobriety was far more fraught by comparison, involving a difficult and nonlinear transformation. On the one hand, his testimony speaks to Brother Ioann's abilities as a spiritual guide, whose combination of compassion, discipline, scriptural knowledge, and spiritual insight served as a steady compass for the individual as they navigated toward full sobriety. On the other hand, his case suggests that at the heart of the trezvennik conversion to sobriety was not only the individual's embrace of Scripture as a guide to life but also a growing awareness of the self as a moral agent; it hinged on a growing consciousness of sin and the difference between good and evil, as well as the need to take responsibility for one's actions toward the self, others, and God.

The Testimony of Vasilii Arsen'evich Guliaev

Like Krylov, Vasilii Arsen'evich Guliaev was a man broken by drink when he first met Brother Ioann. By his own admission, he was violently dangerous, the member of a gang of thieves whose main strategy was to lie in wait at night under the American bridge on the major road from St. Petersburg to Moscow, and then mercilessly beat, undress, and rob passersby.[51] He spent everything he stole on alcohol. His only inkling of faith was the trust he had for his partners in crime, and when one of them found God and sobriety with Churikov's help, he felt deeply betrayed. Thus Guliaev first attended a beseda not with the intention of becoming sober or repenting, but with the goal of exacting revenge on Brother Ioann by means of the large knife tucked in his boot. Fortunately for both of them, things did not turn out as Guliaev had planned.

According to his testimony made in 1913, when Guliaev met Brother Ioann on that fateful day, he was devoid of all faith and even the barest conception of sin. A tough guy on the outside, inside his soul was "hardened" too, full of "bitterness, resentment and strongly sown with hatred." But as he approached Churikov with "Cain-like malice," the instant his eyes met Brother Ioann's, "something unbelievable" happened: "I broke into a terrible fever," he recalled, "and I shook as if I had touched a bare electrical wire." Although physically large and strong enough to take on anyone in the room, he felt suddenly and utterly powerless: "I lost my composure, and my physical strength fell; I was totally exhausted, and my soul [*dusha*] beat like that of a bird in a cage. Everyone around me looked at me in surprise. I turned pale, as happens out of great fear, and all of a sudden, I was struck by the thought: what am I doing? What a crazy idea!" Instantly, Guliaev reconsidered his decision to kill. Then, as if pushed he fell at Churikov's feet. "My soul had awakened," he explained. With tears in his eyes, he begged for forgiveness, and as Brother Ioann's hand touched his head to offer a blessing, an "inexplicable force" rushed through his body. Drained of energy, he struggled to rise to receive the blessing, as if "a very sick person just getting out of bed." As he staggered to the door, he realized that he had just witnessed truth (*pravda*) on earth, an experience he had never believed possible until that moment. In other words, he had come to believe in God and in Brother Ioann at exactly the same time.

From that point on, Guliaev's life changed permanently. He gave up his "parasitical" ways, managed to secure a good job as a skilled worker at the massive Putilov armaments factory in St. Petersburg, and began to provide for his family for the first time in many years. At the time, many of his coworkers at Putilov were becoming radicalized, joining trade unions, striking, or demonstrating against the tsarist government for its politically and socially repressive policies. But Guliaev stayed on his own path to salvation. "Since I became sober, I praise God, I love Christ, and I try to live according to the Gospel as Brother teaches." He followed Brother Ioann to Vyritsa, where he bought land to build a house. Although he continued to work in St. Petersburg, he spent his free time on the colony, where he would focus on improving himself spiritually though prayer, reading Scripture, and conversing with Brother Ioann and other trezvenniki. For men especially, this shift from socializing in the workplace to the home—or in this case, the sober community—was an important factor in their ability to stay sober.[52]

Guliaev's account points to several other factors that helped trezven-niki stay on the path to sobriety. The first was regular fasting. While abstaining from food and drink was widely understood as an important form of spiritual discipline, Brother Ioann saw it as an exercise with dis-tinct physical and mental benefits; when a person fasts, he taught, the blood is cleansed, bones are detoxified, and an oil is produced, which in turn clarifies one's mind.[53] For trezvenniki, fasting meant more than abstaining from food, drinking, or smoking, however. Ascetic to an extreme, trezvenniki renounced almost all forms of secular "fun," including card-playing, theatergoing, and dancing, both to keep them-selves from temptation and to redirect their time and energy toward spiritual development. Thus, on holidays as well as Sundays, they read and discussed Scripture, prayed, and sang hymns, and only seldom engaged with secular newspapers or literature of any kind.

The weekly beseda provided another important context for the solid-ifying of the trezvennik self in the context of community, not unlike the mandatory meetings for AA. Comparing Churikov's words to those of the prophets and apostles, his followers described his preaching as a gift from heaven, with the power to bring "dead men back to life," "to cheer up . . . tired souls," and "to awaken[] in us a striving for truth and a pure life."[54] A site of enlightenment, contemplation, and *communitas*, the besedy were also the only place where Petersburg trezvenniki could see Brother Ioann in person. Although even long-time followers contin-ued to use the petition process to ask for his prayers and advice, regular physical contact with Brother Ioann was very important for a lot of people.[55] While it is impossible to say with any certainty that Krylov's long struggle with sobriety was caused at least in part by the fact he had distanced himself from Brother Ioann physically, or by his refusal to take advantage of the empathic community around him, other people clearly found great value in both resources and utilized them regularly.

Trezvenniki attended besedy in part because they provided a safe space where even men could openly express their shame and confront their sinful tendencies. Instead of repressing or hiding their transgres-sions and impure thoughts, they embraced the opportunity to make the contents of their soul as transparent as possible. This included Guliaev who, one journalist observed, exuded a "terrible joy" as he broadcast his former sins to a crowded room.[56] Strangers would unashamedly share the "secrets of their life," the trezvennik Petr Terekhovich recalled, "con-fessing before [other] people, as if before God Himself."[57] Initially these outpourings had made him extremely uncomfortable. But for many trezvenniki, confronting past sins and revisiting pain in this way was an important exercise of emotional and spiritual catharsis. The trezvenniki appeared to love to "tear themselves to pieces" and "spit out" their former lives, the journalist Mikhailov commented.[58]

While the scriptural parables of Lazarus and the prodigal son offered many former drinkers a meaningful framework through which to make sense of their experiences, Guliaev saw himself in the tale of the demon-possessed man (the "Gadarene swine") from Luke 8, in which Jesus heals him by casting the devils out of him and into pigs. This was also a predictable choice given the widely shared understanding of alcoholism as a form of possession at the time.[59]

As he often did, Brother Ioann offered a metaphorical reading of the story, in which the Word of God heals the alcoholic (the possessed) by helping him to get rid of temptation (demons).[60] Demons disorient one's thinking, he would observe, and it is the Devil's work to "remove" (unosit') God's Word from human souls in order to convince them that "drunkenness and theft are not sin." Without the Word of God, people become addicted to debauchery and drunkenness, and this inevitably leads not only to poverty and fighting, but to murders and suicides. But the Word of God will still protect the soul of even those who had lost everything, by working as a kind of talisman against evil: "Listen to the Word of God, and all demons—drunk, depraved, and dancing—will disappear from you; demons will be ashamed to be in you when the Word of God is in you."[61]

As Guliaev testified to his conversion, however, his own interpretation of the possession story had more in common with traditional exorcism accounts than with Brother Ioann's metaphorical (and more modern) version. While lacking some of the dramatic thrashing, shrieking, and animal sounds associated with exorcisms, his account contained exactly the same basic narrative elements and stages. He described, for example, that when he approached Brother Ioann after his sermon, he was overwhelmed by an "incredible" feeling of malice "apparently raised in me by Satan himself, possessing my entire soul"— a description that perfectly matched the script of one of Father Ioann's sermons about the possessed man who rages in anger as his demons are met by "blessed power, which is hateful to them, and stronger than them."[62] Similarly, Guliaev recalled how he was rendered powerless the instant he looked into Brother Ioann's (good) eyes, and then just as Churikov's hand touched him, he felt an inexplicable force rush through his body, as if his demons were exiting. Once the evil spirits were gone, Guliaev staggered to the door like "a very sick person just getting out of bed," still weak but finally "awake."

Given his violent past, it is not surprising that Guliaev preferred the more traditional version of the possession story. While both relieved him of responsibility for his former self to a certain extent (since, by definition, one possessed is not in control of one's actions), in the more literal reading the demons were not abstract representations of "temptation," but actual creatures sent by Satan, who had invaded his body and gained access to his soul. Thus once the demons had been forced out, Guliaev no longer had to fear them, or himself. At the same time, his version departed from the traditional narrative in a significant way—namely, by placing Brother Ioann, rather than the Word of God or the clergy, in the role of exorcist and giving him credit for chasing the demons out. This is an interpretation which both clergy and Churikov would have found problematic.

Nonetheless, this is the version that Guliaev decided to share before an audience of secular and clerical authorities in 1913. For reasons that are not completely clear, Guliaev was able take the floor at a ticket-only lecture given by a Petersburg priest entitled "The Orthodox Church and the Antichrist."[63] In the audience was Bishop Nikandr (Phenomenov), who was leading a formal investigation of Brother Ioann at the time. Aware of the many powerful people in attendance, Guliaev tapped into widespread fears about "hooliganism" among the urban lower classes to defend Brother Ioann as the healer of his sinful soul—and, by extension, Petersburg society. Mindful of the clergy's hesitation about Churikov, he also reassured his audience that Brother Ioann's highest priority and greatest achievement had been to put his followers on the path to God and to the Church. He then took the featured clerical speaker to task for suggesting that Brother Ioann was the "Antichrist" and clarified that the trezvenniki continued to love the Church, but only that "of the saints, apostles, and martyrs, not the persecutors."[64] While certainly not the first to defend Brother Ioann against his critics, the scope and content of Guliaev's comments were bolder than most, and they raised questions about Brother Ioann's ability to control his message in the hands of even his most devout followers. After all, Brother Ioann could offer them powerful, salvific stories with which to reimagine their lives, but it was up to the individual trezvennik to decide what to do with his or her story—how to interpret it, where to tell it, and why.

At some point around this same time, Guliaev become a preacher of holy sobriety in his own right. While in part a practical response to the silencing of Brother Ioann by the authorities, especially after his excommunication in 1914, Guliaev's decision to preach and testify might also be seen as the manifestation of a particular type of "sober" masculinity embodied and cultivated by Brother Ioann. As Steve Smith has observed, norms of masculinity were changing in the working-class environment at this time. Although many workers still associated "manliness" with physical strength and a range of morally questionable habits (such as excessive drinking, swearing, and sexual conquest), others were beginning to embrace a more "modern" form of male identity linked to self-control, social respectability, hard work, and skill acquisition.[65] While this typically involved mechanical, construction, or electrical expertise—as encouraged on the colony in Vyritsa—in the context of the sober community it also meant the skill of preaching the Word of God. Indeed, Brother Ioann was revered in large part for both his spiritual strength (and qualities such as piety, humility, serenity, and generosity) and his ability to bring Scripture to life for others. The Moscow *brattsy* were the most well-known (and controversial) of his male followers to become preachers; given the persecution they would suffer at the hands of Moscow clergy, this was a role that gave them ample opportunity to showcase their spiritual strength as well as scriptural knowledge and expertise. But many others, including Guliaev, were similarly committed to preaching and defending holy sobriety on their own. In doing so, they too embodied a new form of sober masculinity, not only in and around the factories of St. Petersburg, but in other towns as well.

The passion with which trezvenniki individuals like Guliaev and Krylov declared their devotion to Brother Ioann and his teachings struck many contemporaries as unusual and sometimes extreme. In trying to make sense of it, they often pointed to their psychological and emotional vulnerability. For example, the priest-missionary Kesarev explained in 1905 that individuals who were "weak in will, spirit, and faith" or had lost their "mental equilibrium" because of difficult circumstances naturally sought out someone stronger who could help them "heal their psychological [*dushevnye*] wounds." Thus they followed Churikov "as a person . . . more skilled in spiritual life, as a living example of faith and patience [*terpenie*]."[66]

Explanations that hinge on people's weak will or "need to submit" are not wrong as much as they are incomplete, both in their understanding of Brother Ioann's influence and in the way that they objectify his followers as passive actors in their own conversion story. As Catherine Wanner has argued in her work on evangelical Protestant communities, the process of conversion should be seen not as a wholly submissive act by which an individual surrenders to God's omnipotence, but rather as "a redefinition of agency, submission, and empowerment."[67] This approach is useful when thinking about converts to holy sobriety as well. For although the relationship between Chruikov and his followers is best understood as a popular version of the Orthodox tradition of spiritual eldership, as scholars have observed, *starchestvo* was itself a flexible institution involving different types and varying degrees of submission and empowerment.[68] In fact, even with the most extreme surrendering of the self to the demands of an elder, the disciple might still be seen as exercising a measure of spiritual agency. As V. A. Kuchumov has noted, the metaphor of the elder as a blacksmith is useful in that it captures the idea that the "iron" has inherent strength and potential but needs help being shaped into something more useful or perfect by someone skilled.[69] The testimonies of both Krylov and Guliaev would seem to bear this out; at the same time, their submission was far from inevitable, and the end result was not in Brother Ioann's hands.

Individual converts to holy sobriety understood Brother Ioann's ability to empower them in different ways. Some people suffering in the depths of despair were drawn to his extraordinary qualities, most of all his exemplary piety, his capacity for healing "miraculously," and his superior knowledge (both scriptural and prophetic). Others had difficulty expressing what drew them to him, or if they tried, focused on less tangible attributes, such as his gaze, his presence, or his "charisma." Yet the majority saw him as a living image of sanctity and looked to him as a "teacher of life and the highest judge in all matters," seeking out his advice at every step of their lives.[70] Many also took to heart Brother Ioann's own emphasis on Scripture as the source of all meaning and found helpful guidance in his besedy, both the moral messaging as well as the narratives he offered them to make sense of their lives. As in Lobanov's case, the parable of the prodigal son offered a way to locate his troubled life on a positive trajectory, and this gave him hope and the will to change. Yet, as Guliaev's testimony reminds us, Brother Ioann could control the narratives he offered his followers only so far; individuals ultimately had the power to decide how to testify to their own healings.

Testimonies also suggest that the trezvenniki's devotion to Brother Ioann was based on—and repeatedly confirmed by—his ability to connect with people and to sense and address their needs. This meant not only seeing them, but valuing them as human beings. Of all those who commented on the people's attraction to Churikov, the journalist Kondurushkin was the most perceptive when he highlighted the unconditional love and understanding Brother Ioann extended even to those buried in sin and shame. While both Krylov and Guliaev benefited from Brother Ioann's guidance, they were lifted from their former states of despair most of all by his love. More than anything else, his deep "faith in humanity's likeness to God [*bogopodobie*]" set him apart.[71] The clergy, Kondurushkin observed, taught people right and wrong, the state emphasized duty, and politicians stressed the importance of rights and opportunities. But even the most broken people were lifted up by Brother Ioann because he acknowledged the potential for good in *them*, including a fundamental desire for dignity and righteous living. After visiting one of Brother Ioann's besedy, Kondurushkin claimed to be overwhelmed by the realization that it was rare to witness such "love for the individual person [*chelovek*]" in contemporary Russian society.[72]

Trezvennik testimonies also reveal a paradox. Although Brother Ioann's followers believed that they had been healed of their addictions only by virtue of his influence over them, his faith in them was but a crutch for their self-realization; ultimately, they had to—and had to want to—walk on their own. Whatever factors brought them to Churikov's feet, the oath of sobriety was a promise they themselves had to keep. Looking back on his own experience, the trezvennik Zhigachev recalled his fear as he prepared to take the pledge. "I confessed, I communicated and made a promise before the Gospel and the Cross never to break [my] promise not to drink," he remembered, "and when I kissed the Cross, I was afraid I had made such an important promise, [and] I did not know if I would fulfill it."[73] Although he claimed that Brother Ioann's willingness to be there for him every week made all the difference, his repeated use of "I" in his testimony makes it clear that the ultimate responsibility for his actions lay with him.

The miracle of the alcoholic's healing was not the end of their relationship with Brother Ioann, but rather the beginning of a spiritual journey. True sobriety itself was not miraculous—on the contrary, it required hard work, undertaken with the spirit of a pilgrim, demanding sacrifice and courage, but promising great spiritual reward. For some the road from a highly imperfect past to a better future was longer and more winding than for others. Open to the power of prayer and to the miraculous, trezvenniki such as Krylov and Guliaev found in Scripture both the guidance that they needed to reimagine their lives and the comfort they needed to confront uncertainty and pain.

Being sober meant struggling to embrace a sense of self defined by the highest standard of moral purity and perfection; indeed, the selves to which they aspired were a mirror image of their former lives, which they described as "weighted" down by sin and fear. To reject their former state of victimhood and embrace a sense of agency and dignity required no less vision, courage, or commitment than that of the revolutionaries around them. Significantly, though, the trezvenniki assumed their new identities not by rejecting the ideals of the dominant culture but by aspiring to live up to them.

CHAPTER 4

Sober Sisters

Voices of Trezvennitsy

In 1904, the wife of a state councilor and mother of four, Maria Pavlovna Spiridonova, threw her troubles at Brother Ioann's feet. In addition to diabetes, she was suffering the effects of a slowly dying marriage, which included her husband's attempts to commit her to a psychiatric hospital so that he could use their money to cover his gambling debts and purchase gifts for his mistress. Although protection from Tsar Aleksandr III had once secured her freedom from the madhouse, Spiridonova had recently made her husband's desire to lock her away somewhat easier by "falling accidentally" into a spiritualist circle—a five-year preoccupation he tried to leverage as proof that she was insane.[1]

In a letter to the new tsar (Nicholas II) asking for protection, Spiridonova acknowledged that her spiritualist tendencies had been a problem in the past. As a "spiritual medium" she had been tormented for years by an unruly and evil spirit that would not let her sleep or eat and "kept forcing [her] to write down messages." But she reassured the tsar that those days were now behind her. Desperate to break free from these "spiritual manifestations" (which may or may not have been hallucinations related to her diabetes), she had reached out to Brother Ioann in 1904, and because of his prayers and besedy, she was free from her visions, which she now understood—by dint of his "truly Orthodox reasoning"—to have been the work of "Satan."

After her healing, Spiridonova moved to an apartment near Petrovskii Park to be closer to Brother Ioann. She attended his besedy with great regularity, claiming that his scriptural recitations were like "a balm" that healed her "mental wounds," and with equal consistency she solicited his counsel on all the difficulties in her life. Out of gratitude, Spiridonova began gifting him generously. In addition to a fancy carriage, she offered him a gold watch and 275 desiatina of land in Tula Province.[2] Although he refused both the watch and the land, when word got out about her extreme generosity, her irate husband again tried to lock her up. Spiridonova managed to avoid the madhouse and remained a devoted trezvennitsa until her death in 1910.

Given her great privilege and education, Spiridonova was not a typical member of the sober community, but her story was not a complete outlier either. After all, the legal vulnerability and emotional abuse that she experienced within her marriage would have been familiar to many other trezvennitsy. Her desperate need for "protection" from a man she could trust would also have resonated widely. Women were in fact far more likely than men to seek out Brother Ioann for prayers and guidance, and they outnumbered men among his followers by a ratio of approximately two to one. Yet, even as Spiridonova took up the habits of the sober community, attending besedy and petitioning Brother Ioann, her relationship with him was shaped by her privilege. In addition to the lavish gifts, she inundated him with passionate letters about the troubled state of her soul and engaged in long exercises in scriptural exegesis, as if he were her personal confessor.

Spiridonova's behavior was also unusual for the simple reason that she had reached out to Brother Ioann on her own behalf. Women were, on the whole, far more likely to petition Churikov on behalf of other people—usually their husbands, but also their children. In fact, women were crucial to his outreach to the people of St. Petersburg not only because there were more of them, but because as mothers, wives, sisters, and daughters, they took on the responsibility of connecting their family members or neighbors with him. As in the case of Aleksei Krylov's mother, this was often an almost impossible task, involving years of pleading, patience, and prayer. While some women struggled with drinking problems themselves, as Patricia Herlihy observed, women were "more commonly the victims, not of drunkenness, but of drunkards."[3] For this reason their determination to secure Brother Ioann's help stemmed as much from their desperation to save themselves and their children from abuse or poverty as from a desire to rescue the alcoholic. One of the most common themes running through their testimonies is the deep vein of familial (especially maternal) love that enabled working-class families to survive.

For all her eccentricities, the case of Maria Spiridonova reminds us of both the universality of Brother Ioann's appeal, as well as the diversity of the sober community; people of all kinds sought him out, often for different reasons, and they cultivated different kinds of relationships with him. The following profiles of two equally unique trezvennitsy expand our understanding of a sober identity, while also encouraging deeper reflection about the role that gender played within the community—both when it mattered, and when it did not.

Evdokiia Kuz'minovna Ivanovskaia was a young, recently widowed, working-class mother in St. Petersburg when she met Brother Ioann. Like many of the women who submitted petitions to him on their own account, Ivanovskaia complained of "female problems," which she linked to her "loose" sexual behaviors. If there was a female corollary to the male alcoholic among Brother Ioann's followers, it was someone like Ivanovskaia, who identified herself as a *bludnaia doch'* (debauched woman). We might not know anything about her had Ivan Tregubov not passed on the testimony of her "miraculous" healing to leading members of the Petersburg medical community for review. While reflecting on the nature of Brother Ioann's influence, her case offers insight into contemporary doctors' perspectives on Churikov's role as a healer, as well as the way that the trezvenniki navigated between religious and medical sources of authority and their competing discourses on healing.

The other woman profiled here, Maria Kartasheva, testified in the 1920s to her healing as a young woman; at the time she had served as one of Brother Ioann's devoted sestritsy for decades. Although essential to Churikov's ability to tend to his followers' needs, Kartasheva and the other sestritsy rarely drew attention to themselves; on the contrary, they hid in plain sight as his devoted helpers, living almost invisibly on account of their humility and their sex. In 1926, however, the trezvenniki produced a collection of testimonies and reflections celebrating the life they had built with him in Vyritsa. The album, which included entries from Kartasheva and several other sestritsy, offered a unique opportunity for the women closest to Brother Ioann to express their beliefs, perspectives, and priorities. When read in the context of other trezvennik accounts, Kartasheva's testimony encourages further reflection on the nature of women's roles and agency within the community. Because the album was recorded long after Brother Ioann's excommunication from the Orthodox Church, and during the era of official atheism, it is not surprising that the women did not engage directly with questions of Orthodox identity; nonetheless, their accounts suggest ways in which Orthodox influences were still very much at work among them.

The *Bludnaia Doch*

Around 1900, seventeen-year-old Evdokiia Kuz'minovna Ivanovskaia was sent from the village of Nizovo to live with a relative in St. Petersburg after the death of her father. Like many girls from the countryside, Ivanovskaia testified, she quickly fell victim to the "dissolute" life of the big city, and after a year of multiple sexual encounters with different men, became so ill that she had to seek help at a local hospital for "female problems."[4] Her mother was so distressed by her behavior that she cried until her voice was gone. After a year-long recovery, Ivanovskaia vowed to live a more "honest" life, suggesting that she perceived a connection between her sinful behaviors and her illness, as most Orthodox did.[5] She moved to a dacha on Vyborg and, shortly thereafter, met and married a soldier, to whom she was faithful. Ten months after their daughter Elena was born, however, her husband was killed in a training exercise, leaving her a young widow and single mother. Devastated, she returned to St. Petersburg and began drinking heavily and seeking comfort in her old ways, with old friends. Her health declined again.

Ivanovskaia consulted both religious and medical authorities to help restore her health, but neither offered any relief. Like many working-class people in the big city, she moved around a lot and did not have a regular parish priest to whom she could turn. When she finally found a priest to confess her sins, he refused to receive her until she had paid him the requisite fee. With next to no money left to feed herself and her baby, she walked away unrepented, feeling abandoned by both God and the Church. Without her faith to draw on, she claimed, she became even more lost and engaged in even "deeper debauchery."

With her health continuing to fail, Ivanovskaia was readmitted to the hospital, where she stayed for several months; after her release, she was treated for more than three years for "female problems," which were diagnosed as pelvic inflammatory disease (an infection of the uterus and ovaries caused by sexually transmitted bacteria such as chlamydia or gonorrhea).[6] Her condition worsened to the point that she could no longer walk without crutches, and the medical prognosis was not encouraging. Admitting that he was "not God," her Petersburg doctor told her that he could not heal her and that her only recourse was to go abroad for treatment and surgery (the most frequently prescribed remedy before antibiotics).

Bereft of hope, faith, and money, Ivanovskaia sought out a fortune-teller to try to figure out her fate, at which point someone directed her to Petrovskii Park, where Churikov was preaching and receiving petitioners at the time. Like many others who ended up at Brother Ioann's door, Ivanovskaia followed the advice of a stranger blindly—desperate for free help of any kind. She knew so little about Churikov, in fact, that on her first visit to his beseda she made the mistake of showing up visibly drunk and was promptly turned away. But she soon returned to petition Brother Ioann, identifying herself as an alcoholic and "terribly debauched" woman. At the time, Brother Ioann was prohibited from contact with his petitioners, so she could not meet him face-to-face. Instead, their first "encounter" was conducted entirely in writing, with the help of his sestritsy passing notes though a half-closed door. He instructed her to return to the priest to confess her sins (which also meant that she would need to fast) and reassured her with the hopeful if rather vague message that "the Lord has met you in the mire; you will be happy." As was his habit, Brother Ioann also offered her sugar to signify that her bitter life would now be sweet (and to perhaps ease her body into detox). Unexpectedly, Ivanovskaia refused the sugar and the consolation it was intended to provide, claiming that in order for it to have any positive effect, she would need at least a hundred times more.

Ivanovskaia's self-deprecating remark was not unusual for a woman confessing to sexual impropriety. Given that her testimony was reported through Tregubov, we cannot know exactly how she presented herself to Brother Ioann, but other petitions suggest that women were likely to be brutally honest about their sins, even exaggerating them as if an act of catharsis. As in Aleksei Krylov's case, some men confessing to drunken binges could also be quite emotional and self-critical, but women regularly used the opportunity to unload their sins, especially sins of the flesh. Petitions dealing with sexual transgressions stood apart as longer, more emotionally fraught, and confession-like. According to Nadieszda Kizenko, self-deprecating language was fairly typical for lower-class women confessing to Father Ioann of Kronstadt, as was the tendency to acknowledge departures from prescribed Orthodox norms frankly and without excuses.[7] Letters were often dripping in shame, remorse, and fear. The same was true of women's petitions to Brother Ioann. One woman identified herself as "a great sinner," a "harlot" and a "whore" as she begged for Brother Ioann's forgiveness and prayer. "I am soaked in filth like a stinking dog," she continued; "to the church bells I danced and sang street songs that mention the Lord and the Blessed Virgin Mary."[8] "Dear Brother, please don't turn your face from me. I am a great sinner," another woman wrote. "I have deceived my husband, broken the law; I have stolen, and judged, and been envious."[9] Although "ashamed" to acknowledge all the sins she had committed, she feared that her husband and daughters were being punished by God because of her actions and asked Brother Ioann to protect her family from her sinful self: "Dear Brother pray for my sins, so that I won't do them anymore," She pointed to the rash on her body as a visible sign of her shame.

For all her bitterness, Ivanovskaia must have received a measure of hope from her first encounter with Brother Ioann, because she soon began to attend his Sunday besedy with some regularity. Although moved by his preaching and inspired to turn away from drink by witnessing testimonies by other alcoholics, she continued to suffer physically and decided to pursue surgery to correct the problem. Her only hesitation, it seems, was what it might mean for her daughter (it is not clear how she was going to get the money to pay for it). Before consulting the doctors, she turned to Brother Ioann for a healing prayer. He granted her request, but refused to offer his blessing or support for her operation. On the contrary, he made it clear that he did not believe in surgery, since "The Lord did not teach [us] to heal people with knives and poison,"[10] but rather, to pray for one another.[11]

Instead of an operation, Churikov counseled Ivanovskaia to seek out the blessing of the priest; he also offered her healing oil, along with strict instructions to fast. By these means, he assured her, she would be cured.[12] Since Ivanovskaia's illness stemmed from sin (a problem originating in the soul, not the body), he believed, healing would come through repentance, abstinence, and a commitment to living by faith and Scripture. Thus, after warning her against the surgeon's knife, he instructed Ivanovskaia to embark immediately on a course of fasting to cleanse the body and discipline the soul. By promising that she need only repent and begin living by the "science of Christ" (*nauka Khristova*) in order to return to health, Churikov effectively granted her some measure of agency in her recovery (while taking control away from doctors).[13]

On Brother Ioann's advice, Ivanovskaia abandoned her plans for surgery and followed his prescription to fast. By the time she had finished, her health had returned completely, in spite of the doctor's assurance that her illness was "incurable." At the request of one of her doctors, she returned to the clinic where she had been treated and underwent a full physical examination. To his surprise he found that her tumors had completely disappeared. Deeply grateful, Ivanovskaia thanked Brother Ioann for his prayers for "an unworthy, debauched woman" like herself.[14] Convinced by her healing that God had not forgotten her, she returned to church in part, she explained, to venerate the holy icons—a comment that might indicate that she had relied on the saints as well as Brother Ioann during her illness. Whatever the case, with Churikov's encouragement she had begun to overcome her previous animosity toward the clergy who had let her down.

Ivanovskaia's testimony suggests that her healing experience had helped to restore her faith in herself as well. With Brother Ioann's help, she had come to understand that although her sinful choices had made her ill in the past, she also had the power to decide to make herself well. With the weight of her shame lifted and her health restored, she began to lead a more stable and happier life as a worker, mother, and believer. She also knew that she could turn to Brother Ioann for support whenever difficulties arose. And not long after her own healing, she petitioned him to pray for her young daughter Elena, whose legs became badly infected from a wart medication they had gotten from a doctor. She testified that after three days of applying Churikov's mysterious ointment, her daughter was completely cured, and her own faith reaffirmed.[15]

Ivanovskaia's decision to testify to Ivan Tregubov in 1909 was an act of both faith and gratitude; it was also motivated by a desire to provide church authorities with more evidence of Brother Ioann's healing powers. In fact, the form and content of Ivanovskaia's testimony mimicked contemporary miracle narratives written by other Orthodox believers.[16] Clearly aware of clerical concerns at the time, Ivanovskaia was careful to stress her belief that Churikov's "miracles" were not his own, but rather "Christ's works, shown to [them] through Brother Ioann."[17]

Ivanovskaia's testimony was unusual in that it had not one but two intended audiences, each with its own standard of proof. In 1909, Tregubov brought Ivanovskaia's case and several others to the attention of a group of Petersburg medical experts, including eight male doctors, several of whom had treated Ivanovskaia personally. In an effort to convince the more scientifically minded of her "miraculous" recovery, she pointed out that she was now able to work "like a good horse," whereas before she had been completely unfit for any kind of physical labor and on the verge of death. She also obtained a signed statement by her doctor, a "man of science," Professor Nikolai Ieronimovich Rachinskii at the Petropavlovskaia clinic, confirming that her symptoms had disappeared.[18] To the last, the doctors rejected her understanding of her recovery and argued that Churikov's healings—if they happened at all—were the result of suggestion or hypnosis.[19] However, most were nonetheless willing to elaborate on their observations and, in this sense, to engage in dialogue with her (albeit indirectly). Having personally witnessed the sudden disappearance of her tumors after Churikov's blessing, Dr. N. M. Kakushkin at the Petropavlovskaia clinic explained that her drastically improved condition was "not a miracle"; Ivanovskaia had most likely gone into remission, which was easily explained by her decision to pursue a healthier lifestyle, and this, in his view, constituted Brother Ioann's greatest influence over her. That she insisted on the "miraculous" nature of her cure, he continued, was a symptom of the ignorance common to the Russian people, whom he described as "inert, backward, and weak-willed."[20]

Dr. S. L. Trivus, who had been involved in the famous "miracle" case of Nikolai Grachev,[21] was also personally acquainted with Brother Ioann and had great respect for him. In explaining Churikov's ability to heal, he emphasized his great "moral authority," which made his "[power of] suggestion" very strong, especially during Sunday besedy, where he was able to maintain contact with his followers for an extended period of time and in circumstances where religious excitement was high.[22] Like Trivus, the physician M. D. Lion had known Churikov for a while—since 1898, in fact, when he was the assistant director at the Samara psychiatric hospital, where Brother Ioann had been sent for observation. Lion agreed that Ivanovskaia's "miraculous" healing was completely explicable by science; medicine had come to recognize the body's power to heal itself, he explained, and the spirit (*dukh*) was one of the body's most powerful natural defenses.[23] Even more directly than Trivus, he stressed the functional importance of spiritual means of healing and the degree to which the patient (rather than the healer) had agency in the process: "The more we are able to strengthen the spirit of the patient, the stronger his self-defense will be in fighting illness."[24]

In short, even as medical experts familiar with Ivanovskaia's case denied the possibility of the miraculous, some were willing to assign positive causal value to her belief in it. The important precondition for healing through "suggestion" was the patient's faith in the healer—whether the healer was worthy or not, and whether they were religious or medical in approach.[25] In other words, the fact that Ivanovskaia was healed was understood as a consequence of her *belief* in Churikov as a healer—not necessarily a reflection of his ability to heal. The psychiatrist V. M. Bekhterev likewise observed that faith in the practitioner was instrumental in healings—and conversely, a lack of faith could serve as an obstacle to the process, since "a person who does not believe cannot rely on remedy through faith."[26] Thus, even as medical experts rejected Ivanovskaia's claim that Brother Ioann's prayers had brought her physical relief (as in the way that the application of a medical drug might, for example), they acknowledged that her hope in the efficacy of his prayers contributed to the body's ability to heal itself, first, by encouraging her to take better care of herself and, second, by unlocking her unconscious, so as to facilitate her body's self-healing mechanism.

Ivanovskaia continued to see things quite differently from both the religious and medical authorities who weighed in on Brother Ioann's influence. Convinced that her healing through Brother Ioann's prayers had been evidence of God's work in the world, she rejected the medical consensus that her miracle could be reduced to the power of suggestion or explained away rationally by science.[27] Like many trezvenniki, she argued (inductively) that her faith in Churikov as a miracle worker had evolved because she had *seen* his abilities, not the other way around.

According to Leonid Heretz, resistance to "scientific" understanding was not uncommon among the Orthodox; as in Ivanovskaia's case, attempts to introduce modern scientific concepts often had the "paradoxical effect of reinforcing old beliefs."[28] The fact that it was easy to poke holes in the doctors' arguments likely contributed to the inadequacy of rational explanations for what they had seen and experienced. As Churikov's supporters would point out (logically), if the power of suggestion rested on an individual's faith or capacity for religious excitability, then how could one explain the fact that among many of the individuals who claimed to have been healed by Brother Ioann were those who had previously been lacking completely in belief or any fear of God whatsoever? And if regular contact with Churikov was necessary in order for the power of suggestion to work, how could one explain the many individuals who claimed to have been healed by Churikov's prayers from afar—including those who had never met him before?[29]

Contrary to her claims, it is possible that Ivanovskaia had developed a degree of faith or trust in Brother Ioann before her healing, but the trezvenniki could easily point to individuals who experienced healing through Brother Ioann's prayers "from afar" or without ever having had any direct contact with him whatsoever.[30] While one could argue that adults might have been able to harbor faith in Brother Ioann's abilities from a distance, it was harder to explain how children might have been healed from afar, as in the case of Vera Strazheva.[31] As a very young girl, Vera had contracted typhus and lapsed into an unconscious state for many weeks. When doctors failed to help her, Vera's mother sought out Brother Ioann's prayers and later claimed that her daughter's full recovery had begun at the very moment she knelt before Brother Ioann. While it is not certain that he had anything to do with her healing (even without treatment, typhus was not necessarily life-threatening), Vera and her mother clearly believed that he had.

The Sestritsa Maria Kartasheva

Brother Ioann came into Maria Kartasheva's life in 1898, when her family welcomed the wanderer (*strannik*) into their home to read scriptural passages to them. She was only thirteen years old at the time, but he made a big impression on her by predicting that someday the two of them would travel Christ's path together, but only after sorrow and illness had invited them to do so. And so it happened. Years later, after Kartasheva had left home and began working for a wealthy family in "a mansion where no one spoke about God or acknowledged Him," she fell ill with a crippling bone disease. After doctors failed to help, her desperate parents forced her to seek out Brother Ioann, who, she believed, soon cured her paralysis and several later afflictions as well, including near blindness and a large tumor on her face. Her suffering had been very great but not without meaning, she explained, because, as Brother Ioann taught, "God loves even those He makes sick." The purpose of her modest yet prayerful testimony was therefore to express gratitude to God for his kindness, and to Brother Ioann for his continuing "protection."[32]

By the time Kartasheva's testimony appeared in 1926, she was forty-one and had been living as part of a small circle of devoted sestritsy for nineteen years. In addition to Grusha (Agrippina Smirnova), other long time sestritsy included the biological sisters Anna and Maria (Semenovna) Grigor'eva, who like Kartasheva had made the decision to "travel along Christ's path" with Brother Ioann at a young age. Living by his side their entire adult lives, the sestritsy worked tirelessly to support him and his community through myriad forms of service, much in the spirit of the biblical Martha, whose practical virtues were often extolled in clerical writings on Orthodox womanhood in the late nineteenth century.[33] Their days were mostly taken up by mundane domestic responsibilities, such as cooking, gardening, sewing, laundering, and cleaning Brother Ioann's living space. But they also stood silently by his side as he delivered his besedy, and served as assistants and witnesses to his interactions with many petitioners. This last role took on special importance after 1905, when church authorities prohibited Brother Ioann from meeting personally with his followers. Out of necessity, the sestritsy became his trusted messengers, carrying written notes from

FIGURE 5. Brother Ioann's sestritsy reading petitions from his followers at Obukhovo, ul. Troitskaia, d. 60A. Sestritsa Grusha (Agrippina Vasil'evna Smirnova) stands in the center, and Sister Niusha (Anna Semenovna Grigor'eva) on the right; the box next to Brother Ioann holds bottles of healing oil, which the sestritsy would give to petitioners, along with Brother Ioann's response to their notes. Photograph by M. Stukolkin, around 1912. Reprinted with permission from TsGAKFFD SPb.

petitioners to Brother Ioann and then conveying his responses. This was no small task, given the volume of afflictions and woes laid at his feet.

The sestritsy also displayed the qualities of Mary, who served Christ through faith and love; their unwavering loyalty to Brother Ioann was reflected both in the care they gave him and the prayerful spirit by which they lived. Like him, they embraced an ascetic lifestyle, abstaining from worldly pleasures; even when working, they fasted regularly and devoted what little leisure time they had to prayer, singing hymns, and most of all, reading and discussing Scripture, both on their own and with Brother Ioann. They also committed to celibacy at a far younger age than most women who chose to enter a convent. Although motherhood was central to contemporary models of ideal Orthodox femininity, family responsibilities often presented obstacles to the full realization of a woman's spiritual potential.[34]

Unfortunately, Kartasheva's testimony offers little insight into her decision to take on the role of a sestritsa, save for the impression that it was a natural choice for her at the time. And indeed, by the norms of the day, women were assumed to be more capable than men of caring for others because of their natural abundance of "sympathy, tender-heartedness, diligence, and patience"; moreover, they were expected to devote themselves to "lofty service to others" as the manifestation of their "nature" and Christian "calling."[35] For a young woman like Kartasheva, poor, poorly educated, and new to urban life, working for Brother Ioann and living among the community of trezvenniki also offered a safe way to lead a more spiritually meaningful life. Traditionally, village women who wanted to commit themselves to God could take on the role of "*chernichki*," who wore black and read the Psalter for the dead, or "*spasennitsy*," who devoted themselves to matters of salvation alone or in a small group of likeminded women. But as Brenda Meehan observed, it could be difficult for piously inclined women of the lower classes to lead a life of prayer on account of their poverty (and thus lack of control), their gender (and thus lack of authority), and the relatively few institutionalized Orthodox communities open to them.[36]

The desire to forsake the secular world was a common theme in women's testimonies.[37] Some women explicitly expressed the need to escape the city and the myriad dangers they encountered there, including threats of deception and sexual violence; others were alienated by its pronounced secularism,[38] or ran away from what they saw as excessive materialism. The trezvennitsa Zinaida Grigor'eva, for example, left her parents' home in the Caucasus at a young age to seek an education in

St. Petersburg. Naive and inexperienced, she quickly lost her bearings and started a relationship with a man who turned out to be married. "Tortured" by this discovery, she turned to Brother Ioann and began attending his besedy. Under his influence, she renounced her wealth and got a job; before long, she married a sober man and together they lived peacefully as part of the trezvennik community.[39]

To a certain extent, Kartasheva's account suggests that she too was drawn to the community in Vyritsa in an effort to escape the empty materialism and immorality of the secular world. But the main theme of her life until that point had been her illnesses, and this was likely the driving factor in her decision to devote herself to Brother Ioann. Exactly how she understood the relationship between her health and her decision to become a sestritsa is not completely clear, but if her testimony is read in the context of the other sisters' accounts, several possibilities seem likely. The first is that she felt a kind of debt toward him for her healing, similar to that acknowledged by the sestritsy Maria and Anna Grigor'eva. During their mother's grave illness, they made a vow to God that if she were healed by Brother Ioann's prayer, they would work for him as a way to repay the debt—a common pledge taken by the Orthodox in relation to the saints, and one that could be made on behalf of oneself or a loved one. And once their mother's health returned, the sisters made good on their promise to assume their place at Brother Ioann's side for the rest of their lives.

Another possibility is that Kartasheva made the decision to live with Brother Ioann on the hope that he would protect her from future illnesses—another belief widely shared by his female followers. As Maria Grigor'eva testified, she had become convinced of the miracle of his presence when, as a child, she witnessed his interaction with a woman whose nose was swollen and covered with oozing sores. "To my surprise," she recalled, "Brother took her hand, anointed such a terrible nose with oil, kissed her, and said in the Words of Christ: 'Your faith heals you.'"[40] Although Maria was absolutely certain that Brother Ioann would become infected, he never did—and in fact, when she saw the woman a little later, she had "a clean, white face, not even a pimple, and a healthy nose." While highlighting Brother Ioann's compassion, Maria offered the episode mostly as proof that "the impure will not stick to a pure man"—in other words, as a sign of his extraordinary goodness. As she well knew at the time of her testimony, Brother Ioann was not immune from poor health—in fact, he had recently suffered a near-fatal case of pneumonia. She nonetheless believed that the health of those close to him would benefit from his presence, as in her own case; while living with Brother Ioann for almost two decades, she claimed, she had been immune from infectious diseases.[41] Although she suggested that her proximity and close relationship with him was key, even trezvenniki who lived at a distance claimed that after he had healed them, they too had been completely free from illness for the rest of their lives.[42]

The third and most likely possibility is that Kartasheva's decision to devote her life to serving Brother Ioann related to her understanding of the relationship between her physical and spiritual health. Rather than celebrating the "miracle" of her physical healing as many did, Kartasheva was careful in her testimony to express gratitude to God for the fact that her profound suffering had brought her to a deeper faith. Her choice of title for her testimony, "V bolezni—golos Bozhii" (In sickness [is] God's Voice),[43] aligns with Orthodox teachings, which instruct believers to approach evidence of the miraculous with "patience and humility," and to see illness not as a tragedy to be avoided, but as an opportunity for spiritual growth.[44] In this context, the decision to serve Brother Ioann might have been a way to express her gratitude for God's mercy, while moving through the world with humility and faith.

Working by Brother Ioann's side was often hard, especially because the sestritsy were called on regularly to witness "all the sufferings of the world."[45] Tending to the sick, dying, and troubled was an intimate, often unpleasant, and potentially dangerous occupation. In addition to physical ailments and disease, the sestritsy encountered a great deal of emotional pain and trauma revealed to Brother Ioann by victims of violence and abuse, including children. Thus they remained acutely sensitized to people's suffering and the full spectrum of injustices and uncertainties encountered in modern life.

While the suffering they witnessed likely reinforced the sestritsy's gratitude for Brother Ioann's "protection," each healing had the potential to affirm their faith in Brother Ioann anew. Witnessing also offered opportunities for spiritual growth. For example, the sestritsa Maria Grigor'eva recalled how Churikov had forced her to confront her own fears and weaknesses when an "unkempt [and] sickly" woman approached her one day with a dirty, crumpled note to give to him. Feeling "disgust," Maria made excuses for the note's poor condition as she handed it to Brother Ioann, pointing out that "the woman came with a bad illness." To her surprise, he responded by asking, rhetorically, "What kind of diseases are good?" and then commanded her to kiss the woman as a sign of compassion. Maria obeyed, but the kiss made her feel even more disgust. Sensing this, Brother Ioann kissed Maria in return and reminded her, "I took off all the dirt from you."[46]

For the sestritsy obedience to Brother Ioann and his teachings was an obligation and a virtue, but it would be wrong to reduce their relationship to him to one of complete self-renunciation. Grusha likened it to that between a farmer and his field: "Without you and without your spiritual support," she wrote to Brother Ioann, "we are nothing, like land that has not been worked by the farmer and bears no fruit."[47] The metaphor, gentle in tone and organic in nature, is more paternalistic than the analogy of the blacksmith and iron often used to describe elder–disciple relations. While still acknowledging the sestritsy's dependence on Brother Ioann as a teacher-cultivator, Grusha's framing allowed for spiritual growth on the part of the individual, and emphasized love and nurturing rather than skill or discipline.

Living with Brother Ioann was not always easy; several women testified to his strictness and to their desire to escape his rule at times.[48] Sister Grusha also recalled the shame they felt when they were unable to live up to expectations: "Brother prayed for everyone and about everyone: for the mourners, for those who swim in the sea, for widows, orphans, crippled people, prisoners, etc. Sometimes we were on our knees, [and] our knees would ache, our heads would get tired, and a nap would start to overwhelm us. When Brother noticed such laziness in us, he [would] remove us from prayer, although we begged him with tears [not to]. Brother [then] began to pray alone—and his prayer was even longer than when he prayed with us."[49] "Brother Ioann wanted to cultivate humility and patience in us," Grusha later recalled, confessing that at the time, the women did not always understand his ways.[50]

On the whole, however, the relationship between the sestritsy and Brother Ioann was a fundamentally loving and affective one, reciprocal and mutually beneficial in ways that mirrored Orthodox gender expectations: while the women depended on Churikov's strength, wisdom, and protection, he looked upon them gratefully as "peace-bringers" and valued them for their deep faith, humility, and modesty.[51] The relationship functioned as a marriage of sorts, with each helping the other to develop morally and spiritually, in the interest of their "spiritual family," which was founded "upon an ethos of Christian love, equality, and mutual support."[52] Although the sestritsy Anna and Grusha wielded more influence within the broader trezvennik community by virtue of their exceptionally close relationship with Brother Ioann, all the sestritsy received praise for their model behavior and commitment to helping others lead moral lives and "breathe with a full chest." While conflicts sometimes arose, one trezvennitsa claimed that the sestritsy's love was treasured like "a precious jewel" residing in the hearts of each member of the sober community.[53]

Like many families, Brother Ioann and his sestritsy would endure a lot together, not only as witnesses to the suffering of others, but as victims of persecution. The sestritsy's unusually close relationship to Brother Ioann left them vulnerable to clerical suspicions, especially speculations related to their cohabitation. In line with long-standing assumptions that men (even monks) could not live in such close proximity to women without being tempted by them, and that women were likely to develop "passionate attachments" to the confessors they idolized,[54] the hieromonk Veniamin (Fedchenkov) cast suspicion on Churikov and his sestritsy—a point he reiterated by suggesting that many of Brother Ioann's female followers had once been prostitutes.[55] Such accusations, in part the product of a broader culture of fear around the issue of sexual deviance and the breakdown of traditional social norms after 1905,[56] were particularly widespread in the case of women associated with the Moscow *brattsy*.[57] While none of their female followers were found guilty of sexual misconduct,[58] they nonetheless had to endure humiliating and invasive medical examinations to prove their innocence—the same kind that the police used on suspected prostitutes. One of Koloskov's young female followers was denied a proper Orthodox burial simply by virtue of her relationship to him.[59] Although Churikov's sestritsy would not suffer the same degree of abuse, the suspicions cast on the Moscow sestritsy were deflected onto them as well. Perhaps this too was what Kartasheva meant when she thanked Brother Ioann for his "protection." As discussed further in chapter 8, Soviet authorities would again subject the sestritsy to ridicule, censure, and persecution, especially in 1927—one year after they recorded their testimonies.

In its broader strokes, the spiritual and moral landscape of holy sobriety that emerges from women's testimonies is similar to that painted by men. Like their male counterparts, sober women were drawn to Brother Ioann's compassion and moral clarity; fearful of their own sinful natures and the prospect of divine punishment, they searched for guidance, reassurance, and inspiration in both his conversations and his personal modeling of spiritual discipline, prayerfulness, and generosity. Like men, trezvennitsy also expressed an active love of Scripture and looked to gospel stories as meaningful frameworks for understanding their own experiences. As Churikov taught, they embraced Scripture's transformative potential and aspired to align their lives with it; in doing so, they experienced hope for a morally ordered, safe, and more peaceful world. Women's testimonies also abound with examples of Brother Ioann's spiritual insight and gift of prophecy. If for some his ability to "see" or know the future was terrifying, for others it was a powerful confirmation of his identity as a man of God as well as another source of consolation and protection in an unpredictable and hostile world.[60] Last but not least, women were equal to men in their openness to the miraculous—not simply because miracles promised healing or prosperity, as some contemporary observers liked to claim,[61] but because they served as powerful evidence of God's work in the world. This was true even for former skeptics like Vasilii Guliaev and Evdokiia Ivanovskaia, both of whom found themselves empowered by a faith they had not even been seeking. As the sestritsa Anna Grigor'eva testified, this was further evidence of Brother Ioann's greatness: the "great prophet" had arrived not for those were already looking for God, but especially for those who were not.[62]

While sober men and women expressed needs and beliefs irrespective of their sex, gendered patterns emerge in the ways that men and women characterized Brother Ioann's role in their lives—how they understood it, expressed it, and experienced it. For example, while both described Brother Ioann as a "savior," they tended to mean different things by it. Using the language of "rebirth" or referring to time "before" and "after" meeting him, men emphasized how he had rescued them from a life apart from God and helped them to overcome debilitating shame and thereby restore themselves to their expected roles within their families and society. For their part, women were more likely to portray him as their beloved protector, who understood the weight of their familial responsibilities and women's feelings of powerlessness. Significantly, these patterns were not new; on the contrary, they stemmed from long-standing norms. According to Isolde Thyrêt, Orthodox interactions with the saints had been similarly gendered in Muscovite Russia: "While men's cures tended to restore their position in society at large, women's healings revolved around problems and restrictions specific to their gender."[63]

As we have seen, both male and female trezvenniki were willing to come forth with evidence of Brother Ioann's powers, even when doing so risked conflict with authorities or the public. Yet on the whole men tended to be more didactic, offering up their own stories as models to instruct, inspire, and warn, whereas women usually testified in the defensive mode. While perhaps inspiring to others, their testimonies were primarily meant to defend him and the community against his critics and skeptics, including those in positions of religious or secular authority. In other words, women's stories mattered most of all to the extent that they served the needs of others, rather than their own. This is a subtle difference perhaps, but it corresponds to their roles within the community at large.

The women closest to Brother Ioann and most devoted to him (his sestritsy) were defined by their unceasing service and quiet humility. In contrast to the sestritsy's inward orientation, some of his most devoted male followers, including Guliaev, projected their trezvennik identity outward, becoming highly visible preachers in their own right. This is not to say that women did not proselytize as well. On the contrary, mothers and wives were often relentless in their efforts to bring their families into sobriety, but their tactics and targets differed from those of the men in the movement. Most of all, they tended to pray and plead rather than preach.

When men and women defended Brother Ioann against skeptics and critics, they also tended to do so in different ways. Male trezvenniki always took the lead when it came to crafting collective petitions, and when men took the stage to defend Brother Ioann, as in E.V. Frolov's letters to newspapers or Guliaev's bold defense, their actions were as much an articulation of their own identity as a defense of him. The most obvious example of this pattern was the case of the former workers Ivan Koloskov and Dmitrii Grigor'ev, who in the process of spreading Churikov's teachings developed their own devoted followings largely by imitating him. Given their reputation for exceptional piety and deep familiarity with Scripture, it might have been possible for the sestritsy to cultivate their own following, as in the case of Anastasiia Kerova, a peasant from Samara, who was known among local peasants to possess extraordinary spiritual insight as well as the ability to heal.[64] But again, Brother Ioann's female followers did not aspire to the same public platform as male trezvenniki. In contrast to what I've called "sober masculinity," which called for discipline and self-control, "sober femininity" was more in line with traditional notions of Orthodox womanhood; while this entailed greater humility, it also allowed for more public displays of emotion. Thus women were able to be more openly effusive in their testimonies and in their personal interactions with Brother Ioann, for example, by kissing his hand after a beseda. The sestritsy also benefited uniquely from their sex in that they were allowed to live by his side; even though this made them the target of suspicion, it was a blessing and privilege for those who loved him. Likewise, when skeptics or unwanted outsiders showed up at the besedy, women were more often than not the ones to confront them, defending Brother Ioann and the integrity of the trezvennik community with both their words and their bodies. Thus they stepped up to protect Brother Ioann just as he protected them.[65]

To the extent that trezvenniki differed in their beliefs, two core issues are worth noting. The first concerns the extent to which Brother Ioann's physical presence mattered to their healing or salvation. Although the individual women profiled here are not meant to be representative of all trezvennitsy, the relationships they experienced with Brother Ioann reflect a spectrum of intimacy and dependence that is representative of the sober population as a whole. By definition Churikov's followers demonstrated a willingness to conform to his judgment in the interest of their spiritual and moral health, but as we have seen, the devotion expressed by Maria Kartasheva and the other sestritsy was different in nature and intensity. Yet, even as they lived with Brother Ioann for decades and benefited uniquely from his presence and the full weight of his protection, they did not aspire to be dependent on his person; on the contrary, they stayed close to serve him but centered their lives on the Word of God as he had taught them. Maria Spiridonova, by contrast, craved physical and spiritual proximity to Brother Ioann. While exchanges between elders and their spiritual children could often be intense, one senses both anxiety and addiction in her decision to live close to him and in her excessively long letters asking for his prayers and advice.[66] At the same time, physical distance was completely irrelevant to the experience of other trezvenniki. Indeed, some claimed to have been healed by Brother Ioann from very far away, having met him only in their imagination. While a number of factors could explain these differences, the issue of Brother Ioann's physical presence would have significant implications for how both believers and nonbelievers understood the nature of his spiritual authority, especially after his death.

Another variation in belief related to the most fundamental question of all: Who was Brother Ioann? Unfortunately, on this point individual testimonies (male and female) are less forthcoming. As Nadieszda Kizenko has argued with respect to the followers of Father Ioann of Kronstadt, less educated believers tended to think in terms of a "constellation of Orthodox sanctity" and to position individuals (including themselves) along a continuum to God.[67] The evidence suggests that the same was true for Brother Ioann's followers. While all trezvenniki revered him as a man of great piety and insight in the tradition of spiritual eldership, their understanding of who he was ranged considerably. Some saw him as a righteous individual pleasing to God, a *zastupnik* (intercessor), a saint, or even a prophet. Still others—and only a minority of the trezvennik population at first—came to believe that he was Christ, the Second Coming.

As the following chapters will discuss, these vastly different views on Brother Ioann's identity would become more pronounced over time, even as the continuing efforts to silence Brother Ioann led to a greater tightening of the trezvennik community, based on their mutual appreciation for his teaching and spiritual gifts and the shared experience of persecution.

CHAPTER 5

Not in Good Faith

*The Orthodox Church's Case against
Brother Ioann, 1910–1914*

In 1911, the Petersburg diocesan missionary Dmitrii Ivanovich Bogoliubov (1869–1953) addressed Brother Ioann's growing popularity in a series of articles for the clerical journal *Prikhodskii sviashchennik (Parish Priest)*. Having spent years offering sermons in the same neighborhoods, actively trying to woo away his followers, he had grown to appreciate Brother Ioann's ability to move people spiritually, to speak to their hearts and to their deep "yearning for righteous living."[1] By contrast, Bogoliubov observed, the laity felt insufficiently fed from the clergy's "pastoral table," and thus he urged his colleagues to approach Churikov's example as an opportunity for self-reflection. Rather than focusing on how to excise him from the Orthodox community, he suggested, it would be better to try to meet the laity's need for scriptural guidance and moral leadership.[2]

At the time, Bogoliubov was in a shrinking minority. Although some clergy embraced pastoral work and encouraged lay involvement in missionary efforts, clerical calls to silence Brother Ioann strengthened after 1905. While the rapid spread of Brother Ioann's influence was a factor, a major shift in the broader religious context was equally if not more significant. In the years following the 1905 law on religious toleration, a period described by one Petersburg journalist as "the springtime of sectarianism,"[3] the Church found its influence challenged by an unusually spectacular proliferation of popular evangelical and charismatic figures, as well as unprecedented challenges from within the Orthodox community.[4] Breaking free from their former state of "spiritual slavery," religious scholar V. Iasevich-Borodaevskaia noted, ordinary people were exhibiting "a newly awakened desire for self-determination" in matters of the faith.[5] Among the Orthodox, the so-called "Ioannity," the radical followers of Father Ioann of Kronstadt, were perhaps the most well-known challengers to Orthodox norms and church authority at the time, but they were far from the only example.

In 1908 missionaries at the Fourth Missionary Congress in Kiev debated how best to confront the explosion of lay activity and experimentation. The debate amounted to a version of the proverbial stick or carrot: Was it better to admonish and force those considered "deviants" to come back into the Orthodox fold, or to encourage the people's spiritual development with the hope that Orthodoxy would win out over the longer run? The Church remained divided on this and many other issues in the post-1905 era, but by the end of the Congress, the more aggressive missionary position had won out.[6] Conservatives in the church hierarchy interpreted the new law on toleration as a call to arms, "not with peace but with the sword." At stake, some feared, was more than the souls of the individual faithful; the whole future of the faith was under threat.[7]

In this context, Brother Ioann and his followers soon became a highly visible "other" against which church leaders could reassert their voice and authority.[8] According to the hieromonk Veniamin (Ivan Afanas'evich Fedchenkov, 1880–1961), the case against Brother Ioann seemed especially important to resolve since it involved so many of the issues at the center of the contemporary "religious ferment" (*brozhenie*).[9] In 1910, the Church began to subject Brother Ioann to intense scrutiny and interrogation, led by an ambitious and experienced group of professional Orthodox missionaries.[10] Churikov's besedy were closed temporarily in late 1910 and permanently in 1912, and after a series of extensive interrogations by the Petersburg missionary council, he was barred from the communion table in 1914.[11]

The path toward excommunication was neither smooth nor straight-forward. Along with the devotion and tenacity of Brother Ioann's followers, spiritual authorities had to contend with uneven levels of state support. Although tsarist authorities took a more conservative turn toward religious matters in mid-1909,[12] some Duma members openly championed the sober, hardworking, law-abiding trezvenniki as model citizens. At the same time, the 1905 law on toleration limited the Church's discretion by demanding sufficient evidence that a "sect" or group was "dangerous" if it wanted to silence it. In practical terms, this meant proving that the *brattsy* engaged in practices associated with a sect already recognized as heretical, such as the *khlysty*.[13] But this presented another challenge. While there were similarities between the *khlysty* and the trezvenniki—extreme asceticism, for example—there were obvious differences between the two groups, especially the fact that the trezvenniki lacked the *khlysty*'s defining "cult of religious ecstasy," inspired by the Holy Spirit. And while the *khlysty* claimed their prophets to be a reincarnation of Christ, Brother Ioann rejected all claims of deification.[14]

The Church also faced new expectations from the Russian public, since, with the exception of the far right, most people agreed that religious freedom was an important exercise of the more democratic order established in 1905. While the liberal press criticized the Church's excessive reliance on "police" powers and the missionaries' narrow "institutionalized view of religion,"[15] the more conservative daily *Novoe vremia* pointed out that by refusing to accept the people's right to religious freedom, the church hierarchy threatened to "[push] away people of religious feeling."[16] The outpouring of love for the excommunicated Tolstoy upon his death in late 1910 served as a reminder of this possibility.

A net effect of these various challenges was the Church's need to proceed carefully and deliberately in the Churikov case, and to be clear and convincing in its explanation of the "dangers" he presented to the Orthodox. Leading the way was the young and ambitious hieromonk Veniamin, who published a series of articles on Brother Ioann in *Kolokol* (*The Bell*) in May 1911. The articles were later collected into a pamphlet entitled *Podmena khristianstva* (*A False Substitute for Christianity*).[17] Veniamin's critique was the most thorough attempt to articulate, elaborate, and publicize the unorthodox ("sectarian") nature of Churikov's teaching and behavior, and it was soon corroborated by denunciations from his clerical colleagues, the former missionary Father Arsenii Minin and Father Mikhail Chel'tsov. By 1912, it was clear that a consensus had emerged about the need to sanction Brother Ioann for sectarian and "self-willed" behaviors. While helping to pave the way for Brother Ioann's excommunication, these critiques offered an expansive discussion of Orthodox spirituality, the means of salvation, the laity's right to interpret Scripture, and the state of clerical–lay relations. One of the most striking aspects of Veniamin's denunciation was the way he claimed the authority to decide the question of Churikov's Orthodox identity less directly on the basis of his status as member of the clergy (although this mattered) than on his identity as an Orthodox believer, and a corresponding sensibility to determine the presence or absence of true faith in others.

The Case of the Moscow Brattsy

To understand why and on what grounds Brother Ioann's case would evolve toward excommunication after 1910, it is necessary to turn first to his former followers, the so-called Moscow brattsy, Ivan Koloskov and Dmitrii Grigor'ev.[18] Although not quite as popular as Churikov, Koloskov and Grigor'ev used similar methods when preaching the message of holy sobriety, and their followers were every bit as enthusiastic in their devotion, for many of the same reasons.[19] There were significant differences as well. Aside from the more obvious ones—that Churikov was the original teacher and they were his pupils—Koloskov and Grigor'ev were former alcoholics from working-class backgrounds and could therefore be more legitimately claimed as "one of us" by their followers. Though neither were especially gifted speakers, what they lacked in eloquence they made up for in sincerity and a firsthand understanding of where their followers were coming from. Another difference concerned the generally hostile attitudes of Moscow missionaries and diocesan authorities toward Koloskov and Grigor'ev. In contrast to Churikov, who enjoyed at least some support from parish clergy and members of the diocesan hierarchy, the Moscow brattsy faced deep reservations among local spiritual authorities from the earliest days of their preaching.[20] Even Koloskov's own parish priest, Dmitrii Beliaev, testified against him, charging him with "audaciously attack[ing]" the Church and the Orthodox tradition and falsely preaching that he—rather than the Church or sacraments—had been responsible for his followers' salvation.[21]

On the basis of testimonies from Father Dmitrii and others, the Orthodox Church determined that the brattsy had fallen into "pernicious heresy, profane and blasphemous, similar to *khlystovstvo*" and pronounced "anathema" on them on March 7, 1910.[22] The solemn spectacle of the anathema, which was carried out in churches throughout Moscow, was intended not only to admonish the brattsy and bring them back into the Church's fold, but also to inspire fear in anyone tempted to follow them into heresy.[23] When public opinion in Moscow seemed to take the brattsy's side, missionaries intensified their efforts by disseminating a pamphlet in which the brattsy were demonized as the Antichrist. The claim was not just that the brattsy were "vile heretics," but "wolves in sheep's clothing" and "deceivers of the *narod*,"[24] who had been deliberately misleading innocent laity for their own benefit. By setting up an inverse relationship between the appearance of good and the reality of evil, the pamphlet wove a complex web of doubt around the brattsy, making it next to impossible for them to defend themselves. Try as they would, the more they proclaimed their innocence, the guiltier they would seem to appear.

Back in St. Petersburg

Although the Church's campaign against Koloskov and Grigor'ev was not a proxy war against Churikov, the two cases were connected in important ways, not least because the events in Moscow were known to Brother Ioann and his followers and understandably caused them concern. They also provided a controversial context against which Petersburg missionaries would conduct their own investigation of Churikov. Indeed, Moscow missionaries put active pressure on their Petersburg colleagues to declare Brother Ioann a *khlyst* and to excommunicate him as well.[25] Although Petersburg authorities resisted, in the interest of due diligence they brought Churikov in for questioning several times and routinely monitored his besedy. The 1910 missionary council in the capital soon dismissed the formal inquiry, however, having found insufficient cause to declare him or his movement sectarian or hostile to the Orthodox Church.

For the time being, Brother Ioann was free to continue preaching. The Moscow case had nonetheless raised questions and concerns, and Churikov had moved quickly to disassociate himself from them.[26] He testified on April 18, 1910, that "Ioann and Dmitrii" were simply two "comrades" who had attended his spiritual besedy, but he did not know anything about their activities in Moscow and had had no contact with them in three years.[27] Referring to himself uncharacteristically as a "Russian" and dedicated to sobering up *Rus'*, a term associated with Orthodox nationalism at the time and likely meant to appeal to conservatives,[28] Brother Ioann also specifically warned his "pastors and friends" not to blame someone for finding Christ through "the back door."[29]

To further distance himself from the Moscow case and to build up a defense against his critics, Brother Ioann also published an "open letter to my friends and enemies."[30] Introducing himself not as "Brother" but as "I. A. Churikov," he professed that the "only goal" of his life has been "to live and to labor in the Orthodox Church for the glory of God's Name, in praise of His Gospels, saving the souls of [my] brothers and myself in strict obedience with Holy Orthodox teachings." "With God as my witness," Churikov continued, "[I] speak only one truth. For the last fifteen years I have worked in Petersburg. Anyone who has during this time listened to me knows that I have never criticized a single dogma of the Orthodox Church, nor have I defied her sacraments, nor swept aside her divine principles [bozhestvoe ustroistvo]." He denied some of the various rumors circulating about him as well—that he forbade his followers from seeking out medical help and that he was a khlyst because he counseled them to give up meat and surrounded himself with unmarried women. Moving away from a purely defensive position, he also accused his critics of trying to shut down his besedy simply because he refused to walk the "hackneyed" paths that others had tried. In conclusion, he used a scriptural passage to protect and empower himself against his critics: "Do not forbid me," he warned them, "Christ did not give you the right to do that," as written in Luke 9:49–50, "Master, said John, we saw a man driving out demons in your name and we tried to stop him, because he is not one of us." To which Jesus replied, "do not stop him, for whoever is not against you, is for you."[31]

At the end of the letter, Churikov invited anyone who had doubts about the Orthodox nature of his preaching to his besedy. His offer was soon taken up by the young hieromonk Veniamin. By this point in time, clergy had been attending Brother Ioann's besedy for years, and most had not found them harmful in any way. But from the start Veniamin appeared skeptical of both Churikov and his followers. In fact, on his first visit to a beseda in October 1910 he left abruptly, claiming he felt alienated by the "abnormal" atmosphere. He returned later that month, and it was on the basis of his second visit that he wrote the articles to appear in Kolokol the following spring.

Having received his own theological training at the Tambov Spiritual Seminary and the St. Petersburg Spiritual Academy, Veniamin was highly educated but relatively inexperienced when he began his investigation into Brother Ioann. The recent case against the Moscow brattsy and the prosecution of the Ioannity provided important context; as the historian Aleksei Beglov has argued, the Ioannity served as the paradigmatic example against which the Church and state would judge other faith-based movements.[32] At the same time, both cases had caused a lot of controversy and no doubt put pressure on the young priest-monk to make a very convincing case. He was also mindful of the need to tread carefully with his criticisms, given the widespread admiration Brother Ioann commanded among St. Petersburg's working population. Seeing in his role an equal amount of professional opportunity and sacred responsibility, he worked hard to persuade his readers of Churikov's deviance based on his understanding of Orthodox teachings and traditions. While milder than some of the scandal-mongering religious press in Moscow, the tone of Veniamin's analysis simmered with a sense of injury and outrage as it pointed to behaviors he found offensive or dangerous.

Before launching into an extended assessment of Churikov's beliefs and practices, Father Veniamin attempted to unsettle what people thought they knew about him. To do this, he introduced two fertile sources of doubt. First, he challenged the idea that Brother Ioann had meaningful support among the clergy by questioning the role of the press in distorting his image, pointing out that the only positive assessments in the religious press had been written by a single person, the missionary D. I. Bogoliubov.[33] Second, and more importantly, he played into contemporary anxieties about the ubiquity of dissimulation by suggesting that Brother Ioann was not who he pretended to be—by then a common missionary strategy. Reminding his readers that "vinegar smells a lot like wine" and that appearances do not always reflect essence, Father Veniamin challenged Churikov's repeated professions of faith and allegiance to the Holy Mother Church on the grounds that "even the sincerest declaration of Orthodox confession does not constitute a completely sufficient sign of Orthodoxy."[34] Likewise, the performance of Orthodox rituals was not in itself evidence of an Orthodox sensibility or consciousness. On the contrary, Veniamin maintained, the final determination about an individual's Orthodoxy should be based not on their words or actions, but rather on the *spirit* with which they approached their faith. Determining whether or not Churikov and his followers were Orthodox "in spirit" was thus the task that Veniamin had assumed for himself as he observed Brother Ioann's beseda.[35]

As mentioned, Veniamin's first visit did not go well. He instantly rejected the meeting's atmosphere as "spiritually unhealthy" and reminiscent of a "sectarian" gathering.[36] Evidently, his own skepticism was matched by that of the trezvenniki, who deliberately ignored him at first; after more than fifteen years of persecution, many were not very welcoming to clergy they did not know and trust. When a middle-aged woman exacerbated his discomfort by claiming that he needed permission to be there (which was untrue), he concluded that the trezvenniki found Orthodox priests "strange" and "hostile."[37] He was also disturbed by the way the woman had referred to her fellow trezvenniki as "we," since this suggested that they saw themselves as a distinct community apart from his own.

As Father Veniamin waited for the prayer meeting to begin, he made note of the unusually large (10x14-inch) framed photograph of Brother Ioann on display next to various icons, and later commented on the way in which Churikov's right hand was held near his heart, as if to suggest that his stance linked him visually to a portrait of a well-known *khlyst*, as well as the recently excommunicated Moscow brattsy.[38] He also made special mention of Churikov's rather large pectoral cross. Though he conceded that it was hung by silk rope and not silver chain (as a priest's would have been), he was clearly convinced that Churikov's choice of outfit was a visible sign of his unauthorized claims to religious authority. "Who gave him the right [to imitate the clergy by his dress]?" Veniamin demanded, reminding his readers that "the Church has the right to send those who will preach [Romans 10:15]."[39] He left the meeting within minutes, claiming that he was short on time.

After returning for a longer visit on Sunday, October 10, 1910, Veniamin witnessed what appears to have been a typical beseda in every respect. The large hall was packed, and as news of Brother Ioann's imminent arrival circulated, the crowd began to cheer and chant loudly— behavior he described as shocking and un-Orthodox. After requesting a blessing from the priest, Churikov led a hymn and began to preach. The scriptural passage of the day was Luke 5, the story of the fishermen and their "miraculous catch,"[40] which was followed by a brief account of the life of St. Pelagia, during which Churikov reiterated the importance of the Word of God and prayer in the salvation of the sinner. Periodically, he interrupted his preaching to draw his audience in by singing a hymn and, occasionally, calling them to repent. Afterward, many waited in line for Churikov's blessing.

Father Veniamin's account of the beseda made it clear that the experience had left him deeply troubled on many levels. Reading like a list of wounds to his Orthodox sensibilities, it highlighted points of mild discomfort (as when the audience erupted into a "frenzy" at Churikov's arrival), to moments of serious injury caused by behaviors he deemed alarmingly un-Orthodox. He identified four main forms of deviance, related to (1) Churikov's approach to Scripture; (2) the implications of his preaching with respect to issues of salvation; (3) the nature of his relationship with his followers; and (4) Churikov's lack of humility and unwillingness to submit fully to the authority of God and God's Church.

With respect to the first point, Father Veniamin characterized Brother Ioann's scriptural interpretations as simplistic and dangerously mundane. Comparing him to the *besedniki*, he also took him to task for being "utilitarian," by which he meant preaching on "the organization of earthly life and earthly contentment," rather the divine or the eternal.[41] The priest acknowledged that the Church did not forbid people to worry about their daily lives—indeed, it not only allowed but actively encouraged believers to rely on saints for help with earthly life.[42] But he also made it clear that if the saints could be called on to assist in the negotiations of everyday life, "this is by no means [the ultimate] goal," and true Orthodox should know better than to allow the privileging of mundane concerns over eternal ones. Thus he found fault with Churikov for offering lessons from the Gospels and the Acts of the Apostles not for the (correct) purpose of meditation or reflection, but rather as rational (and therefore false) "plans" for bettering their lives. The problem was compounded by the fact that "the common people [*narod*]" in his audience did not seem to understand that this was wrong. On the contrary, they appeared both captivated and inspired by Churikov's theatrical style and cleverness with words, as if he was offering them "deep thoughts" and true meaning.

More significant still was Veniamin's concern that Churikov was cultivating in his followers a false understanding of salvation. Here his analysis shifted from Brother Ioann to his followers, whom he found to be lacking in "true" (*istinnoe*) religious feeling. Pointing to their unbridled enthusiasm as they "repented" their sins at Churikov's command, he denounced their almost celebratory energy as inappropriate, as if they did not mean what they said or did not grasp the gravity of their sinfulness.[43] The priest admitted that he found it difficult to articulate precisely how and in what way he sensed this, but he added that the problem would be obvious to any true Orthodox believer. To illustrate, he noted the response of an "intelligent" Orthodox laywoman, who claimed that an evil spirit had entered her soul during a beseda, and that she felt so violated she had to pray for days on end in order to eradicate the "spiritual poison."[44]

Expanding on the nature of the trezvenniki's deviance, Veniamin elaborated on the difference between two distinct means of salvation, the mental (*dushevnyi*) and the spiritual (*dukhovnyi*). In this sense, the priest's concern was not one-dimensional, but two. The first dimension related to his perception that the trezvenniki's joy was exclusively a function of their rational, not spiritual, faculties. This in turn indicated an incorrect (un-Orthodox) understanding of sin on their part. As Irina Paert has discussed, the nineteenth-century elder Amvrosii expressed a similar concern when confronted by one of his correspondents who kept a chart of his sins. The monk deemed the practice un-Orthodox, Paert explains, "because it made his correspondent feel good about himself, especially when he seemingly managed to overcome particular vices." On the contrary, "what mattered to the elder was a feeling of remorse, not a neat accounting of committed and avoided sins." This, Paert argues, was a "striking example of the Orthodox understanding of sin, understood not in a computational sense, but as a general sense of one's weakness before God."[45] Like Amvrosii, Father Veniamin perceived in the trezvenniki's exclamations of repentance a false, artificial sense that was fundamentally "mental [or] carnal" (*dushevno plotskie*) rather than "spiritual" (*dukhovnoe*) in nature, as if they were not so much acknowledging their sins as they were accounting for them, as if problem-solving. In other words, their joy stemmed from their relief that their lives were better, rather than from the hopefulness or gratitude associated with the promise of God's grace.

Here, Veniamin also made a distinction articulated in the work of the Orthodox bishop and spiritual guide Ignatii (Brianchaninov) and elaborated upon by the religious historian Vera Shevzov.[46] Writing in the nineteenth century, Ignatii explained the essential difference between two kinds of sight in the context of the miraculous. Whereas one kind of sight is conditioned by "a mind that is set on the flesh," another is "enlightened by spiritual reason [*dukhovnyi razum*]." According to Ignatii, the former kind of sight leads to false consciousness, and belongs to individuals too focused on the human condition and worldly concerns, and out of touch with "longer-term moral or spiritual considerations." Seeing the body as the "barometer of life," these individuals view illness as a "calamity" and health as an indicator of well-being. Thus when the body is "miraculously" healed, they understand the "miracle" as a "display of wondrous power" and an end in itself. But the other type of individual knows better. Approaching the miraculous with "patience and humility," they embrace the opportunity for spiritual growth, understanding that its purpose is less to heal the body than the soul. Based on what he had witnessed at the beseda, Veniamin put the trezvenniki into the category of the unenlightened.

The second dimension of Veniamin's concern related less to the trezvenniki's expression of "joy" at the moment of repentance than to their apparent failure to experience the deep and essential sense of grief that was expected of the Orthodox as they acknowledged their sins. While the Orthodox typically experienced a sense of hope that they would be saved through their faith, he explained, that hope was not the same as a firm belief in their salvation, as among Protestants. Thus ideally, "Orthodox grief [*pechal'*] is mixed with joy [*radostvornie*]," but it is nonetheless *real* "distress" (*sokrushenie*). In other words, the proper Orthodox response would have centered on an emotionally fraught recognition of loss and even shame. Unlike some clerical witnesses such as Father Grigorii Petrov, however, Veniamin found the grief and humility expected of the Orthodox entirely lacking among Brother Ioann's followers. On the contrary, the celebratory spirit they exhibited at the time of repentance reflected a feeling of empowerment, even spiritual arrogance.[47]

According to Father Veniamin, a third aspect of the trezvenniki's deviance from Orthodoxy related to their extremely "unhealthy" devotion to Brother Ioann. Whatever suspicions Veniamin might have had on this score before his visit were confirmed during an episode following the beseda.[48] After listening in on a heated conversation between Churikov and Veniamin through a closed door, several of Brother Ioann's female followers allegedly greeted the priest with "evil looks" and in a distressed state reminded Veniamin how Brother Ioann had saved them from miserably sinful pasts. When the priest castigated them for their anger and judgment, suggesting that if they were of "a truly Christian mind" they would never speak to him in such a disrespectful tone, the women were temporarily chastened. But several other trezvenniki were provoked by Veniamin's comments that their devotion to Brother Ioann was abnormal and "not Orthodox," and that Brother "Ivan" (not the more respectful "Ioann") lacked the grace that priests had. One accused the clergy of being useless and lacking in grace, and another claimed that he "could not live without Churikov," adding defiantly, "it's all the same to us: go ahead and excommunicate us all; it won't matter. We will still not leave our Brother."[49]

Significantly, the highly emotional exchange confirmed for Veniamin that the trezvenniki's devotion to Brother Ioann was stronger than their attachment to the Church and that they believed him to be their savior. As the priest made clear, his concern was not simply that Churikov was unworthy of the praise attributed to him, but that his followers' devotion to him was diverting them from the true path of salvation. Although the trezvenniki participated in the rituals of the faith, including the sacraments, Veniamin was convinced that they nonetheless "preferred [his] besedy to prayer." His point was not simply that the beseda had become the geographical and spiritual center of their faith practices, in effect displacing the Liturgy; after all, there was a long tradition of rural people worshipping most of the time at home or in chapels, rather than a church.[50] Rather, Veniamin's charge was that the trezvenniki did not believe that the sacraments were essential to their salvation: "in their hearts [Churikov's followers] do not feel that mediation of God's grace [blagodatnyia posredstva] is necessary."[51]

The fourth and final concern articulated by Veniamin related to Brother Ioann's spiritual constitution and his relationship with the Church. Directly after the beseda, the priest confronted Churikov directly, pointing out that some of his followers had addressed him as their "savior" and considered him "everything for them," including "a priest, a bishop, and the church, and almost Christ Himself."[52] Moreover, Churikov had encouraged his followers to believe in his holiness. When Brother Ioann protested that he was powerless to stop them, the priest accused him of insincerity and extreme "self-importance." When Churikov tried again to defend himself by reminding the priest of his deep commitment to prayer and Scripture, Veniamin countered that other "sectarians" could claim the same. Good deeds did not necessarily indicate a good soul, he explained; even miracles were not a precondition of holiness, since goodness stems most of all from one's spirit, not actions. In spite of the fact that Brother Ioann appeared to possess many of the qualities associated with a spiritual elder—asceticism, devotion to the Word, a facility for counseling the suffering—the priest was convinced that he lacked the "internal holiness" and humility of a "true servant of God." "In the depths of his soul," the priest concluded, "in the most internal makeup of his spirit, he is delusional [v prelesti], that is, completely abnormal."[53]

Again, the writings of the nineteenth-century monk Ignatii are relevant to Veniamin's reading of Churikov's spiritual state. Prelest', which was understood as a kind of spiritual and mental illness indicating the influence of evil spirits (or the work of the Devil on the soul), was, according to Ignatii, the natural state of humanity since the fall, since Satan accessed the human soul constantly and used lies to stimulate the passions. Through grace one could be rescued from the state of delusion, but only by following the commandments and not trusting one's own will and reason. Veniamin made it clear that he did not think that Brother Ioann was capable of this, since he lacked the humility it would require. As the priest explained, "without humility, all goes to rack and ruin. Many religious zealots [podvizhniki] have ruined their spiritual feats [podvigi] in this way." Thus, Veniamin predicted, it was only a matter of time before Churikov's un-Orthodox spirit would eventually distort his thoughts and behaviors as well. The priest warned him that he was on a "dangerous path" and demanded he submit himself to the authority of the church elders at the Spiritual Academy for further counseling.[54]

Churikov's transgressions against the faith, Veniamin would conclude, had to be understood as part of a broader process of secularization in the post-Enlightenment period. When the Devil found himself unable to attack Christ directly, he explained, he turned to deifying humans, making them more powerful in relation to God. "This faith [vera] in the individual" was exceedingly dangerous, Veniamin continued, because "in the end [it] translates into belief in the Antichrist."[55] Drawing on the language used at the Fourth Missionary Congress in 1908, he determined that Churikov's followers constituted a "sect similar to khlystovstvo, with the fundamental premise [being] the deification of this or that individual, the pure substitution of the human for the graceful [blagodatnyi], the mental and carnal for the spiritual, and belief in the individual for belief in God." Although Veniamin conceded that the trezvenniki had not gone quite as far as the Ioannity, who believed that "God has appeared in the flesh within the Kronstadt priest [batiushka],"[56] he nonetheless found them equally guilty of attributing too much power and authority to their spiritual leader and of forming a "community of like-minded devotees" who demonstrated an "unwillingness to be directed by church and state authorities."[57]

By directly charging Churikov with self-willed behavior, tying the trezvenniki to the khlysty, and characterizing them as a "community apart," Veniamin was setting the stage for shutting them down as a dangerous sect, either by excommunication or by legal action. While not all clergy had been convinced of Brother Ioann's deviance, those who had defended him now found themselves increasingly under pressure to reconsider. Among them was the former synodal missionary and Athonite monk, Father Arsenii (Minin), who in late 1911 published an article highly complementary of Churikov's preaching. Having read

Brother Ioann's besedy and found them firmly based on Scripture and the teachings of the Holy Fathers, Father Arsenii concluded that he had the potential to be of great benefit to the Orthodox, showing the narod the "true path to salvation." Further praising Churikov's preaching as "permeated by a deep religiosity, Christian simplicity, and compassion for those who are confused and perishing," Arsenii also recommended that his clerical colleagues set aside their "pride and envy" and "rejoice at the emergence of such an evangelist during a time corrupted by unbelief, atheism, and immorality."[58] Curiously, however, Father Arsenii backpedaled on these claims only weeks later. After stating that he had found nothing heretical in Churikov's besedy, he counseled his Orthodox readers who might be under Brother Ioann's influence to be "careful" and to listen to their own priests. The determination of whether Churikov was a "sectarian" or not, he noted, was better left to local religious authorities.[59]

Just a few months later, in early February 1912 Father Arsenii issued a full retraction of his support for Brother Ioann in Skvortsov's *Missionerskoe obozrenie*.[60] His change of heart, he explained, was based on a (re)reading of Churikov's besedy, which (he now realized) encouraged his followers to engage in behaviors similar to other "sectarians," such as "spiritual Christians, *shtundisty*, and Baptists." These included claiming that Holy Scripture can be interpreted by each individual and calling upon his followers to "partake of [*prichastit'*] the Word of God spiritually," to be "healed by the Word of God," and "to answer to the Word of God," as if to suggest that the Word was the only true source of salvation and that confession and sacramental life were irrelevant. Although Arsenii had never attended a beseda in person, on the basis of printed versions of his preaching he determined that Brother Ioann was a man of great arrogance, "possessed" of "diabolical charm."[61] As evidence, he pointed to the way he "deif[ied] himself," by signing his photographs as "Brother Ioann the Samaritan [*Samarskii*]," a clear reference to John 8:48, in which Jesus is called a "Samaritan." In this way, Arsenii argued, Churikov sought to identify himself with Jesus Christ and should therefore be seen as one of the "false prophets" spoken about in Matthew 24:24.

Arsenii's criticisms were no doubt damaging to Churikov's case, especially since they underscored many of the claims made by Veniamin. According to Tregubov, however, his retraction had been forced. The leading antisectarian missionary, V. Skvortsov, had sent a copy of the alleged denunciation to him along with a "request" that he sign and submit it for publication. If he agreed, Arsenii was told, he would be transferred from the Crimea to his beloved Voskresenskii monastery near Liuban; if he refused, his two benefactors (both wealthy Petersburg merchants) would cut off his only means of support.[62] Already elderly and unwell with no other financial recourse, Arsenii signed the retraction, which Skvortsov quickly published.

Whether Tregubov's account is entirely accurate or not, it seems that Arsenii's retraction deliberately misquoted Brother Ioann in an effort to suggest that he did not privilege Orthodoxy as a source of salvation. "The Orthodox Christian believes that only by belonging to the Orthodox Church will he or she receive eternal salvation," the article stated, "but according to Churikov's interpretation, it does not matter which faith one belongs to; confession has no meaning with respect to salvation." As evidence of Churikov's confessional indifference, Arsenii pointed to a quote from his November 7, 1910, beseda, "Joseph enjoyed the confidence of the Egyptian, even though the Egyptian was of a different faith," and another from a beseda on September 5, 1910, "he who becomes enamored of [*uvlekaetsia*] Scripture will be saved, whether he is a sectarian, *khlyst*, [or] *pashkovets*."[63]

While it is true that Brother Ioann received believers of all backgrounds, the original text of the September 5 beseda was taken out of context. In fact, the sermon that day—as it was recorded by Tregubov and verified by Churikov himself—centered not on questions of confession (as missionaries insisted), but rather on the importance of Scripture as a source of life and faith: "if a person rejoices in the Word of God, no matter how much, this is better than debauchery and drunkenness. Therefore, no matter what they call me—sectarian, *khlyst*, *pashkovets*— I will nevertheless [try to] captivate [*uvlekat'*] the people with the Word of God."[64]

While clearly a defiant statement, Churikov's claim that he intended to preach Scripture at all costs was not the same as asserting that confessional identity did not matter. This misrepresentation of Brother Ioann's views, combined with the forging of Arsenii's article, suggested that the tactics used by the missionaries in St. Petersburg were beginning to resemble the morally and ethically questionable means seen in the Moscow case against Koloskov and Grigor'ev, which had included fabrication of evidence and false accusations.[65]

In late 1912, the Petersburg priest and diocesan missionary, Father Mikhail Chel'tsov, also changed his position on Brother Ioann. A leading member for church reform after 1905, Chel'tsov had recently spoken out in highly positive terms about Churikov's efforts to bring Scripture to a working-class population desperate for spiritual leadership.[66] Yet, in the final issue of *Tserkovnye Vedomosti* in 1912, the priest published an extended denunciation of Brother Ioann's teachings.[67] Noting up front the divisiveness of the debate over Churikov's Orthodox identity at the time, Chel'tsov framed his comments as a dispassionate inquiry into his teachings, based on a careful reading of his printed besedy—that is, unenhanced by Brother Ioann's own emphases or emotional rendering of the text. Although some of his conclusions were drawn from circumstantial evidence,[68] Chel'tsov's analysis was less impressionistic than Veniamin's and far more systematic than Arsenii's, and thus his observations went a long way in supporting their key points.

One shared concern was the way that Brother Ioann used metaphor to connect sacred text with daily life, and his tendency to engage in the "materialization of Christ's teachings"—that is, the consistent application of Scripture to questions of material well-being and earthly life, not eternal salvation. According to Chel'tsov, at the core of Churikov's teachings was a single, problematic message: "Christ came to earth to save us from grief, need, illness, and suffering; for this reason, those who listen to and embrace the Word of God will be wealthy, healthy, joyous, and live without any kind of need."[69] In this way, Brother Ioann exhibited a tendency to reduce the Word of God to its functional significance as a guide to material success and life's comforts, rather than acknowledging that the Word calls believers to moral and spiritual *podvigi* (feats) and the *renunciation* of earthly happiness. Moreover, Chel'tsov agreed with his colleagues that by holding forth the Word of God as the only true source of hope and healing, Churikov effectively negated the possibility of God's grace—or at least, equated Divine Grace with the Word. While Churikov did not dismiss the sacraments out of hand (as, say, a Baptist would), by stressing healing and reconciliation with God through Scripture, he effectively taught that they were not important to salvation—and thus redirected people's energy away from them.[70]

Chel'tsov was also troubled by the way in which Churikov's besedy in effect humanized Christ, repeatedly portraying him as a great Teacher of life, but never once acknowledging his divine nature as the Savior, and referencing his identity as the Son of God only a handful of times.[71] While indulging his love of metaphor, Churikov spoke frequently of spiritual—not physical—resurrection, teaching his followers that Christ's place was no longer "in the tomb, but rather, in those who were drunks and became sober, those who were proud but became meek, those who were blind but now could see." In effect, he "reduced" Christ's resurrection to "its historical meaning" and interpreted it to mean that he now lived through his Word. While neglecting any mention of the afterlife, he also incorrectly (and consciously in disregard of the Church's teachings) interpreted Final Judgment to mean the judgment of nonbelievers in Christ.[72]

Primarily on these grounds, Chel'tsov concluded that Churikov's beliefs should be designated as "sectarian."[73] Curiously, he chose not to engage claims about Brother Ioann's divinity as directly or extensively as the others. Perhaps he understood the problematic nature of Veniamin's assumption that he could sense what was in another person's "heart," or the difficulties of basing a case on the clergy's ability to discern the "spirit" of a person's faith. Perhaps he took issue with the idea that Brother Ioann should be held responsible for the fact that some (but not all) of his followers made dangerous claims about his identity. Whatever the reason, Chel'tsov's decision to use the pejorative title "Churikovshchina" reflected his understanding of Brother Ioann's teachings as dangerously un-Orthodox; indeed, he went so far as to claim that Churikov was in effect proposing a "new Christianity."[74] The fact that these claims came from one of the more reform-minded members of the clergy in St. Petersburg suggested a widening consensus that Brother Ioann's identity was problematic. It was in this context that missionaries would intensify their campaign against him, and the trezvenniki would, in turn, ramp up their efforts to defend him.

By late 1912, Orthodox missionaries and clergy had gone to great lengths to make their concerns about Brother Ioann known. While all of his critics took issue with his interpretations of Scripture and expressed concerns about his views on salvation, Hieromonk Veniamin went further in challenging the nature of Churikov's faith and beliefs, and in asserting the importance of intangible over tangible forms of proof in matters of faith. While explicating distinctions between true (*istinnoe*) and untrue (*poddel'noe*) forms of piety, and between external and internal manifestations of Orthodoxy, Veniamin argued that neither Brother Ioann nor the trezvenniki were Orthodox "in their hearts," despite the fact that they outwardly acted according to the rules of the faith.

In that Veniamin's impressions of Brother Ioann and his followers rested not only on the (un-Orthodox) nature of their expressed beliefs or actions, but also on the un-Orthodox nature of their *spirit*, his denunciation was based less on what he had *observed* at the besedy, than on what he, as a "true" Orthodox, had *felt* (*umnym chuvstvom*) while in their presence. Veniamin's determination to essentialize Orthodoxy (and non-Orthodoxy) would in turn make it difficult for anyone to object to his conclusions. If they did not see evidence that Brother Ioann was dangerous, it was because he was not unlike the Devil, who is clever and "always acts hypocritically, under the cover of good."[75] And if they did not "feel" his deviance, it meant that they themselves were not truly Orthodox either. Veniamin's strategy, in other words, was not simply to call into question the spiritual authority attributed to Brother Ioann by his followers, or even to challenge Churikov's own claims of devotion to the Orthodox Church, but to deny the ability (and right) of both Brother Ioann and the trezvenniki to assert any claims related to issues of belief or spiritual authority.

CHAPTER 6

An Unorthodox Conversation
Sober Responses to the Church

By 1912, the controversy over Brother Ioann's Orthodox identity was widely known throughout St. Petersburg, but many lay Orthodox were still not sure what to make of the clergy's claims against him. One curious believer, an older woman of means, decided to attend one of his besedy to find out for herself.[1] Although pleasantly surprised by the "highly reverent mood" of the crowd, her impressions shifted when a young trezvennitsa announced Brother Ioann's arrival by shouting, "here comes our savior [*spasitel'*]!" Claiming injury to her "religious feelings," the older woman scolded the younger: "Dear, you (*ty'*) forget that our Savior is Christ, not (your) brother." The young woman, in turn, shared how her alcoholic father had "tyrannized" her family before Brother Ioann came along and sobered him up. Given all he had done for them, she asked, "How could we not consider him our savior?"

As the encounter between the two women suggested, the heart of the debate over Churikov lay in the distinction between "savior" and "Savior"—that is, between the everyday, moral-spiritual salvation the trezvenniki had found with Brother Ioann's help, and the eternal salvation that only God could provide. As discussed in chapter 2, many educated secular observers extolled Brother Ioann and the trezvenniki for their moral aspirations and clean lifestyle.[2] At the same time, however, the older woman's skepticism echoed the thinking of the clergy and missionaries who remained deeply troubled by the nature and degree of Brother Ioann's influence. In short, the two women embodied the debate; the fact that they were *women*—and from different classes—also reflected the extent to which the issues at the heart of the Churikov debate had engaged the whole Orthodox community.

Writing not long after the publication of Veniamin's denunciation in 1911, the religious scholar A. S. Prugavin seemed convinced that the missionaries' case against Churikov would not go far, in part because of the negative public response to the Church's handling of events in Moscow, and in part because of his large and devoted following. After all, past attempts to incarcerate Brother Ioann in prison or the insane asylum had only served to galvanize support for him. Given the circumstances, "what consequences could one expect from anathema and excommunication?" he queried.[3] As it turned out, Prugavin was both wrong and right. While the Church would move toward excommunicating Brother Ioann between 1912 and 1914, it would not anathematize him; on the contrary, it stressed the promise of reconciliation and the hope that Brother Ioann and his followers would come back into the Church's fold. As Prugavin had predicted, however, the missionaries' persecution of Churikov pushed him and many of his followers further away from the Church, in effect solidifying them as a "community apart."

As the possibility of excommunication became more evident, the trezvenniki worked hard to defend Brother Ioann and their sober identity to church authorities and the public, even more fervently than in the past. They responded directly to missionary claims, both defending their beliefs and practices and voicing their right to claim Brother Ioann as their "savior," a term they intended in the same way the young trezvennitsa had. Although their community was far from homogeneous, the trezvenniki found common ground in the belief that it was their right to read and interpret Scripture as a "living Gospel" and, of course, in their belief in Brother Ioann's goodness and gratitude toward him. Yet, even as they asserted their identity as Orthodox believers, they insisted that their community was not *religious*, as Veniamin charged, but rather moral, joined together through a common set of values. It might also be seen as an emotional community, bounded by affective experiences rather than a shared set of beliefs about God or the Church. Over time, as the Church's repression of Brother Ioann intensified, it would also evolve into an "interpretive community,"[4] as its members became more closely united through a common narrative of persecution.

FIGURE 6.   Brother Ioann and his followers in the prayer house at Vyritsa, photographed by the Bulla studio, 1911. Plaques on the table read: Joshua 24:15 "As for me and my house, we will serve the Lord," and John 6:37 "whoever comes to me, I will never cast out." Reprinted with permission from TsGAKFFD SPb.

Without a foundation of trust, confrontations between clerical authorities and Brother Ioann and his followers resulted in further polarization: the more the trezvenniki defended him, the more evidence there was to suggest that they "deified" him; the more he defended himself, the less he seemed to possess the requisite humility expected of a true son of the Orthodox Church; and the more ardently the clergy challenged the trezvenniki's devotion or humiliated them through ridicule or condescension, the more they pushed those same individuals away from the Church, thereby undermining the very authority they sought to assert. More forcefully than ever before, Brother Ioann advanced Scripture as a source of consolation, legitimation, and self-defense against all those who tried to define him. And the more loudly he asserted the right of all Orthodox to do the same.

The Trezvenniki Respond as Spiritual Partisans

By the fall of 1910, the trezvenniki were feeling the pressure of increased scrutiny by clerical authorities. When the priest-missionary Veniamin sensed hostility on the part of a trezvennitsa during his visit in October 1910, he did not imagine it. One month later, the diocesan missionary Dmitrii Bogoliubov faced a similar response when he asked to address the audience at Brother Ioann's beseda on November 21. In spite of the priest's relatively sympathetic stance toward Brother Ioann, the trez-venniki made it clear that they were not interested. When Bogoliubov insisted that he had been "empowered by Bishop Nikandr" to address them, they refused outright, saying that they had come only to hear their Brother. Churikov made an effort to calm them, telling them, "I did not teach you this," but to no avail. Bogoliubov grabbed the leaf-lets he had intended to distribute and rushed out.[5]

Afterward, authorities closed the besedy temporarily. By order of the bishop, Churikov recanted in a signed apology, affirming that he was not a heretic, and if he had done anything wrong in his besedy, it was due only to his lack of education; in the future, he promised, he would seek out help from clergy with respect to his interpretations, pronunciation, and proper prayers. He professed to be deeply troubled by the fact that several of his followers had compared him to Christ and the apostles—behavior he deemed to be gravely sinful—and reiterated he had always encouraged his followers to value and participate in sac-ramental life.[6] Following the apology, authorities allowed his besedy to reopen. But the November 21, 1910, episode had revealed what was becoming a pattern: missionaries would challenge Brother Ioann in some way, the trezvenniki would respond passionately (and often in ways that bordered on disrespect and even blasphemy), and the Church would then assign the blame to Churikov. More than before, Brother Ioann seemed unable to control his followers' response to clerical attacks, and thus became more vulnerable before religious and secular authorities.

The attitude of Petersburg trezvenniki toward missionaries deterio-rated over the course of 1911. That spring, just as the first of Veniamin's scathing critiques of Brother Ioann appeared in print, they watched the church's campaign against the Moscow brattsy intensify. In an effort to build a criminal case against Brothers Koloskov and Grigor'ev, mis-sionaries conducted multiple late-night searches of the brattsy's private living spaces, as well as their followers' homes, in search of physical evi-dence of their alleged "fanatical" and "immoral" acts (such as soiled bed linen).[7] Although no physical evidence was found, on the basis of hun-dreds of pages of sworn testimony, on March 27, 1911, over a hundred police accompanied missionaries to Koloskov's and Grigor'ev's homes and arrested them, along with some of their close female followers. All were sent to the Butyrskaia prison and placed in solitary confinement.[8]

In December 1911, as the Moscow brattsy and some of their followers remained confined to their prison cells, two Petersburg trezvenniki by the name of Davydov and Frolov issued an extensive response to Father Veniamin in a published pamphlet entitled *Dukhovnyi partizan* (*The Spiritual Partisan*). Deeply wounded, frustrated, and angered by his critique of Brother Ioann, they addressed every issue he had raised— from the oversized cross around Churikov's neck to the nature of his teachings and his reputation as a miracle worker. As they pointed out, they were not as well educated as their clerical critic, and not only in matters of church doctrine; their arguments are occasionally muddled, and in places repetitive and even contradictory. Nonetheless, as their editor, R. Ia. Bereskov, highlighted in his foreword, they wrote "simply but sensibly," with "great conviction" and a remarkable sense of authority, drawing on their extensive knowledge of Scripture as well as their firm belief in their right to choose their own spiritual advisor.[9]

Dukhovnyi partizan reads as a lengthy profession of faith, bearing witness to Brother Ioann's spiritual influence, while also working hard to place the trezvenniki's devotion to him within the limits of the Orthodox tradition.[10] Given the diversity of their experiences and perspectives, Davydov and Frolov could not speak for each and every one of Brother Ioann's followers, but tried instead to highlight the shared concerns of the community. While repeatedly voicing their commitment to the Orthodox faith, above all they stressed Churikov's role as a positive moral influence in their lives.

As in earlier trezvennik attempts to defend Churikov from clerical attacks, Davydov and Frolov offered personal testimonials as evidence of his goodness, stressing how Brother Ioann's prayers and guidance had helped them to take responsibility for their sins, to live by the Word of God, and to become more conscious (indeed, exemplary) in their attention to their Orthodox duties.[11] Rather than imagining themselves now free from sin (as Veniamin implied), they had come to realize the importance of committing themselves to the highest moral (and in their view, Orthodox) standards. To this end, they affirmed, "we think that it is safest and best to trust the words of Scripture, for they were written for our guidance."[12] They stressed that they did not value prayer or the sacraments any less; on the contrary, "the only difference between us and [other Orthodox] is that we celebrate [the sacraments and holidays] with the singing of psalms and church prayers, instead of with drunkenness and dancing."[13] With no apologies, they admitted to rejoicing because they had overcome their formerly sin-ridden selves and the danger they had posed to their families and others. At the same time, they fervently rejected the priest's impression that they celebrated with complete abandon; they were now more than ever aware of their sins and fearful in the knowledge that someday they would be called to account for them. In other words, with Brother Ioann's guidance they had become more conscious Orthodox believers.

Like the young trezvennitsa introduced earlier, Davydov and Frolov insisted that they did not think of Brother Ioann as a divine figure, but rather as their savior with a small *s* because he had helped them to overcome a life apart from God. His influence on them was tied very much to their experience in this world, not eternity. While agreeing with Veniamin that devotion to an individual could be dangerous, they maintained that "attachment to a good and moral person is not only not harmful, but directly useful and good for the soul."[14] Under Brother Ioann's influence, they had committed themselves to enlightenment and aspired to bring their lives in line with the faith. To an extent they also agreed with Veniamin that it was not enough to act Orthodox externally (by the performance of prescribed rituals); a true believer had to embrace faith internally and work to keep their inner and outer selves morally aligned. At the same time, however, they aspired to live their faith beyond their ritual obligations. As Brother Ioann preached, "if we attach ourselves only to the tomb of the saint, but we do not attach ourselves to his words and his life, then this is of no use to us." But when "people attach themselves to the life of a saint, whole cities appear, because God is rich and gives wealth to his zealots."[15] Thus, having escaped a world of lies, doubts, and deception—a world that many of them, especially alcoholics, had once helped to create—they aspired to live transparently, with honesty, humility, and faith.

On the subject of Brother Ioann's miracle-working abilities, Davydov and Frolov pointed out that the witnessing of miracles had confirmed the holiness of other individuals, and on these same grounds they offered evidence of Churikov's healing powers.[16] According to the Orthodox tradition (as they understood it), it was their duty as believers to testify to what they had witnessed, since "the miraculous constitutes a fundamental [part] of [the Orthodox people's] faith."[17] Though confident in their right to proclaim the sacred—both in terms of the miraculous, and in terms of what they saw as good and just—they also knew to tread carefully here. Like Evdokiia Ivanovskaia, they made it clear that they proclaimed Brother Ioann's healings as "miraculous" not out of a desire to glorify him, but rather out of a sense of their right and duty as Orthodox to acknowledge evidence of God's "gifts, whomever He gave them to: whether it be priests, laymen, or anybody else."[18] "No one should think that I write in defense of Brother Ioann and attribute [my healing] to him; no, I am defending the mercy of God as revealed to me because of Brother Ioann's prayers," Frolov wrote, in a manner consistent with other trezvenniki. "I would not write at all, but I fear God's wrath," he continued; "[I write] so that I will not get sick again for concealing miracles and God's works."[19]

Throughout the pamphlet, Davydov and Frolov were also careful to proclaim their love, need, and continued respect for the clergy.[20] The moral transformations Brother Ioann had inspired, they believed, were important not only to their personal salvation, but to that of the Orthodox community as a whole, especially urban priests. They acknowledged the sense of alienation and helplessness that many clergy experienced in the face of rampant "hooliganism," highlighting the anguish expressed by one Petersburg priest about the way people treated him, especially the young. "It's horrible . . . there is no fear, no respect or reverence. Even [for] our spiritual fathers, [it] has become impossible to walk down the street, especially on Sundays and other holidays. Everywhere there are drunken people [engaging in] inappropriate conduct and conversations. Not paying attention to our sacred dignity, they shout all sorts of abuse in our faces and call us 'parasites.'"[21] By bringing people to sobriety, they pointed out, Brother Ioann was helping the clergy in their efforts both to cultivate a healthy Orthodox life and to regain their rightful place and dignity within their communities.

Davydov and Frolov also made it clear that their relationship to the clergy had become fragile and tenuous, however. They voiced a profound sense of disappointment and frustration with church authorities as a whole, who had ignored them when they were drunk, depraved, and Orthodox in name only, and now that they had embraced holy sobriety, paid attention only in order to deny them as Orthodox. They also confessed their dissatisfaction with what most ordinary priests offered them in the way of spiritual comfort, adding that "if only [the Orthodox clergy] could be of help to the common people [narod] as Brother Ioann has been, then the people would love them just as much."[22] Rather than understanding their need for spiritual leaders who could speak their language, Father Veniamin had chosen to ridicule Brother Ioann for his "simple" language and everyday thoughts, preferring instead to use words and concepts that were incomprehensible to ordinary people like themselves.

Significantly, the trezvenniki did not see a conflict between their devotion to Brother Ioann and their love of the Church. On the contrary, they saw Churikov's spiritual leadership as complementary to that of the Church, since he had helped them to carve out a new space for their spiritual and moral growth. In claiming that Churikov was unique in providing them, as Orthodox, with spiritual and moral guidance they could find nowhere else, their main point was not to criticize clerical behaviors, but rather to assert the right of each person—lay or otherwise—to try to save the other; if it was considered morally right for a person to help someone drowning, "then why should not ordinary laypeople who have been gifted the ability to understand Holy Scripture save those drowning in drunkenness and debauchery?"[23] They further emphasized that Churikov's goal was to spread Scripture as a guide to life (not to teach dogma), not to distract them away from faith but, on the contrary, to encourage them toward the Church and its teachings.

With respect to the question of salvation, and whether or not the trezvenniki truly believed "in their hearts" that their salvation could be secured through Churikov's teachings and prayers alone, Frolov and Davydov's text suggests that they understood salvation in two distinct dimensions (human/moral and eternal/divine); but as believers in the modern world, where the religious and secular tended toward divergence, they were seeking a way to bridge the two in their everyday lives—and to not have to privilege one over the other. As Churikov taught them, they rejected as hypocritical those Orthodox (including their former selves) who continued to sin and then "purify" themselves through the sacraments, only to sin again. They also pushed back on the tendency of some clergy to tolerate believers' sins (including drinking) as long as they indicated that they understood the correct behavior.[24]

In their thoughts on the cycle of sin and repentance, it is fair to say that the trezvennik position had something in common with Baptists and Evangelical Christians; this did not necessarily mean, however, that they rejected the sacraments as irrelevant, even if this is what Veniamin and the Church eventually determined. On the contrary, Davydov and Frolov tried hard to reassure the clergy that they understood Brother Ioann's insistence on Scripture as a guide to earthly existence rather than as a substitute for the sacraments. To Veniamin's concern that they had come to value Brother Ioann's besedy above all else, they replied, "we reject neither prayer nor divine services, but only recall that the Savior did not bring prayers to the world, but preaching, as one of the most important means for renewing the world that was fraught with sins."[25] Without his preaching they had not been Orthodox, but rather "drunk in the streets, becoming like pagans." "Isn't that a substitute for Christianity?" they asked, turning the title of Veniamin's pamphlet to their own purposes.[26] In other words—and this was one of their most important points—Churikov's preaching of God's Word, and the moral discipline and guidance they received from it, was essential to their Orthodox identity.

With respect to Veniamin's charge that they constituted a "community apart" from the Orthodox, the trezvenniki agreed only to the extent that they thought of themselves as those who had already been healed by Churikov's counsel and prayer, as opposed to the countless others who continued to live in debauchery and darkness. The attachment most felt to Brother Ioann was primarily affective in nature—that is, a function of emotional and moral need. In this sense, theirs was both a moral and *emotional* (not religious) community, centered on the shared experience of overcoming a life of sin and degradation, and a set of attendant emotions, including shame (for their sinful lives, and the many people they had hurt), pride (at having transformed themselves), and last but not least, gratitude and love (for Brother Ioann, since he had led them to a better place in their lives, and for each other).

In all these ways, Davydov and Frolov worked to defend the beliefs and behaviors of the trezvennik community within the framework of what they understood to be the Orthodox tradition. Although some trezvenniki had claimed to Veniamin that the threat of excommunication did not frighten them, the numerous attempts by Churikov's followers to defend Brother Ioann indicated that the Church's approval mattered to others quite a lot. For this same reason, they made it clear that they did not approve of the disrespectful way in which some followers had treated Veniamin after the beseda, behavior they considered to be wrong but also atypical. After all, Churikov refused to acknowledge as his followers anyone who defamed the clergy, reminding them of Paul's warning to "respect one another" (here, as in many places in the text, a double meaning was clearly intended).[27]

For all the ink spilled over the course of 1911, little would be resolved between the trezvenniki and their clerical critic. In writing the preface to the published version of *Dukhovnyi partizan*, Bereskov likened the written exchange between Veniamin and the trezvenniki to a collision between two opposing worlds.[28] Their emotionally fraught in-person encounters likewise suggested the near impossibility of engaging either side in effective dialogue. The trezvenniki had made the hieromonk feel uncomfortable and disrespected during his visit to the besedy, and he responded by losing his composure and using his status to intimidate and lash out at them.[29] The trezvenniki's attempts to reassure him of their respect had done little to assuage him, and in concluding his account, he made it clear that he did not expect they would listen to his concerns.[30] The trezvenniki, in turn, accused Veniamin of lacking empathy for their plight and "shutting his heart and ears" to their needs, like the man with a full belly who is indifferent to the cries of the hungry.[31]

As a consequence of the trezvenniki's profound confusion over the Church's persecution of Brother Ioann, and especially after the publications of Veniamin's articles in 1911, a complex of negative emotions (fear, betrayal, anger) began to strengthen the bonds of their community as much as positive ones (hope, love, gratitude) had in the past. Thus, even as the trezvenniki's words expressed continued devotion to the Church in the abstract sense, their tone—and, increasingly, their actions—indicated a collective need to recoil from the clergy in defense of both Churikov and the community with which they so strongly identified.

The Kolesnikov Scandal

On January 24, 1912, just one month after Davydov and Frolov published their response to Veniamin, Petersburg missionaries held a special meeting to discuss Churikov and his besedy. With eleven members of the missionary council present, Bishop Nikandr (Phenomenov) addressed Brother Ioann disrespectfully as "Ivan" and then accused him of being a liar for going back on an earlier promise to stop publishing his besedy. "Your besedy are being recorded by a sectarian," the bishop charged, and "[they are] imbued with a sectarian spirit."[32] Brother Ioann asked him to show him exactly what was sectarian about them, so that he could make corrections. He added that priests had regularly attended his spiritual-moral lectures and that none had found anything wrong with them up to that point. So, he implied, what had changed?

In response, Nikandr informed Brother Ioann that if he refused to cease his besedy at once, he would be officially designated as a "sectarian" on account of his failure to act as a "son of the Church." While

Churikov promised that he would "not blaspheme any dogmas or criticize any religion or clergy" (as he had agreed in the past), he drew a line in the sand: "I cannot be silent or stop preaching the Word of God because at the present time the *narod* is perishing because of drinking and debauchery. The Word of God is the best healing remedy for all evils, and [yet] you want me to stop preaching [it]. Do what you will with me, for I am prepared to suffer. But know that my blood will fall on the clergy."[33] Clearly taken aback by Churikov's refusal and unusually threatening tone, the missionary council fell completely silent for several minutes.

At the time, Brother Ioann's popularity among laypeople was not only steady but growing. On Easter Sunday (March 25, 1912), the meeting hall at Petrovskii Park was overflowing with people wanting to hear his beseda; an additional four hundred could not get into the building, so they stood for hours, listening from the courtyard. In all, 2,255 individuals came to kiss Brother Ioann's hand after the conclusion of the beseda—an impressive increase over the recorded 1,900 admirers who had sought Brother Ioann's Easter blessing in 1911.[34]

Later that spring, Brother Ioann prepared to open his new meeting space in Obukhovo, built to accommodate his expanding population of followers. The local diocesan council had tried to prevent the opening of the new preaching site, but secular authorities had allowed it.[35] As a sign of respect, Brother Ioann requested the local parish priest, Father Ioann Kolesnikov, to bless the new hall. The priest refused, however, allegedly on the grounds that Churikov was not a priest and therefore (in his opinion) not authorized to hold prayer meetings. The awkward exchange immediately set off an emotional chain reaction that fed on the fears of clergy and trezvenniki alike.

The fact that Father Ioann refused Churikov's request was likely not a surprise to anyone, given he had long been openly hostile to the trezvenniki's presence in his parish and had regularly labeled Brother Ioann a sectarian, a heretic, and even the Antichrist. In fact, Kolesnikov's rantings were so extreme that local trezvenniki had written to the Synod, asking for protection and expressing fear that other parishioners might come after them.[36] So Brother Ioann had quickly moved on and, after securing the blessing of another priest, went ahead with his plans to preach in the new space. When Father Ioann found out, however, he became outraged and showed up at a prayer meeting unexpectedly, demanding his right to address the trezvenniki gathered there.[37] Churikov was amenable to his demand, but the crowd was not, and when the priest persisted, they shouted him down "with one voice": "*Batiushka*, go to your own church and preach what you like, even curse us [there], but here we won't let you."[38] Panic and chaos quickly ensued as Father Ioann was ushered out of the church. When the trezvenniki spilled into the streets, Orthodox workers from the nearby Obukhov plant were waiting to beat them up as retribution for the disrespectful way they had treated the local priest. Several were arrested, many were seriously injured, and the violent encounter was sensationalized in local papers for several days.[39]

Whether or not Father Ioann had deliberately provoked the confrontation (as some trezvenniki would charge), he nonetheless made the most of it. In a report to the bishop the following day, he accused Brother Ioann of preaching for a long time so that his followers would not want to listen to anyone else, and he portrayed the trezvenniki as hooligans, who attacked him so violently that "it seemed like my life was hanging by a thread, and that I might be torn to pieces."[40] Assuming the heroic role of a "defender of his Orthodoxy," he explained how he had asked God to help him as he "suffered humiliation and abuse for truth [*istina*]." As he left the hall, Kolesnikov elaborated, he was greeted by a "large crowd of people enthusiastically welcoming him and expressing their sympathy with tears in their eyes." He escaped without further injury, as did the deacon, but another priest, Mikhail Akimov, had received both insults and blows to his ear and back.[41] His report concluded by accusing Churikov of distorting the holy texts, "exploiting the simple people," and "[cultivating] in them such brutal feelings toward the Orthodox clergy." Days later, Bishop Nikandr wrote to local Petersburg authorities to insist that Brother Ioann's besedy be shut down completely, on the grounds that the Church did not need preachers who are "ignoramuses" such as the "peasant Churikov."[42] Churikov's besedy were closed once again.

News of the priest's "disgrace" was rapidly circulated by the sensationalistic press, provoking outrage among the broader Orthodox public. Violent confrontations were still far from common, and the one with Father Kolesnikov was the first—and ultimately last—of its kind between the clergy and the trezvenniki. But its impact was significant, and it is clear that the workers of Obukhovo were not the only lay believers to harbor hostility toward them. While it is impossible to gain an accurate sense of its scope, evidence suggests that animosity came from diverse parts of the capital, and from different classes of believers.[43] If many people had been relatively indifferent to the case up to that point, the loud cries of the outraged priest surely swayed some opinions against the trezvenniki, especially in Vyritsa and Obukhovo.

At the same time, however, a June 19 article in the new newspaper *Pravda*, by "N.S." (K. Samuilov), spoke out in support of the trezvenniki. It questioned the well-substantiated claim that workers from the Obukhov plant had participated in the beatings but nonetheless defended the trezvenniki by arguing that it was not right for the "proletariat" to play a role in their "persecution" or to mock their "sincere" and "deep religious-moral feelings."[44] And while challenging the idea that drunkenness was the main cause of workers' misery (or that religion was the answer to either problem), it acknowledged that the battle against drunkenness was a good thing and that the trezvenniki should be tolerated because the law was on their side. Partly on the logic that "the enemy of my enemy is my friend," Samuilov also raised questions about the clergy's motivations: What were the Churikovtsy guilty of exactly? Reducing the fees that would otherwise go to priests? Or was the problem that they were being led by a "simple peasant" who dared to preach Scripture?

Churikov clearly sensed a shift in the atmosphere following the Kolesnikov incident and was uncharacteristically quick to respond. In the immediate aftermath, he turned for protection to secular authorities, petitioning the Ministry for Internal Affairs (MVD) for permission to reopen his besedy so that his followers would not go back to drinking. As in the past, he reassured secular authorities that his respect for the clergy was great and his devotion to the Holy Mother Church complete. But his version of events on June 12 differed considerably. While acknowledging that the situation had quickly spun out of control, he claimed that the crowd's panic had started in direct response to someone shouting "fire" in the hall. Aside from the details of that day, he charged, over the longer run the clergy (including Kolesnikov) had brought the situation upon themselves not only by failing to tend to the needs of their "flock," but also by persecuting those who did. At the same time, Brother Ioann seized upon the opportunity to express his own frustration at years of clerical suspicion and persecution, by again comparing his situation to that of David when he had angered King Saul. Clearly identifying with David, the former shepherd who bravely battled with demons and beasts, Churikov cast the clergy in the role of Saul, the king who was jealous of his feats and sought to kill him.[45]

A trezvennik petition to the MVD backed up Churikov's claim that the violence had been perpetrated by Father Ioann's "half drunk and rowdy" parishioners, who had caused them to fear for their own lives.[46] After accusing the priest of trying to "wash the blood off his hands" by rushing to the press, they complained that local police had done nothing to protect them during the beating and reiterated Brother Ioann's request that their meetings be permitted again. In an effort to do further damage control among the public, the trezvenniki also attempted to use the press to their own advantage. Although the popular daily *Peterburgskii listok* turned them away,[47] they were able to publish a letter to the editor in *Nevskaia Zvezda*, assuring the Orthodox public that Brother Ioann had taught them to respect the Orthodox Church and its clergy, while encouraging them to refrain from drinking and smoking and all kinds of disreputable behaviors.[48] As Brother Ioann had two years earlier, they then invited anyone who continued to harbor doubts about their activities to come to one of their prayer meetings. They concluded with a desperately worded plea to those workers who had condemned them, asking for compassion and solidarity: "We are also workers, just like you, and we are striving toward the same goal as you. Why then are you spiteful toward us and why do you cause us evil, which we don't deserve at all? Wouldn't it be better for us all to strive for truth [*pravda*] and to live in peace and love?"[49]

For all their efforts, Brother Ioann and his followers were painfully aware that the balance of clerical opinion had turned against him as a result of the incident on June 12. While the extensive arguments offered by the hieromonk Veniamin and the priest Chel'tsov gave church authorities the logic they needed to move forward with formal sanctioning, the Kolesnikov scandal had given the case the emotional gravity it had previously lacked. The disorder in Obukhovo gave local secular authorities pause as well; whereas they had been generally supportive of the trezvenniki's right to meet in the past, the violent incident on June 12 forced at least a temporary change in their position until a formal investigation could be completed.[50] As Natalia Zarembo has observed, changes in diocesan leadership in 1912–13, especially the death of Metropolitan Antonii in the fall of 1912 and the replacement of the more sympathetic Dmitrii Bogoliubov with the ultraconservative antisectarian missionary Ivan Grigor'evich Aivazov, who had been leading the case against the Moscow brattsy, also helped to shift the balance of clerical opinion against Churikov.[51] In this context, Metropolitan Vladimir took another step toward excommunication by calling Brother Ioann in for a requisite meeting with the missionary council (*uveshchanie*) the following spring.

In the meantime, Churikov's besedy remained closed, but state authorities allowed Brother Ioann personal contact with his followers on major holy days. The turnout at Christmas was striking, as waves of people arrived throughout the day, seeking his blessing; according to one newspaper, in all, there were twenty-two train cars, each with one hundred to four hundred people on them.[52] Another group of followers walked on foot for miles from all corners of the city, in freezing conditions, carrying with them the gifts of gold, frankincense, and myrrh. In return, Brother Ioann gave them a kopek to symbolize prosperity, frankincense as a symbol of a healthy, pure life, and oil as a symbol of healing. In the absence of regular contact with Brother Ioann, the trezvenniki invested the holiday exchange with enormous meaning.

Among Churikov's visitors was none other than Father Ioann Kolesnikov, who came to offer Christmas blessings. The gesture evidently moved Brother Ioann very much, but the trezvenniki once again tried to turn the priest away.[53] Inspired by the holiday spirit, a deputation of Churikov's followers also sought out the popular priest Father Filosof Ornatskii, head of the local Orthodox mission and soon to be rector at the Kazan Cathedral. Hoping to make a peace offering and shore up an ally, they asked him to visit Brother Ioann. "We love Christ and the Church," they reassured him. "We are fighting only with the tavern-keepers and distillers." Although he refused their request at the time, Ornatskii visited Obukhovo soon after and, in a meeting described as "touching," blessed Brother Ioann and his followers. The priest did not accept their "gifts," however, making it clear that Brother Ioann needed to demonstrate that he was a faithful servant of the Church by holding off on his besedy until religious (as opposed to secular) authorities granted him permission to restart.[54] While siding with the church hierarchy, Ornatskii was careful not to alienate the trezvenniki entirely. After delivering a brief sermon, he had tea with them and listened as they testified to Brother Ioann's "miraculous" healings. Christmas, in short, had resulted in a fragile peace between Brother Ioann and local clergy, at least for the moment.

A few months later, in May 1913, the trezvenniki also received a welcome dose of public support from a vocal group of secular elites outraged by the developments in the ongoing criminal prosecution of the Moscow brattsy. At a special hearing led by the Octobrist faction of the Duma, journalists, scholars, and statesmen denounced the Church's campaign against the brattsy as a "witch hunt" motivated by fear.[55] One after the other, distinguished speakers stepped up to defend

FIGURE 7. Scenes from Brother Ioann's colony in Vyritsa. "The Struggle against Drunkenness near St. Petersburg: Sketches from Nature for the Magazine *Ogonek*," by the artist S. V. Zhivotovskii and photographs by K. K. Bulla.

the trezvenniki in both Moscow and St. Petersburg, and together they wove a glowing counternarrative stressing the moral effects of the brattsy's preaching. Typical was the claim from Professor Karl Eduardovich Lindeman, who suggested that the trezvenniki "should serve as a model for the masses by [virtue of their] sobriety, diligence, clarity of mind, and devotion to the existing system."[56] The published speeches clearly reflected the participants' shared belief that the issues at hand in the case of both Brother Ioann and the Moscow brattsy were much bigger than the fate of the individuals involved. At stake was nothing less than the fate of religious freedom and the possibility of Russia's social and moral progress.

The Final Steps toward Excommunication

During multiple meetings over the course of 1913-14, the Petersburg diocesan missionary council tried to wear Brother Ioann down with their interrogations, while Churikov tried to remain composed as he emphatically denied the charges against him and asserted his devotion to the Holy Mother Church. Although a necessary part of the formal process, the inquiries were a maddening experience for everyone. Transcripts suggest that Brother Ioann was becoming bolder in declaring his right—as an Orthodox Christian—to interpret Scripture, as well as his need to preach for the spiritual health of others. He also intensified his critique of the clergy.[57] By this point—in fact, as of early 1912—he appeared to have given up on the idea of convincing his interrogators. They repeatedly seemed to ignore, for example, his vehement claims of indignation when his followers compared him to the apostles or Christ, and made little of his willingness to submit his scriptural interpretations to review by the clergy. Having arrived at the hard realization that truth was not an effective defense, he exhibited deep despair over his situation, especially the clergy's lack of compassion toward him. He would later characterize these formal conversations with the "angry and hate-filled" missionaries on the council as exercises in "moral torture."[58]

Even after the debacle with Kolesnikov, Churikov's supporters remained hopeful that the besedy could be reopened, and sent petitions to the tsar and empress as well as secular authorities in the MVD, but all of their appeals were denied.[59] Then, on February 4, 1914, not long before the Church's final decision, Churikov was interrogated by the diocesan missionary council one last time. The assembled were an impressive and unsympathetic group, including Bishop Nikandr and I. G. Aivazov, professor of the History and Unmasking of Sectarianism at the Moscow Theological Academy, as well as Father Kolesnikov and another parish priest.[60] As his witnesses and support, Brother Ioann brought three of his followers, identified only as Lypandin, Orlov, and Sergachev. The ensuing debate over whether or not the lay guests were allowed in the room was telling of the state of broader clerical–lay relations at that moment. When missionaries tried to eject the trezvenniki from the room entirely, Churikov protested that their conversation should be "in the open," so the council decided to allow the three men to sit in an adjoining room with the door ajar, effectively leaving them on the margins of the discussion. The compromise made everyone unhappy. The meeting thus got off to a tense start and continued in that vein for the next five hours. In terms of the line of questioning, as well as the tone and substance of Brother Ioann's answers, the meeting was typical of the interrogation process as a whole, and therefore worth a close look.

The missionary Aivazov conducted the interrogation, which he directed first toward Brother Ioann's relationship with the Moscow bratsty. As in the past, Churikov flatly denied the accusation that their "very dangerous sectarian" teachings were the "fruits" of his own preaching— and instead blamed missionaries for having embittered them and chased them out of the Church. Then, in words no doubt intended to apply as much to his own situation as to theirs, he advised: "you should approach them with love, and if they are mistaken about something, then you should correct them and they would be good helpers to you and workers on behalf of the Church."[61] Missionaries also raised the subject of the excommunicated Tolstoy, and the fact that Brother Ioann had publicly showed respect for him as a "wanderer for Christ" and admitted to praying for him upon his death. In response, Churikov defended his right to pray for him on the grounds that one should pray for both the righteous and the sinners. But when Aivazov suggested that he believed that the Church had been wrong to excommunicate Tolstoy, Brother Ioann countered, "the Church didn't excommunicate him, you excommunicated him," making a clear distinction between the "true" Church and the false missionaries who pretended to speak on its behalf.

Citing letters from Brother Ioann's followers, Aivazov then turned the interrogation to the question of deification. Of course, the missionaries already knew Churikov's views, since he had repeatedly and unequivocally condemned as sinful any claims made by his followers suggesting his divinity. But this time he elaborated: "we all should bring Scripture to life and be like Christ, and then there would be no disasters: no drunkenness, no illness, no revolution." Careful not to suggest that he harbored a "*khlyst*-like" belief that individuals could "become Christs," he clarified: "We cannot be Christs, but Christ can exist within us. And one can see from one's actions in whom Christ lives." He then took a moment to point out that the missionary Aivazov was an exception, since he spent all his time persecuting "the science of Christ" (*nauka Khristova*), and that is the same thing as persecuting Christ himself. For his actions, Churikov warned, "there will be final judgment, both on earth and for eternity."[62] Such disrespectful language was unusual for Brother Ioann, and surely indicative of his frustration at that moment.

When Aivazov later mentioned that the authorities wanted to prohibit him from receiving petitioners by note (having already shut down his besedy and prohibited his personal receptions), Churikov protested emphatically.[63] As early as 1911, he had begun to use more secular arguments in defense of his besedy: "Shame on you for talking about closing besedy and stopping prayer receptions," he had told the missionary

FIGURE 8.   Brother Ioann in front of the image of Jesus praying in the garden at Gethsemane, a place of suffering, ca. 1910–14. Reprinted with permission from TsGAKFFD SPb.

during a highly publicized debate in February 1911. "All of Russia, following the lead of our Sovereign Emperor, is talking about sobering up the *narod*, and you are suggesting the closing of prayer receptions. People are asking for prayers so that they can become sober, and you are chasing them away. Shame on you. For this you will have to answer before God."[64]

Brother Ioann's besedy remained closed in spite of his protests, and in April 1914, after almost two more years of interrogations and discussions, he was found guilty of multiple "sectarian-heretical" and "self-willed" (*samovol'nye*) behaviors. The charges included freely interpreting Holy Scripture without direction from the Holy Fathers and Church, preaching a false understanding of the relationship between the Holy Sacraments and salvation, and "blasphemously" comparing himself to the "Evangelical Christ" and posing as a miracle worker.[65] Compared to the Church's decision to pronounce anathema against the Moscow brothers, excommunication alone was a less serious sanction; Churikov had been barred from the communion table but not from the Church, and the hope was that he would reconsider his ways and submit fully to religious authorities in the future. Moreover, church authorities made it clear (most of all to priests) that his followers had not been excommunicated, and therefore should not be refused rites—as trezvenniki had been by local parish priests in Moscow.[66] Significantly, no criminal investigation followed.

Nonetheless, the sanctioning of Churikov was a devastating blow. On April 1, 1914, the day that the Church announced its decision to excommunicate him, Brother Ioann responded with a letter published in the journal *Nov'*. He had avoided the press for twenty years but claimed that false accusations in the missionary press were forcing him to speak out. He once again attested to his identity as a faithful Orthodox believer, yet also—as if to preempt the impending exercise of clerical authority against him—confessed that he had refrained from the communion table for almost a year by that point. How could he receive communion when there was no peace between him and the clergy?[67] His letter also refuted the Church's claim that its primary goal was to reconcile him with the faith. Given the terms set by church authorities—namely, that he agree to stop preaching the Word of God—such a reconciliation was (they knew) impossible. "In the name of saving our perishing *narod*," he begged, stop looking down on the "simple people [*prostoi narod*]" as if they were children. "We are adults, just like the missionaries, and we should have the same rights [as the clergy have] to preach the Word of God." In unusually politicized language, he further pleaded: "in order to save our dying people, I, as a native of the people, appeal to all the authorities to free the Word of God out from under the yoke of missionary captivity" and to allow the laity to interpret it, except as it concerned dogma and rituals.[68] To the accusation that he had encouraged his followers' tendency to glorify him, he cited Scripture in his defense: "If I glorify myself, my glory means nothing. My Father, whom you claim as your God, is the one who glorifies me" (John 8:54).[69]

The Church's "small excommunication" (*maloe otluchenie*) seemed only to encourage more people to seek out Brother Ioann, as well as to increase the amount of love and respect they demonstrated toward him. A June article by N. Leonidov in *Dym otechestva* (*Smoke of the Fatherland*), a patriotic weekly known for its critiques of the church hierarchy and the radical right, estimated that since the Kolesnikov scandal in 1912, Churikov's followers had increased by about eighty thousand, and now totaled around two hundred thousand, not including children.[70] On April 19, 1914, thousands of Brother Ioann's followers traveled to Vyritsa for an emotional exchange of Easter greetings. Lacking official permission to greet them personally, Churikov blessed them from his window; observers noticed that many in the crowd were moved to tears. The following Monday, some ten thousand more people came.[71] In light of Brother Ioann's success in bringing both former alcoholics and people of other faiths to the Church, Leonidov urged clergy and missionaries to check in with their own "conscience" and reconsider their decision to silence Churikov's preaching.[72]

Several months after the Church's formal denunciation of Brother Ioann, which came out in August 1914, just as war was breaking out, a defiant Churikov sent an *obiasnenie* (explanation) to the MVD, responding to the final charges against him with the hope of getting state permission to reopen his besedy.[73] With his excommunication now a fact, he boldly characterized the missionary council's claims as "shameful" and "lies"—for example, the "senseless" and "blasphemous" accusation that he had compared himself to the Evangelical Christ. Who is to be believed, he asked, the missionary council that fishes for any kind of lie or the honest trezvenniki, who number in the thousands? While he acknowledged that he had read the Word of God to people dying of alcoholism without the bishop's blessing, he reminded his readers that when he had turned to the authorities in the early days of his preaching, he had been imprisoned without a trial. Likewise, he allowed that some of his interpretations might have been mistaken or misguided, but also pointed out that instead of explaining his errors, the clergy had rushed instead to label him a "sectarian" and "heretic."

Churikov argued to secular authorities that the clergy's actions against him had been based on a combination of fear and pride, and he compared his situation to that of the beloved and deeply pious Ioann Zlatoust (John Chrysostom), who was envied and persecuted "because the *narod* loved him and listened to his influential preaching" and thus refused to listen to the official clergy.[74] With this analogy, he was able to defend (and legitimize) his own actions on the grounds that he was meeting the spiritual needs of ordinary laity, while at the same time suggesting the inability or unwillingness of clergy to do the same. Although caught uncomfortably between the expectations of church officials and those of the *narod*, Brother Ioann consoled himself with the knowledge that clerical decisions were fallible and temporary, whereas the love of the faithful was eternal. Anticipating that clerical authorities might find his comments "heretical," he added that Holy Scripture had been written "so as to vindicate those persecuted for the Word of God and to condemn the evil for their hatred," and "everyone knows that the truth hurts," but all can be healed by the Word.[75]

For all his anguish and anger, Brother Ioann concluded the document by declaring himself a "true Orthodox Christian and a faithful [*veryni*] son" of the Orthodox Church. He then asked secular authorities to respect the laws of April 1 and October 17, 1905, so that he could continue to read the Gospel freely to those dying of drunkenness, to their benefit and that of the Holy Church. In a follow-up to the Ministry of Internal Affairs in February 1915, he was even clearer: "If we in the Orthodox Church do not have the right to speak freely about the Word of God to simple laypeople, then believe me, we will have only disabled people [*invalidi*] who are unable to defend Orthodoxy, because the brave soldiers in Christ will all go into sectarianism. And to me, a zealot of the Word of God, the missionaries also point the way there [to sectarianism]. I look at this case with sorrow and pain."[76]

In a photograph published in a popular Petersburg newspaper in late March 1914, on the eve of his excommunication, Brother Ioann posed at his desk in Vyritsa, next to a small plaque carefully angled toward the reader: "As for me and my house, we will serve the Lord" (Joshua 24:15).[77] Even more than his carefully worded statements of that year, the well-known scriptural quote made clear his response to the Church's decision.

FIGURE 9. Brother Ioann in his office in Vyritsa, photograph by A. Mikhailov, *Vsemirnaia panorama*, no. 257 (March 21, 1914): 12. The caption notes that the various items on and around his desk portray him as a man of intellect and curiosity, including a telephone (connecting him to his followers in St. Petersburg) and binoculars; it also mentions the large portrait of Peter the Great, whom Churikov admired mostly for his tolerance of those of different faiths.

Although the Church's decision to excommunicate Brother Ioann had been issued with the hope of reconciliation, the trauma caused by years of questioning and conflict made the possibility remote, at least in the short term. Whether motivated by fear, ambition, jealousy, or faith, the clergy's complete unwillingness to believe a word that Brother Ioann or his followers said had been deeply offensive to the trezvennik community, leading to a further erosion of trust. Moreover, in spite of the Church's commitment to "unmasking" false prophets and leaders in the interest of preserving Orthodoxy, their own tactics—especially in Moscow, but in Churikov's case too—had involved lies and deliberate falsifications. The case had rested in part on the testimony of unsubstantiated lay witnesses and disgruntled parish priests, especially Father Ioann Kolesnikov, and the trezvenniki's beliefs had been measured according to a highly subjective standard of proof—Veniamin's ability to assess what was "in their hearts." And while officially Churikov had been charged with multiple "sectarian-heretical" and "self-willed" behaviors, his case had been made to the public largely on the grounds that he was not what he seemed or claimed; from the earliest days of his preaching, he had been the target of unsubstantiated innuendoes and insinuations that he was a fraud, an exploiter, and a sexual predator.

As the missionary Dmitrii Bogoliubov had predicted, the Church's decision to approach Brother Ioann with hostility instead of understanding had alienated many of his followers from it; in fact, some (although not all) stopped going to church and seeking out priests altogether.[78] As Churikov argued, in the end the clergy had been the ones responsible for sending his followers away from the Church and toward the moral certainty of Scripture. By ridiculing them for their beliefs in the miraculous power of healing, they had grown cold toward all that is "holy," all but ensuring that they would continue to choose Churikov over the clergy; "the stone the builders rejected has become the cornerstone" (Matthew 21:24), he observed.[79] One of the most significant consequences of the Church's case against Brother Ioann was the way it united his followers around a common narrative about who he was and what he was trying to do (and why he was misunderstood)—a narrative best articulated in *Dukhovnyi partizan*. In this sense, after 1911 or so, we can talk about the trezvenniki not only as a moral or emotional community, but also as an interpretive community, centered on a shared narrative of hope and persecution.

This is not to say that the clergy did not have legitimate reasons to be concerned about the tendency of some of Brother Ioann's followers to deify him; on the contrary, such beliefs had been acknowledged (and denounced) by Brother Ioann himself on numerous occasions. Yet many others—including Davydov and Frolov—looked upon Brother Ioann as a savior in the moral rather than divine sense, and thus continued to struggle with the fact that the clergy and missionaries involved in the case had treated Brother Ioann with suspicion rather than respect (let alone, compassion) from the start. The case thus revealed the church authorities' inability—or at least, unwillingness—to acknowledge such distinctions, even if some individual clergy did.

The Churikov case also revealed a growing divide between religious and secular authorities. As news of the excommunication was sinking in, several well-known moderately conservative state and political elites visited Brother Ioann in Vyritsa. Like the Octobrists who had spoken out the year before, they had been impressed by the trezvenniki and wanted to voice their disapproval of the Church's attempts to marginalize them. Typical of the comments to appear in *Dym otechestva*, a platform for a progressive nationalist agenda, were those of Petrograd Duma member G. A. Fal'bork, who praised Brother Ioann as a "very talented Russian *samorodok*" (intelligent in spite of his lack of education). The secret to Churikov's popularity, he suggested, was the way he "combine[s] his spiritual powers with practical knowledge. Mystically attuned, he deeply believes in God's help, but [when] speaking about the heavenly, he combines it with the earthly." "To forbid such people to communicate with the people is a terrible sin," Fal'bork continued; "you cannot kill the people's faith, extinguish the spirit of religion. This is not only a mistake; from the point of view of the Church, society, and family—this is a state crime." In line with those Octobrists who saw the trezvenniki as exemplary workers and citizens, he concluded that people like Churikov should be encouraged in every possible way. Much for the same reasons, State Duma member L. A. Velikov called on his colleagues to "denounce their haters" and support the trezvenniki.[80]

The fact that local security forces in St. Petersburg also spoke positively about the trezvenniki helped their case. In January 1914, a police investigation concluded Churikov and his followers had consistently shown "unconditional loyalty" to the state and the tsar. Finding them completely harmless, even "useful" to the social order in the way they contributed to the overall "health" of the proletariat, local police found no reason to object to the reinstatement of the trezvenniki's right to meet for religious-moral meetings.[81]

Although Churikov's besedy would be not permitted again under tsarism, the state continued to support the trezvenniki's right to exist as a community after the excommunication. His followers formed a mutual aid society, and many continued to gather in private homes to testify and to read and discuss Scripture.[82] In this way, the Church's decision to assert control over the trezvenniki had, paradoxically, resulted in a significant loss of oversight. And as the war in Europe dragged on and the mood and resources in Petrograd dwindled, the popularity of Brother Ioann and holy sobriety began to spread again, like mushrooms after the rain.

CHAPTER 7

Revolutionary Sobriety

Challenges and Opportunities, 1917–1927

When revolution erupted on the streets of Petrograd in early 1917, Brother Ioann was living on the sober colony in Vyritsa, where he had been for the duration of the war. The lingering wound of excommunication and strict limits on personal contact with him had left his followers bereft and alienated. But with permission from secular authorities, the trezvenniki had carried on the work of sobriety on their own. In Petrograd, small, "secret" groups led by lay preachers from the community gathered in private apartments for prayer, Scripture readings, and testifying, and in July 1914, members of the trezvennik community officially registered as a mutual aid society; additional branches opened during the war, including one at the Serafimovskaia Church with the support of Father N. Vostokov.[1]

In spite of all he had endured, Brother Ioann continued to advocate for obedience to existing authorities, including the call to serve in the Imperial Army during the war. Even as the conflict's devastation began to turn public opinion against the tsarist regime, Churikov saw the war as justified; he instructed his followers not to accept state pensions and instead paid for soldiers' families out of mutual aid funds from the colony.[2] Nonetheless, after years of loss and struggle most trezvenniki experienced the collapse of the tsarist regime in early 1917 as a moment of liberation, especially when, for the first time in five years, they were able to hold public besedy with Brother Ioann.[3] On the first day of Easter, April 2, 1917, just weeks after Tsar Nicholas II's abdication, Churikov and his followers rushed to their old meeting place in Obukhovo to celebrate their new freedom—the absence of police was a noticeable sign of the revolution's promise.[4] After the beseda, thousands approached Brother Ioann to receive his blessing.

This reunion no doubt went under the radar of many observers distracted by the myriad events associated with the "revolutionary spring" of 1917, and it has certainly missed the attention of historians who have tended to ignore anything that did not speak of direct revolutionary impact. Yet Orthodox authorities remained wary of Brother Ioann. Metropolitan Antonii Khrapovitskii, for example, made it clear that he continued to fear the purveyors of "spiritual delusion" (*dukhovnaia prelest'*), a group in which he included Brother Ioann by name. As he despaired from his monastery prison cell in 1919, "the war, and even more the Revolution, has significantly cooled their ardor, but spiritual infection like this is too deep for it to be destroyed by even the most radical political upheavals."[5] As time would tell, he was not wrong about Brother Ioann's potential to live on as a popular spiritual force.

For Churikov and his followers, as for most Petrograders, the spring of 1917 was a hopeful time in spite of the ongoing war and increasing poverty and uncertainty. The trezvenniki naturally wondered about their status as believers in the new order: Would the democratizing trends within the Orthodox Church alter the decision to excommunicate him in 1914? Was a reconciliation between Brother Ioann and the Church now possible? But long before answers would come, subsequent events further complicated their situation. The prolongation of war through the summer of 1917 brought acute shortages of food and fuel in the city, and the radicalization of the revolution brought new and pressing challenges.

Publicly at least, Brother Ioann responded to the usurpation of power by the Bolsheviks in October 1917 with equanimity, in no small part because his traditional unwillingness to engage politically was reinforced by a daily struggle to survive. At the same time, the new regime's policies inspired a sense of both outrage and opportunity. In spite of lingering bitterness over the excommunication, trezvenniki shared the distress of the Orthodox community over the Bolshevik assaults on the Church, the clergy, and sacred objects. However, as sober workers they also found reason to sympathize with the social aims of the new regime, and for a brief time Brother Ioann contemplated joining the so-called

"Red" or "Living Church," led by Orthodox clergy who had broken away from the new Patriarch Tikhon in an effort to reconcile their faith with socialism.

In practice, the trezvenniki's designation as "sectarians" who had been formerly persecuted by the tsar allowed them a significant degree of autonomy in the early days of Soviet rule when the need for sober, productive workers was especially acute. Although Bolsheviks privileged those who advocated "scientific" (atheistic) communism, they understood the advantages of allying with religious sectarians in the building of socialism. Thus, while the trezvenniki would find themselves subjected to godless ridicule, bureaucratic harassment, and heavy tax burdens, they were for the most part able to live according to their own beliefs. Indeed, as paradoxical as it sounds, when asked in 1928 about the "October liberation," the long-time trezvennik Ivan Frolov publicly expressed his gratitude to the godless Bolsheviks for giving them the full right to talk about Christ—a right that the Orthodox had long denied them.[6]

In the fall of 1918, Brother Ioann officially registered his followers as a community (obshchina) dedicated to holy sobriety, thus resurrecting his long-silenced mission of besedy and healing through prayer.[7] With a renewed sense of optimism, the trezvennik community worked to maximize the common ground between their own goals and those of the communist project, as they understood it. To this end, the obshchina dedicated itself to "the development of spiritual and moral life in keeping with the commandments of God and on the basis of abstinence, solidarity, and humanity," and to the unification of the people "in brotherly love" and "communal working life" organized according to the scriptural verses, "all the believers were together, and had everything in common" (Acts of the Apostles, 2:44), and "if a man does not work, he should not eat" (2 Thessalonians 3:10).[8]

In line with these goals, Churikov was granted permission in the fall of 1918 to turn the colony in Vyritsa into an agricultural commune. As he preached in December 1920, the BICh commune (named after "Brother Ioann Churikov") was imagined as a place where the trezvenniki could live out their commitment to building the kingdom of God, "a kingdom of love, equality, and brotherhood," a framing he believed to be fully in sync with the key socialist principles of communalism and hard work.[9] And indeed, the trezvenniki found the land of the godless to be relatively fertile soil for building their kingdom—at least for a while. While other successful religious communes emerged at the same time, the BICh commune evolved a very distinct cultural and social habitus, and its history reminds us of the diverse ways in which the revolution was experienced and imagined by the working people of Russia.

Preaching Sobriety in Revolutionary Russia

During the civil war years 1918–20, the trezvenniki were focused—as all Petrograders were—on the daily struggle for survival. Brother Ioann continued to live in Vyritsa, but he traveled into Petrograd once a week to preach and to meet with petitioners. His prayers and advice as well as the weekly ritual of the beseda provided much-needed support and stability during a period marked by deepening poverty, myriad anxieties, a rise in alcoholism, chronic health problems, political uncertainty, and the violent persecution of religious believers, especially the Orthodox.

When interviewed in the fall of 1918, Brother Ioann estimated that the size of his following in the Petrograd region was about fifty thousand, mostly factory workers and their families.[10] This figure is significantly lower than the journalist Abramov's estimate of one hundred thousand in 1916,[11] but much higher than Soviet estimates in the mid-1920s, which suggest the number of trezvenniki remaining in the city and environs was down to between three and ten thousand, 80 percent of whom were still factory workers.[12] While it is important to approach these estimates cautiously, several factors likely contributed to a decline in the sober community in the Petrograd region in the early Soviet years, including the spread of atheism among workers and the proliferation of other alternative healers and preachers during the period of the New Economic Policy (1921–27). But the biggest was the massive out-migration that took place during the civil war period, as many Petrograders scattered into the provinces in search of food, fuel, and work. Vasilii Arsen'evich Guliaev, for example, moved to Kostroma for several years after the revolution; in addition to preaching there, he would travel back and forth to Petrograd to bring healing oil from Brother Ioann to his followers.[13] Thus the population of Churikov's followers living outside the Petrograd region in Moscow, Kostroma, Yaroslavl', Ivanovo-Vosnesensk, and Omsk appears to have swelled in proportion, reaching anywhere from forty thousand to one hundred thousand by the mid-1920s.[14] According to one godless source, other trezvenniki fled to Siberia during the Civil War, while the sizeable community in Tallinn (then Reval) drifted away as Estonia became independent from Russia.[15]

Churikov's preaching in Petrograd and Vyritsa nonetheless remained popular during the first years of Soviet rule; in spite of repeated attempts on the part of local authorities to requisition his prayer house for more secular purposes, his besedy were said to be the most attended of any in the region. In 1924 a godless reporter estimated at least a thousand people at a meeting in Obukhovo, which had quickly regained its reputation as an important site of *obshchenie*, where people gathered from different corners of the city to hear Churikov preach, share their stories, and take comfort in each other. When the Soviet expert on sectarian movements, A. I. Klibanov, attended a beseda later in the 1920s, he estimated the crowd at four hundred to five hundred.[16] By his calculations, the number of Brother Ioann's followers in Leningrad by the mid-1920s was three times that of Baptists, evangelicals, and Adventists *combined*.[17] Accurate or not, the impression speaks for itself.

Unfortunately, existing records of Brother Ioann's besedy or written statements from the 1920s vary greatly in terms of their accuracy and reliability. While he was required to file his beseda with officials regularly, inaccurate transcriptions circulated as well. As far as we can tell, he stayed very much on message with respect to the evils of alcohol and related vices and, in spite of the climate of official atheism, the importance of bringing life in line with Scripture. At the same time, he was careful to welcome the revolution and to make his respect for Soviet authorities visible, while also placing limits on what he deemed as acceptable behavior. Over the course of the 1920s, Churikov would be visited by many state officials, party activists, and even literary figures, as well as individuals of different backgrounds, education, and nationalities. He received all of them with "great love and an open heart" and continued to embrace his one and only "politika": to believe in God and love the Holy Church, to work, and to reject drinking and smoking. When asked directly how he felt about the fact that the Soviet government negated belief in God, he replied: "I know people who worked at the factories, at Putilov and others for twenty years, and never once laid eyes on their employer nor heard his voice, but they continued working."[18] In this way, he let it be known that his highest priority was to serve the Lord.

What Brother Ioann actually thought about Bolshevik rule is hard to say.[19] When interviewed by I. M. Matveev, a Soviet investigator evaluating his petition to set up a commune in the fall of 1918—that is, only a few weeks after the unleashing of the Red Terror—Brother Ioann made no secret of his distrust of those who denied God. Citing Scripture

(Matthew 10:14–15), he made clear that God's Law was above all other authority and that any government that was built without it would be destroyed, just as in Sodom and Gomorrah. When asked directly about the revolution, however, his answer was cleverly ambiguous and easily applied to the current as well as the former tsarist regime. Revolutions occur, he observed, when people see only "madness" in their leaders and the abuse of power and lies. People cannot trust those in power when they only "carry the sword." "You ask how I look at the Bolsheviks? Well, Christ said: 'Whoever wants to become great, let him be the servant of all' (Matt. 20:26)." He observed approvingly that Bolshevik policies had produced both fear and awe in "criminal people," but he reminded his interviewer that "Christ said, 'Thou shalt not kill' and the Bolsheviks have killed." He then elaborated by referring to a passage in Matthew (21:41–44): "Have you never read in the Scriptures that the evildoers will be brought to a wretched end [and] the vineyard [owner] will rent the vineyard to others?"[20]

The intense political climate of the civil war period sometimes pressured Brother Ioann into preaching in more distinctly "revolutionary" ways. In December 1920, for example, in response to accusations in the press that his nonpolitical sermons could be considered "counterrevolutionary" (and therefore prohibited), he delivered a beseda on intentionally "religious-revolutionary" themes, before a crowd of approximately 1,600 people—an impressive turnout at the time.[21] He began with a discussion of Matthew 22, the parable of the wedding feast, which he reworked to be more sympathetic to the Soviet story. The "divine feast," Churikov explained, was the project of building a new kingdom along communal lines (rather than the "partaking of Scripture"), and the privileged classes from tsarist times—the kings, capitalists, landowners, merchants, and high clergy—were cast in the role of those who "would not feast" at the great banquet. Preoccupied with their own interests, they refused to attend "the wedding banquet, that is, a new, universally communal life." Worse, they killed the servants (revolutionaries) who had tried to call them to the table. The angry "king" then dispatched his troops, destroyed the murderers, and burned their towns, "because they lived only for themselves, for their personal property, and for the oppression of the poor, working people." And thus they were subjected to the Final Judgment (the revolution).

Brother Ioann also celebrated the Bolshevik revolution as a new Easter (or resurrection) for the people, which was a common trope at the time.[22] On Easter on April 16, 1922—a tense moment for many

Orthodox believers, following the Bolshevik campaign to requisition church valuables as famine raged in the Volga region—Churikov delivered one of his most important besedy,[23] introducing a refrain that he would repeat many times in years to come: although the current authorities "do not know God," they were in fact committed to doing God's work—to feeding the hungry and dressing the poor.[24] "If someone wages war for capital, for the wealthy, then he is ruled by the Devil," he continued, "but one who wages war for the poor is ruled by the Lord."[25] He then described how "God's enemies," those who "lived for themselves," had disappeared during the revolution like "smoke" and "melted like wax on a fire." Although clearly laying out the common moral ground between socialism and Christianity, however, Brother Ioann again issued a subtle warning to those in power, preaching that "the time will come when [the authorities] will find out that God rules over them [vladet']."[26]

Brother Ioann had walked a fine line between obeying and challenging religious authorities before the revolution, and he was careful to temper his criticism of the Soviet government with equal praise.[27] He honored Lenin publicly at the time of his death, for example. According to trezvennik testimony, on Sunday, January 27, 1924, at the precise moment that Lenin's body was being placed in his tomb in Moscow, Brother Ioann paused his beseda to acknowledge the Bolshevik leader as "a great prophet in work and deed," comparable to Moses. He also remarked on the severe snowstorm that had paralyzed the cities on the day of Lenin's death, as if to suggest that Nature had taken a holiday in his honor. "Nature always gives preference to people who do not live for themselves, but live for the people."[28]

The Trezvenniki and the Orthodox Church in the Revolutionary Context

As troubled as Brother Ioann's relationship with the Orthodox Church had been after his excommunication in 1914, revolutionary events made the religious landscape even more difficult to navigate after 1917. The Church's bold efforts at reform in 1917 had been a promising sign for the trezvenniki, but they were quickly eclipsed by the Bolsheviks' violent campaign against the clergy and the faith, which included the silencing of the religious press, prohibiting religious teaching in schools, closing churches, disinterring saints' tombs, and requisitioning church valuables. Beginning in 1918, the clergy were also subjected to waves of violent repression, especially against those in the positions of authority. In response, the newly elected Patriarch Tikhon anathematized the Bolsheviks and issued a call to the Orthodox to resist the new government, making it very clear that any effort to comply with the atheistic regime was the equivalent of working for Satan. Although the Bolsheviks backed off somewhat for a few years, conflict erupted again in 1922 during the Volga famine and the related controversy over church valuables. Patriarch Tikhon was put under house arrest in May 1922 and excluded from participating in worship and church governance.

The relationship between Churikov and his followers and Orthodox clergy remained extremely fraught. On the one hand, for Brother Ioann—as for all Orthodox believers—the atheistic state's repeated assaults against the Church and the faith were deeply painful. On the other hand, he and many of his followers remained estranged from the clergy because of the confusion and crisis within the Church itself, and because of the lingering effects of his excommunication. Thus in his Easter sermon in 1922, he pointed to the way that wealth had corrupted the Orthodox Church, but he also implicitly warned Soviet authorities not to make the same mistake by forcibly requisitioning church valuables.[29] In what amounted to an essentially secular moral argument, Churikov pointed out that all valuables were a form of exploitation, so neither the state nor the Church had a right to them.

Around this same time, Brother Ioann explored the possibility of joining the so-called "Living Church," although little is known about his motivations. The match between the church "renovationists," pejoratively dubbed "red priests" for their willingness to work with the Bolshevik regime,[30] and the "sectarian" trezvenniki was far from perfect, but several issues provided them with common ground. These included an emphasis on the social dimensions of Orthodoxy, a desire for a more accessible liturgy, and hostility toward the "black" (monastic) clergy who had been responsible for Brother Ioann's excommunication. For their part, renovationist clergy were anxious to grow their flock and likely drawn to Brother Ioann on account of his popularity. In late 1922, Fathers A. I. Boiarskii and A. I. Vvedenskii reached out to him proposing cooperation in promoting the "religious enlightenment of believers" and normalizing the "relationship between faith and science, church and state, religion and socialism."[31] Then, on December 1, in preparation for Brother Ioann's reconciliation with the faith, they held a general confession (*obshchaia ispoved'*) after vespers at the Church of

Zakariah and Elizaveta, and the next day he received communion for the first time since 1914.[32] Soon after, a priest at the "Red Church," Father Nikolai Syrenskii, a long-time friend and temperance organizer, filled in for Brother Ioann at a beseda when he fell gravely ill with pneumonia.[33] His sermon praising Brother Ioann and his teachings was well received by the thousands of followers who had gathered to pray for his recovery. The relationship between the red clergy and the trezvenniki broke down irrevocably, however, when the renovationists refused to comply with their demand to eliminate wine from the sacrament of communion, making it clear that they were unwilling to acknowledge the trezvenniki's commitment to sobriety.[34]

After the split with the renovationists, Brother Ioann and his followers moved further away from any kind of contact with Orthodox clergy. Although it is difficult to tell how many trezvenniki regularly attended the Divine Liturgy or performed their annual obligation of confession and communion in the early years of Soviet rule, some clearly maintained relations with their parishes.[35] But the evidence also suggests many began to move permanently away from Orthodox liturgical life and the communion with God it provided, as well as any active relationship with clergy.[36] At the time, it was not uncommon for believers to form religious networks around charismatic leaders outside the parish structure; in fact, less formal spiritual networks connected to individual clergy were vital to the survival of the Church throughout the Soviet period.[37] But the loss of clerical influence over the trezvennik community was particularly acute and long-lasting. At the same time, the addition of newer converts without any active relationship to Orthodoxy resulted in a further shift of the community away from the teachings and practices of the faith. In this new context, Brother Ioann's followers turned more exclusively toward Scripture and his teachings as the foundation of their beliefs. As later chapters will discuss in greater detail, this development would mark the beginning of a major split within the sober community over Brother Ioann's identity, as well as a fragmentation of his authority.

New Converts in a New Age

In the early 1920s, Brother Ioann attracted new followers from a broad cross-section of the population. The many epidemics and the high frequency of accidents, combined with the lack of sufficient medical facilities and the generally poor health of the urban population, made it even more likely that people would turn to alternative forms of healing, including prayer, than they might have before 1917. In what would quickly become a crowded marketplace of healers, Churikov remained extremely popular. People "argue about [him] everywhere in the corners of Leningrad, especially in the outskirts," noted one disgruntled godless reporter in 1924.[38] While some came just to find out what Brother Ioann was all about, others became followers, including young workers who might otherwise have identified with the Bolsheviks.[39] According to the historian Natalia Lebina, by 1928 approximately one quarter of Churikov's followers in Leningrad worked at local factories, including Nogin, St. Khalturin, "Rabochii," and "Krasnyi Shveinik."[40] The Soviet historian Aptekman estimated that the figure was closer to a third, among whom were card-carrying members of the Bolshevik party.[41]

Surviving first-person testimonies from the 1920s are unfortunately far fewer than before the revolution, and those that remain were often recorded much later by family members or other trezvenniki. But the evidence suggests little change in terms of the reasons people sought out Brother Ioann or the patterns of interaction between him and his petitioners.[42] For example, the healing account of a potential suicide by the name of Androsov, originally told by the feldsher caring for him, Il'ia Moiseevich Moiseev, in the 1950s,[43] began with unbearable suffering. Paralyzed and confined to bed for three and a half years, the young sailor begged Moiseev to get him poison so he could end his life, but the feldsher referred him instead to Brother Ioann. In spite of his atheistic beliefs, Androsov agreed to petition Churikov, who responded to the effect that doctors are human, but that "what's not possible for humans is still possible for God," and for this reason, he should understand that his illness was calling him not to death, but to God. The sailor followed instructions to put Brother Ioann's oil in his tea and then to fast, and he was soon healed of his paralysis, both physical and spiritual. He got out of bed, procured a Bible, and began to read it, in spite of the mocking he faced from almost everyone he knew.

In the early Soviet context, the derision that Androsov encountered was not unusual—at least not in Petrograd. Yet neither was his pragmatic approach to healing, nor his openness to faith and the possibility of the miraculous.[44] While the Bolsheviks did a good job exposing the Church as a flawed, exploitative institution that profited from people's desperation, they struggled to minimize let alone eradicate the need for miracles or the willingness of people to believe in them. Once the clergy had been marginalized and their influence curtailed, alternative spiritual leaders like Brother Ioann became an even more important resource.

Drinking problems remained the other major reason people were drawn to Brother Ioann in the early Soviet period. In spite of official prohibitions on the sale of alcohol and the Bolsheviks' insistence on almost puritanical discipline, the new regime did little to address a deepening crisis. On the contrary, their first response was to deny the problem altogether, while wiping out the Church's temperance infrastructure. After seizing power in 1917, they extended the existing dry law put in place by the tsar in 1914, following the lead of the always sober Lenin, who explained that the proletariat had "no need of intoxication," since it derived its "strongest stimulant to struggle from its class position and from the communist ideal."[45] Yet, even as the deprivation of the civil war years, including the severe shortage of grain, decreased the amount of available drink, a sharp increase after 1923 proved Lenin wrong. Over the course of the 1920s, levels of alcohol consumption, much of which was illicitly made or traded samogon (homebrew), would not only overtake prewar figures, but lead to a significant rise in alcohol-related deaths; in Leningrad alone, the increase was sixfold in four years. Indeed, a "wave of alcoholism engulfed the whole country," observed the neuropathologist V. M. Bekhterev.[46]

In addition to chronic illness and alcohol addiction, the emergence of new cultural norms also produced converts to holy sobriety, as in the case of the factory worker O. Bogdanova, who moved to Vyritsa in search of a meaningful spiritual life. Bogdanova continued to work in a factory as she actively identified as one of Churikov's followers, but the situation eventually became untenable. When her coworkers found out that she "went to the Brother" they ridiculed her and tried to force her to give up her beliefs. As an antidote to her "delusion" (zabluzhdenie) they elected her as a delegate to the women's section, which forced her to study political literacy and fill her free time with meetings. The conflict between her faith and work environment turned into crisis when her Sunday obligations as a delegate prevented her from hearing Churikov preach. "I needed to go to the beseda," she recalled, dismissing a party meeting as a colossal waste of time. She ended up going to neither and was soon kicked off the list of delegates. For this she was relieved, having found that "in general [Communists'] life was not attractive or upright." She quit her job and moved permanently to the commune in Vyritsa, where Brother Ioann rescued her from "the maelstrom of secular life," and where she found satisfaction for "the demands of [her] soul."[47]

Another convert seeking a new way of life was the young worker Petr Terekhovich, who initially turned to holy sobriety to save himself from the immoral and undisciplined habits of his generation. As historian Anne Gorsuch has discussed, the mid-1920s were a time of rampant crisis and growing pessimism among working-class and Komsomol youth, reflected in a troubling upswing in cases of alcoholism, "hooliganism," depression, and suicide.[48] Of these, hooliganism was the most widespread and diverse, manifested in rape and murder on one extreme to more mundane forms of mischief (such as smashing things, running naked, and urinating in public spaces) on the other. To Bolsheviks envisioning "new" people capable of building socialist society, these trends signified a disturbing lack of discipline and purpose among youth and the failure of proper acculturation. Although contemporary observers debated the root causes, they could not dispute that drinking alcohol was, as always, a magnifier of destructive and "uncivilized" behaviors. Or that such behavior threatened the welfare of society as a whole.

In this context, Terekhovich turned to sobriety as an alternative path. Born into a "typical" working-class family in St. Petersburg, he was a factory worker by day and an aspiring musician by night. When his older brother disappeared while working as a medic during the civil war, his mother had turned to Brother Ioann and soon became a devoted follower.[49] Content in his own "godlessness" at the time, Terekhovich hoped to join the Komsomol, but when that plan failed, he became a musician and spent a lot of time in nightclubs indulging in drink and other "loose" behaviors. His mother's incessant pleas to reconsider his lifestyle fell on deaf ears until he landed in jail and felt the need to reflect on his life. Following his release, he began to take Brother Ioann and the promise of holy sobriety seriously.[50]

Around the same time, Terekhovich joined a community of young trezvenniki who shared his values and supported him intellectually and emotionally. Guided by sober elders, the group met *nightly* in private apartments throughout the 1920s and maintained a highly rigorous routine of prayer, Bible reading, and spiritual edification.[51] "We youth grew, strengthened in faith, enlightened by the wisdom of the Word of God, in close contact with each other, and prepared to lay our souls down for the other."[52] Though they conceived of their group as a *kupal'nia* rather than a *kruzhok*—that is, a place for spiritual reflection rather than secular enlightenment—it is clear that Terekhovich embraced his new identity at least in part because of the intellectual rewards it held for him. In line with the norms of "sober masculinity," he was proud to be able to impress the older members with his "serious relationship to the Word," which involved not only personal mastery of the texts and the refashioning of his life accordingly, but also preaching Scripture and sobriety to others at similar home-based besedy.

Youth groups such as Terekhovich's grew "not by days but by hours" until 1928 and played an important role in keeping sober culture alive throughout the decade.[53] They also helped produce a new generation of future leaders of the movement, including Ivan Smolev. Born in 1900 to a family of trezvenniki, Smolev had been involved in a sober youth circle since 1912 and started his own group, Rassvet (The Dawn), in 1919 with eight friends.[54] Officially Rassvet was registered as "religious," in line with the bureaucratic rationale that there was no alcohol for sale in the Soviet Union so no one needed a group devoted to sobriety. As before the revolution, the youth in Smolev's circle socialized together exclusively, although the meetings were open to all, young and old, including trezvenniki from other regions. As adolescents, their activities had been largely leisurely—walking, berry picking, and playing games; as they came of age in the Soviet era, they participated in voluntary forms of labor known as *subbotniki*, such as hauling firewood, shoveling snow, or working on the commune. But their collective pursuits in the 1920s also became more intensely spiritual.[55] In addition to gathering to discuss Brother Ioann's weekly beseda, study the Gospel, and sing prayers and hymns, they petitioned him on Mondays and then met the next night to discuss his responses. They also studied Brother Ioann's life and activities. Whatever the topic, however, the meetings served as an important site of *obshchenie*, fostering a sense of emotional and spiritual communion.

Youth activism was an encouraging sign of the vitality of the trezvennik movement in the 1920s. "The youth circle is like a flower greenhouse, a hothouse [where] young plants grow, bloom," the journal *Trezvyi Rassvet* observed. While it was "cold" (hostile to faith) outside and "people are dying in snowdrifts," the article continued, "you, sober youth, brought up by dear Brother Ioann, the teacher of life, the savior of fallen people, are blooming, fragrant in the midst of a drunken, cold human world."[56] Smolev's group was such an inspiration that a delegation from Luga approached them in 1927 asking how to set up a society there, and among them were representatives from the regional soviet. However, the same spirit of autonomy and purpose that allowed for youth to organize in the 1920s sometimes led to unintended consequences, including fanaticism and the distortion of Brother Ioann's teachings.[57] For his part, Churikov apparently expressed concern that these circles were unnecessary and sometimes excessive, but he preferred not to meddle in them. Thus, while youth groups generated welcome energy and enthusiasm, they also reflected a diminution of Brother Ioann's authority, as well as a decentralization within the community as a whole. As discussed in chapter 8, later in the 1920s they would also become a source of vulnerability for the movement.

From Colony to Commune

Vyritsa remained the spiritual center of holy sobriety throughout the 1920s. More than ever a welcome place to escape the pressure of secularization of the proletarian city, the settlement continued to play a central role in the trezvennik imagination as the promised land where the kingdom of God could be brought into being. This is not to suggest that it was a paradise; in fact, the road to a more perfect future presented myriad obstacles and sources of uncertainty, including extreme poverty, heavy economic burdens, an unstable political context, and an increasingly hostile state bureaucracy. But Vyritsa remained a place of hope and faith, and a site where the principles of holy sobriety could be cultivated.

Soon after the Bolsheviks took power, the trezvenniki on the colony in Vyritsa moved to conform to the demands of the new regime. The first step was to elect a soviet, which over the course of 1918 met regularly to decide pressing issues such as the registration of all local men eighteen to forty-five for service in the Red Army, plans for bridge repair, and the selection of a veterinary feldsher. Confronted with an increasingly scarce food supply, it also took up a collection to buy flour and set up a committee to purchase potatoes and cabbage for the local population.[58] The next stage of "sovietization" occurred with the August 19 election of a committee of the poor (kombeda), which organized local food and fuel supplies.[59]

The biggest transformation on the colony came on September 24, 1918, when Brother Ioann and the trezvenniki petitioned Soviet authorities to allow them to register as an agricultural commune.[60] With grain, meat, and dairy in devastatingly short supply, the trezvenniki in Vyritsa shifted their efforts toward planting and animal husbandry. The decision reflected new economic priorities and stemmed primarily from the hope that the commune would receive critically needed state subsidies.

As part of the approval process, the colony underwent an investigation by local authorities, which resulted in a somewhat mixed assessment. At the time, thirty members lived there permanently, along with about two hundred temporary members, the majority of whom worked in the factories but traveled to Vyritsa to tend their plots whenever possible. In addition to some thirty-seven desiatina of swampy land, the trezvenniki were in possession of six horses and five cows that fall.[61] In spite of its limited resources, in October 1918, the local (Tsarkosel'skii uezd) soviet and committee of the poor determined that the colony was made up entirely of "kulak elements" and citizens who did not respect the new Soviet constitution.[62] Whether or not lingering resentment toward the trezvenniki among the local population influenced their assessment is hard to say, although Churikov suggested it did.[63] In any case, local opinion was soon outweighed by state representatives. The first of several reports by an agricultural instructor that fall concluded that there were in fact no "exploiters" on the new commune, just "honest toilers" (truzhenniki); it also praised Churikov as an excellent organizer and director.[64]

The trezvenniki would soon find protection from several authorities higher up in the Soviet administration. This included, most importantly, Vladimir Bonch-Bruevich, one of the most outspoken defenders of "sectarians" in the early Soviet period. In a letter to the commissar of Internal Affairs dated March 1919, he defended Churikov and his followers on the commune as deserving "special consideration on the part of Soviet authorities" because they belonged to the "depressed [upadochnyi] element of the working class" who had fallen into the "lumpenproletariat" because of vodka. To strengthen their case, he stressed that the BICh commune had been created "literally out of nothing" and that its members were dedicated to "a communist way of life," having suffered persecution under the tsarist regime.[65] Moreover, Churikov was the kind of sectarian who "hates money with his whole soul"; he had not only fully cooperated with state demands but exhibited "a completely open heart toward Soviet power." Although Bonch-Bruevich's support would not free the commune's members (kommunary) from heavy obligations to the state, it did enable them to maintain a legal status under the new regime, which in turn gave them a fair amount of autonomy to live according to their beliefs.

The commune was officially approved on November 6, 1918. At the time, the state deeded the commune a portion of a farm formerly owned by a local "bourgeois" officer named Miniukh. Although the additional land was welcome, three-fifths of it was marshy and forested and would therefore take "colossal" effort to clear and dry out before it could be arable.[66] While Churikov would prove as adept at making worthless land productive as he was at transforming troubled people into good citizens, the first four to five years of the commune were undeniably difficult for everyone. In addition to the poverty, hunger, and illness common during the civil war period, the kommunary were challenged by a lack of modern equipment and their collective inexperience. The commune members included factory workers, plumbers, cooks, carpenters, dressmakers, shopkeepers, shoemakers, actors, schoolteachers, and at least one former monastic. Some arrived with skills related to farming or animal husbandry, but most did not. The occupation of Vyritsa by both the White and Red Armies compounded the commune's woes, as did the constant threat of a hefty and increasing tax burden. The civil war further undermined the commune's chances of survival by taking away some of its best workers to serve in the Red Army.[67]

High turnover was typical of communes in the 1920s, and BICh was no exception.[68] "Almost everyone left," the trezvennitsa Nina Maslova recalled, "one after another."[69] Indeed, by 1928, only twenty-three of the original members of the commune remained; seventy-two had joined between 1919 and 1924, and eighty-nine had joined since 1925, by which time the commune was doing quite well.[70] Because Churikov rarely turned anyone away, the commune appears to have taken in as many people as it lost, and thus membership hovered rather consistently around 200–250 throughout the 1920s. This made BICh about five times bigger than the average-sized commune at the time.[71]

Perhaps to offset the uncertainty and fluidity of the moment, the commune's labor culture was highly disciplined and unapologetically patriarchal. An elected council (soviet) of six older males made all the important decisions with respect to the daily functioning of the commune. If any member of the commune was suspected of disobedience of any kind, a general meeting of all men over eighteen was called. The commune's charter explicitly stated that members had to abide by the council's findings and could not appeal to the courts.

Labor tasks were assigned according to an individual's age, ability, and sex—a fact much in line with earlier trezvennik practices, but out of sync with the Bolsheviks' aspiration to ensure gender equality in the workplace. Men and boys were responsible for all the heavy labor in the fields as well as the higher skilled jobs in the commune's many workshops, while female members took care of cooking and household labor. The younger children were taught to work and to be neat and thorough (*akkuratnyi*), and then at age nine or ten, they were expected to take on defined responsibilities, beginning with the task of tending to the chickens and keeping them from the hawks. At twelve or thirteen they tended to the sheep and calves, and at fourteen or fifteen, they would take on regular work like the adults. In the winter, younger girls worked in the sewing workshop, while boys helped out in shoemaking, blacksmithing, and metalworking. Although workdays were long, kommunary were quick to point out that each individual worked to their own "level."[72]

For all its challenges, by 1924–25 the commune became successful and went on to win recognition from the state for its high levels of productivity.[73] In addition to impressive harvests, the commune maintained productive workshops devoted to everything from shoemaking to metalworking. Along with a dairy, the commune boasted an expanding stock of poultry and animals, including sheep and horses.[74] As on the colony, the kommunary's achievements were at least in part the result of their ability to innovate. Churikov's expansive knowledge of various forms of technology was especially useful in the early Soviet years of destruction and deprivation, and within a few years, the commune managed to develop a respectable inventory of agricultural equipment out of little more than machine scraps.[75] Although the commune did not qualify for state subsidies, it did manage to secure the use of a powerful tractor; all the other machines, with the exception of several motors, were made "in large part out of rubbish, purchased for next to nothing, and rebuilt by the commune members under Churikov's personal direction."[76] The massive project of drying out the marsh was undertaken with the help of a *kanavnikov*, a device invented by Churikov and attached to the big tractor. Given the low level of technology in rural areas and the peasants' resistance to modernization at this time, the commune's emphasis on its willingness to conform to the Bolsheviks' technological dreams seems a deliberate attempt to curry favor with authorities. In addition to a lot of talk about their "big" tractor, the kommunary also hung a banner: "Down with callouses, long live machines!"[77]

Nonetheless, the commune's members were convinced that their success resulted most of all from their faith in Churikov and in God, as illustrated by the 1926 testimony of one of the sestritsy.[78] In 1923, only one year after famine had subsided in the Volga region, the weather in Petrograd turned out to be unusually hostile; it was cold and rainy, and the harvest was so poor that the locals in Vyritsa didn't even want to waste their energy and strength to bring it in. Neither did the kommunary. But with Brother Ioann's uncompromising insistence, and by his example, they spent four brutally numbing weeks in the wet fields, pulling out the dirty oat stalks by hand and washing them in manmade ditches. The general mood of the workers was poor, and uncharacteristically, many of them admitted to being unhappy with Brother Ioann for making them do such difficult work. But he ignored their complaints and ordered them to dig a large pit, with walls supported by planks and covered with clay, into which they then threw green oats. Once it was full and covered by planks and earth, Brother Ioann told them "we have buried Lazarus, but he will be resurrected." At the time, most of the laborers could focus only on the fact that they had just buried four weeks of backbreaking work, but in the spring of 1924 they rejoiced as they uncovered the pit to discover aromatic and fully ripened oats, perfect for feeding their growing herd of livestock. To the kommunary who witnessed the unveiling of the oats, it was nothing less than a miracle, "manna" from heaven. In line with popular Orthodox beliefs, the tendency to look for evidence of the divine in natural sources would become increasingly common in the Soviet era, especially as officials destroyed or closed access to traditional sacred sites, such as churches and shrines.[79]

For the first nine years of its existence, official reports on the commune's labor practices were largely favorable. In May 1924, a group of students at the Leningrad Communist University (im. Zinov'ev) specializing in agricultural cooperatives reported that the commune's "organization of labor was marked by cohesion and unity at every step." They also commented positively on the kommunary's use of mechanization, clever use of substitutes for feeding the animals, and "rational use of all elements of production." While acknowledging the unbelievably difficult labor expended, however, their report further noted that the commune's religious convictions "kept the members from a true understanding of all powerful meaning of labor and cooperation and solidarity."[80] Curiously, when V. Shishkin, the chairman of a circle on agricultural cooperatives, surveyed the commune that same year, he concluded that the trezvenniki's religious approach to their labor—that is, their reliance on faith and prayer as much as technology—served as a source of "undeniable moral and physical strength," and explained their determination to battle a hostile natural environment. Echoing the earlier inspector Matveev, Shishkin found Churikov to be

FIGURE 10.   Brother Ioann proudly standing amid the oat stocks harvested between 1922 and 1924 by the BICh Commune. The sign behind him connects their hard work drying out the swamplands with their successful battle against hunger. Photographer unknown.

"an outstanding personality" in terms of both his agile mind and ability to work in many different capacities, and his facility for bringing out the best in people. He went so far as to declare it "a pity" that the Land Department had not yet provided proper support to the commune, comprised as it was of "honest proletarians."[81]

All Work and No Play Makes Ivan (or Maria) a Good Kommunar

Communal life at BICh, like communal labor, was subject to a strict disciplinary regime, based on a clear set of rules and rituals. As the Soviet state stipulated, members of all communes were expected to pool their material resources, eat together, and live in communal housing. But on BICh, the regulation of behavior—and the degree of "leveling" associated with communal living—was even more extreme. Indeed, the daily routines—not only the "what" but the "when"— extended to the smallest details and tasks, not unlike a monastery or military camp. Although the colony had been governed by a similar set of behavioral norms, gone was the autonomy of the prerevolution- ary period. At least in part a compensation for the extreme chaos and unpredictability of early Soviet society, the increased regimentation was also a response to the diversity and fluidity of the commune's population, which included both dedicated trezvenniki seeking an intentional way of life and individuals and families drawn to Brother Ioann out of desperation.

The kommunary's daily schedule began with tea and breakfast from 6:00 to 7:30 a.m. in the big house where Brother Ioann and the sestritsy lived. After crossing themselves before the icons, which still covered the walls from floor to ceiling as before the revolution, commune mem- bers sat down at a T-shaped table to wait for Brother Ioann to arrive; they were usually segregated according to sex, with women to his left, and men and youth to his right. Brother entered at precisely the same time every day, led the "Our Father" hymn, and then went back to his quarters. When they had finished their simple meal, he would return to offer a prayer and lead another hymn before blessing them as they went off to work. At 11:30 the entire commune would break to eat lunch (outside during good weather), followed by an hour or so of prayer, discussion, the singing of hymns, and a conversation about "practical matters."[82] Then after another four or five hours of work, they would reconvene for dinner with Brother Ioann in the dining room.

In addition to surrendering their worldly goods, all kommunary were expected to commit themselves completely to a sober, strictly ascetic, Scripture-centered lifestyle. Whereas many communes established rules to ensure just and peaceful interactions between members, much of BICh's statute was designed to regulate individuals, so as to protect them from their own sinful nature. Laziness was expressly forbidden, according to the scriptural prescript "those who do not work shall not eat" (that is, out of obedience to Apostle Paul, not the Bolsheviks). And what little leisure time the kommunary had was to be devoted strictly to the pursuits of the spirit. The commune's regulations stipulated that all secular forms of fun and entertainment were forbidden as a turning away from God.[83] They prohibited playing cards, going to the theater or "other happy places," smoking, or doing anything else that might stupefy a person's "common sense." Instead life at the commune revolved around the many scheduled opportunities for prayer, the singing of hymns, and of course Brother Ioann's besedy, which were typed up on mimeograph paper and filed with local authorities. More informal discussions of Scripture continued around the table. It seems that later in the 1920s at least, discussions sometimes revolved around issues in the contemporary press, including *Pravda* or *Bezbozhnik* in spite of the general ban on secular literature.[84]

The rules of behavior on the commune were clear and nonnegotiable, providing a sense of order and stability in a time of chaos and anxiety. But the consequences could be harsh for those who deviated from them, even if for good reason. In 1920, for example, the commune's council heard the case of Anna, the wife of the Red Army soldier Varfolomei Alekseevich Plotnikov, who had committed a "vile act" during her husband's time at the civil war front from June 1919 to March 1920. Specifically, without her husband's consent, she had left the commune with a strange man and allegedly engaged in "speculation," bartering away all of her belongings. And when her husband returned from war, she did not appear in order to explain herself. Given that her act was thought to cast shame on Brother Ioann and the entire community, she was banned from the commune from that point on.[85] Because the rules of the commune stipulated that no one could appeal to the state courts, Anna had no recourse and was forced to leave. Her husband stayed.

Tales of the Kommunary

In contrast to the colony, where people lived together because of shared beliefs, the commune attracted a broad range of people, men and women, old and young, from different regions, professions, and classes, and even with different thoughts on God.[86] While a core of long-time trezvenniki lived and worked on the BICh commune, Churikov's widespread reputation for healing made it an attractive place for many other people to land as well. The commune's inventories, mandated by Soviet authorities and punctiliously maintained by local officials, reveal strong evidence of familial ties at work, as well as evidence of *zemliachestvo*. But like many communes in the 1920s, BICh also attracted struggling individuals in search of work, food, and safe, affordable accommodations. It was an especially strong magnet for young girls and widows with no family and nowhere else to turn. The community associated with BICh through faith or labor was bigger still. Although culturally set apart from the secular world outside, its boundaries were easily traversed, with goods, people, and news regularly flowing in and out. As before 1917, many residents continued to work in Petrograd/Leningrad (most in factory jobs), and everyone connected to the commune devoted their time and energy to the fields during the growing season. As noted, many of Churikov's followers traveled to Vyritsa to hear him preach on Sundays. At certain times of year the number of trezvenniki making their way from the city to the commune was so high that the local trains were overwhelmed, causing irritation among nontrezvenniki.[87]

In 1929, Timofei Zaitsev wrote to Soviet authorities to explain why he had left his position as a railroad foreman to live and work on BICh. Until 1922, he drank heavily every day, even while on the job. When he fell extremely ill with dysentery and doctors failed to help, his wife traveled to Vyritsa to petition Brother Ioann. Zaitsev was soon cured, and when he suffered another debilitating illness, he sought out Churikov again. With Brother Ioann's help, he became sober, quit his job in the city, and went to live and work on the commune, where he and his wife finally found peace and stability. There he knew "no worries" and learned how to work the land and handle the livestock. Clearly aware of the new premium placed on labor by Soviet officials, Zaitsev highlighted his transformation into a productive citizen under Brother Ioann's guidance: "I was a drunk and now I am sober, I was sick and now I am healthy, I used to bring harm to the state and now I am useful."[88]

Women often joined the commune in search of a more spiritually fulfilling or purposeful life.[89] Like Olga Bogdanova mentioned earlier, D. Sirotkina was driven into a "frenzy" by all the "noise and din of the machines" and by "people's different views" in the paper factory where she worked. In search of "peace in [her] soul," she turned to Matthew 6:33 and found hope in the idea that where the Gospels reign, truth reigns. So she moved to be with Brother Ioann in Vyritsa.[90]

For those who arrived at the commune less out of choice than circumstance, the learning curve was often steep. Around 1920, for example, thirteen-year-old A. Ivanovna was sent to Brother Ioann by her aunt. Having lived in a state orphanage since 1917, she had been raised an atheist and was far from excited by the idea of living on a religious commune. Sensing her ambivalence, Brother Ioann hesitated to let her stay and told her plainly that the road would be hard. But eventually he took her in and taught her about everything, especially the spiritual value of physical labor. With time Brother Ioann became like a father to her, and she adopted the culture of the commune as her own.[91] A similar transformation was experienced by Elizaveta Builova, a formerly middle-class widow whose alcoholic husband had been cured by Churikov. When she found herself penniless and homeless after her husband's death, Brother Ioann took her in and put her to work with her hands for the first time in her life.[92] After a rocky transition, Builova came to appreciate the commune as a safe refuge from the violence and instability of early Soviet society.

Not everyone learned to adapt to the commune's way of life, however. Those who arrived only in search of a safe place to live and work sometimes found themselves either at odds with the strict rules or alienated by the expectations of communal life. A young woman by the name of Efrosina Petrovna Matina, for example, had joined the commune partly "under pressure from [her] parents, and partly out of [her] own desire," but hated it from the start. "Everyone was a slave," she complained, and had to work dawn to dusk in the summer, with limited rest time and no pay. She also didn't like the fact that everyone ate and slept together. Other kommunary also found conditions less than ideal and stayed only long enough to get on their feet. This included Brother Ioann's own cousin and her family.[93]

Communal property issues regularly provoked tensions as well. While most people seemed willing enough to comply with the legal requirement to pool their resources upon entering the commune, those leaving under less than happy circumstances were often displeased that they could not get them back. One clearly disgruntled individual by the name of Drovenikov wrote to Churikov after his departure from the commune, demanding payment for the labor he had done from October 1928 to February 1929, and threatening to take him to the people's court if his request was denied.[94] In 1928, a woman by the name of Brovina had done just that, claiming that she had become religiously "intoxicated" by Churikov and joined the commune in 1921, but then found herself in a desperate situation with two young and very ill children, no money or property, and no work after she decided to leave.[95]

Medical care was another regular source of conflict on the commune, with the biggest complaints registered by parents who had lost a child. One particularly controversial case involved the Baburov family whose thirteen-year-old daughter Olga died in 1919 of what an autopsy revealed as brain swelling caused by typhus. At first the parents had taken comfort in Brother Ioann's reassurance that their daughter would recover and followed his instructions to bathe her. But when Olga's condition worsened, they departed from the norm on the commune by consulting a local feldsher. When she died soon after, they held Brother Ioann responsible and took their case to local authorities.[96] Although no effective treatment for typhus aside from rest and symptom control was available at the time,[97] the Baburovs' complaint got the attention of both state authorities and the official press. In fact, the secret police would later use their testimonies to build a case against Brother Ioann and as justification for shutting down the commune.

The Commune in a Comparative Context

The way of life cultivated on BICh had much in common with the communes set up by Baptists and Evangelical Christians in the early Bolshevik period. As described by the Evangelical Christian leader Ivan Prokhanov, for example, the Gethsemane commune established by eleven Evangelical families in 1919 in Tver province was organized according to "the principles of faith, collective labor, technology, hygiene, creativity, sober habits, and the striving for self-perfection."[98] There was also significant overlap between BICh and Tolstoyan communes, including a shared commitment to vegetarianism, abstinence from drinking, smoking, and swearing, and emphasis on "the great moral significance of productive labor."[99] At the same time, the degree of self-renunciation expected of each individual on BICh was comparatively extreme.[100] Whereas Tolstoyans allowed some room for individual self-expression,[101] originality and ambition were frowned upon in the BICh commune, much as on the peasant *mir*, famously described by the Slavophile Konstantin Aksakov as "a union of people who have renounced their egoism, their individuality, and who express their common accord."[102] According to one young female member, the first lesson she learned from Brother Ioann was to strive for "self-abasement" and to "consider others higher than oneself."[103] Living

selfishly and acquisitively, "according to the word 'I,'" was unaccept-
able, as was any attempt to surrender anything less than one's whole
body and spirit to the commune.[104] When an enthusiastic young man
claimed that he would be "good for the commune" because he could
"do anything," Brother Ioann surprised him by responding that the
commune did not need workers who gave their hands but not their
heart.[105] This expectation was a clear departure from Churikov's earlier attitude on the colony, when he had denounced communalism
as contrary to the spirit of individual freedom and independence he
hoped to cultivate there. Whether or not his new stance was a conscious embrace of Soviet collectivism is hard to say, but it seems
clear that communal norms and values were trending away from the
bourgeois individualism that had governed the trezvenniki in Vyritsa
before the revolution.

Another unique feature of the BICh commune was the central role
played by Brother Ioann. Whereas the Tolstoyans were united by their
vision of "a worldwide brotherly, stateless society, free of violence and
exploitation,"[106] the majority of kommunary on BICh devoted their
labor above all to the man whom they saw as the embodiment of righteous living. To be clear, the trezvenniki made much of their commitment to the virtues of holy sobriety, but their defining quality was their
dedication to Brother Ioann rather than his beliefs. Although the all-
male council was technically empowered to adjudicate all transgressions
or conflicts on the commune, in practice, Churikov was the ultimate
authority and decision-maker. His uncontested authority no doubt
helped to minimize conflicts on the commune, or at least to return it
to a state of order and stability when disputes arose.[107] But as discussed
earlier, many of his followers sought his approval at virtually every
step—not only when it came to eating or working, but also when nam-
ing their children or approving their children's marriages. "Living with
Brother was easy," one young trezvennitsa recalled, "because as long as
Brother blessed [something] then everything would be good, [and if he
didn't] then you wouldn't do it."[108] Such faith in a time of uncertainty
was likely reassuring, but it was also extreme, since many believed that
without Churikov's consent, any action constituted a punishable trans-
gression or sin. In this sense, kommunary considered themselves equal
not as laborers or citizens, but rather as subjects of Brother Ioann's
judgment. For the majority this was a personal choice, rooted in a particular form of self-realization. In fact, even those "godless" observers who denounced Churikov's authority as oppressive—tyrannical

even—seemed to recognize that he did not usurp authority as much as it was given *to* him by his followers.[109]

With few exceptions, the majority of kommunary exhibited a similar sense of indebtedness to Churikov for his energy, his protective concern for each of them, and his closeness to God. The 1926 collection of testimonies was the most extensive expression of praise and gratitude put together by commune members, but it was far from the only one. "Our dear Brother fed us in body and spirit, gave us [water] to drink, kept us warm, dressed us, put shoes on our feet, and coddled us like a good hen with her children," wrote Timofei Zaitsev when petitioning the Soviet state on Churikov's behalf.[110] In a similar vein, others emphasized how the biggest sacrifices had been his, not theirs, and that it was primarily because of his love and prayer that they had become better versions of themselves. In an interview in the 1990s, E. A. Ermolova, the daughter of trezvenniki who lived on the commune as a young girl, recalled how Brother Ioann had "consecrated" his life for the people (*narod*). "Brother gave his life to the *narod*," she remembered, "and the Lord rewarded him with divine power."[111] Consequently, as in the case of Orthodox saints, many followers perceived a certain reciprocity in their relationship with Brother Ioann and felt obliged to repay all of his good deeds, leadership, and love with their hard work and unquestioning obedience.[112] As Zaitsev explained, the kommunary worked "not for money, gold or silver," nor for the sake of Soviet power, but solely for "honor and glory of such a teacher as Dear Brother."[113]

By the mid-1920s, the BICh commune had achieved a great deal, although the experience of being sober under early Soviet rule had not been easy. In addition to the poverty, uncertainty, and loss of life experienced in those years, Brother Ioann's followers faced many challenges on account of their faith. The commune was taxed heavily and unpredictably, and the obshchina suffered harassment when they lost their lease on their meeting place in 1923 and were blocked in their efforts to find another. Churikov's followers were criticized by some as *kulakskie* (kulak-like), and individual trezvenniki encountered ridicule or harassment from coworkers in the factories, or lived in fear of being fired if their beliefs were discovered.[114] Brother Ioann was also the target of a brutally critical godless press, especially after 1924.

But with these unprecedented challenges came new opportunities. Through hard work, discipline, obedience, ingenuity, and faith, the trezvenniki not only survived but expanded on their sober vision under early Soviet rule. As proof of the hope they shared, trezvenniki on the commune proudly documented their lives through a new series of photographs capturing the symbols of their success—new faces, healthy families, the "big, big" tractor, and bountiful harvests. By the mid-1920s, the commune had become a place of peace, equality, and hope, and it remained a site of faith and imagination. Like other sectarian groups grounded in Scripture, the trezvenniki aspired to recapture what they believed had been lost since the early days of Christianity, in order to lay down a foundation for a new, more perfect society. As the trezvennik Ivan Frolov would proudly tell a shop full of fellow workers in 1928, Brother Ioann's vision was one of a "heaven on earth" rooted in sobriety, work, and social harmony. "While the Prophet Elijah ascended alone into heaven, Brother lifts everyone up high," he observed, "[and] while the priests promised paradise in heaven, [Brother] says that we should live here on earth as if in heaven, [and then] milk and honey will flow from us."[115]

Anyone familiar with Stalin's brutal collectivization of the peasantry will know that the world the trezvenniki were building in Vyritsa was not to last. But what sustained them was a belief not only in the compatibility of sobriety and socialism, but in the idea that the ultimate success of socialism lay *in* sobriety. Taking a long view, they believed— and openly confessed throughout the 1920s—that "the teachings of Jesus Christ, which Brothers preaches, are necessary for everyone, the pious and the godless; without Christ's teaching it is impossible to live."[116] Their hope might be seen as naïve, but only in retrospect. After all, the commune was created at a time of almost boundless idealism, when the very imperfect present was seen not as an obstacle to a more perfect future but a necessary stage leading to it. As Richard Stites noted with respect to the recurring conflicts between "experimental striving" and the many real challenges of the 1920s, "the practitioners viewed these experiments not as the 'impossible dream' . . . but as the only antidote to the impossible reality."[117] So too, in their own way, the trezvenniki looked around them at the "cold" (secular, atheistic) environment aspired to by many socialists and still believed that Churikov's teachings—sobriety and hard work, respect for authority and nonviolence—were not only completely compatible with the revolutionary project, but also vital to its successful "ascension into socialism."[118]

This pattern of thinking was not new for Brother Ioann, of course; just as he had always believed that Scripture was an essential means by which to deepen the laity's identity as Orthodox, so he believed that sobriety was a precondition for the socialist self. Moreover, just as his followers before the revolution believed that because of their sober life-style and rejection of sin, they modeled ideal Orthodox behavior, so too the kommunary of the early Soviet period persisted in the belief that they were exemplary Soviet citizens, worthy of the state's protection. Although this was not to be, it remained their sustaining hope not only throughout the 1920s, but into the Soviet future.

CHAPTER 8

The Soviet State's Campaign against the Trezvenniki, 1924–1933

For the first decade of Soviet rule, the trez-venniki occupied what they believed was a fairly secure if marginal space in Soviet society, especially during the period of greater cultural pluralism associated with the New Economic Policy (NEP).[1] Like all religious believers, they were periodically harassed by local officials and the *bezbozhnik* (godless) press, but their largely working-class origins combined with their reputation as sober and productive laborers kept them safe from overt repression,[2] as did their careful compliance with all Soviet laws and procedures.[3] They elected representatives to the local soviet, paid their taxes, and in contrast to other religious groups, including the Tolstoyans and Baptists, willingly provided male recruits for the Red Army.[4] Support from Bolsheviks in high places—especially V. V. Bonch-Bruevich—also protected them, as did the fact that Churikov's relationship to Orthodox leaders (especially those faithful to Patriarch Tikhon) remained distant.

Brother Ioann was savvy enough to understand the unstable political parameters of the early Soviet period and to perform his allegiance to the new regime and its ideals at key moments. He openly preached obedience to Soviet authorities and occasionally alluded to the common ground between socialism and *trezvennichestvo*, stressing the "usefulness" of sober workers. Following his lead, the trezvenniki expressed their loyalty to the October Revolution by hanging red stars on official holidays and displaying portraits of Lenin the "father" next to images of Brother Ioann and Jesus Christ. And when Lenin died, members of the commune sent a memorial wreath to Moscow, calling on "proletarians of all countries" not only "to unite" but also to become sober and "to struggle against all vices!"[5]

Yet even as Brother Ioann praised the state's goals of feeding the hungry and clothing the poor, there was never any question that he could embrace the Bolsheviks fully. As the historian M. Iu. Krapivin has pointed out, the trezvenniki could not conceive of the possibility that the building of socialism could be carried out by "sinners."[6] Thus, while perhaps not as actively committed to proselytizing as the Baptists or Evangelicals,[7] Brother Ioann continued to preach Scripture and holy sobriety, and his followers took advantage of their relative autonomy during the NEP era to build society as they thought it should be. Committed to nonviolent change, they aspired to live as models of faith, sobriety, productivity, and communalism as they welcomed people of all kinds into their community. Significantly, for most of Brother Ioann's followers, holy sobriety formed the basis of a shared vision—rather than a specific program or recruitment plan—that they believed to be in sync with socialism's fundamental values. Yet, as argued in the previous chapter, most claimed an even stronger allegiance to Brother Ioann than to his specific *politika*.

In the 1920s, however, not all trezvenniki held the same views or adhered to the same timeline. Under Soviet rule and the discursive framework that privileged forward thinking and ideological progress, some trezvenniki—mostly youths—came to understand holy sobriety as a revolution in its own right. Consequently, they began to organize around this alternative path to both individual and collective salvation in the late 1920s—not only as a complement to Soviet socialism but as a stage beyond it. This shift was partly a reaction against the Bolsheviks' repressive stance toward religious groups and partly a natural extension of their belief system influenced by broader currents of politicization particularly strong among Soviet youth.

The scope and scale of sober activism remained limited, but its political potential clearly concerned Soviet authorities and ultimately became one of the factors they cited in justifying repression against the entire community. After a decade of relative tolerance on the part of Soviet authorities, a series of official actions in 1927–28 made it clear that the trezvenniki's position had become more precarious; in the words of the youth leader Ivan Smolev, the atmosphere "thickened."[8] Within a year police, journalists, and bureaucrats launched a combined attack on the trezvenniki on multiple fronts. The first wave of repressions coincided with the persecution of other religious and sectarian groups, including Baptists and Evangelical Christians, as well as the assaults on the remaining Orthodox monasteries;[9] the second wave was part of the much more extensive process of collectivizing the peasantry and transforming them through a cultural revolution.

Some scholars have argued that the relationship between religious sectarians and the Bolsheviks was bound to break down eventually in spite of the efforts by influential individuals like Bonch-Bruevich to highlight their common ground. Kathy Rousselet, for example, has argued that the sectarian commune, with its own rules and beliefs, was "a state within a state," incompatible with Stalin's shift toward more centralization and atheism in the late 1920s.[10] Historian Richard Stites also saw the split as inevitable, although for different reasons. "Stalinism," Stites wrote in his classic, *Revolutionary Dreams*, "was a rejection of 'revolutionary' utopianism in favor of a single utopian vision and plan, drawn up at the pinnacle of power and imposed on a society without allowance for autonomous life experiences."[11] Thus, while the trezvenniki's vision of socialism could grow on the fertile field of social experimentation that characterized the NEP, it could not survive the transition to the much more narrowly defined ambitions of the industrializing Five-Year Plan. The deciding factor in their elimination, Stites suggested, was not simply their faith-based approach to life or work, nor even Brother Ioann's authority, but more fundamentally, the fact of their autonomy as a "community apart." As Stites observed, Stalinist conceptions of collectivism "resembled the belief of Zamyatin's antihero that only the collective 'we' has rights," and thus it could not tolerate the "'little we's' of experimental life."[12]

The Soviet state's attacks on the sober community in Leningrad and Vyritsa between 1924 and 1933 began with a propaganda campaign in the godless press, followed by mass arrests, the destruction of the commune, and the dissolution of the obshchina. If in many ways the rationale and timing of official actions against Brother Ioann and his followers were in line with a wider state assault on believers, the experience of persecution was specific to the sober community and their way of life. It was not a fair fight, and the trezvenniki could do little to stop an armed state bent on their destruction. But the state's campaign to silence Brother Ioann and shut down the obshchina and the commune was neither simple nor straightforward, and authorities worked hard to justify their actions. A closer look at the dynamics of the commune's liquidation is revealing in terms of the relationship between the trezvenniki and Soviet authority, and shows how the process impacted both.

The Godless Campaign Begins

By 1924–25, as the Soviet Union's political and economic situation was stabilizing under the New Economic Policy, the trezvenniki began to see the fruits of their labor on the commune. For the first time in many years, life seemed to be getting better. Yet, even as the state rewarded them for their high levels of productivity,[13] godless propagandists attacked them in the press. In the fall of 1924, a sprawling six-part article in *Leningradskaia Pravda* by V. Marovskii offered a highly unflattering portrait of Churikov and his sober movement. In line with the anticlerical tradition that guided much of the atheists' propaganda, the primary goal was to "expose" and "unmask" Brother Ioann as a fraud and exploiter of the poor and ignorant.[14] Constructed out of loosely connected yet colorful anecdotes and "testimonies," Marovskii's narrative also had much in common with the emergent Bolshevik genre of agitation-plays, which relied on ridicule, shame, and embellishment to establish a clear moral and ethical framework.[15]

In the same sarcastic tone used to report the unmasking of Orthodox saints, Marovskii cast Brother Ioann as the antihero of his own biography, portraying him as variously profit-driven, corrupt, and sexually deviant. Each virtue attributed to Churikov by his followers was twisted into a vice: Rather than a "meek lamb [of God]" living in poverty and dedicated to prayer and people's spiritual needs, he was caricatured as a cunning "swindler" who hid his "moneyboxes" much like "a chicken with her eggs" and worked with his conniving "virgins" to fleece his followers by falsely promising "heaven on earth." Rather than healing, he prevented people from getting medical help, and instead of enlightening people by teaching them Scripture, he kept them ignorant of the saving truths of Marxist-Leninism. Finally, Brother Ioann was characterized as a tyrant, who controlled his followers' "every step," and was so greedy that he took everything he wanted from them—including, it implied, their beautiful, young daughters for his sexual pleasure.[16]

Many of these charges had been levied by Churikov's Orthodox missionary critics before 1917, and Marovskii relied on many of the same rhetorical tools—exaggeration, abstraction, guilt by association, and fabrication. But the corrupting role of Churikov's (bourgeois) class roots and the related claim of financial exploitation were far more pronounced in Marovskii's denunciation, as were charges of his political unreliability. In an anecdote that would be repeated in godless circles, Marovskii claimed that when Vyritsa was occupied by the Red Army during the civil war, the trezvenniki "anathematized" the "White bandits"; but when the Whites took the town, they "anathematized" the Red Army soldiers. Churikov allegedly pointed to the corpses of the communists killed by the Whites, saying "their brains are now being licked by dogs"—as if to suggest that the same would happen to others who wanted to live by their own will.[17] Given that a significant number of trezvenniki had served in the Red Army with Brother Ioann's support, the story was likely a fabrication—but effective nonetheless. Not unlike missionary efforts to paint the Moscow brattsy as agents of the Antichrist, the accusation that Brother Ioann had taken part in "counterrevolutionary" activity derived its power from doubt and suspicion and was thus next to impossible to refute convincingly.

Typical of godless accounts in the 1920s, Marovskii's assessment of Brother Ioann revealed a contradiction. On the one hand, he dismissed "the Churikovshchina" as "a piece of the old world" that had "no place" in the "new peasant-workers' Russia."[18] Implicitly casting the trezvenniki as Churikov's innocent victims, he worked hard to suggest that Brother Ioann was a relic of the past—and that a healthy dose of collective ridicule and godless "enlightenment" would be enough to check his influence. On the other hand, Marovskii, like the hieromonk Father Veniamin,[19] appears to have been genuinely concerned about Brother Ioann's influence over his followers and the trezvenniki's status as a "community apart" from the Soviet masses. He would be the first in a long line of godless activists to point out that Churikov's followers were—and intended to remain—immune to the influence of the Soviet project. Willing to conform outwardly to the state's demands, they were permanently resistant to the transformation of self that "becoming Soviet" meant. In spite of Churikov's preaching that the revolutionary government was "a power granted by God," Marovskii pointed out, he forbade them to read political materials of any kind and diverted them from contact with the "Soviet plague," including the Komsomol. Indeed, under Brother Ioann's leadership the trezvenniki were creating a *novyi byt* (new way of life) of their own, based on honest labor, sobriety, and communal living.

The high profile of Marovskii's series of articles in *Leningradskaia Pravda* suggested that at least some party authorities understood that trezvennichestvo was not to be written off lightly. In fact, while even the most damning portrayals of Churikov before 1917 could be found only in missionary papers or pamphlets and in some conservative papers, Marovskii's piece appeared right across the page from articles on the Trotsky-Stalin debate in the fall of 1924—that is, front and center in a significant contemporary political space.

As in the past, the trezvenniki refused to let a public attack on Brother Ioann stand uncontested. The manager of the Vyritsa commune and members of the local soviet quickly penned a letter to the editor of *Leningradskaia Pravda*, dated October 8, 1924, in "defense of the truth."[20] They pushed back hard on Marovskii's suggestion that Brother Ioann had exploited them by amassing a small fortune at their expense and argued that the cause of Marovskii's "error" was his "hatred of sobriety, and hatred of communal life." Confident that they had nothing to hide, they extended an invitation to him to visit the commune to meet them and see for himself what was really going on.

From the trezvenniki's perspective, godless propaganda was harmful not only because it was irreverent and based on lies, but also because it empowered their critics and opened them up to other attacks both in the press and in the courts. As mentioned in chapter 7, the former trezvennitsa Brovina took Churikov to court on the claim that "under religious intoxication" (the title of Marovskii's article) she had been unlawfully duped into giving Brother Ioann all her possessions when she joined the commune.[21] After much time and expense, the case was eventually dismissed due primarily to inconclusive evidence, but the scandal lived on in the press, damaging Brother Ioann's reputation and leaving him vulnerable to other accusations.[22]

A Revolution of Their Own?

The real turning point in the state's treatment of the trezvenniki came in March 1927 with the arrest of Vasilii Arsen'evich Guliaev, Brother Ioann's devoted follower for many years, a preacher in his own right, and one of the Leningrad obshchina's leading members. The grounds for the arrest included concrete evidence of what authorities understood to be a political threat to Soviet power. During a search of Guliaev's apartment police had discovered a notebook allegedly belonging to him and containing scriptural quotations and various talking points deemed anti-Soviet. "The lesson of the Russian revolution" was that it was all "a blatant lie," the notebook read, and "instead of freedom, we received oppression, constraint, cold, and hunger. Instead of wealth, [we received] poverty, extortion, and taxes, and [for] those who do not pay—arrests, inventory, and the sale of property. Instead of peace, [we got] civil war and prolonged strife with all [other] governments." Under Bolshevik rule, "evil became good, and good became evil, and their deception became known to all." Thus, it concluded, "socialism as an idea is unsuitable to life, [and] communism is unrealizable."[23]

Although notebook entries dated back to 1921, the more overtly anti-Soviet statements had evidently been entered since 1924. Police attributed the shift in part to the fact that Guliaev had begun to witness what he considered "completely debauched" behaviors among communists at the Putilov factory, where he had worked for many years.[24] This was a concern shared widely by trezvennik youth groups at the time. What police files neglect to mention is that in December 1924, Putilov workers collectively voted to close the factory church. The decision prompted a major backlash from clergy and religious workers, which included a massive petition campaign, and by the end of the January 1925, the disruption had spread to other factories. The church's desecration the following month occurred amid the protests of some eight thousand believers, some of whom denounced the iconoclasts as the "Antichrist."[25]

Although it is unclear if Guliaev took part in the Putilov unrest, he certainly would have been aware of it. The notebook's references to the campaign against the faithful equated the Soviet state with the "power of the Antichrist" and accused it of serving to "embitter" and "corrupt" the *narod* while "preparing the Russian nation for self-destruction." According to police reports, Guliaev pitted the new government, which was ruled by Jews (*zhidy*) known for their "trickery and speculation," and other "unscrupulous" people and "scum," against the builders of a "Great Russia." It is difficult to know what to make of these nationalistic and antisemitic claims, although they too appear in the notebook after 1924. On the one hand, the language was not in keeping with Brother Ioann's statements (at least not those made in public) and had more in common with those associated with the "Black Hundreds," the prerevolutionary right-wing movement that had attracted some clergy (including Father Ioann). On the other hand, the connection between Jews and Bolsheviks was widespread among the (still predominately Orthodox) population in the early 1920s. In part a reflection of the disproportionate number of Jews among revolutionaries and now in positions of authority—including the leadership of the League of Militant Godless—the association was also a product of the binary framework through which many believers made sense of the world: because neither Jews nor the "godless" were "for" Christ, they were necessarily "anti-Christ."[26]

Questions also remain about the authenticity of Guliaev's notebook, although at least one witness, Efrosina Petrovna Matina, offered evidence linking him to denunciations of Soviet power as the "Antichrist" and "the beast."[27] Given her own reputation as an outspoken critic of Brother Ioann and the commune, Matina's testimony is somewhat suspect.[28] But letters sent by other trezvenniki from around Leningrad were written "in the same key" as Guliaev's journal, suggesting that at the very least, he was not alone in his condemnation of Soviet power.[29] Indeed, in the weeks following Guliaev's arrest, police amassed numerous testimonies connecting other Leningrad trezvenniki to similarly anti-Soviet statements, suggesting a broader culture of anti-Soviet dissent.

Among those accused of preaching in an "anti-Soviet spirit" was the youth group leader Ivan Smolev, who produced a journal, *Trezvyi Rassvet* (*Sober Dawn*), in 1926–27.[30] While the journal gave voice, energy, and a coherent vision to the sober youth movement, its militant language, which referenced armies, battlefields, commanders, "unremitting struggle," and "victory," had more in common with the Bolsheviks' lexicon after the civil war than with the trezvenniki's usual vocabulary. A 1926 article by the youth leader A. Puchkov was representative.[31] "With a gospel sword and a shield of faith," Puchkov declared, Brother Ioann "went out into the battlefield" with a cry: "Stop! Stand, do not back down, do not give yourself to death, there is still salvation, just repent and believe in the Gospel, change your way of life and victory will be ours." Hearing the call of their "brave commander," he continued, thousands "united into one army and with faith in God went against drinking. And in the near future, a young army of sober troops under the banner of Christ with Leader Brother Ioann will give the last and decisive battle to drunkenness."[32] While an understanding of sobriety as a war against drunkenness was not in itself new, Puchkov's framing suggested that the battle against drunkenness was not simply a personal struggle but a crusade to be waged by and for the masses, and led by Brother Ioann, who was sometimes referred to as "'the vozhd' of the sober avantgarde."

Understandably, the militancy of *Trezvyi Rassvet* might have alarmed authorities into thinking that the trezvenniki were preparing a battle against the socialist state as well. And indeed, police files note that its editor, Smolev, "hate[d] Soviet power" every bit as much as Guliaev and regularly predicted its downfall: "In the Soviet Union, business is not going well, and we see destruction instead of creation, and soon such a moment will come that power will be in the hands of Brother." Once the Bolsheviks were gone, Smolev predicted, "we teetotalers, the despised, will soon be blessed."[33]

While police reports suggest that other trezvenniki were similarly convinced that Soviet power was disintegrating, there was little clarity with respect to who would be responsible for taking down the regime or what would take its place. On the one hand, the trezvennik K. Borisov echoed Guliaev's notebook when he denounced Soviet authorities as exclusively "Jews, thieves, and robbers" who persecuted the faithful, and preached that Brother Ioann must "save the Russian people from destruction": "LENIN walked against God and God destroyed [him], and Brother [Ioann] will finish his business and will be the ruler not only of Russia but soon of the whole world as well." "Sober people, especially the youth, should rally," Borisov proclaimed. "Brother suffered to give us the kingdom and the kingdom we will get. . . . So Brother says, [and] Brother's word is holy."[34] On the other hand, other trezvenniki predicted that the communist party would wither and collapse on its own or soon be destroyed by foreign powers— a common claim in the context of the 1927 war scare, when rumors circulated to the effect that the British were planning an invasion.

As the historian Aleksei Beglov has discussed, the severe sense of crisis and uncertainty of the revolutionary era opened the floodgates to eschatological expectations and movements; in line with A. A. Panchenko's findings on the origins and evolution of *khlystovstvo* into the nineteenth century, many believers engaged in a search for a new "savior" and counted themselves among the "chosen" or the "saved."[35] Rumors of the impending apocalypse were especially widespread during Stalin's collectivization of the countryside, when they became a call to protest for peasants who understood collectivization to be the work of the Antichrist in advance of the Second Coming.[36]

When Brother Ioann emerged as a spiritual leader around the turn of the twentieth century, apocalyptic thinking had also been very widespread,[37] although his own besedy typically did not engage in it. Nonetheless, it is possible that the unprecedented chaos and destruction associated with the revolution and civil war era altered how some trezvenniki understood the state of the world and Brother Ioann's role in it. As discussed in earlier chapters, rumors about his alleged divinity had been circulating for decades, and likely intensified in the 1920s as clerical oversight receded and eschatological expectations were heightened. This tendency was especially evident in the statements of one Klokov, who allegedly referred to Churikov as "the Second Jesus Christ" and, equating Soviet power with the mythical beast with three heads—in this case, "Kerensky, Lenin, and Rykov"—predicted that all those who followed the beast would be branded and then perish.[38] Nonetheless, even some of the more apocalyptic claims attributed to the trezvenniki might have been intended not as direct threats to Soviet power or a call to arms, but rather dire (and implicitly hopeful) predictions of divine justice. The apocalypse would come, they implied, because God willed it (not because *they* did). At the same time, the trezvenniki's predictions might be seen as teleological, born in response to the violence and uncertainty of the moment but rooted in their confidence that holy sobriety would ultimately prevail.[39]

Whatever their personal beliefs about the imminent fate of Soviet power, in the 1920s some young trezvenniki exhibited an unprecedented tendency toward purposeful activism and the goal of motivating their generation to improve society.[40] In this sense, their militancy might be read as a matter of identity as much as faith or politics. Like members of the Komsomol and Baptist youth groups (the *Bapsomol*), sober youth shared a commitment to self-improvement, both the conscious adoption of new cultural habits and higher ideals, and the energetic struggle and sacrifice that they demanded. Just as communist youth committed themselves to "building socialism," the so-called *trezvomol'tsy* devoted themselves to building "a new Church," founded in "fear of God, faith, and firm hope [*upovanie*] in Brother Ioann's grace." Petr Terekhovich, for example, wrote about the deep sense of "joy" and the "great deal of responsibility" he felt toward his work on behalf of sobriety, which he understood as a higher form of truth. *Trezvennichestvo* was the rising "sun of God's truth in our Soviet Government," Terekhovich reflected, as if to suggest that with time, Churikov's teachings could save Soviet power, just as they had saved him.[41]

1927: Repressions Begin

The degree to which Brother Ioann shared any of his followers' more apocalyptic or political beliefs or perspectives is unclear. While there is some evidence that he prophesied that believers would eventually triumph over the godless and the sober over drunkards,[42] there is no mention of a timetable or promise of an imminent victory.[43] Moreover, the militant language attributed to Guliaev and others was unusually political for Brother Ioann, and Borisov admitted under interrogation by Soviet officials that he might have misinterpreted some of Churikov's words when speaking out (of course it is possible that he claimed this to protect him).[44] Nonetheless, Soviet authorities would do their best to link Brother Ioann to his followers' alleged anti-Soviet statements both by documenting his close and ongoing relationship with them and by gathering witnesses who would testify that he had preached against Soviet power.

For the time being, however, authorities decided to leave Churikov alone. When police showed up at the commune in May 1927—two months after Guliaev's arrest—they came not for Brother Ioann but for some of the people closest to him. Among them were two members of the commune's soviet, Sergei Fedorovich Andrianov and Varfolomei Alekseevich Plotnikov, as well as four of Churikov's sestritsy, his beloved Grusha (Agrippina Smirnova), Maria Kartasheva, Maria Grigor'eva, and Anastasiia Dmitrievna Vasil'evna.[45] Charged on the basis of Article 58 of the criminal code for counterrevolutionary and/or anti-Soviet behavior, they were sentenced to three years in exile. Rumors circulated to the effect that Brother Ioann had been spared either on account of his advanced age or, more plausibly, because Soviet authorities had wanted to send a warning but had been afraid to touch him for fear of inciting protest.[46] What seems clear is that Brother Ioann's sestritsy were considered expendable in the eyes of the authorities. As women of faith and Churikov's intimate companions, they had already suffered years of ridicule and misogynistic innuendo, and now they had become collateral damage in the state's campaign against Brother Ioann and the male leadership. In other words, the women were arrested not because they were perceived to be dangerous but because they were *not*.

For the next several months, police authorities interrogated both former and current commune members in an effort to "prove" what had been rumored on the pages of the godless press: that Churikov and his "sisters" were exploiting their followers and practicing "criminal witchcraft." Authorities alleged that Brother Ioann and the sestritsy "lived in luxury" on the commune, while everyone else, including children under the age of sixteen, were forced to work sixteen hours a day and teetered on the "edge of poverty," "half-starved," dressed in clothing made out of sacks, and unable to afford boots.[47] In order to procure material evidence to justify the arrests, police raided the house where Brother Ioann and the sestritsy lived and confiscated an assortment of manufactured items, including nice bedsheets. Although these items had been gifted to them by well-meaning followers over the course of the previous thirty years, the authorities insisted that they had been confiscated from people for profit and were therefore the result of "theft."[48]

Based in part on testimonies from former commune members, authorities further alleged that the sestritsy were complicit in Churikov's reign of fear and exploitative practices, including beatings and forced marriages. Taking advantage of their close relationship with Brother Ioann, they not only lived better than everyone else, but treated commune members rudely and demanded bribes in exchange for access to him.[49] Rumors also circulated to the effect that the sestritsy liked to sell necessary items to the impoverished commune members for a profit, and because Brother Ioann's authority on the commune was so extreme, the victims had been too afraid to complain.[50] The charge of "criminal witchcraft" related to the fact that the women regularly administered sugar, incense, and oil to those seeking to be healed from alcoholism and other illnesses.[51] Drawing on the complaint filed by the Baburov family, authorities also claimed the sestritsy had refused to allow doctors to heal the sick, leading to unnecessary deaths, including a number of children.[52] Although it is difficult to disentangle truth from rumor, the sestritsy's relatively privileged position on the commune likely stirred feelings of jealousy and made them vulnerable to false accusations. Whatever the case, the godless press was quick to capitalize on the charges against the women, disparaging them as *bogoroditsy* who feasted on jam and "little boxes of chocolate" and sold off clippings of Brother Ioann's hair and nails to fill their own pocketbooks.[53]

Members of the commune were devastated by the sestritsy's arrest and sent several protest petitions to the state. In one dated May 14, 1927, they labeled the authorities' decision "especially harsh" in light of the fact that the arrested had been registered and law-abiding citizens, fully engaged in sobriety and agricultural work on the commune. Reiterating that the BICh commune was a "labor commune" in compliance with state laws, they suggested (perhaps naïvely) that a mistake had been made and demanded that Soviet authorities consider assigning the women "cultural work" rather than resorting to more repressive tactics. This petition, as well as those to follow, would be unsuccessful, and the sestristy were forced to live out their three-year sentences.[54]

The women would not be forgotten, however; trezvenniki kept up an active correspondence with them in exile, and their letters were read to the whole commune. In a letter destined to fall into police hands, one trezvennitsa praised the women for their love and faith and "heroic" struggles against drunkenness and immorality, while scolding those who accused them of living selfishly and acquisitively, "according to the word 'I.'"[55]

More challenges were soon to come. In March 1928, Ivan Smolev was also arrested and sent into exile, drawing a large crowd at the Moscow station desperate to show him support and say goodbye.[56] Not long after the arrests of the sestritsy, authorities also began efforts to shut down the obshchina. When the trezvenniki attempted to reregister their charter in late 1927, they were informed that the name of the organization (and thus its official stamp) had been changed (and politically demoted) from the category of "struggle against alcoholism" to "religion"—a sign that their identity as useful workers was now considered secondary to their beliefs. The trezvenniki appealed, affirming that their goal was "exclusively the education of our members in the spirit of absolute labor and sobriety, [and] not at all the pursuit of any kind of anti-Soviet ideals or propaganda contrary to the government."[57] Nonetheless, the state denied all their requests to renew their lease on their old building or to find a new meeting space.[58] The Obukhovo location was shut down permanently in early 1928, allegedly with plans to turn it into a center for children—an effective tactic for ensuring the support of the local population, which was desperate for social services of all kinds.

In addition to increased police surveillance, the commune endured another full investigation by agricultural authorities in the spring of 1928.[59] The report found that the commune had adequate equipment for industrialized collective agricultural production, and for this reason continued to show economic potential for the future. It also pointed out that some of the commune's methods (for example, the drying of the swamp) demonstrated "great creative initiative" and that "the labor discipline of each and every member of the commune" had a positive "instructive" effect on the local peasant population.[60] At the same time, investigators voiced serious concerns about the commune's commitment to faith-based temperance and its role as a "headquarters" for religious propaganda; they also raised questions about the excessive amount of authority wielded by Churikov, pointing out that members took little if any part in the production planning process. Their report

ЛЖЕ- КОММУНА „БИЧ" СЕКТЫ ЧУРИКОВЦЕВ

FIGURE 11.   Image of the BICh commune, late 1920s. Brother Ioann is on the big tractor on the far right. The banner held by commune members (on the far right) says, "We will defeat hunger, BICh commune." The caption, likely added when the image was displayed at a Soviet antireligious exhibit, reads: "The False Commune—BICh of the Churikov Sect." Reprinted with permission from TsGAKFFD SPb.

concluded that BICh did not deserve to be called a "commune" in any official sense, since it functioned more like a "monastery."[61]

In order to justify the state's attack on the obshchina and commune to the public, the press launched a new assault on the trezvenniki in 1928 in Leningrad and in provincial cities. The most extensive study of Brother Ioann and his followers in the 1920s was published by a leader of the godless movement, I. Ia. Eliashevich.[62] At an impressive eighty-one pages, Eliashevich's *Pravda o churikove i churikovtsakh* (*The Truth about Churikov and the Churikovtsy*) was an elaboration on Marovskii's arguments from 1924, embellished by now requisite quotes from Lenin and supported by a much wider base of research, including an extensive examination of prerevolutionary materials on Brother Ioann's life and interviews with current and former trezvenniki. The methodology was also similar; concerned less with the factual record than ideological "truth," Eliashevich appealed to his readers' emotions and sense of class justice in a tone alternately mocking and condescending. As he cast Brother Ioann as an exploiter, hypocrite, pervert, and tyrant hiding behind the mask of a man of God, his arguments rested on a creative

manipulation of the factual record by means of exaggeration, false juxtaposition, selective omission, and the assigning of guilt by association. The resulting portrait of Churikov was not unlike a Rodchenko
collage—fragmented, disjointed, and contradictory.

While Eliashevich's "othering" and essentializing of Brother Ioann
as a fraud and exploiter contributed to the shaping of the atheists'
moral narrative, the primary aim was more political and, in this sense,
reflective of a broader propaganda trend. "By decade's end, antireligious strategy had shifted towards explicit politicization of the secularization campaign," Daniel Peris has observed. "Where religious belief
had earlier been treated as an obstacle to social development, by 1929 it
was presented as a direct threat to Bolshevik rule from enemies within
and abroad."[63] As Eliashevich stated in the conclusion, every form of
religion (including "sectarianism") was "a brake on socialist construction and the cultural revolution," and thus the duty of every Soviet
citizen was to "do battle" against faith as a means to "clear the path to
socialism." In this new context, Eliashevich's task was different from
Marovskii's; by 1928, conforming to the immediate demands of Soviet
power in the absence of full class consciousness or faith in Marxist-
Leninism was no longer a tenable position. Therefore, in his capacity
as a leading godless missionary, Eliashevich set out to reveal Brother
Ioann as the Soviet equivalent of the Antichrist—that is, anti-Soviet in
a political and ideological as well as moral sense.

Pushing back on claims by Bonch-Bruevich and others that Churikov
possessed a "communist" cast of mind, Eliashevich set out to show
that Brother Ioann's beliefs made him "an enemy of Soviet power."
Churikov considered "Soviet power [to be the work] of the Antichrist,"
he explained, because it "distort[ed] the divine and the true proletarian,
revolutionary teachings of Christ, [and encouraged] violence against
religion and destruction of sacred objects." Brother Ioann also refused
to acknowledge classes or class struggle, believing that all people are
"brothers in Christ" and "socialism will arrive only when all people
become true Christians."[64] Moreover, Eliashevich spelled out, "by proclaiming [the individual's] worthiness before God" and stressing the
importance of moral living as essential steps toward the "imagined
'kingdom of God' on earth," Churikov "obscure[d] the working mass's
consciousness of their class interests, and [led] them away from revolutionary struggle, and in our times—from the building of socialism."[65]

Eliashevich also accused Brother Ioann of more directly political
statements. For example, he connected him to Klokov's prediction

about the inevitable death of Soviet power under "the three beasts of the apocalypse: Kerensky, Lenin, and Rykov," and the "happy times" that would follow when the government would be transferred to none other than himself.[66] In the same vein, he named several other young sober activists, including K. Borisov, who had been preaching in a similarly "anti-Soviet spirit" while setting up a network of agitprop stations around Leningrad. Most of all, Eliashevich highlighted the danger of Churikov's central teaching that "the root of all evil is—vodka," that "poverty comes from drunkenness," and that once drunkenness was overcome, heaven on earth would become possible. On the contrary, he explained, holy sobriety was an especially dangerous form of "spiritual enslavement of the masses," because it spread "the harmful illusion of being able to fight this social evil without a radical transformation of the social system." Drunkenness is not the "traveling companion of poverty," he emphasized, "but the result of poverty and exploitation, and can only be addressed through the building of socialism."[67] Thus Brother Ioann's understanding of socialism, grounded in scriptural principles, sober living, brotherhood, and peaceful means of change, was fundamentally incompatible with the Bolshevik project, not only politically but morally and ethically.

Eliashevich's account lay the groundwork for the shutting down of the obshchina and the silencing of sober preachers, while also raising serious concerns about the commune. Not coincidentally, his arguments aligned closely with those made recently by the agricultural commission; even the phrasing was similar. Eliashevich reiterated the point that Churikov's authority over his followers was both excessive and unhealthy—not only patriarchal but tyrannical. Pointing to Brother Ioann's alleged claim that "the commune is me," he observed that the soviet was democratic in form only (since he picked all the candidates); likewise, he described members of the commune as "hypnotized" by Churikov, who told them that they were nothing without him and then deluded them further with sermons that "in the future we will eat and drink better, but now we must work."[68] Thus they labored "uncomplainingly and tirelessly," though starving in conditions of great poverty, victims of both ignorance and exploitation, and "cut off from life." In spite of Churikov's "boasts" that the commune's agricultural achievements had "surpassed that of state farms," Eliashevich concluded, it was nothing more than "a peculiar sectarian monastery with forced labor and discipline, in which people are transformed into a flock of sheep." After declaring that "the Churikov commune is a false (*lzhe*) commune, and there is nothing communist about it,"[69] he devoted the remaining discussion entirely to one of his underlying goals: to introduce the *novyi byt* (new way of life) into Soviet villages, and to advertise the bright promises of the emergent cooperative and collective farm movement.

In June 1928, as part of his campaign to enlighten the public about the "truth" of Churikov and to justify the state's actions against him and the trezvennik community, Eliashevich invited the long-time trezvennik Ivan Frolov to a public debate on the floor of his typography shop. Spread out over two lunch periods and staged before large crowds of workers, the debate raised the kinds of questions and doubts the public harbored about the trezvenniki, while also planting new ones.[70] Topics ranged from more serious concerns such as the trezvenniki's position on the clergy, medical healing, labor practices on the commune, and Soviet power to issues clearly piquing popular curiosity at the time, including the scandal surrounding the former trezvennik Antonov convicted of rape. In one of several feisty moments, Frolov pushed back on Eliashevich's attempt to assign the guilt of a "single good-for-nothing" (Antonov) to the entire trezvennik community, saying in effect that the Communist Party would not want to accept responsibility for the sins of all those who had been associated with it.[71]

The final question of the debate concerned Brother Ioann's perspective on Soviet power. Firmly rejecting the insinuation that Churikov was against Soviet authority, Frolov claimed that in the twenty-two years he had known him, he had never heard him say that he was either for or against *any* authorities. He also vehemently countered the godless claim that Brother Ioann had met the White Army with "bread and salt"; in fact, he noted, when General Iudenich arrived in Vyritsa, two armed trezvenniki (Iakov Kononov and Efim D'iachkov) went after the white troops with weapons. He added that the people's authority (*narodnaia vlast'*) was the most just form of government, since the people knew best what they needed, how best to live, and which laws were important. After qualifying this statement with the suggestion that everyone should live according to the teachings of Christ, he reassured his audience that Brother Ioann's goal was to make everyone sober, but not necessarily "Churikovtsy."[72]

The staged debate between Eliashevich and Frolov might be seen as the atheist equivalent to the *uveshchaniia*, the requisite meetings with missionaries that Churikov had endured before his excommunication. If the stated goal was to publicize the trezvenniki's false beliefs and behaviors, the godless missionary Eliashevich nonetheless sought simultaneously to establish norms among the "faithful" while cultivating support for the expulsion of "heretics" from the "orthodox" community. But aside from the obvious differences in the nature of their respective beliefs and transgressions, there was another key difference—namely, the absence of any hope of reconciliation between Brother Ioann and the Soviet state. Indeed, many of the charges brought by Eliashevich matched, sometimes word for word, those that had been gathered through interrogations by the secret police (OGPU) in the spring of 1927 and were used by officials to justify future waves of arrests of trezvenniki, including Churikov. Although the exact correlation or sequence of events is difficult to reconstruct, Eliashevich's goal was to make the state's case for the arrests in the court of public opinion and thus grease the wheels of the prosecutorial process.

Later publications, including Pavel Petrov's 1929 book, *The Vyritsa Christ*, expanded more specifically on the "conspiratorial" nature of the trezvennik movement. Supplying further justification for the arrests that had already taken place—including the arrest of Guliaev, whom he accused of rape (a "fact" allegedly "covered up" by other trezvenniki)— Petrov documented the counterrevolutionary nature of the "trezvomol," which, he argued, had evolved intentionally as a "counterweight" to the Komsomol and drew strategically on the experience of ex-Mensheviks and "even communists."[73] As evidence of their conspiratorial intent, he pointed out that trezvennik leaders had been encouraging members of the community to apply to the Communist Party not for ideological reasons, but rather "in order to learn the methods of the party in the fight against us."[74] Finally, Petrov linked the enduring success of trezvennichestvo to money from abroad, a claim that tapped into associations of sectarianism with foreignness (a link long made by Orthodox missionaries) as well as contemporary fears about capitalist agents working to undermine socialism. While living off the three thousand U.S. dollars he had received from Germany in 1928, he alleged, Brother Ioann had been able to undermine Soviet power by influencing his followers to vote for "the faithful" or more "independent" (read: better-off) candidates to the soviet.[75]

By the spring of 1929, the trezvenniki had grown justifiably anxious. Contrary to widespread reports, Brother Ioann and his close followers did read newspapers at least some of the time and were very aware of the propaganda campaign against them. In early 1929, commune members discussed a piece published in the Moscow paper *Bezbozhnik*

u stanka titled "In the Nets of Religion: The Churikovtsy." In addition
to the now requisite godless refrains about the anti-Soviet nature of
holy sobriety, the article featured a large caricature of Brother Ioann
encircled by his white-scarved sestritsy dutifully grooming his hair and
washing his feet.[76] Over tea Brother Ioann asked his followers how they,
as the "dark, simple, and trusting people" referenced in the article, felt
about being caught in his "religious net"; according to a trezvennitsa
present, all responded with enthusiastic gratitude.[77] This acquired
knowledge of godless arguments, painful as it must have been, would
prove useful to the trezvenniki as they crafted petitions to authorities
in the coming years.

As atheists worked to shape public opinion against Brother Ioann
and the trezvenniki through the press, the secret police were actively
planning an assault on the community, with the aim of silencing it
once and for all. In early 1929, ten more of Churikov's closest followers,
including the leadership of his commune in Vyritsa and obshchina in
Leningrad, were deprived of the right to vote.[78] Then, on April 19, 1929,
just days after the introduction of the new law on religious associations

FIGURE 12.   Cartoon drawing of Brother Ioann surrounded by his white-scarved sestritsy. From
an article by Kii, "V tenetakh religii: Churikovtsy," *Bezbozhnik u stanka*, no. 1 (1929): 6.

increased state control over all forms of religious life,[79] Brother Ioann and several more of his closet followers—five in Vyritsa and five more in Leningrad—were arrested. In addition to engaging in anti-Soviet agitation in his capacity as the founder, leader, and preacher of the obshchina (Art. 58-10), Churikov was accused of "believing himself to be the 'second Christ' and the sole spiritual leader and rescuer of mankind," inciting religious hostility (Art. 59-7), and having organized a "fictitious" and exploitative commune (Art. 169).[80] The final charge involved possession of unauthorized weapons (Art. 182). To the shock and despair of his many followers, he was led away to prison, along with the twenty-one pairs of crutches belonging to trezvenniki he had helped regain the ability to walk, which OGPU agents took as material evidence of his claim to healing. After hanging prominently in the communal dining room next to the icons, they would from that day forward remain in the OGPU archive until the end of the Soviet era.[81] Brother Ioann would never return to the commune or live freely again. On September 14, 1929, he was sentenced to three years in prison, and on March 7, 1932, he received an additional three-year sentence; he died on October 8, 1933, after being transferred to the Butyrskaia detention center.[82]

The End of It All

Immediately after Churikov's arrest, state officials took over the management of the commune and began to reorganize it into a collective farm. Initially at least, the justification for the reorganization centered squarely on labor issues, as if the state was legitimately stepping in to save workers from what authorities believed was a highly exploitative situation. A six-page document, dated July 6, 1929, and written by the agronomist A. Miliutin (one of the new "bosses" since Churikov's arrest),[83] outlined the logic of the reorganization. While acknowledging the commune's successes, the report highlighted problems in productivity and labor management, including the lack of a scientific plan, leading to undercultivation. Under Churikov's direction, Miliutin pointed out, the kommunary did not correctly cultivate the soil by alternating usage and applying mineral fertilizer, and they appeared to work the land without any kind of agronomist instruction. He added that most of the commune members had no clue what to do on their own.

In contrast to the report made by investigators in 1928, which had been critical of Churikov's patriarchal authority but made no other substantial claims against him, Miliutin characterized Brother Ioann's leadership as despotic and exploitative in every sense and justified the commune's reorganization on the grounds that he had been hoarding its profits and keeping his followers in poverty. It noted that workers were paid in food rather than money, and only in the form of cabbage and black bread equal to twenty-one kopecks per day. These rations were especially low for people expected to work the land, and the lack of nourishment had had the effect of increasing their passivity as well as their tendency to feel no "need to work for society [*obshchestvennost'*] whatsoever."[84] No mention was made of the excessive tax burdens routinely imposed on the commune, nor of the fact that at the time the commune was founded, wages were expressly forbidden by the new Bolshevik state, and that legally property was supposed to be communalized.

The third concern raised in Miliutin's report also related to issues of productivity and, specifically, the opportunity costs of their religious life. Refuting earlier observations that the kommunary's shared religious convictions *enhanced* their productivity, Miliutin charged that they wasted a lot of their time engaging in religious rituals, the most damaging of which were their many fasts. Fasting, he charged, had led to underperformance, and thus the need to employ far more workers than would otherwise be necessary. After calculating the number of labor days lost to religious needs and malnourishment, he declared that religious rituals were not just a waste of time, but actually harmful to workers—especially to those who did not personally engage in them, yet suffered the consequences of those who did. While preventing correct labor discipline, the status quo had also been detrimental to the kommunary's intellectual development, resulting in "dimwittedness" and mass psychological problems, including "fanaticism."[85] To allow the situation to continue, Miliutin concluded, would be irresponsible.

Under Miliutin's watch religious rituals were expressly forbidden in public spaces. Meat was served regularly, allegedly to promote better health, but in flagrant disregard of the kommunary's ethically based vegetarianism; the new administrators even slaughtered some of the commune's own livestock for food. Those kommunary who remained faithful to Churikov and the old system were deemed "psychologically ill" and forced to leave the commune as "foreign class elements"—a decision that called into question the transformative potential of the new labor regime. Forced expulsion was mandated even when it was acknowledged that many commune members were impoverished and had nowhere else to go.

Brother Ioann's arrest was, not surprisingly, a highly traumatic event for his followers, especially those close to him on the commune.[86] The liquidation of the commune was a full-out assault on their way of life. Though initially shocked and unprepared, they soon began to protest against the state's actions, petitioning collectively for Churikov's release and return and for a halt to the reorganization process. A handwritten letter by commune member Timofei Zaitsev, drafted on August 1, 1929, reflects the confusion, anger, and fear that dominated the commune at this time.[87] It also reveals some of the kommunary's assumptions about their rights as laborers. Declaring the commune "in complete ruin," Zaitsev protested against the sudden and violent usurpation of authority by the two new administrators, who had wrested control of the ninety-three keys to the storehouse and use of the commune's official seal. Playing to the state's alleged concerns about labor democracy, he emphasized that "all of this was done without any kind of general meeting of the *narod*; the people know nothing." He then inverted the atheists' denunciations of Churikov, accusing the new bosses of exploitation and complaining that they lived and ate better than the workers while ignoring the welfare of the commune's weakest members. In addition to embezzling from the collective, they had slaughtered one of the commune's cows and eaten it themselves. Taken together, Zaitsev emphasized, the actions of the new administrators had "driven communism away" and worked against the idea of "proletarians of the world unite," causing many tears for the working "*klas* [*sic*]." Zaitsev ended his appeal with the following charge: "Leninin [*sic*] fought against capital, and you tell us to 'unite' but then force us to live for wages, to smoke, drink wine, and you don't pay any attention to orphans or widows—our life was much better before, because we believed in God."

In a collective petition to regional agricultural authorities later that August, the kommunary detailed how the new managers had "offended their religious feelings" by forcibly removing their icons and treated them "rudely" by swearing vilely at them and threatening that they would be expelled or even shot if they did not comply with their orders.[88] Like so many petitions sent by peasants to Kalinin or Stalin during the years of collectivization, they expressed faith that the higher authorities had their best interest in mind and would defend them from godless activists. But they were also quick to point out the hypocrisy of the authorities' claims—and, again like many peasants, denied the legitimacy of the kolkhoz imposed on them from above. They demanded that an investigatory commission be established and concluded by comparing their situation to a second serfdom (a tactic that would become widespread but was still rare in the summer of 1929):[89] "So it appears that neither they nor we want to work together," and "all their behavior suggests that they are not our comrades, but rather some kind of lord who does not want to work with us but rather rule over us," which is why the community's official seal was taken from the chairman of their soviet and given to the communist B. Rozov.[90] Ivan Tregubov signed the trezvenniki's petition as well, along with a note dated October 12, 1929, stating that the once prosperous commune had been "completely destroyed." "Almost all the members have fled, and in place of a friendly, sober, and upright life [now rules] chaos."[91]

Although well crafted, the kommunary's petitions had no visible impact on the liquidation process, which continued into harvest time. "Because this is a religious commune," they were repeatedly told, "it will be dissolved and a different, nonreligious commune will be set up in its place." All members were instructed to comply by joining and electing a new soviet, and their request for their old charter (reregis-tered in 1929) was denied.[92] On August 20, the new administrators, Rozov and Miliutin, put up a notice that everyone had to appear for work by 8:00 a.m. or they would not be allowed to work and therefore receive no food; those who refused would be given dried food supplies for two weeks and forced out. But these threats failed to influence most of the 250 or so members of the commune; only twenty complied, and the rest refused to work at all. The commune came to a standstill, in spite of the urgent need to tend to the harvest.

Although the new kolkhoz managed to attract around sixty new adults and their children, conditions were so poor that many left shortly thereafter.[93] In spite of the new management's claim that set wages would improve the kolkhozniki's standard of living, the new salaries totaling ₽24–60 per month amounted to far less than the ₽150 per month that the kommunary had been effectively making, and now the kolkhozniki had to pay for their food, clothes, sheets, and shoes. Rozov, the first manager of the kolkhoz "Trezvyi put'" recruited from Churikov's commune, responded to the reduction in wages by embez-zling ₽4,600 and all the clocks on the property (as Zaitsev had observed); he was taken to court and soon fired.[94]

The story of the BICh commune did not end well for anyone. The kolkhoz began a downward spiral, undergoing three name changes in less than three years, in an attempt to cover up its repeated failures. When Tregubov visited the following year, he found the whole place dominated by a "deadly silence."[95] In March 1930, shortly after Stalin's famous "dizzy with success" article, he petitioned the state on behalf of the trezvenniki, demanding that the "anti-Leninist mistakes" with respect to liquidating sectarian communes be corrected according to Bolshevik principles (*po-bol'shevistki*) and that Churikov and the trezvenniki be acknowledged as "communist-sectarians" (*sektanty-kommunisty*) rather than "sectarian proprietors" (*sektanty-sobstvenniki*). To this end, he offered a comprehensive account of the commune's achievements under Churikov, along with a detailed portrait of the kolkhoz's "agony" under the watch of "atheist-fanatics." In stark contrast to the clean, orderly buildings he had once found there, Tregubov reported, the kolkhoz was filthy and falling apart. All progress had been reversed; the electricity and heating systems were no longer operating, and the well was broken, so instead of spring water, the kolkhozniki—and the inhabitants of Vyritsa who had long benefited from the well—were forced to drink unhealthy water. Upon his arrival at the kolkhoz, he had been forced to wait in a dirty smoke-filled office full of *chinovniki* (officials), both local and from away, and then initially refused a visit, because he had not received permission through the proper channels. The kolkhoz, he quickly determined, was now "ruled by the office" at great and unnecessary expense to the government.[96] The administration's inefficiency was coupled by a lack of useful knowledge and experience, as well as vital equipment for workers. In short, nothing and nobody worked anymore.

Although Tregubov's petition had done a good job tapping into the Bolsheviks' pressing concerns around social hygiene, labor discipline, and rational management techniques,[97] like the many petitions sent in by Churikov's followers before, it too would fail to influence authorities. The fate of the commune had long been sealed.

The Final Appeals

In the months following Churikov's arrest, additional members of the trezvennik community were "purged" (arrested) and sent to Arkhangel'sk, Murmansk, Solovki, Central Asia, and the Urals.[98] Although the leadership of the commune and obshchina had already been arrested, another group of seventeen trezvenniki in the Leningrad area was "liquidated" following widespread protests after Churikov's arrest. According to a secret police report, the protestors were primarily "traders" and property owners (NEP men), organized under the leadership of Aleksei Fedorovich Novikov, who allegedly blamed "Jew-ish [*zhidovskii*] authorities" for persecuting Christians, labeled Soviet power the "Antichrist," and warned fellow trezvenniki away from unions and medical help.[99] "Little brothers" living outside the region also soon became targets. In September 1929, for example, the Kostroma paper *Severnaia Pravda* reported on the "unmasking" of twenty local "sectarian-activists" associated with Churikov, including three work-ers at the local "Lenin" factory. It was unconscionable, the article con-cluded, that this "bouquet of sectarians" had not lost their right to vote and continued to receive benefits (such as rations and housing) from Soviet institutions and organizations, even as they "conduct[ed] coun-terrevolutionary work against the social structure."[100] True or not, the charges clearly reflected widespread Bolshevik anxieties about trezven-nichestvo and its potential to live on even after Brother Ioann had been locked up and silenced.

In October 1929, six months after his arrest, Brother Ioann wrote to Soviet authorities from the Butyrskaia prison in Moscow, protesting his arrest on the grounds that he had served the Soviet state faithfully as a director of the commune, which had been in full compliance with local policies since its founding. Like many petitioners seeking offi-cial rehabilitation, Brother Ioann evidently understood the need "to assert a Soviet self," which included, most importantly, claims to be performing socially useful labor.[101] He offered the commune as "a liv-ing example" that the measures undertaken by the Soviet government had taken deep root in the "national field of labor" and were bearing "beautiful fruit for the benefit of the working people."[102] His definition of the "fruits" of that labor was left ambiguous, perhaps intentionally.

Ivan Tregubov was more specific with respect to Brother Ioann's "usefulness" in the multiple petitions he filed on his behalf. Pushing back on official attempts to brand Churikov as anti-Soviet or coun-terrevolutionary, he stressed his success at preaching socialist values as found in Scripture, curing people of their addictions, and raising the commune's agricultural productivity.[103] Rather than impoverished and exploited, he had found the commune members on BICh to be "completely free and happy." And while he personally did not like how some trezvenniki worshipped him, he rejected the claims that Brother Ioann was thought of as a "tsar" or "God" as 95 percent a lie (or only 5 percent true).[104] Even more boldly, Tregubov petitioned for Churikov's release on the grounds of his religious "genius." If Brother Ioann had been guilty of anything at all, he argued, it was only to bring about communism on a religious basis—a comment that suggests that he either did not yet understand this to be a problem or saw this as an opportune moment to voice his own protest as a Free Christian. Whatever the case, Tregubov's defense was spectacular. Churikov's entire movement, he argued, "should not be defamed, but scientifically studied, and Churikov himself should not be imprisoned, but put into a scientific laboratory corresponding to his activities."[105]

For their part, the trezvenniki were more careful and strategic in their claims. In May 1930, following the sentencing of Brother Ioann to three years of political isolation in Iaroslavl', 1,200 trezvenniki, identifying themselves as "workers in factories and plants in Leningrad," petitioned the local soviet chairman P. G. Smidovich requesting Churikov's release. "We do not find that he taught us anything counterrevolutionary," it declared; "on the contrary, for thirty-nine years he taught us according to the Gospel, to be sober, industrious, honest, and [responsible] workers in [the area of] production and in fulfilling the directives of Soviet power." They also noted how Churikov had given his "mental and physical" energy to their successful agricultural commune, which a government commission had valued at the sizeable sum of ₽300,000.[106]

Another petition seeking Brother Ioann's release, signed by 1,800 trezvenniki and directed to the procurator of the OGPU Katanian on October 20, 1930, offered four distinct arguments in Brother Ioann's defense. In addition to his usefulness to the state as a healer bringing "the dregs of society to a working life," it offered the trezvenniki's tax payments and voluntary service in the Red Army as evidence of their political loyalty. Moreover, they underlined Churikov's efforts to celebrate the "establishment" (*vodvorenie*) of Soviet power by preaching the people's "resurrection" thanks to "the late comrade Lenin." Employing an "our enemy's enemy is our friend" argument, they reminded Soviet authorities that it was *only* under Soviet power that Churikov had been freed after his persecution under Father Filosof Ornatskii (who had been shot for counterrevolutionary activities in 1918) and his supposed arrest by Aleksandr Kerensky acting on behalf of the Provisional Government in 1917. Finally, the trezvenniki appealed to the authorities' sense of humanity, arguing that to keep the now elderly Brother Ioann locked up was equal to a death sentence.[107]

The trezvenniki attached typed excerpts from two of Brother Ioann's final besedy to their petition. In the first, delivered on March 10, 1929, he denounced tsarist society as no better than Sodom and Gomorrah and framed the revolution as a day of judgment. After the old regime had been justifiably destroyed by "fire, by the sword, and by hunger," the poor of all nations were united according to Scripture, as Jesus had predicted. Again, as in the past, Churikov reiterated that although the current authorities do not acknowledge it, they are doing God's work and preparing the way for the kingdom by feeding the hungry and caring for the poor. In the second beseda, delivered on March 24, Brother Ioann had called his followers to continue to renounce drunkenness in the name of Jesus and to join in building the "social [sotsial'noe] kingdom based on the Gospels."[108] It is hard to say whether these prophecies were intended to convince Bolsheviks of Brother Ioann's loyalty to the socialist regime or, conversely, offered in protest as an assertion of their own continuing faith.

What is clear, however, is that many trezvenniki refused to concede to godlessness and embraced martyrdom instead. "We were ready for anything," youth leader Smolev recalled, "[and] ready to take any hits, with the knowledge of the absolute correctness of our sobriety [trezvogo dela]."[109] Recalling Churikov's final words, they meditated on "the sufferings of Christ, [and] persecution of His students and follower-Christians," in whose image they saw themselves. To prepare themselves emotionally for the struggles that lay ahead, they looked for comfort and courage not only in the Gospels, but also in the Cossack heroes of "Taras Bulba." In spite of their sometimes militant language, they pursued only nonviolent forms of protest, primarily collective petitioning and prayer. And when an older and beloved trezvennik by the name of Nikitin died, they used his funeral as an opportunity to demonstrate on behalf of sobriety, employing a tactic well known to revolutionary workers trying to gather legally during tsarist times. Although peaceful, the trezvenniki's protests would nonetheless serve as a justification for further persecution.[110] While Brother Ioann remained in prison, another wave of arrests occurred in May 1931, including Petr Terekhovich, who was incarcerated for eight months, followed by three years of exile in Kazakhstan.[111] Yet another round of arrests came in 1933. Faced with an impossible cycle of persecution, the trezvenniki would eventually be silenced—at least publicly, and only for a while.

When all was said and done, godless activists, local agricultural authorities, and OGPU agents—working independently and in tandem—had expended an extraordinary amount of time and energy investigating and justifying the decision to persecute the trezvenniki, who had earned a reputation as some of the most gentle, peaceful souls to walk the earth. Secret police files house copious materials documenting the youth activists' beliefs and activities, in an effort to prove anti-Soviet intent among them. Although the "trezvomol" had nowhere near the following or "organizational dynamism" of the so-called *Bapsomol*, and although their language was far more militant than their actions, Bolshevik authorities evidently worried about the sober activists' ability to compete with communist youth groups in their quest for converts to their version of faith. As Heather Coleman has observed with respect to Baptist youths who aspired to shape the future of Soviet power, it was precisely the "intertwining" of what Bolsheviks regarded as "incompatible identities" that troubled them most.[112] Indeed, in the context of the so-called "cultural revolution" that accompanied the building of socialism, the opposition between religious and socialist beliefs formed a key dimension of the class struggle that would lead to the victory of socialism.

Much like class warfare in the village, godless propagandists had from the early 1920s sought to undermine the trezvennik community's strength by pitting the "exploiter" Brother Ioann and his close circle against the sober rank and file—and then allying with the "exploited." Over time, propagandists working in tandem with agricultural bureaucrats on the ground developed the case against Brother Ioann around issues of exploitation and social justice in the commune. Following Eliashevich, a short book published in 1930 justified the commune's dissolution as an act of proletarian justice on account of its exploitation of "backward, ignorant people."[113] Yet, even as state authorities were cast as saviors of poor, ignorant, exploited trezvenniki, the process of "saving" them had exposed the contradictory moral choices at the heart of collectivization. The same officials who professed concern for the trezvennik families suffering on account of the commune's poor diets or inadequate medical care soon after desecrated their living spaces and subjected these same individuals to homelessness or exile on account of their beliefs. While this could be justified within a Stalinist framework, that mattered little to those, like the trezvennik Timofei Zaitsev, who shed some of the "many tears of the working class" after the communists took over their commune.[114]

By 1931, much of the world the trezvenniki had created in Vyritsa to that point had been destroyed and forever relegated to the realm of collective memory. But the persecutions of 1929–33 amounted to the end of a chapter, not the end of their story. To be sure, the Soviet assault was devastating. But expulsion from the ranks of the godless was of an entirely different order than the alienation from the Orthodox community they had experienced in 1914. And although we cannot know how many trezvenniki pursued different paths as a result of Soviet threats or arrests, prison letters and memoirs suggest that the experience of persecution often intensified the trezvenniki's commitment to their faith in holy sobriety and in Brother Ioann, much as it had under the tsar.

As Petr Terekhovich reflected in his memoir, he survived his incarceration and exile with the knowledge that secular authorities could control his body but not his soul, and like many religious believers at the time, he found the experience of repression on account of his faith cause to rejoice.[115] Letters written by the sestritsy from their exile in Perm reflected a similar willingness to embrace suffering on Brother Ioann's behalf.[116] While detailing the myriad physical, emotional, and psychological challenges of exile, the letters suggest that the women bore their sentences in the same spirit with which they had served him and holy sobriety up to that point—with humility, conviction in the rightness of their cause, and hope. Encouraged by trezvenniki still in Leningrad to remember the scriptural passage that "suffering produces perseverance; perseverance, character; and character, hope" (Romans 5:3–5),[117] they promised to carry on the work of holy sobriety. Likewise, the exiled Grusha reassured Brother Ioann in a letter that her spirit remained strong in the knowledge that "all is God's Will" and that if God had decided she needed to suffer in exile, then he could decide to bring her home too.[118] Knowing that her letters would likely be read by Soviet authorities, she also promised that his work would not be sacrificed to "oblivion," but would, like "lush shoots," continue to grow "everywhere."

Yet in spite of their continued faith in holy sobriety's ultimate victory over godlessness, and the powerful memories of their accomplishments in Vyritsa, in the short term the trezvenniki were left with a lot of questions. When, if ever, would Brother Ioann return from incarceration? What would happen if he did not? How would the experience of Soviet persecution impact holy sobriety moving forward?

CHAPTER 9

Promises of an Afterlife

Holy Sobriety after Brother Ioann's Death

In February 1931, Stalin summoned Brother Ioann from the prison cell where he had been held for almost two years. According to his bodyguard, Achmed Alma, the revolutionary leader was curious to meet a man who had been arrested even more times than he had.[1] As Stalin and the war minister Voroshilov entered the room, so the account goes, Brother Ioann greeted them with a raised cross and a back-handed blessing: "May the Devil lose his grip upon you." After two hours of interrogation, Churikov directly challenged Stalin: "all that you think is wrong," he announced, and "all that you do is false." He also warned that he would never be silenced. After Brother Ioann was taken away, Stalin labeled him a "freak" and promised to "find some way to wean him away from his delusions."

Alma's description of the encounter between Stalin—the supreme atheist, responsible for the deaths of millions, including many thousands of clergy—and Churikov, the now elderly yet still feisty man of God, was likely apocryphal. But it nonetheless offers a framework for characterizing the relationship between trezvenniki and the Soviet state for the next several decades. As Stalin threatened, he would try to silence Churikov's influence once and for all; Brother Ioann would be held in captivity until he died in 1933, one of countless believers to suffer for their convictions under Stalin's rule. Shortly before his death, godless curators at the newly opened Museum of the History of Religion and Atheism in the Kazan Cathedral in Leningrad hung his image in the "sectarian" exhibit, labelling him simply "charlatan."[2]

Meanwhile, Stalinist authorities continued to suppress all forms of public religious life by attacking clergy, closing and destroying churches, discriminating against believers in the workplace, and refusing to register faith-based groups. While religious leaders were especially vulnerable, persecution of the lay faithful was also harsh, if uneven and unpredictable. While some believers were targeted more than others, efforts to eradicate religion from socialist society were interrupted by moments of "pragmatic" accommodation—especially during the Great Patriotic War, when Stalin allowed a partial reconciliation between the state and the Orthodox Church in the interest of martialing the country's spiritual reserves against the German invasion. Another period of increased scrutiny and persecution followed in the late 1950s and early 1960s under Khrushchev.

Under the circumstances of official atheism, historian Irina Paert has observed, "all Christians had to become monks and nuns in the sense that in order to live in the new Soviet society they had to build invisible walls."[3] For some religious communities, including the True Orthodox, the demands of faith necessitated a total rejection of the secular world and therefore Soviet society.[4] For many believers, however, "living socialism" meant adapting to—and navigating through—the secular demands of Soviet life, especially work, while remaining true to their convictions and finding ways to nurture their religious and spiritual selves. This meant hiding their beliefs in public and retreating to private spaces whenever possible, in effect leading a double life. As the Orthodox believer V.Ia. Vasilev'skaia wrote, life "under the guidance" of her spiritual elder in Zagorsk, Father Serafim (Batiukov) in the 1930s–1940s brought her great peace and joy, but "the constant need to conceal and deceive lay heavily" on her.[5]

The trezvenniki had no choice but to reimagine their lives in the context of official atheism during the 1930s–1960s, and their community, beliefs, and practices would be shaped by both external and internal challenges. Survival was especially difficult for those who stayed in the Leningrad region given the pronounced secularization and surveillance of urban life there, as well as the trauma of the wartime siege, when Nazi troops occupied Vyritsa and some trezvenniki were sent into forced labor in Germany. But for all of Brother Ioann's followers, the single most disruptive and painful event of all was his physical departure, first as a result of his arrest in 1929, and then by his death in prison four years later. They "needed him as light, as air, as the sun," his devoted sestritsa Nina Maslova once remarked, and "without HIM they had an unthinkable life."[6]

As the sociologist Max Weber observed, the death of an individual spiritual leader typically signals a transitional moment within a faith from charismatic authority to a more institutionalized form.[7] In Churikov's case, however, the timing of his forced departure coincided with a rapid deinstitutionalization of all forms of public religious life, leading to both the disruption *and* eventually the strengthening of trezvennik communities. The rich legacy of texts, rituals, and memories Brother Ioann left behind helped to guide his followers as they moved on. For some, their Orthodox inheritance, including a tradition of prayer, fasting, icons, eldership, and veneration of the saints, continued to shape their beliefs and behaviors, but most of all they would be led forward into socialism by Scripture, especially as it had been interpreted by Brother Ioann in the texts he left behind, including his besedy and letters. Thus even as their sober identity left them marginalized and vulnerable to harassment and persecution, the trezvenniki's experience of "lived socialism" cannot be reduced to one of alienation, victimization, or opposition. The alleged confrontation between Brother Ioann and Stalin notwithstanding, their relationship to the socialist world around them was marked by conflict and accommodation, resistance and adaptation, repression and resilience.

Brother Ioann in Absentia

By the time of his arrest in spring 1929 Brother Ioann had been separated from his followers many times against his will. In addition to prolonged periods of official prohibition against contact with his followers, he had suffered incarceration in the mental asylum in 1898, another arrest and imprisonment in 1900, and years later, a life-threatening illness in 1923 that had kept him isolated from many of his followers for an extended period of time. Although these absences had been temporary, they had forced Churikov's devoted followers to contemplate what their lives would be like without him and to find ways to carry on the practice of holy sobriety in his absence. New preachers had emerged, his teachings had been disseminated, and smaller groups had become accustomed to meeting on their own. In short, they had already become adept at what Tamara Dragadze has described as the "domestication" of religious life under Soviet communism, by which believers relocated religious practices from public to private spaces (usually apartments), and allowed individual believers (typically, "elders") to take over the role of preaching and spiritual advising.[8]

Nonetheless, the simultaneous and violent disruption of the BICh commune and the broader sober community would be profoundly disorienting for quite some time. Adding to the trezvenniki's sense of confusion and suffering after 1929 was the mystery surrounding Brother Ioann's disappearance. Likely in an effort to forestall protest, Soviet authorities suppressed the news of his death in prison on October 8, 1933. Word of his demise would trickle out slowly to the scattered community, but the mystery of his final days lasted until the 1980s, when his official rehabilitation by Soviet authorities gave hope for real answers; more concrete information came only with the opening of police archives in the 1990s, however. In the meantime, the disappearance of Brother Ioann's body precluded the possibility of a proper funeral and burial for a man adored by so many, as well as any kind of physical shrine or relics as a site or means of worship. Later the trezvenniki would compensate for their loss by visiting surrogate sites of mourning, including Churikov's father's grave, as well as that of his longtime spiritual confidante, sestritsa Grusha.[9]

To fill the void of information at the time of Brother Ioann's disappearance, his followers circulated rumors and consoling myths that both reflected and confirmed their beliefs. One story was that Brother Ioann had been much loved in prison and won over many people there, including the prison head, whose wife Churikov had allegedly brought back from a stupefied state. As rumor held, the director had arrived at the prison one morning to discover that Brother Ioann was no longer there and that no one had any information about what had happened to him—as if to suggest that he had managed to escape or, perhaps, disappeared miraculously.[10] One possible explanation was that the episode was an official fabrication trying to hide the fact that Churikov had died or been transferred, but the implication was that Brother Ioann had escaped to a better place—or been resurrected, like Christ.

Given the value followers had typically placed on his presence, including his gentle, penetrating eyes and physical touch, Brother Ioann's absence was no doubt experienced as a profound loss for many. Yet, the same tendency to endow him with saintlike qualities meant that his physical death did not necessarily present an obstacle to his continued presence in their lives, since it represented a transformation rather than an end of their relationship.[11] This tendency was also reinforced by (and related to) the Orthodox tradition in which many had grown up, especially the intimate relationships they imagined with the saints.[12] Along these lines, the godless writer Pavel Petrov reported in 1929, some followers had acquired clippings of his hair and nails (presumably as relics) while he was still alive.[13]

The impact of Brother Ioann's arrest and imprisonment had been magnified by the forced closing of the BICh commune, after which many trezvenniki found themselves in prison or exile for the better part of ten years. Those who managed to avoid arrest were cast out into the street and denied a passport, making it impossible for them to stay and work in the city where their families lived.[14] Those scattered to remote corners where the godless presence was thin were relatively lucky and able to live more freely; for example, an elderly, kind, and well-educated "churikovets" in the Molvotitsii region in Novgorod province came to enjoy a remarkable degree of respect among his fellow villagers.[15] For the many trezvenniki who remained in more urban areas, however, the eyes of the godless (activists, authorities, and ordinary citizens) were far more ubiquitous, especially in the 1930s. In this context, visibility became a distinct liability and meeting in private the norm.

Lidia Konstantinovna Gavrilova (then, Skvortsova) was only sixteen years old when the commune was liquidated. Although she was not especially visible within the community at the time of the mass arrests, her status remained fragile, and she too suffered a close call with the authorities. While working at the commune, she and her mother had attended Brother Ioann's besedy, sometimes with a male friend who, unbeknownst to them, was also employed by the secret police. When he learned that the police had started a file on them, he tried to convince the women to deny Brother Ioann, lest they too be arrested. They refused but in the end escaped arrest nonetheless, for reasons that Skvortsova interpreted as more than "luck." First, the agent in charge of their case was arrested himself before he could follow up. Then, when she again refused to renounce Churikov in exchange for a much-coveted passport, another family friend with clout stepped in on her behalf and recommended that she be allowed to go free and be given a passport.[16] Brother Ioann had protected her, Skvortsova believed, because she had protected him.

Entering into close relationships with nontrezvennik individuals after the repressions quickly became challenging. While it was usually

possible to hide one's identity in public and at work, the urban housing crisis in the 1930s and 1940s meant that trezvenniki found themselves in difficult living arrangements with people who did not respect
their beliefs or way of life. For example, one trezvennitsa shared a small
room with another single woman in a communal apartment; when
the roommate discovered that she believed in God and abstained from
meat and alcohol, she relentlessly taunted her, calling her a "crazy person" and "sectarian." She also started smoking on her bed just to upset
her. When the woman began threatening that the trezvennitsa should
be "burn[ed] at the stake!" concerned neighbors stepped in. Although
it is unclear whether the roommate genuinely cared about the trezvennitsa's beliefs or whether her goal was to get the room to herself, even
the simple practice of praying or fasting could result in accusations
that the trezvenniki were imposing their beliefs on others in communal
spaces.[17] Whatever the case, when the trezvennitsa managed to escape
the woman's taunting by securing a space of her own, she attributed
the miraculous feat to Brother Ioann.[18]

School was another difficult context, since young members of the
trezvennik community often encountered ridicule from teachers and
students alike. In spite of the potential risks, some nonetheless professed their beliefs openly, even defiantly, well into the 1930s. Elena
Lappo (born in 1917) was the daughter of a struggling boot maker who
became one of Brother Ioann's followers after overcoming his drinking problem. His wife soon identified as a trezvennitsa as well, so they
brought up their daughter accordingly. Raised to read the Gospel and
the lives of the saints and to respect holy sobriety, Elena refused to
participate in sports, sing secular songs, or watch films in school in
the 1930s. When confronted by her teachers, she revealed that Brother
Ioann had taught her that these were inappropriate behaviors. In
response, they smirked and ridiculed Churikov for living with unmarried women and for wearing a "silk shirt," to which she replied that he
also wore chains and "suffered for the people."[19] While pointing out
that she was "a very good girl, better than the others," they asked her
why she believed in God—to which she replied, "I am better than others,
because I know God." Proclaiming that she was personally "against the
[secular] authorities," because "all authority is from God," she challenged their right to question her beliefs. While such confrontations
further isolated her, they also likely strengthened her identity as a trezvennitsa. Although she was able to finish high school, Elena's boldness
soon caught up with her; in 1938, while living in the working-class

district along the Obvodnyi canal and working as a furrier, she was arrested—along with her mother—and exiled from Leningrad.[20]

Records of trezvennik activity in the first two decades following Brother Ioann's death are unfortunately scarce, but traces of their continued prayers and meetings can be seen in a small collection of "petitions" they scribbled on the back of blank factory forms dating from 1930 (so, after his arrest). With Brother Ioann no longer there to receive their petitions, they penned them instead to their "Brothers and Sisters," and asked for collective prayers to be said on their behalf.[21] The trezvennik community remained fragmented through the 1930s, and many of those who returned from prison or exile were subject to rearrest; after completing his initial sentence around 1930–31, for instance, Ivan Smolev was immediately sentenced to ten more years of exile with his family.[22] In 1936, sestritsa Grusha (Agrippina Smirnova) was arrested for the third time, along with eight other trezvenniki, and sent to Aktobe, a camp for the elderly, disabled citizens. She soon fell ill and, after suffering paralysis, died on November 23, 1939. Someone managed to bury her in a coffin, which was almost unheard of for exiles at the time.[23]

The widespread fluidity of the labor market made relocation a common practice as well. As part of a cleansing process led by the secret police, almost eighty thousand people were denied passports in the first eight months of 1933, mostly for being "kulaks," but some for their religious views.[24] The war further disrupted the trezvennik community, especially when the German army occupied Vyritsa and Leningrad was put under siege for nine hundred days. While some trezvenniki served in the Red Army to fight the fascists, others were sent into forced labor in Germany.

Not unlike the period of mass arrests in the late 1920s and early 1930s, the war both disrupted the trezvenniki's collective practices and intensified their "spiritual hunger."[25] Although the postwar period was one of continued deprivation, it was also one of increased public religious practice among the Orthodox, following Stalin's partial reconciliation with the Church in 1943. To be clear, the situation was still dangerous for religious believers, especially "sectarians." After surviving an arrest in 1929, the trezvennik Varfolomei Plotnikov, for example, was arrested again in 1948 under Article 58 (anti-Soviet activity) and sentenced to twenty-five years.[26] In spite of the risks, trezvenniki began to look for one another to reconstitute some form of faith community. Among them was Ivan Smolev, who settled in Gatchina and worked as a factory superintendent after serving in the Red Army from 1941 to 1946. As one of Brother Ioann's oldest and most devoted followers and a former youth group leader, he took up this role naturally and began to gather people, often just a few at a time, for spiritual conversations.[27] Other trezvenniki did the same, and over time more small communities formed, scattered like a sober archipelago across the northwestern region of the Soviet Union.

As with many faith groups during the Soviet era,[28] the biological family remained the single most important site for the sharing and spreading of sober beliefs; while not all individuals born into trezvennik families embraced holy sobriety, many did. This had been true before the revolution and in the 1920s too, but the added degree of marginalization after Churikov's death intensified the tightly knitted nature of local communities. Children would play together, grow up together, and some would even marry one another, leading to multigenerational families. Indeed, the post-Stalin communities would include many of the children of Churikov's contemporaries, since it was typically the case that second-generation trezvenniki followed their parents' sobriety and were raised with a deep respect for Brother Ioann. Consequently, the fifth generation of a trezvennik family is still practicing in St. Petersburg today.[29] If a trezvennik married outside the sober community, the new spouse was expected to embrace a sober lifestyle—or at the very least, tolerate it completely. When they did not, the situation often led to conflict. As one couple testified, the fact that the husband was an "active worker [on behalf] of the Soviet Union" and the wife was an "active worker [on behalf of] Churikov" made it impossible for them to "get along," so they divorced.[30]

Vyritsa, a site of sobriety and the place where Churikov had lived and worked for decades, remained a kind of mecca for Brother Ioann's followers, especially for those who had known him personally. Although returning could be legally difficult, some trezvenniki tried to resettle there after their period of exile or incarceration or after the war. As if to suggest that the trezvenniki's absence was unnatural in the years after Brother Ioann's arrest and the destruction of the commune, rumors—especially powerful in a society where information was controlled and manipulated from above—spread that the land had grown infertile, just as it had been before they had arrived in 1905. Many believers imagined that God had punished the godless for their destructive behaviors; as the historian A. Beglov has observed, the idea that the natural environment was reflecting divine judgment—in this case, on behalf of Brother Ioann—was not uncommon in the Soviet era.[31] For this reason, the poverty of the place might have actually made Vyritsa even more meaningful to trezvenniki. Either way, the fact that Brother Ioann and his followers had prayed there for so many years likely contributed to its identification as a sacred place, in the same way that other Orthodox pilgrim sites were thought to be *namolennye*—that is, made more holy by the many prayers of the faithful that had been made there.[32]

The presence of the popular elder Father Serafim (Murav'ev) in Vyritsa between his release from prison in 1933 and his death in 1949 was another draw; according to Klavdia Vasil'evna Sedova, who grew up in a family devoted to Brother Ioann, many trezvenniki turned to Serafim for healing prayers in Brother Ioann's absence. In her own experience, devotion to one enhanced the other. Although she did not identify fully as a trezvennitsa and worked as a medic though the war (a profession Brother Ioann would have frowned upon), she nonetheless returned to Vyritsa for spiritual support many times. In her words, "Every second [of my medical career] I felt the aid of these two great startsy [Churikov and Serafim], and their concern about everything."[33] How typical her experience was is hard to say, but according to Irina Paert, there was "a surge of lay interest in elders in Soviet society" for many of the same reasons as before 1917, especially health concerns or a need for psychological support.[34] Given the people's thirst for spiritual guidance, Serafim's presence enhanced Vyritsa's reputation as a special place, while doing nothing to detract from the faith that Brother Ioann's followers had in him.

Texts, Ritual, and Community in the 1940s–1960s

After Brother Ioann's death—and to this day—the weekly prayer meeting (beseda) remained a powerful ritual through which to express and cultivate a sober identity, for both individuals and communities. Compared to the mass meetings held when Brother Ioann was alive, postwar gatherings were by far smaller and more intimate. But the pattern he established continued: his followers would set aside several hours each Sunday afternoon to privilege their spiritual selves and to open themselves up to prayer and scriptural enlightenment. Instead of engaging in more common weekend activities such as sports, movies, or housework, trezvenniki would dress in nice clothes and gather before icons and a large portrait of Brother Ioann to pray, sing religious hymns, testify, and most importantly, reflect together on scriptural passages and Brother Ioann's teachings.

While *obshchenie* (communion) with Brother Ioann had typically meant experiencing the gift of his presence, even before his death the authorities' multiple attempts to limit his contact with his followers, combined with the challenges of distance, had forced his followers to engage with him through a variety of written means. This included reading and reciting his besedy and corresponding by petition, note, or letter. After his death, however, Brother Ioann's written texts took on even greater importance, as his followers naturally looked to them for the kind of moral and spiritual instruction and comfort that he had provided while alive. Copies of Brother Ioann's written works could be hard to obtain after the war, however, so longtime trez-venniki took the lead in tracking them down and restoring Brother Ioann's spiritual inheritance. Others devoted themselves to making copies by hand.

Testimonies suggest that Brother Ioann's texts took on their own sacred quality in the postwar period, serving not only as spiritual nour-ishment but also as a vital means of communion. In 1958, for example, Ivan Smolev shared with a circle of trezvennik friends a find from the archives of the Leningrad public library, an account of one of Churikov's besedy from January 1910, which he had personally attended at the age of nine. In Smolev's retelling, the reading "resurrected in each soul the dear image of Brother Ioann and the spiritual peace [found] in Broth-er's hall,"[35] bringing the community together through shared joy and grief. The reading also fostered Smolev's reputation as a living link to Brother Ioann.

To elude suspicion and possible arrest, the trezvenniki's Sunday meetings were usually held in a private apartment and on the pretext of a birthday. They were off limits to outsiders, but newcomers were welcome if accompanied by a sponsor. After the more formal part of the meeting, the trezvenniki would break for tea and conversation, just as Brother Ioann had done. The gatherings went on for hours, without regard to time or the schedules that dominated everyday life. As in the past, the trezvenniki remained highly ascetic—fasting from alcohol and meat—but after the beseda they allowed themselves the opportunity to indulge a bit in shared fruits, sweets, and baked goods. In line with Brother Ioann's emphasis on modesty, the spread was never extrava-gant; on the contrary, it was intentionally simple so that none of the trezvenniki—even the poorest—would feel embarrassed by their lack of means and thus unable to host. And during fasts, there was typically only a loaf of bread with tea, sugar, and jam on the table. The sharing of food of any kind, especially in the lean postwar years, was an act of generosity and nurturing.

A truly non-Soviet space, the weekly gatherings offered trezvenniki a site of *bytie* (spiritual being) rather than *byt* (everyday life), and of community and *communitas*. Referring to each other as "brothers" and "sisters," the trezvenniki tended to think of the sober community as a "spiritual family," descended from Brother Ioann and bonded together by shared beliefs and a common experience.[36] "God has no leaders," claimed V. Stepkina; "[he] who knows faith better, then speaks. All Christians are equal before God. And we have one spiritual master, dear brother."[37] New leaders or elders nonetheless emerged within the community after Brother Ioann's disappearance, and the patriarchal structure that had reigned both on the colony and in the commune also remained intact. Although some individual women were highly respected within the community, with few exceptions men led gatherings even when women dominated numerically.

Community leaders tended to be those who had been part of Brother Ioann's inner circle—that is, those to whom he had regularly turned for help and advice. Some had been preachers in their own right, led youth circles in the 1920s, or lived on the commune. And in the Stalin years, most had suffered arrest(s) and imprisonment or exile. According to Olena Panych, within the Evangelical Christian-Baptist community the experience of faith-based repression during the Soviet era almost automatically gave an individual special authority and was often a path to leadership.[38] For trezvenniki, however, the criteria were somewhat different. On the one hand, the experience of prison or exile tended to intensify the faith of those who survived, and this in turn increased the likelihood that they would serve as role models upon their return; thus, those who suffered in prison or exile were accorded a great deal of respect within the local communities.[39] On the other hand, in terms of leadership potential, an individual's personal acquaintance with Brother Ioann in his lifetime mattered at least as much as, if not more than, their identity as a martyr.

Those who had once known Brother Ioann personally, or "in the flesh"—whether male or female—were accorded a special status in the community and served as links to him through their personal experience. This included Ivan Smolev and Petr Terekhovich, for example, and Nina Maslova. Yet even Smolev, who was said to have "replaced" Brother Ioann, did so only as a son takes on the responsibilities of the father after he dies.[40] In other words, he devoted himself to carrying on his legacy, not taking his place. To be sure, elders could wield a significant amount of influence and authority, especially when it came to interpreting Brother Ioann's written legacy. But for the most part, they assumed a kenotic posture toward the community, much as Brother Ioann had, devoting themselves to serving the needs of others rather than aspiring to positions of power. The smaller they made themselves, the bigger Brother Ioann's image loomed.

Of course, the criteria for one's status in the community would naturally change over time, as the older generation of trezvenniki died off in the 1960s and 1970s. Although no single factor determined leadership potential, a new common marker of an individual's place in the community was the number of years they had been sober.[41] V. Glinskii, the leader of the Petersburg trezvenniki, for example, embraced sobriety as a young boy in the 1960s, following his alcoholic father's suicide. After leading the community to petition for Brother Ioann's rehabilitation in the late 1980s, he continued to serve in his leadership role until his death in April 2021. Revered at the end of his life for his kindness, wisdom, and big-heartedness, Glinskii was known above all for his devotion to God and selfless leadership.[42]

While these same qualities, especially piety and humility, were characteristic of other elders as well, the leader of the trezvennik community in Vyritsa in the post-Soviet period, Aleksei Sinnikov, cut a different profile. Born in 1912, Sinnikov moved to Leningrad in 1930—the year after Brother Ioann's final arrest—so the two never met in person. After working in construction, managing a store, and fighting at the front, he came to holy sobriety in the late 1940s. By the 1970s, however, he had established his own reputation as an elder possessing unique spiritual insight, capable of both healing and prophesizing. For these reasons, Sinnikov was the only elder considered by some trezvenniki to be Brother Ioann's spiritual successor; in fact, some go so far as to believe that he was Brother Ioann returned.[43] While his example reflects a continuing desire for charismatic healers and prophets as well as the need for a leader in the flesh, his legacy among the trezvenniki is hotly contested to this day. He might therefore best be seen as the exception that proves the rule of Brother Ioann's irreplaceability.

Soviet-Era Testimonies and the Sober Imagination

Among their many roles, sober elders regularly encouraged people to testify to Brother Ioann's impact on their lives, even after his death. As discussed in chapter 3, prerevolutionary trezvenniki tended to share their personal stories with several goals in mind: to express gratitude; to assert their commitment to sober values; to speak to potential converts outside the community; and to speak *for* the community by protecting Brother Ioann from his critics. These same patterns would continue to a greater or lesser extent after Brother Ioann's death, but with three differences. First, given the extreme realities of Soviet repression, bearing witness usually involved sharing one's story with a small circle of trusted people, often in conditions of great risk. Second, for those who had known Brother Ioann, testifying was also an exercise in active remembering and, as in Smolev's case, fostering communion with him. Third, the recording of testimonies acquired a new kind of sacred purpose as they became part of a grander narrative of Brother Ioann's life and influence and, therefore, a constituent part of his legacy.

Some stories with a moral purpose were told over and over—like parables. In the late 1950s, for example, the feldsher Il'ia Moiseevich Moiseev recounted the healing of the paralyzed sailor and atheist Androsov who had been saved from paralysis and thoughts of suicide in the 1920s, a story that spoke both to Brother Ioann's ability to heal body and soul and to the power of faith over medicine and atheism.[44] Also popular was the cautionary tale of the former trezvennik Dmitrii Danilovich Losev, who had been one of Brother Ioann's most visible and respected followers before the revolution. In 1918, he became one of the leaders of the commune, but as he became more successful, he lost his humility and began to drift away from sobriety. Eventually, he lost his battle against alcoholism as well.[45]

In the 1960s, as the community aged, a number of the elders took on the task of collecting and recording trezvennik testimonies; these included the former youth activists Petr Terekhovich, Ivan Smolev, and Elena Feliksovna Liadova, who had identified as a trezvennitsa since 1922 and been very active in the Leningrad youth circle, Rassvet, until her arrest in the early 1930s.[46] Another was Nina Maslova who had served as a secretary on the commune in the late 1920s.[47] Most testimonies were delivered orally and recorded anonymously, likely in an effort to protect the speaker from discrimination or persecution, and then circulated in self-published (*samizdat*) form. Some were longer and more personal, but many were extremely brief and episodic. In fact, Liadova left out notebooks for followers in Vyritsa to record their recollections of Brother Ioann as they wished; in all, their memories—which included episodes, predictions, snippets of conversations, and quotes (from Brother Ioann and Scripture)—filled eight volumes, organized completely randomly in terms of theme, context, and chronology.[48] Although most entries were anonymous, one senses an inclination on the part of the witnesses not only to document Brother Ioann's life and teachings, but also to inscribe themselves in his sacred path and, by extension, to write themselves (sometimes anonymously) into the history of the sober movement. Lacking the cathartic quality that often characterized oral testimony, they have a more meditative quality, as if timeless notes written to posterity, or to God. Together, however, the recollections prove greater than the sum of their parts, producing an image of Brother Ioann not necessarily as he was (or even wanted to be), but rather as his followers wanted to remember him.

The trezvennik Sergei Palamodov, who has spent the last few decades documenting an accurate history of Brother Ioann's life, warns that testimonies collected during the Soviet era need to be approached carefully, since there are clear distortions and falsifications.[49] At least two factors contribute to the problem. The first relates to the ideological and militantly secular nature of official Soviet history, and the way in which personal or private histories offered a non-Soviet space in which individuals had almost limitless agency to tell their stories and craft the terms of their own identities. At the same time, the broader Soviet tendency to privilege ideological over factual or empirical truth might have further contributed to the (mis)shaping of individual memories. The second and even more significant source of distortion stemmed from the desire of some of Brother Ioann's followers to offer evidence of his divinity. While this was also the case before his death, the tendency toward mythologization of his identity was even more pronounced among later generations, the result of both changes in trezvennik belief and again, perhaps, the fluidity of truth in the Soviet era.[50] Yet, in spite of these caveats and limitations, the testimony collections were a rare exercise in the sober imagination, illuminating the spectrum of ideas and experiences associated with Brother Ioann.

To a great extent, testimonies gathered after 1933 reveal patterns of belief and behaviors similar to those seen while Brother Ioann was still physically alive: they document his ability to heal, to protect individuals from illness and harm, to predict the future, and to "know" what others could not. Common themes include Brother Ioann's response to illness, historical events, life on the commune, and problems of everyday life. Many also have a moral lesson to share, as if passing down the kind of advice that Brother Ioann was known to give—comforting at times and reproachful at others. Most of all, they attest to the widespread tendency of his followers to look for evidence of Brother Ioann's continuing presence in their lives at every turn, and especially during times of confusion or crisis, illness or accident.

According to Ia. V. Plotnikov, for example, when Brother Ioann's sestritsy came back to Vyritsa in 1932 after their arrest and period of exile, they did not have permission to stay. But because the husband of a trezvennitsa, Vera Krasovskaia, was a party member and vouched for them, they were allowed to live there.[51] Rather than recognizing this gesture as a form of *blat* or a matter of luck, they believed that it was a sign that the Lord had intervened on their behalf. Likewise, when the trezvennitsa Anna Ivanovna Kuznetsova was finally able to secure a living situation in Vyritsa, she too insisted that her good fortune, "without complications and without *blat*," was due solely to the many collective prayers made by other trezvenniki on her behalf.[52] Such claims were not uncommon; on the contrary, the trezvenniki's tendency to attribute to Brother Ioann all good things and outcomes—from decent housing and food rations to the avoidance of all kinds of catastrophe—was so widespread throughout the Soviet era that it routinely drew the chagrin of secular authorities, who thought that "man" (i.e., the Soviet state), and not God, deserved all the credit for people's welfare.[53] Even after his death, trezvennik testimonies suggest, Brother Ioann was doing more good work in the socialist world—finding people housing, curing their illness, keeping them safe—than all the workers in the massive Soviet bureaucratic network put together.

Indeed, faith in Brother Ioann's continuing protection was what defined some trezvenniki; remarkably, this was true even for those who joined the community after his death. The difference between trezvenniki and other people, one woman explained, was that while others experienced "troubles, sorrows, and difficulties," in life, "for us trezvenniki everything strangely turns out somehow, everything [works out] on its own."[54] They were, in other words, not only uniquely blessed, but "chosen." Yet at the same time, Brother Ioann helped even people he did not know. A young convert by the name of Gavril Andreevich was suffering from throat cancer when he asked an older trezvennitsa how to approach Brother Ioann since "he is no longer here." She instructed him to write a note and ask for his healing. "It is impossible to take him from the people," she explained. "His Body is no longer with us [but] He will always be present among us in spirit—like Christ." She further instructed him to pray with a pure heart, and then to light the note on fire and scatter it to the wind.[55]

For most trezvenniki, engagement with Brother Ioann's written works was a constant preoccupation, and not only on Sundays. It also took different forms. As Vladimir Glinskii recalled, one trezvennitsa painstakingly embroidered a white tablecloth with scriptural sayings and quotes from Brother Ioann, and then gifted the precious cloth to his family; from then on it covered their table on all celebratory occasions, reminding them of both Brother Ioann's teachings and the woman's exemplary devotion.[56] A more common practice was to devote one's free time to copying besedy by hand for hours at a time, or annotating a Bible with Brother Ioann's comments. Both exercises encouraged the individual writer to engage deeply with his words and teachings, while also providing a service to others. As in politically dissident circles at the time, the ritualized practice of reproducing and spreading texts considered subversive likely played a role in bonding the trezvennik community as well.[57]

While all trezvenniki looked to Brother Ioann's writings as a source of enlightenment, however, some came to attribute them with additional meaning and power, as in the case of an alcoholic who claimed to have been cured "by Brother's word" after attending trezvennik meetings.[58] Unfortunately, as this example suggests, the type of power assigned to Churikov's words is often ambiguous in the sources: did the alcoholic believe that Brother Ioann's words had saved him by convincing him to embrace sobriety, or did he ascribe healing power to the words themselves? What is clear, however, is that for those followers who believed in his divinity, Brother's word was the Word of God. In fact, among their descendants in Vyritsa today, Maria Masagutova has found that "Churikov's sermons relate to Scripture in the same way that the figure of Churikov itself [relates] to the figure of Christ—as the same thing, but renewed."[59] Exactly when this belief took root or how widespread it might have become is difficult to determine.

Although less important than his words, Brother Ioann's image remained an object of reverence as well; his followers hung his portrait on their apartment walls near their icons, displayed it at prayer meetings, and wore it around their necks or carried it in their pockets.[60] Many trezvenniki also wore znachki (pins, badges, or brooches) featuring one of a trilogy of images that spoke to the different aspects of his mission—Churikov battling the snake of drunkenness, holding out a Bible in his hands, or standing amid stalks of wheat on the commune.[61]

Followers ascribed different powers to Brother Ioann's image, includ-ing the power to heal and protect, not unlike a saint's relic. One trez-vennitsa, for example, confessed to holding Brother Ioann's image to her cheek after scalding herself with boiled milk; although she claimed to know that the various material objects (such as the flasks of oil) that Brother Ioann had handed out were not in themselves effective in the healing process, she nonetheless took some comfort in holding the image to her cheek.[62] Another woman who had struggled to get sober told how she was finally able to secure a job simply by showing her prospective employer a brooch with Brother Ioann's image on it.[63] Although the employer likely saw the image as a sign of her potential as a sober worker, the trezvennitsa clearly invested the image with less rational powers. In an even more dramatic case, several women claimed that they had miraculously survived the German bombing of Lenin-grad because of Brother Ioann's image. While many trezvenniki (includ-ing those who had served at the front) believed that Brother Ioann had kept them alive during the war, the women's claim was more literal: his image had protected them because they held it up in the air as they walked the streets during the bombings.[64]

In contrast to the copious and highly visible amounts of Soviet swag devoted to celebrated leaders and heroes, images of Brother Ioann were usually hidden from public view for fear of attracting negative atten-tion. While employers typically valued trezvenniki as reliable workers and were therefore willing to overlook their religious beliefs,[65] those who dared to expose themselves as believers in the workplace could face serious consequences, ranging from ridicule and ostracization to demotion, dismissal, or even arrest.[66] Thus many hid their relationship to Brother Ioann from their coworkers very carefully. As mentioned, this was not an uncommon reality for many people who held alterna-tive beliefs in the Soviet era; "subcultures survived by means of dissimu-lation," Oleg Kharkhordin has observed, "a minimal demonstration of loyalty at work, in the guise of an obedient member of the kollektiv, satisfied both the regime and the individual."[67]

But the decision to conceal one's identity as a trezvennik remained a difficult one, since hiding was thought to be a potentially dangerous betrayal of Brother Ioann's memory, and of the transparency between life and faith that was central to a sober identity. For example, a young widowed trezvennitsa claimed that before her husband's untimely death, he had been a good, sober factory worker, devoted to Brother Ioann. But when he was promoted from the factory floor to an office position at the forestry exchange on the Obvodnyi canal, he was afraid to hang Churikov's image openly for fear that administrators would not approve. So he hid the image behind a shelf instead. Soon afterward, he fell ill and started drinking again, and then died. His wife's testimony suggests a belief that his rapid and unexpected demise was punishment for hiding either his sober identity or Brother Ioann's image—possibly both. Either way, the image was central to the way she made sense of her husband's misfortune.[68]

Many Soviet-era testimonies also continued the tradition of documenting Brother Ioann's prophetic powers, suggesting that people continued to derive comfort from a belief in his ability to know the future.[69] Some testified that he had forecast events occurring long after his death, inspiring hope that his other long-term forecasts (for example, that someday everyone would become sober) might also come true.[70] Other testimonies circulated about the dangers of not heeding Brother Ioann's predictions.[71]

Pushing back on a culture officially devoted to rational and scientific explanations of phenomena, trezvennik testimonies repeatedly affirmed their belief in the miraculous—the inexplicable as well as the irrational—and thus an acceptance of the limits of human understanding. To ordinary humans, the world was a mysterious and largely unknowable place, the trezvennik A. Kozlov told a Soviet researcher: "The Lord has many secrets. They are revealed through human affairs, but only as it pleases God, and people cannot find out why."[72] Related to Brother Ioann's rejection of medical authority, the retelling of prophetic stories in the context of Soviet authoritarianism (both scientific and ideological) was itself a form of resistance, if not subversion—that is, a way of undermining the experts (or "pharisees") and the various powers-that-be.

While offering a way to understand a world of uncertainty in a meaningful way, belief in mystery and the miraculous also reassured trezvenniki that secular authorities were less powerful and less permanent than they thought they were. Indeed, some trezevnniki believed that those who claimed to know too much would be punished for their arrogance. During a serious drought in the late 1950s or 1960s, for example, older trezvenniki circulated a letter written by Brother Ioann explaining that all misfortunes and natural disasters were a punishment for state-driven efforts to control nature by secular means.[73] In this same spirit, the trezvennik A. Skachenkov allegedly advised others to turn off the radio when the widely celebrated space mission was being broadcast, claiming, "This is of no interest to us. The sputniki fly high, but the science of Christ [*nauka Khrista*] flies higher."[74] Like Brother Ioann, the trezvenniki remained deeply suspicious of the proponents of modern science; while they acknowledged the value of certain innovative technologies, especially those that lessened the need for human labor, they stressed the dangers of science in the hands of those who ignored God's will—as evidence, they pointed to the massive human losses caused by the atomic bomb.[75]

Divided Legacy, Divided Community

During Brother Ioann's lifetime, the trezvennik community had been divided into roughly three concentric circles, defined by the closeness of the individual's personal relationship with him or by the degree to which they embraced holy sobriety in their daily lives. These distinctions continued to exist in the postwar period, even as tensions between insiders (believers) and outsiders (nonbelievers) naturally reaffirmed the boundary *around* trezvennik communities. Because of the generally repressive conditions of Soviet life, the personal networks (*sviazi*) among members of each trezvennik community served as important sources of knowledge as well as spiritual and material support. Given the trezvennik community's physical fragmentation, semiclandestine status, and lack of coherent leadership, it was inevitable that a degree of fluidity in practice and belief would emerge after Brother Ioann's death. This was especially the case with respect to issues that had been subjects of debate when he was alive, including the question of whether or not to seek out medical care,[76] the nature and extent of engagement with the Orthodox clergy and sacramental life,[77] and the acceptability of reading secular papers or participating in other secular forms of leisure.[78] Curiously, these differences did not always map neatly onto the older distinctions within the community— for example, elders who had known Brother Ioann personally might disagree on any given issue. The politics of each local community appear to have mattered more.

As discussed in earlier chapters, even during his natural lifetime Brother Ioann struggled to control his own message and to curb some of the more extreme interpretations of his identity and authority. After his death, his identity became even more a product of interpretation, mystery, and imagination. A trezvennitsa's claim that an "invisible force" had lifted her body from train tracks just as a train was approaching—as if to suggest that Brother Ioann had rescued her from beyond the grave—was but one example of his vulnerability to mythologization.[79] Another was the claim that he had once fixed a broken tractor on the commune by means of prayer alone, and then turned around to save a train from crashing—as if he were a hybrid of two ideal types, the (religious) miracle worker and the (socialist) Stakhanovite.[80]

By far the most important—and the most divisive—issue within the postwar trezvennik community was the question of Brother Ioann's relationship to God. As discussed, the clergy had voiced concerns about the trezvenniki's deification of Brother Ioann as early as the 1890s. And in response Churikov had repeatedly admonished his followers for glorifying him. While his reproaches had little effect, many trezvenniki nonetheless revered him as a righteous person and a saintlike figure, "our protector before God,"[81] but not God himself. This included Nina Maslova, who considered Brother Ioann divinely inspired—that is, uniquely touched by God, like a prophet or a saint—but still accepted his humanity. Nonetheless, in the absence of oversight by either the Orthodox clergy or Brother Ioann throughout most of the Soviet period, the belief that Brother Ioann was "God in the flesh," the Second Coming of Christ, took deep root within the trezvennik community. Although some followers had insisted on deifying Brother Ioann even during his lifetime, belief in his divinity spread significantly from the 1930s on.

According to the historian A. Iu. Saperova, the case made by some trezvenniki in support of Churikov's divinity rests on nine distinct points, each of which draws a parallel between his life and prophecies in the Bible.[82] In addition to evidence of his "miracles" and his tendency to frame his actions and relations to others by quoting the Gospels, they point to the fact that he was born in 1861 (the year of the emancipation of the serfs), that he began to preach at age 33.5 (the age Jesus was when he died), and that he lived during a time of revolution and great bloodshed, which they understand to be the fulfilling of the prophesy that when Christ returned to earth, he would bring "Judgment." In addition to Scripture-based arguments, some followers claimed that Brother Ioann had offered clues to his own identity as Christ. Ivan Smolev, for example, recalled a time when he had been sitting on a train with Brother Ioann and realized that he was the predicted "God-Man," the Second Coming; at that very moment, Smolev testified, Churikov looked at him and confirmed his thoughts with a slight smile, a knowing look, and a nod.[83]

Another factor shaping the debate around Brother Ioann's identity was the belief that Churikov's "real" beliefs had become manifest only after 1917; until then, it was argued, his claims—including his professed devotion to the Orthodox Church—had allegedly been guarded, the product of circumstance rather than belief.[84] While casting doubt on Churikov's repeated insistence on his own Orthodox identity and humanity, this line of thinking also gave greater credibility to his post-revolutionary besedy and oral accounts, even though many of them had been written and rewritten by his followers and never verified by him personally. In this context, Brother Ioann's control over his identity eroded further, and "evidence" of his divine nature produced by his followers (including Smolev) found fertile soil.

Similar to the way in which Brother Ioann's excommunication had led to the creation of a united front among trezvenniki in 1914, the ongoing threat of discrimination or persecution under Soviet rule helped to mask the deep interpretive chasm that opened up after Brother Ioann's death. While individuals on either side of the divinity issue still treated each other with respect through the Soviet period,[85] the issue remained divisive and corrosive.[86] Those who believed that Brother was the Second Coming criticized the other trezvenniki for their doubt and unbelief, and the latter rejected the divinity argument as heresy.[87] Although less apparent to outsiders during the underground years of the Soviet period, the debate ate away at the heart of the community for decades and still divides the trezvenniki today.

Sober Memories

In the 1960s and 1970s, elders on both sides of the divinity issue worked to shape Brother Ioann's legacy by writing expansive "historical" accounts in the form of either biography or memoir; during the Soviet period, the texts were circulated only secretly in small quantities as typed manuscripts. Although each account can be seen as a form of testimony and exercise in sober imagination, their approaches to Brother Ioann's past, teachings, good works, and spiritual feats are distinct. For our purposes, the texts are revealing not only because they suggest how each writer saw themselves in relation to Brother Ioann, but also because each worked in their own way to position the sober movement vis-à-vis the socialist project, as well as dominant Soviet norms and values. By confronting and highlighting different aspects of the trezvennik experience in the past, they also aimed to keep alive a particular vision and hope for the future.

Of the three accounts under consideration here, Petr Terekhovich's "brief autobiographical sketch [ocherk]" was by far the most personal. Written toward the end of his life in the 1970s, it covered his fifty-five years as one of Brother Ioann's devoted followers. Intended for fellow trezvenniki as well as "anyone into whose hands [it] might fall," Terekhovich's prose is also the closest to Brother Ioann's in language, meditative tone, and in its extensive quoting of Scripture, which is used as both evidence and argument. Thus, although he claimed to be writing for everyone—and posterity—is it unlikely that his account would have been accessible to a broader public. On the contrary, it reflects the discursive distance between his own sober perspective, rooted in a deep engagement with scriptural verse and concepts, and the secular and atheistic norms of Soviet society. That Terekhovich held on to this voice after more than forty years of Soviet life is in itself striking.

Terekhovich's choice of an ocherk as the format for his narrative is also interesting. A popular Soviet genre in the 1950s, the ocherk is unique in that it centers on the narrator's life for structure, while allowing them to shed light on aspects of Soviet reality that fall outside of official narratives. Thus, as Terekhovich recounted his evolution as a trezvennik, he frequently punctuated his story with exultant words of praise and gratitude to Brother Ioann (rather than Comrade Stalin or Soviet achievements) and repeatedly interrupted his narration to remind his reader of his personal sinfulness, on the one hand, and of the fundamental truth of divine rule on the other.

Terekhovich's account of his life is anchored by two moments of acute spiritual struggle—first, when he fell victim to his own "sins" as a young man in the early 1920s, and then when he became a victim of Soviet repression in the early 1930s. The first part of the narrative, which testifies to his decision to embrace holy sobriety, covers much of the same ground that other testimonies did—how he fell into an immoral lifestyle, suffered on account of his pride, was supported by his mother's love, and eventually came to follow Brother Ioann and live by Scripture. The second part of the memoir details his experiences in the Soviet prison system and in exile in the 1930s.

In the final pages Terekhovich offers an overview of his life's trajectory after his release from exile in the 1930s, including information about his marriage and children, his service in the Red Army during the Great Patriotic War, and his job at a factory. The discussion makes clear that in spite of many difficulties—including his family's experience during the siege of Leningrad, when his daughter was permanently injured—he felt blessed and deeply grateful. But the brevity with which he recounted those decades also suggests their relative unimportance to the story he wanted to tell. Indeed, even as he acknowledged his sense of duty to the Soviet system, which he enacted through his job and his service in the war, he made it clear that his experience as a Soviet person was a long struggle that had not led to a deeper and more meaningful engagement with socialism. On the contrary, rather than "rising together with the people," as the Stakhanovite Pasha Angelina famously said, his "Soviet experience" had been an ongoing trial that ultimately led him to a deeper and more meaningful engagement with God.[88] In this way, his account reversed the dominant narrative associated with religious believers at the time, which, Emily Baran has observed, traced "their lives as a journey from religion and toward the truth found only in communism."[89]

Terekhovich openly voiced his confusion about the Soviet regime's persecution of Brother Ioann, and of all those who led honest, sober lives and never spoke out against the revolution.[90] In another comment on the abuses of Soviet power, he recalled his incarceration and exile in great detail, including the harsh conditions, the arbitrary rules, and the loss of close friends and loved ones—aspects found in many other gulag accounts. Yet, rather than dwelling on his suffering or victimization, Terekhovich's point was to narrate his own spiritual survival in an effort to praise God, and to accentuate the saving power of holy sobriety and its core values of patience, humility, and hard work. While years of sober living enabled him to find meaning in the asceticism of prison life as a form of penance, he had been sustained by his deep knowledge of Scripture and the realization that he remained "free" because of his spiritual integrity, just as Brother Ioann had been during his own incarcerations.[91] Indeed, it was precisely in this way—that is, by finding peace through faith—that he had been able to subvert the power of Soviet authority over him. As Brother Ioann taught, Terekhovich believed that everything happens for a reason, even when it seems arbitrary at the time, both because God is always in control and because suffering is a source of spiritual growth.

Like Terekhovich, Ivan Smolev and Nina Maslova could claim to be living links to Brother Ioann, and they shared a common desire to shape, preserve, and spread Brother Ioann's legacy. Although they did not see eye to eye on the issue of his divinity, all three shared faith in the project of holy sobriety as the only true path to the kingdom of God and acknowledged their responsibility to carry on as sowers in Brother Ioann's "sober vineyard." "Our task," Smolev wrote, "is to unite our ranks as closely as possible to strengthen the struggle for holy sobriety in word and deed, for the correct understanding of the teachings of our Master, for the implementation of what he taught us."[92] Likewise, Maslova reminded her fellow trezvenniki of Brother Ioann's final words to them before his arrest in April 1929: "When my love abides in you, then you will see me,"[93] which was likely a reference to a gospel passage in John,[94] in which Jesus asks his disciples to carry on in his absence by living according to his teachings and loving others as he had loved them.

As a lifelong trezvennik and zealous youth organizer in the 1920s, Smolev (b. 1900) had grown up in Brother Ioann's shadow and was the single most prolific member of the community after his death. Although the energy and militancy of his younger days had long been muted, he continued his work as a sober activist both in his capacity as a community leader and through his prose and poetic reflections on Brother Ioann's life.[95]

Claiming to be the most "authentic" witness of Brother Ioann's life, Smolev intended his 1962 one-hundred-plus page biography commemorating the hundredth anniversary of Brother Ioann's birth as the fullest history of Brother Ioann's spiritual legacy and of the trezvennik movement written from the "inside." To this end, his *povest'* carefully reconstructed Brother Ioann's beliefs, activities, and teachings, drawing on his personal memories as well as extensive research, an indication that his intended audience went beyond the sober community that knew the history well.

Smolev's account also went further than others in its efforts to write Brother Ioann and his followers into bigger Soviet narratives, tying them not only to major historical events (especially the Revolutions of 1917) but also to contemporary socialist values.[96] Indeed, Smolev's emphasis on hard work, patriotism, internationalism, and fraternity among peoples spoke pointedly to the priorities advanced in 1961 at the 22nd Party Congress and articulated in the "Moral Code of the Builder of Communism" as a guide for the Soviet future. While it was not uncommon for Soviet citizens to use "the language of Communist morality" to promote their own interests, including religious beliefs,[97] Smolev's efforts in this respect were also in line with the trezvenniki's ongoing attempts to highlight the congruence between sober and socialist morality; although imperfect, it was far from insignificant.

On the contrary, Smolev could legitimately point to the BICh commune as a living example of the trezvenniki's commitment to Soviet values, including the spirit of collectivism, brotherly love and communal ways, and the love of labor.[98] In his words, the commune was "a model for many, a model of people's endurance, devotion to work for the common good, a model of struggle in any conditions in the name of a bright future." Likewise, Smolev highlighted the ecumenical nature of trezvennichestvo and the universality of the message of holy sobriety. Brother Ioann "prayed for everyone," and his legacy was that of a peace-bringer, "fighting evil and hostility, sowing the seeds of peace between people, calls for brotherly love, community, and not stopping on the principle of peace of man with man," but even "call[ing] man to peace with animals."[99]

With its themes of hope and healing, Smolev's account of Brother Ioann's life fits well into the context of Thaw memory practices. As a victim of Stalinist persecution in the late 1920s, Smolev had personally suffered multiple arrests and years of incarceration, and he took advantage of the new political context to point out the "irreparable mistake" committed by those who had violently silenced all the messengers of holy sobriety under Stalin. Yet, aside from this brief (yet passionate) denunciation, the focus of his *povest'* was not the trauma or suffering that he or others had experienced under Soviet rule, but rather his unwavering faith in Brother Ioann and the enduring promise of holy sobriety as part of the socialist project. In this sense, his account offered a "narrative of healing" and resiliency very much in line with Thaw-era patterns of destalinization, which were oriented less around past suffering than toward a better, more peaceful future.[100] Given that he was writing not only as Gulag survivors were returning home following state amnesties, but also as trezvenniki remained under threat of persecution for their beliefs, his decision to choose reconciliation and hope over anger and despair would seem to be deliberate.

Like Smolev, Nina Maslova was inspired to bear witness to Brother Ioann's life and accomplishments toward the end of her life (she also died in the 1960s). The result was a comprehensive, detailed account of the BICh commune, based in large part on her own experience living and working there for ten years in the 1920s.[101] Composed in the literary form of a *povest'*, Maslova's narrative begins by acknowledging the unique challenge of capturing Brother Ioann's legacy, since his good works were inscribed not "in books" but "in innumerable human hearts." Thus rather than claiming the authenticity of her own voice as Smolev had, she used the written page to weave together the voices of the many believers whose testimonies she had collected over the years. In this way, she enacted her role as author in keeping with her identity as a faithful sestritsa—that is, as Brother Ioann's devoted witness, and an obedient messenger between him and his followers.

On the one hand, Maslova worked hard to ground her portrait of the Vyritsa colony and commune in extensive research; in addition to her own personal memories, she read widely in the press and relied on both the commune's records and official reports in order to recreate life there in great detail.[102] On the other hand, her account reveals a clear tension between factual accuracy and emotional truth, especially when it relies quite freely (and uncritically) on oral histories that included rumors and secondhand evidence. Indeed, in keeping with the spirit of a *povest'*, her primary goal seems to have been less to tell the story of what happened on the commune than to convey how it *was* living with Brother Ioann. To this end, her priority was to capture the complex of feelings and values that dominated life there and, in turn, to inspire others to carry on in Brother Ioann's spirit—most of all, with love, respect, humility, patience, and hope.

While admitting that the early days of the commune were a time of great want, Maslova—again, like Smolev—resisted any temptation to dwell on negative or traumatic memories. On the contrary, her tone is both joyful and reverent as she paints the commune as a modern incarnation of early Christian communities, built on faith, equality, and peace. In contrast to Smolev's portrayal of the BICh commune as an authentic expression of socialism, she boldly proclaimed "our whole life on the commune" as "a miracle created by Brother Ioann."[103] A place of honest labor and communal living, the commune as she conjured it was a uniquely sacred site, created and nurtured by faith and the power of the Holy Spirit.[104] Although the commune received official recognition from secular authorities, she emphasized, it was Brother Ioann—not Soviet officials—who had sustained people through crises and desperate hardship.[105]

In many ways, Maslova's portrait of Brother Ioann was in line with that of his other followers. He was unfailingly good, loving, and protective, and his skills were limitless (he even made the food taste better!). Like Smolev, she characterized Churikov as ecumenical in practice, demonstrating love and concern not just for the Orthodox, but for all people. Even local nontrezvenniki came to him with their grief and their troubles, and he treated everyone who visited the commune—no matter their class, education, nationality, or religious views—with "great love and an open heart."[106] Even more central to her portrayal of Brother Ioann, however, was his likeness to the biblical figure of Moses. Just as Moses had led his people to the promised land, so Brother Ioann had led the sober out of "slavery" to their addictions and brought them to the commune. There, like Moses, he had given his people the commandments that would lead them to salvation. Most importantly, Brother Ioann was a prophet, whose ability to know transcended worldly ideas, ideologies, and institutions. In fact, in a subtly subversive claim, Maslova pointed out that Brother Ioann had known his fate even before Soviet authorities decided to arrest him.

Given that Maslova composed her *povest'* at a time when Stalin's rule was being subjected to intense criticism, it is hard not to see in her portrait of Brother Ioann an alternative model of heroic leadership, a leader whose authority was grounded not in ideology or violence, but in love and scriptural law. Yet she made it quite clear that Brother Ioann stood not only outside of Soviet political space, but outside of time itself. "Everything in life, in the history of mankind changes," she concluded her *povest'*; "only the soul of the RIGHTEOUS does not change: he is patient, even and unshakable in all circumstances."[107]

Both Smolev and Maslova used historical narrative as a tool not only to preserve a lost past, but also to shape trezvennik culture in the present and to project a more perfect future. Yet, whereas Smolev's account stressed the fundamental complementarity between sobriety and socialism, Maslova was more interested in crafting an "alternative utopia," in Mark Edele's usage,[108] based on the desire for a future that promises not only the proclaimed socialist values of universal brotherhood and peace, but also an abundance of patience, kindness, tolerance, stability, and the absence of fear—that is, those values and qualities that had been lacking in Soviet society. At the same time, however, Maslova's *povest'* articulated a nostalgia for the more perfect past of early Christianity. In this sense, it might best be understood as an exercise in what Walter Brueggemann has called the "prophetic imagination." By vividly depicting Brother Ioann as a righteous man of God, and as a source of both law and love, Maslova worked to keep him alive in the present, not only as a healer for those in pain, but also—and even more importantly—as a prophet, whose vision of a peaceful, sober world would unconditionally be realized in the future. Here again, she (as sestritsa) acted as the messenger in his absence, giving voice to his prophecies for those in need of hope and inspiration. As Brueggemann wrote, "it is the vocation of the prophet to keep alive the ministry of imagination, to keep on conjuring and proposing future alternatives to the single one the king wants to urge as the only thinkable one."[109]

Much of Maslova's account was devoted to documenting evidence of Brother Ioann's gift of prophecy, including forecasts that spoke to the future of the Soviet secular project. For example, she shared a memory from the anxious days before Brother Ioann was arrested, when he was discussing an article on the trezvenniki in the godless press. Clearly sensing his followers' fears, he reassured them that the future would be sober: "How much better it is for us to follow Christ than to deny Christ. People went to the cross inspired by Christ, they knew that they would be satisfied by life in the future. Christians have everything, and nonbelievers who deny Christ nothing. So it will be for those who are sober, and for drunkards nothing."[110] While acknowledging that the sober would need to suffer for their faith, he reassured them that the future belonged to them, the faithful: "a time would come when all the churches would be open all the time, and people would have faith and the fear of God again, and the canons would be replaced by the living word."[111] By sharing Brother Ioann's predictions, Maslova was affirming both the community's collective agenda to carry on in his absence, as well as her belief in his prophecy as the foundation of hope, an unimpeachable confirmation that the future would belong not to the godless, but to those who believed.

When considered together, the texts by Smolev, Maslova, and Terekhovich reveal the lack of a single interpretive lens through which trezvenniki viewed the relationship between their beliefs and Soviet society. While all three highlighted the core values of holy sobriety that were in sync with the Soviet project (discipline, hard work, respect for authority and each other, and love of humanity), each author positioned trezvennichestvo differently with respect to the Soviet present: while Terekhovich framed the relationship as dialectical, Smolev stressed its complementarity, and Maslova posited sobriety as an alternative mode of living. Not unlike the Thaw generation, which focused energetically on extensive searching for a viable path to socialism, Smolev and Maslova both offered up sobriety as the missing link in the chain to the radiant future. By contrast, Petr Terekhovich's reflections on his life suggest a far more de-territorialized perspective, centered on spiritual conflict and struggle.

Nonetheless, all three were equal in their expressions of love for Brother Ioann, as well as their shared belief in holy sobriety as a higher form of the socialist imaginary, and the hope that "SOBRIETY on earth would RISE AGAIN [*voskresnet'*]!" to save humanity.[112] As Brother Ioann had prophesied, it was only a matter of time. In the meantime, Terekhovich observed, the trezvenniki would always be useful to the state and society because they lived according to scriptural precepts, including obedience, patience, and humility. And while none of them could conceive of a perfect society in the absence of God, they believed that everything was for a purpose, and that suffering was necessary not because of the logic of class struggle, but because it brought people closer to God. As they had in the past, they would continue to bear any "cross of suffering" with patience.[113]

As suggested at the outset, the trezvennik experience under Soviet rule was one of both ongoing struggle and adaptation. Yet, for all their suffering and setbacks, the trezvenniki's emotional center of gravity continued to be dominated not by sorrow, fear, or anger, but rather by hope and joy. If Stalin made good on his apocryphal promise to Brother Ioann, the reverse is true as well: Brother Ioann had prepared his followers well for living under the spiritual authoritarianism of the Soviet period, bequeathing to them a rich legacy in words, images, and memories, and a set of "workable" beliefs—that nothing ever happens without a reason, that God is always in control, and that the socialists were doing God's work even if they didn't know it. Even in the face of traumatic disruption and ongoing persecution, trezvennik communities lived according to their faith, carrying Brother Ioann's spirit and teachings with them into the future long after Stalin had been put to rest. To be sure, the transparency between life and faith to which Brother Ioann's followers had traditionally aspired was no longer possible without great risk. But in spite of all the challenges of being a person of faith living in Soviet society, holy sobriety remained central to their experience of "living socialism."

The impact of Brother Ioann's arrest and death on their beliefs and practices was significant, and it was magnified by the realities of atheistic rule. Two parallel developments—the loss of his presence and oversight, and the forcing of religious practices underground—resulted in contradictory effects, unleashing both centrifugal and centripetal forces within the trezvennik movement. The result was both more coherence within the community and more disruption. On the one hand, communities grew stronger through the bonds of their shared faith, hopes, and fears. On the other hand, the realities of physical fragmentation and the loss of guidance from Brother Ioann and the Orthodox clergy gave greater space for interpretation within the trezvennik community as a whole. This in turn led to deep fractures over issues of belief, most significantly around the question of Brother Ioann's divinity. In this way, the greater cause of holy sobriety would in fact be profoundly scarred by Stalin's militant atheism.

As it was for many believers, the trezvenniki's collective survival story in the Soviet period was one of both adaptation and spiritual resistance. Harassment or persecution was always a possibility for believers, and at times the trezvenniki found themselves caught in a "mutually reinforcing dynamic" as their attempts to resist state repression by living their faith were then used as justification for their further persecution.[114] But especially after the early Stalin years, the majority found ways to live and work both soberly and peacefully, often within the context of a supportive community. As in the 1920s, their ability to find a workable equilibrium resulted in part from their reputations as sober and hard-working, and from their relatively moderate views, since, unlike some religious groups, their faith did not demand that they refuse to vote, to work in state-run enterprises, or to serve in the military.

To be sure, throughout the Soviet period, trezvenniki remained deeply at odds with the regime on account of its godlessness, and over its refusal to accept their belief that the country's drinking problem was a consequence of the people's widespread rejection of God. There thus remained an inalienable and permanent space between their understanding of what was sacred (God's Word) and official secular and atheistic norms. At the same time, some trezvenniki acknowledged the compatibility of holy sobriety and the moral and ethical tenets of socialism; rather than rejecting the Soviet project outright, they viewed "scientific communism" as more religious than scientific, but also "incomplete" and therefore "flawed." While communism had resolved many of society's more challenging economic problems, the trezvennik truck driver P. Rozotov acknowledged, "it did not indicate the path of spiritual development for the individual person." For him and his fellow trezvenniki, holy sobriety filled a void and represented "the highest achievement of human thought," without which communism could not survive.[115] In this sense, they understood their position vis-à-vis the Soviet project as neither marginal nor oppositional, but rather much as Brother Ioann had seen himself in relation to Orthodoxy, as the cornerstone of the future kingdom on earth. Instead of dwelling on their repression or actively protesting the Soviet state, the trezvenniki remained determined to carry on in Brother Ioann's spirit, united in a single goal: to spread to seeds of holy sobriety, especially Scripture, and to cultivate the "sober vineyard" among themselves and those around them.[116]

CHAPTER 10

Sober Truths during Late Socialism

In 1963, not long after the Soviet leadership under Khrushchev declared that the country had launched its next and final phase, the building of communism, the atheist Nikolai Ivanovich Iudin published a new book on Brother Ioann and his followers. "The construction of a new society is inextricably linked with the formation of a new person," it began, and "to build communism requires people who are capable of great daring, confident in their abilities, qualified experts in their field, [and] armed with advanced scientific knowledge, [and] clear-thinking."[1] As Iudin would then spell out, the trezvenniki had no place on the aspirational landscape of a communist future. Although sometimes still useful as human foils to the ideal Soviet person, they were but "surviving remnants" of an exploitative and backward past and, as such, destined to be swept aside to make way for the new generation of men and women that would build the communist future.[2]

The trezvenniki were not being singled out in this way; all religious believers would find themselves targets of Khrushchev's antireligious campaign. While religious faith remained a legal right, now more than ever it was framed as an immoral and unethical choice. "To believe or not to believe in God is the personal [*lichnoe*] business of each individual," wrote the journalist N. Rusakov in 1959, but "one ought not to forget that in most cases religious beliefs cause harm to our society, destroy families [and] health, [cause] trauma to children's psyche and consciousness, [and] tear our citizens away from participation in social life."[3] And while atheism was not explicitly listed as a value in the 1961 Moral Code of the Builder of Communism, it was understood as a precondition for the kind of scientific and social consciousness required by the collective tasks that lay ahead. If at certain times in the past the performance of allegiance to the communists' cause had been sufficient, during this final period of societal transformation—the most revolutionary phase since Stalin's great break in 1929—ideological orthodoxy was expected of all. The transition away from a regime that was less overtly coercive during the Thaw demanded that individuals and communities be "conscious" enough to discipline themselves. For these reasons, at this new and final stage of class struggle, the victory of the Soviet future needed atheists, and thus the final defeat of believers.

The campaign against religion was waged by godless activists on many fronts and involved the closing of almost fifty percent of working churches, legal prosecution, and "enlightenment" work in the press and in lecture halls across the country.[4] Yet, for all the hope and effort that Iudin and others would devote to the atheist project, their successes ultimately fell short of their ambitions. For one thing, many Soviet people—believers and nonbelievers alike—continued to assume that "religion and Communism get along very well." In fact, the historian Victoria Smolkin has observed, rather than seeing faith as antithetical to communism, many people "considered Communism to be the manifestation of Christian ideals." "Believers build communism alongside atheists," atheists noted with dismay in the fall of 1963, and "many of them sincerely try to combine in their consciousness socialist ideas with religious beliefs."[5] In this context, religious communities—including trezvenniki—continued to renew themselves, not necessarily in opposition to but often in ways complementary to the socialist project.

In the 1950s and 1960s, as the Soviet Union looked forward toward communism, the trezvennik movement continued to welcome new members from different generations and walks of life. Most had benefited from Soviet society in some ways but found it wanting in others. Among them was A. Kozlov (b. 1924), who enjoyed all the trappings of a comfortable life—a decent job, a wife, a place to live, food to eat, and free health care—but whose alcohol addiction and infidelity drove him to attempt suicide.[6] Another was Anna Ivanovna Kuznetsova (b. 1914), a single woman who had survived the Leningrad blockade and distinguished herself as a tram driver, but struggled with the feeling that something was missing in her life. After exploring different religious groups, she joined the trezvennik community in the 1950s and declared her new sense of belonging "a miracle."[7] Yet another convert was Maria Iakovleva Kotiurova, a mother and shopworker who joined the sober community in Leningrad in 1968 and was followed in later years by her husband and son. Her family's conversion experience, profiled in this chapter, speaks to some of the spiritual and moral limitations and challenges of the "socialist way of life" under late socialism, and in turn, the longevity of holy sobriety as an alternative set of beliefs and lifestyle.

The ongoing efforts of godless journalists to criticize and marginalize the trezvenniki were much in line with antisober discourse in both the prerevolutionary and socialist past, but their claims also reflected an intensification in violence and distortion. In addition to the psychological impact of godless critiques, sober communities also had to endure the lingering threat of persecution, which began to lessen only in the mid-1960s. Around that same time, Smolkin has demonstrated, the resilience of faith-based groups like the trezvenniki would force a significant shift in the way that atheists approached questions of religious identity and spirituality and, ultimately, compel them to confront their own blind spots when it came to matters of the soul.[8]

Sobriety as a Soviet "Swamp"

In the summer of 1959, during the launching of the Seventh Five-Year Plan under Khrushchev, the trezvenniki found themselves the target of another propaganda campaign. In an article in *Gatchinskaia Pravda*, coauthored by I. Voronov and B. Novikov, the sober community in Vyritsa was profiled as an isolated swamp of backwardness amid a sea of Soviet progress. As other citizens celebrated "on the road to communism" with their televisions, radios, parades, and pioneer camps, "all is static among Churikov's followers."[9] Instead of building communist society, the trezvenniki gathered in secret prayer meetings, preached false promises about heaven and the afterlife, and spread the misguided claim that alcoholism was the single root of all social problems. They prayed "secretly" and refused to register as a "sect" not because they feared discrimination or persecution, but because they knew their "fanatical activity" was deeply harmful.[10]

Voronov and Novikov's narrative suggested that little had changed in terms of the basic tropes of antireligious propaganda since the last major campaign in the late 1920s. Their brief history of the sober movement levied familiar charges of financial, sexual, and psychological exploitation against Brother Ioann (and by extension, his contemporary followers), stressing his tendency toward dissimulation and political unreliability. Once again, Churikov was mocked variously as the "Vyritsa Christ," an unscrupulous exploiter, a "liar and rogue" (*obmanshchik i prokhodimets*), a sexual pervert, and a political "chameleon" who had supported "White terror."

The continuity between the first and second wave of godless narratives was both ideological and methodological. In fact, virtually every detail in Voronov and Novikov's piece was lifted directly from literature produced in the 1920s, including unsubstantiated and deliberately falsified claims or rumors; the authors also adopted many of the same strategies first pioneered by Orthodox missionaries and then repurposed by the first generation of *bezbozhniki* (godless activists), including the blending of rumor and fact, innuendo and exaggeration, abstraction and class-based essentialism, and guilt by association.

What distinguished Voronov and Novikov's portrait of Brother Ioann from earlier accounts, however, was the degree of exaggeration in many of the claims, and the pronounced mocking and hostility. To be sure, godless denunciations in the 1920s were far from objective or flattering. But the accusations made in 1959 were more extreme in every respect. As in the classic game of "telephone," aspects of Brother Ioann's life first recorded by Orthodox missionaries or scholars before 1917 and then retold with no small amount of ideological spin by *bezbozhniki* in the 1920s were once again given new life—and a greater degree of distortion—in the 1950s. The retelling of Brother Ioann's relationship with his wife is particularly striking. In place of the once widely accepted interpretation that his wife's demise had been related to their daughter's death, and that Churikov had consequently renounced his material wealth in order to devote himself to God, Voronov and Novikov claimed that Churikov—now vilified as a "monster-husband"—had beaten his wife within an inch of her life, an assault so devastating that it led her to hang herself, but only after setting the house on fire and burning all of her husband's money up with it. Brother Ioann turned to the Gospel after his wife's death, therefore, not out of grief, but only because he knew that preaching would be lucrative.[11]

The combination of ridicule, condescension, and demonization in the *Gatchinskaia Pravda* piece was part of a newer pattern of sensationalist reporting targeted toward religious groups. Given the partial rehabilitation of the Orthodox Church during the war, the press under Khrushchev was especially harsh toward "sectarians," who were mocked as "moral freaks, fanatics, parasites."[12] Adding to this list was Voronov and Novikov's accusation that Ivan Frolov, one of Brother Ioann's most loyal followers, had collaborated with the fascists during the Nazi occupation of Vyritsa.[13] While unmasking and "othering" were old missionary techniques, Miriam Dobson has observed, "identifying and castigating transgressors" became a particularly useful way to articulate and "consolidate" morals and values during the anxious and unstable process of de-Stalinization.[14] Seen in this light, Voronov and Novikov's attempts to "other" the trezvenniki could be read as extolling Soviet virtues such as transparency, legality, active engagement in the collective, sexual morality, the renunciation of violence (including domestic abuse), and loyalty to the fatherland.

The authors' juxtaposition of the trezvenniki's "inertia" with the celebratory movement of the rest of Soviet society was a variation on the long-standing contrast between the "backwardness" of religious believers and the "progressive" agenda of atheistic socialists. But it was also a gendered distinction, which linked religious believers with *byt*, often associated with women and the feminine, private (and hidden) sphere, as well as the banality of everyday life, materiality, corporality, immobility, and irrationality. By contrast, atheists were linked to *bytie*, which at the time tended to be associated with men and the masculine, and the world of intellect and spirit, movement and rationality.[15] While this juxtaposition was by no means new, for godless writers it took on new relevance and a more extreme form as the Soviet Union entered a new revolutionary stage. Although the two categories might be seen as complementary, *byt* was always understood to be secondary to *bytie* and could be seen as a drag on it.

The Moral Failings of "Spiders" and "Flies"

The godless denunciations of the trezvenniki first articulated in the summer of 1959 gained new momentum in the fall of 1961 with

Khrushchev's declaration that the next Soviet generation would live under communism.[16] Not long after, Iudin published his detailed study of the trezvenniki under the auspices of Znanie (Knowledge), formerly the Society for the Dissemination of Political and Scientific Knowledge. The pejorative title, *Churikovshchina*—first used by Orthodox priests before 1917—was to be expected from the career atheist, who had joined the ranks of godless lecturers in the 1920s and served as a lead librarian for the antireligious section at the Saltykov-Shchedrin library in Leningrad in the 1930s. As an activist, Iudin had met Brother Ioann on the commune in the late 1920s, but rather than winning him over, the visit had apparently confirmed the rumors that Churikov was "a crafty, ignorant demagogue, a kulak, a sanctimonious person and despot, who used the 'fear of God' as a tool to keep his followers in line." In fact, Iudin took part in liquidating the commune in 1929, which he dismissed as a "nest of spiders," where "former people" (i.e., exploiters) from the tsarist era were hiding out.[17]

Bringing decades of recycled research and godless outrage to the project, Iudin crafted much of his sixty-three-page book by embellishing earlier histories of Brother Ioann's life in light of contemporary events. For example, yet another round of "telephone" led to even more extreme versions of Churikov's depravity, including Iudin's claim that Brother Ioann was not only a wife-beater but a murderer, so angry at having failed at business and lost all his money that he took it out on his wife and *beat her to death*.[18] Given that even Eliashevich's 1928 account, from which Iudin drew freely, ascribed to the pre-1917 version of Churikov as broken-hearted, this further vilification of Churikov's image seems both deliberate and noteworthy. While catering to the Soviet public's love of scandal, it might also be read within the context of de-Stalinization, when the arbitrariness and violence of earlier Soviet authorities were being discussed and rejected. Another embellishment related to the alleged connections that the trezvenniki had with "foreign powers." Against the backdrop of the cold war, Iudin claimed that the sestritsy's arrest in 1927 had been related to espionage; drawing on Petrov's 1930 booklet, he referred to the women by degrading nicknames such as "Australia," "Africa," etc. (an allusion to the global aspirations of the sober movement), and then updated the claim to reflect cold war realities by noting that "Europe" and "America" had been the main offenders in the spy ring.[19]

Because Iudin's ideological lens distorted previous claims about Churikov beyond plausibility, his account begged multiple questions: If

Brother Ioann were such an outrageous swindler, murderer, and sexual deviant, why did so many people follow him? If he and his followers were so wealthy, then why did they all live in poverty? If he didn't actually cure people of their alcoholism, then why did they say he did? To guard against the reader's suspicion that things didn't quite add up, he did what other atheists before him had done: assign responsibility for any inconsistencies to Churikov himself—to his extreme "cleverness," to his talent to self-fashion and to "mask" his authentic self, to his crafty "chameleon-like" nature—and to portray his followers as agentless, ignorant victims. Within the binary framework that continued to dominate Soviet atheistic discourse through the Thaw, Miriam Dobson has observed, religious perpetrators were portrayed as "irrational and even violent fanatics" while their victims were made out to be hapless "dupes in need of enlightenment."[20] In this way, the poles of power and powerlessness, and of agency and victimhood, were exaggerated, and any measure of understanding of the relationship between them became elusive.

Iudin's main contribution to the godless shelf in the Soviet library was his research into the postwar trezvennik community. Skipping over three decades of arrests, incarcerations, and deaths (including Brother Ioann's) under Stalin, his account introduced his readers to several "pure" trezvenniki (chistye), most of whom were respected leaders and elders after the war. In an effort to unmask these "pure" types as "polluting and corrupting Soviet life,"[21] he recorded an alleged exchange with a young leader by the name of Zakharin. Pushing back on Zakharin's claim that communism needed God to succeed, Iudin pointed to all the industrial and scientific achievements the Soviet people had accomplished since Brother Ioann died, "not only without 'god' [bez 'bozhen'ki'] but in decisive struggle with the very idea of god."[22] He then challenged Zakharin's belief that it was acceptable "to retreat from the world and save oneself through spiritual life." On the contrary, he argued, the search for personal happiness and the salvation of the individual soul was a form of "antisocial, egotistical individualism," hostile to "the new Soviet order."[23] "Pure" trezvenniki like Zakharin were backward-looking and lacked any "common language" with socialist society; they lived entirely for themselves, he stressed, and "everything that serves to develop and increase social welfare is alien to them."

As in the 1920s, class identity continued to determine an individual's moral and ethical tendencies; but because class differences had been significantly muted by the 1960s, the tactic of essentializing class actors took different and sometimes perverse forms. For example, Iudin used evidence of the trezvenniki's persecution under Stalin as *proof* of their corrupt and disloyal characters, pointing out that one *chistyi* had been in prison for "anti-Soviet" activity, another had been fired from his job, and a third had refused to fight the fascists and was sent to a camp.[24] As evidence of both their hypocrisy and parasitic relationship to Soviet society, he also noted that while each worked to "save souls from the secular world," they seemed to have no problem "[eating] Soviet bread" and enjoying other "Soviet gifts," such as mass transit. At the same time, the "pure" trezvenniki prevented others from taking advantage of all that the Soviet system had to offer, especially health care. Like godless activists since the 1920s, Iudin offered heartbreaking stories of sick children barred from medical treatment by trezvennik parents.[25] While still effective at eliciting concern and outrage, the accusation had recently been given even sharper teeth with the addition of Article 227 to the 1960 criminal code, mandating a five-year prison term or exile for withholding medical care.[26]

From an ideological perspective at least, the "rank and file" trezvenniki were less dangerous than the *chistye*, but evidently no more relatable, as suggested by Iudin's profile of a middle-aged working-class trezvennitsa, Elena Petrovna Kalupina. An abandoned wife with a small child, Kalupina had suffered from extreme emotional distress that led her to bond with some compassionate trezvennitsy. Soon after meeting them, she began hanging portraits of Brother Ioann on her wall, although according to Iudin, she actually knew very little about him. Her mind was filled with nothing but "kasha (porridge), confusion, utter confusion," he elaborated, and "to all the speeches of her comrades in the factory, she stubbornly and stupidly responded: 'I found comfort in religion . . . I believe in God, I believe.'"[27] Thus she remained isolated and ignored in her workplace—a comment intended to suggest both her marginality and the lack of responsible vigilance on the part of her coworkers.

Moving little beyond traditional explanations of poverty or ignorance to explain Kalupina's attraction to trezvennichestvo, Iudin's profile flattened her emotions and experiences to the point of caricature, much as he had done with the *chistye*. In the spirit of the agitational plays popular during his early days as an activist, he cast Zakharin as a "spider" and Kalupina as a helpless "fly." But Iudin was far more concerned with demonstrating the ultimate power of communist truth than in dehumanizing the "enemy." So to complete his analysis, he juxtaposed Kalupina's example with that of E. I. Savel'eva, a seventy-year-old victim of an abusive husband, who had also turned to the trez-venniki for comfort. After they warned her away from secular life—the "temptation of Satan"—and told her to accept her husband's abuse as a trial sent by God, she rejected them as poorly educated and "dispir-ited" people (*udruchennye*). After a brief time among Baptists (whom she found deceitful), Savel'eva freed herself from religion and the world of *byt*, and began going out to enjoy Soviet life. "Why would [people] want to waste their best years in a prayer house?" she wondered. "There were too many better things to do!"[28]

Working under the auspices of the godless enlightenment project of the early 1960s, Iudin's main agenda was not to understand why people were still attracted to holy sobriety, but rather to make it clear why they should not be—and in doing so, to reinforce communist val-ues and behaviors among the broader public. Thus he concluded—in a modernized iteration of the "opiate" metaphor—that the problem with the trezvenniki was not that they were religious per se, but rather that their beliefs worked like an "anesthetic," lulling people into a state of "passive vegetation." Although they claimed that holy sobriety had "ennobled" them, the opposite was true. Their faith had turned them into "enemies of culture and knowledge [*nauka*]" and prevented them from contributing to and sharing in socialist progress.[29] Above all, Iudin pressed on, this was a moral failing, a sin of omission (so to speak). He concluded his study with a reminder to all Soviet people that "[as] the builders of communist society," it was their responsibility not only to serve each other as "friend, comrade, and brother," but also to "[clear] the road to communism of all mold, garbage, and filth, [and] of 'the darkness of the soul' of the old exploiting world, including the *churikovshchina*."[30] Here again, the language of purification juxtaposed the health and vitality of Soviet society with the threat of contaminants connected with religious *byt*, the recesses of the soul, and the capitalist past. Whether or not his readers actually followed his call was far less important than making sure they knew that they should.

Trezvenniki on Trial

The impact of godless propaganda on the general public is hard to mea-sure. However, evidence does suggest that certain aspects—for example, charges of conspiracy, duplicity, or the capacity for violence—imprinted strongly on the popular imagination.[31] While these fears and anxieties might have had far more to do with the traumatic legacies of Stalinism and the Great Patriotic War than sectarians of any kind, the godless press took full advantage of them. In fact, the press's stoking of fear around the sectarian snakes and spiders allegedly hiding in Soviet corners was so effective that it prompted pushback by the Council for the Affairs of Religious Cults by 1965.[32]

Behind closed doors, the trezvenniki referred to Iudin as "Iudas" and circulated rumors that he had gone blind and lame as punishment for all the lies he had told.[33] But public protests of any kind were risky, given the trezvenniki's unregistered status, or at best counterproductive. For example, a Leningrad trezvennik named Tarasov responded to Voronov and Novikov's attacks in 1959 with a letter to the editor of *Gatchinskaia Pravda* defending Brother Ioann as a "genius of the Russian people," a "warrior against drunkenness and immorality," and "a communist with the Gospel in his hand."[34] The paper's editor then used the letter as an opportunity to reiterate all the disparaging claims from the first article and to raise further suspicions about the trezvenniki. "Between communism and the *churikovshchina* lies an impassable chasm," the editor concluded, "and to assert [this] means to shamelessly deceive people."[35]

The demonization of the trezvenniki in the popular press could and did have real consequences for the community. Although persecutory practices were generally less harsh than under Stalin, trezvenniki—like other religious believers—continued to face ridicule or discrimination in their jobs and living spaces and, in some cases, legal persecution. On May 29–30, 1963, two of Brother Ioann's followers were put on trial in the court of Luga, another known center of trezvennichestvo 136 miles south of Leningrad, on the Warsaw railroad line. The trial proceedings were then broadcast in the local edition of *Pravda*, which was tied into a national network of newspapers.[36]

The first defendant, I. P. Loskutov, was a middle-aged bookkeeper at the Luzhskoi smelting-mechanical factory, where he had worked for fifteen years. A longtime widower, he had two daughters, a textile worker and a doctor, and one son in the army. As a former alcoholic who beat his wife and children, Loskutov had come to the brink of suicide but was then healed of his addiction after writing a note to Brother Ioann. Since then he had remained sober, hardworking, and devoted to his family. In court, however, he was described as having "two faces": while posing as "a regular soviet worker," he was a "careful, hypocritical, and ambitious" leader of a "secret sect." The fact that Loskutov was both well-educated and smart supposedly made him especially threatening, and he was credited with the goal of becoming "a second Churikov." The characterization of his nature as duplicitous and seditious was strengthened by mention of his earlier arrest in 1932 for "anti-Soviet activity."[37]

The other defendant, Aleksandr Vasil'evich Skachenkov—one of the *chistye* profiled in Iudin's book—was said to have a "stormier biography" and portrayed as a recidivist criminal in light of two previous arrests: the first in 1929, when he was a member of the Leningrad youth circle, Rassvet, and the second in 1942, when he was imprisoned for allegedly refusing to fight against the fascists. After being freed by amnesty in 1956, the trial report read, Skachenkov had moved to Luga and immediately began to gather a group of Churikovtsy around him. "Like a spider" he began to weave a web of religious "obscurantism," in order to "seize the souls of ignorant, morally unstable people." Although less educated than Loskutov (and therefore less "crafty"), the fact that Skachenkov was unmarried and moved around a lot enabled prosecutors to make him seem rootless, and thus physically and morally threatening.

Using witness testimonies at trial, prosecutors showed how the "sanctimonious" trezvenniki had combined their unique brand of religious fanaticism with the exploitative ways of the "kulak" (the self-interested entrepreneur who exploited others) to ruin innocent lives and devastate families. Among the hapless flies caught in Skachenkov's web was E. D. Krivenko, a mother of seven. According to emotional testimony given by her seventeen-year-old daughter, Liuba, Krivenko had routinely abandoned her children when under the trezvennik's spell, leaving them "dirty, hungry and cold." And whenever she returned home, she would force them "to study prayers, and to pray. If we made mistakes, she would beat us, and swear at us." After several years, the children resorted to begging and stealing just to survive.[38]

The transformation of Krivenko from victim to perpetrator in the courtroom and on the pages of the press is striking. On the one hand, Krivenko came off as a simple woman who had fallen prey to a sober "spider." Sectarians needed "simple women," it was argued, in order to spread their influence to other unwitting victims. On the other hand, and in line with a newer tendency to acknowledge the agency of believing women—both mothers and grandmothers—the Luga case suggested that Krivenko had to be held accountable not only because she had abandoned her children to satisfy her own personal needs (religious and sexual), but because she had perpetrated her backwardness on her own children. Her crime was not simply that she had forced her faith on them, although the court made clear that the right to believe necessitated the right *not* to believe and, presumably, to be free from unwanted religious proselytizing.[39] Rather, her main guilt lay in the fact that by expecting the children to spend so much time in prayer, she had failed to socialize them properly. While exposing them to dangerous ideas, she prevented their access to Soviet means of enlightenment—going to the movies, reading books (other than the Bible), listening to radio, attending parades, and engaging in social work.

If on the whole, men were still more likely to be identified as "spiders," as the traditional family became an important site of enlightenment and stability from the late 1930s on, women came into sharper focus for the state, either as facilitators or obstacles to the desired evolution of the next generation of Soviet citizens.[40] This new level of attention was especially noticeable in the case of believing women in the Khrushchev era. As atheists confronted the fact that many believers had been born and raised after 1917, women and the elderly were no longer simply dismissed as "backward" on account of their faith, but "cast as dangerous channels through which religion was being reproduced."[41] Although there were many exceptions, the image of the "bad (grand) mother" quickly evolved as a corollary to the negative male identity of the unpatriotic deserter, the "irrational fanatic," or the predatory religious "spider."

The trial proceedings and related news reports made it clear that Liuba was to be lauded as a heroine for her willingness to testify against her own mother—that is, for standing up to those trying to lead children astray, at whatever the personal cost. Parenting, after all, was understood not as an individual right but as a duty to the collective: "the upbringing of children . . . is not only personal, but also a great societal affair," read a contemporary pamphlet.[42] In the interest of protecting the Krivenko children and, by extension, Soviet society, state authorities declared Krivenko an incompetent parent and sent her children to a boarding school. In a parallel finding, the court determined that both Skachenkov and Loskutov were guilty of breaking Soviet law by encouraging people to retreat from healthy social activities and negatively influencing youth. Skachenkov was sentenced to five years' loss of freedom, and Loskutov was exiled from the Leningrad region.

A New Approach?

For all the apparent vitality of the godless campaign under Khrushchev, atheist authorities were becoming more aware of the limited impact of their efforts to curb people's inclinations toward religious belief. By the mid-1960s in fact, a big shift was underway, guided by the realization that if religion were to be defeated, atheist work would have to "go much deeper, to touch on all sides and all levels of consciousness where religion might make a nest [*gde mozhet gnesdidtsia religiia*]." According to the director of the Academy of Social Sciences (the party's highest organ charged with producing ideology), Iurii Frantsev, this meant, in theory, taking into consideration people's life experiences and the needs that led them to seek out faith: "We need to find out what a person stumbles on as he walks along the Soviet path of life, what stones we need to remove from his path, what holes we need to fill, so that he would not stumble."[43]

In order to do this, atheists further acknowledged that the study of religion needed more rigorous inquiry and scientific research, leading to the founding of the Institute for Scientific Atheism in 1964, and the development of the sociology of religion by the early 1970s.[44] As Victoria Smolkin has argued, a more scientific approach entailed an active engagement with the "spiritual" as a legitimate and productive category of inquiry.[45] Moving beyond the persistent yet unsatisfying diagnosis of poverty and backwardness to explain the appeal of religious belief, researchers began to acknowledge a broader range of social problems and traumas (including alcoholism, old age, and war) as well as psychosociological and emotional factors.[46]

In this shifting context a young researcher, D. M. Aptekman, began an extensive inquiry into the "worldview, psychology, and way of life [*byt*]," of the trezvenniki in Vyritsa and the Leningrad region.[47] Deliberately setting his work apart from previous studies, he criticized atheist-propagandists, including Eliashevich and Iudin, for their primarily ideological and "subjective" approach, the unreliability of their factual information, and their superficial treatment of the trezvenniki's beliefs and religious-ethical perspectives. Although his goal remained the same—that is, "to show the incompatibility of the views of the followers of sobriety with the tasks of building communism"—he aspired to a "more or less systematic analysis of the doctrine and activities of the sober sect at various stages of its existence."[48] To this end, between 1961 and 1964, he and his team of researchers carried out extensive interviews and archival research, pushing far beyond the typical purview of the godless press. The result was an unprecedented attempt to make sense out of the trezvennik experience, even as researchers continued to assume its fundamental pathology.

Aptekman's most extensively researched case study involved Valentina Kren' (Stepanova), a young wife and mother who became a trezvennitsa in the late 1950s.[49] At the time of her first encounter with holy sobriety, Kren' was in her late twenties and experiencing difficulties in her family life. Although once a decent student with an interest in theater, she had married at sixteen (around 1952) before she could pursue a career of her own. Her husband turned out to be a heavy drinker, who led an "immoral life," and the couple argued a lot. "Fatigued by the drunken sprees and fights," she recalled, "everything became hateful" to her.[50] After an especially distressing episode, she confided in a friendly neighbor, Evlampiia M., who invited her to a sober gathering.

Until that time, Valentina's relationship to any kind of faith had been unremarkable. Like many young women of her generation, she had been raised by her grandmother, who had taken her to church on Sundays. Although she recalled that the "chanting" had appealed to her, she had not continued any religious practices as an adult. Her decision to accept Evlampiia's invitation, she told Aptekman, was made on impulse; with little faith in her own family members, she had welcomed the comforting words of a stranger who saw her pain, as well as the warm attention showered on her by other trezvenniki. Although very far removed from anything she had encountered before, the sober, Scripture-inspired community brought her enormous solace. She became a regular at their meetings and adopted their habits and practices, including strict fasting and immersion in Scripture. Wearing a black headscarf, she began to pray "day and night" to Brother Ioann, whom she saw as an advocate, although of course she had never met him: "Before going to the judge, a person goes to consult a defender," Kren' explained, "So Brother is our protector before God, and [since] we are all sinners, God will not listen to us."

As her story unfolds, it becomes clear that Kren' was drawn to the trezvenniki in order to save herself from a life that had proven disappointing in many ways. Yet Aptekman, like Iudin and other god-less before him, struggled to grant the young woman agency in her decision to embrace sobriety, implying instead her behavior was largely performative, as if she were on stage acting out a new identity—in line with her earlier aspirations toward a career in the theater. At the same time, one can see in her decision to identify as a trezvennitsa an element of defiance (as well as self-fashioning). Kren' explained: "My husband and brother laughed when I brought home a copy of the Gospels and books containing Churikov's talks. This made me believe even more deeply." Her asceticism became so extreme, in fact, that she stopped having sex with her husband (which she now deemed a "sin"), and her health eventually began to suffer from a lack of proper nutrition. Indeed, her recounting of her ascetic behavior reads almost like a work slowdown on the factory floor. She didn't leave her husband physically, but she performed her wifely obligations only in the most minimal sense. In addition to her strike in the bedroom, her repeated fasting had disastrous effects in the kitchen since it prevented her from sampling her own cooking—leading to oversalted soup and other culinary problems. In spite of her husband's displeasure, the situation continued for two years, and "things got worse still."

Like many trezvenniki, Kren' struggled with her new identity in public spaces, especially at work. Her scarf-wearing and weight loss likely attracted the attention of those she knew, but she managed to conceal her beliefs from her coworkers for almost two years. When her colleagues eventually learned of her affiliation with the trezvenniki, they went to her home and confronted her husband about it. She also experienced a lot of peer pressure from friends who invited her to the movies and to go dancing. In the end, she explained, her "youthfulness" won out and she gave in to these temptations. Ashamed to tell other trezvenniki the real reason for her absence at Sunday meetings, she claimed that her husband would no longer "let her" attend, and they left her alone.[51]

According to Aptekman, many aspects of Valentina's experience were shared by the other women he interviewed, although they typically did not cut ties to the community as she had. This was especially the case among older, less educated, women as well as victims of "severe psychological trauma" (such as war or domestic abuse). Many women also gravitated toward sobriety because of the tremendous support the community offered, as in the case of "Antonina B." whose husband died accidently as a result of his drunkenness, leaving her alone, depressed, and impoverished, with four children to raise on her own.

To the extent that Aptekman's research represented a clear shift from demonizing "perpetrators" of religious belief to understanding "victims," his work was in sync with a new "humane" trend in atheist activism.[52] For the first time, Miriam Dobson has observed, ordinary believers were given "new importance: they were not just a hangover from the prerevolutionary past, destined for extinction as a consequence of socioeconomic progress, but individuals whose personal experience and thoughts mattered."[53] And indeed, Aptekman's portrait of Kren' was both detailed and sympathetic to many parts of her experience.

Yet, as a whole, Aptekman's study was no less subjective, ideological, or gendered than previous accounts. For all his apparent willingness to interrogate the social and psychological foundations of the movement, he accepted the notion of a single, superior Soviet path and considered it his job to figure out why some people "stumbled." Thus Aptekman's research repeatedly brought him back in line with traditional godless narratives. Like Iudin, he proclaimed the commune in Vyritsa a "petty bourgeois utopia" and went on at length about the trezvenniki's hostility to "[scientific] knowledge and culture" and their tendency to submit to God's will rather than science.[54] Moreover, even as he implied certain deficiencies with Soviet life, including a lack of material or moral support for victims of alcoholism, he cited the trezvenniki's advanced age and low social status as explanatory factors in their worldview. And in spite of his awareness that alcoholism remained a serious problem for many Soviet people, he insisted that it would go away once exploitation and ignorance had been eliminated and the "full harmonious development of the person [*lichnost'*]" could take place.[55]

Aptekman also struggled to make sense of the trezvenniki's emotions and, when confronted by the intensity of their faith, pathologized them. Certain feelings—for example, the peace and calm that Kren' experienced at sober meetings—were for Aptekman both comprehensible and acceptable. So too was her love of chanting and the passion for dancing that eventually led her away from sobriety. But other emotions associated with faith experiences were more problematic. For example, while exhibiting a cautious willingness to acknowledge Antonina's need for the kind of emotional support the trezvenniki provided, he pointed to the fact that she had been religious as a young person and her low level of cultural education as the source of instability in her worldview, and characterized her decision to become sober as "religious recidivism." After joining the trezvenniki, he observed, "her religiosity attained the level of extreme fanaticism, bordering upon a religious psychosis."[56]

Aptekman's account suggests, in other words, that the turn among social scientists toward the emotional life of believers did not come easily or lead to a deeper understanding of religious experience. On the contrary, a believer's emotional life often remained a reason to marginalize them. Although the trezvenniki's behavior was measured when compared, say, to the Pentecostals' "excessive emotions (uncontrolled dancing, crying, and moaning)" and "hysterical, strange, and 'savage' (dikii) behavior," it nonetheless provided an effective foil to "the rational and disciplined habits of the Soviet world."[57] In 1967, when the Soviet scholar of sectarianism, A. I. Klibanov, wrote up his observation of one of Brother Ioann's healings in the late 1920s, he confessed that as an atheist and a scientist he was greatly disturbed by the "dark force" emanating from Brother Ioann and by the crowd's sobbing, wailing, and gesturing.[58] Indeed, even as he attempted an "objective" reporting of the event, he admitted to experiencing both "awe and disgust" as he watched Brother Ioann rouse the crowd into a state of ecstasy and then quickly shut it down. Unwittingly echoing the hieromonk Veniamin who had claimed that Churikov was demon-possessed, Klibanov declared "something not only 'pathological' but 'satanic' in his conducting [dirizhirovanie] of people's will and feelings." Of course, their respective definitions of satanic differed; whereas Veniamin had been concerned primarily by the nature and extent of Brother Ioann's "spiritual delusion" (prelest'), for Klibanov the problem was one of irrationality and of the predominance of the spiritual over the material forces at work. Yet they both insisted upon the superiority of their own respective emotional regimes and positions of knowledge and, as a result, failed to appreciate fully what they were witnessing, the needs that it reflected, or "what was in the hearts" of the trezvenniki. In this sense, there was deep irony in Iudin's claim that holy sobriety—or religious belief, more generally—threatened to "anesthetize" people, since scientific atheism seemed to have left many Soviet oysters stuck in their own ideological shells. As Soviet researchers like Aptekman and Klibanov wrestled with the persistent phenomenon of religious faith, they remained convinced of the incompatibility of faith and socialism, and thus caught between a desire to understand believers and to explain them away.[59]

Yet, as Catherine Wanner has persuasively argued, the relationship between believers and atheists and between religious groups and the Soviet system was "mutually constituting,"[60] since in the process of interaction one inevitably changed the other. Just as the orchid would never become a wasp, the analogy goes, the believer would never become a "Soviet citizen" in the fullest, secular sense of the term, yet in the process of interrelating "the orchid acquired some waspness."[61] Importantly, the opposite was true as well; in spite of Klibanov's confidence that it was the believer who would change in the context of Soviet secularism, in fact some atheists leading efforts in the battle against religion changed as well. By the end of the 1960s, atheists would suffer a crisis of meaning and, as Victoria Smolkin has demonstrated, begin to come to terms with the possibility that the persistence of religious belief in its many forms signaled something inadequate about Soviet atheism as a spiritual project—that it didn't speak sufficiently to people's souls or emotions. Eventually coming to see the problem as moral and spiritual rather than political or ideological, Smolkin has argued, atheists began to accept that in order to reach the "backward" masses most vulnerable to religious belief, they would need a "positive atheism" that addressed "life questions" as well as "emotions and everyday concerns."[62] This, of course, was a realization similar to that which Brother Ioann had forced on Orthodox clergy and missionaries some sixty years earlier.

The Testimony of Maria Kotiurova

Around the same time that atheists began to readjust their lens on religious believers, a forty-year-old mother, wife, and shop attendant, Maria Iakovlevna Kotiurova (b. 1925), began adjusting her perspective on her own life, and in 1968 she converted to sobriety. Of course, no single voice can speak for the trezvennik experience, especially given the profound fracturing of belief within the movement after Brother Ioann's death. And the fact that Kotiurova testified in the post-Soviet period also needs to be taken into account when considering her story.[63] Nonetheless, Kotiurova's detailed account of her family's conversion over the course of two decades offers insight into the tensions between sober and nonsober culture in late Soviet society, while also providing a meaningful complement—and contrast—to atheistic studies of holy sobriety. Her testimony also provides an interesting point of comparison between late Soviet conversions and those of earlier generations.

In line with Soviet autobiographical traditions, Kotiurova's account of her life begins with her birth (in 1925) and a brief social and cultural profile of her parents. She was born in "a most ungodly time," she explains, to a very religious and modest mother, who did not drink or smoke. Setting up a clear moral contrast between her two parents, she describes her mother's life as one of simple poverty, dignity, and moral integrity, while dismissing her father as a gambler and adulterer, and the cause of her mother's great suffering. As much as she looked upon her mother with both sympathy and admiration, however, Kotiurova chose not to follow in her footsteps in her youth; although baptized as many people of her generation were, she lacked innate religious inclinations and found her mother's world "backward" and out of step with Soviet society. "After all, everything in the world was not like mom taught," she reminded her twenty-first-century audience, and thus she chose to live "as the majority of the people in the Soviet era." Once an adult, she no longer attended church or observed fasts or "knew how to pray."

Kotiurova came of age during the war years; she was married at age twenty-four in 1949 and gave birth to a son in 1956. She describes their lifestyle as stressful and poor in the moral and spiritual sense—a fragile balance between work and "play," which typically involved a lot of drinking and smoking. Her son, Sasha, was born with an umbilical hernia, which made him cry a lot and unable to eat. Helpless in their efforts to treat the baby, doctors recommended that the infant be baptized, so he was. When he continued to suffer, Maria's mother found someone in her parish to offer a special prayer, and her son's health improved. But by 1958, Kotiurova's discontent and "anger" overwhelmed her, and she left her husband, taking to the road with her mother and small child, "in search of happiness."

After a series of jobs and moves, Kotiurova took her small family to Malaia Vishera, about two hundred kilometers from Leningrad. She soon met Aleksei, whom she married in a civil ceremony in 1964. He too turned out to be a big drinker, and thus, "my story was repeated: wedding, vodka. . . . And all the time, vodka, vodka." Soon they moved to Sologubovka, some forty-five miles southeast of Leningrad, where she worked in a confectionary shop. Again, Maria stressed that they "lived as many lived" in those days, drinking to excess. Even when her beloved mother died in 1968, they commemorated her death by getting drunk, in spite of the "harm" her mother believed such a sin would cause her soul.

After her mother's death, Kotiurova was a mess, emotionally and physically. By then in her early forties, her body had begun to suffer normal signs of aging (sciatica, hemorrhoids, and blurred vision), as well as other chronic problems, including eczema and a persistent sore throat. Her poor condition, she implies, was tied more to lifestyle than physical aging. She had a decent job, and because of that, she was provided for in a strictly medical sense; she underwent several surgeries to remove an ectopic pregnancy, a tumor on her shoulder, and a cyst on her ovary. Yet the combined weight of her health problems, a husband who was drunk all the time, a marriage dominated by scandals and fighting, and the death of her beloved mother caused her profound unhappiness. At one point, she found herself contemplating suicide. In retrospect, only the thought of her twelve-year-old son kept her alive.

In spite of support from concerned family and friends, Kotiurova struggled hopelessly with depression until she met two sober "angels," whom she came to believe had been sent to save her. In February 1968, they invited her to attend a celebration at the home of a couple commemorating ten years of sobriety. Although hesitant to attend a sober event, her apprehension was quickly dissipated by a series of positive physical and emotional experiences. In colorful detail, her testimony highlights how the celebration engaged all of her senses at once—the gentle aroma of cakes and pies, the taste of apricots and candy, the sight of clean, neatly dressed people, and beautiful spiritual singing. Although modest, the spread of lovingly prepared and "hard to get" foods signified a generosity of spirit that she found unusual and deeply meaningful. The evening was also rich in terms of spirit and conversation, on topics ranging from Scripture and the lives of the saints, to stories about Brother Ioann and problems of everyday life. Like generations before, the trezvenniki expressed gratitude for God's compassion and recalled how they had been saved from drunkenness, or smoking, or sexual immorality. They also shared stories about their families and how they had been saved too—these gave Kotiurova hope for her own. Most of all, she was struck by the way that the people treated each other with openness, warmth, and compassion—a stark and welcome contrast to the behaviors she was accustomed to, which included not only drinking and smoking but also a lot of showing off by means of anecdotes and jokes.

Kotiurova had never experienced anything like that evening in her life. As she described it, entering the sober apartment was like crossing a threshold from the outside world of the mundane and the everyday (*byt*), into a more meaningful space of *bytie* and enlightenment.

In the new (non-Soviet) space, both her body and soul were nurtured and cared for, and the atmosphere was one of profound acceptance, respect, and the kind of spiritual unity associated with *communitas*. In only a matter of minutes, she felt transformed from an outsider to a witness, and recipient, of "sober love"—that is, the unbounded and liberating joy, warmth, and generosity of spirit that came from people who had been lost and found. Even without drugs or alcohol, she felt high, as if in the "clouds," and thought to herself, "this is real paradise!" Everyone was "happy, cheerful, happy! All thanks to the Lord. And I spent the whole evening drenched in tears. . . . If someone asked me why I was crying, *I could not explain what was happening to me.*" Indeed, the entire evening was beyond her realm of experience, beyond her (Soviet) vocabulary.

At some point, one of the older trezvenniki asked Kotiurova Brother Ioann's standard question, "What do you want from God?" and she asked to be healed. They told her to write a note asking God to protect her from all her unhealthy habits—drinking, eating meat, and even smoking (even when she told them that she never smoked). Wanting to be *like them*, she followed their instructions to the letter. By the end of the evening, Kotiurova had taken a vow of sobriety, in spite of her initial apprehension about attending the event at all.

As for many trezvenniki before her, Maria Kotiurova's decision to commit to holy sobriety was both sudden and the beginning of a long struggle and journey, a prolonged process of taking leave of her "old life" and beginning "a completely different, spiritual one in the Law of Jesus Christ." As with many women (including Valentina Kren'), her embrace of sobriety was, initially at least, not so much about faith-seeking as it was about escaping the dominant culture of drunkenness and addiction that was threatening her own well-being and that of her family. Although raised by a pious mother, Kotiurova seems to have understood her vices as unhealthy in a physical, moral, and psychological sense; only later did she begin to see them as sinful. Indeed, in contrast to those born with a natural inclination toward spiritual searching, it was her body—not her mind or her soul—that first drew her to the trezvenniki. Only when she physically fell apart did she seek help, and only later did she start to worry intentionally about her spiritual life. Clearly, though, that first evening among the trezvenniki had awakened her spirit, making her one of many trezvenniki who would claim to have experienced Brother Ioann's unique ability to "spark" faith, even long after his death.

After taking the vow, Kotiurova relied on other trezvenniki to tell her "how and what to do" to live soberly, and she began to attend besedy regularly. She quickly adapted to their disciplined lifestyle; she learned to fast on Wednesday and Friday, and on every Monday morning, before penning notes to Brother Ioann to express her gratitude and needs. Afterward she would burn the notes as instructed. When she continued to suffer from health problems, she trusted the advice of the elders (startsy) to keep a strict fast, even as she continued to work full time. In fact, she specifically mentions that the more she fasted, the better she became as a worker. This was one of several signs that she understood her conversion not in opposition to Soviet norms but rather as a way to enhance her ability to live up to them.

"Trying to live a Christian life, as Dear Brother Ioann taught," took time and great effort, Kotiurova reflected, "but it [was] better and easier than rotting alive and swallowing a bunch of chemical drugs." In this respect, she found the elders' logic as compelling as their faith: "If we go to a hospital, doctors prescribe medicine. If the patient does not take them regularly, of course, he also doesn't recover. It is the same in spiritual life. Christ cures us if we execute his precepts, that is, in everyday life we apply and we carry out all his instructions—leave behind our former life, and we begin a completely different, spiritual life according to the Law of Jesus Christ." Although "not easy," she persisted in her commitment to a new vision of self, and gradually, as her behaviors began to align more fully with holy sobriety and as she began to see and speak about her experiences through a sober framework, "the Lord began to remove all my illnesses, and my sorrows, and all the horrors of my life, and everything in my life began to change."

Among the many factors—the words, ideas, rituals, and emotional practices—that worked together to help Kotiurova along the path to sobriety, one of the most important was the emotional support provided by the community. From day one, Maria was moved and buoyed by the trezvenniki's unbounded kindness, respect, and hopefulness, and her experience of their love and concern was reminiscent of the way that earlier generations had found healing through the nurture and support they received from Brother Ioann. As the journalist Bereskov had commented in 1910, Churikov's ability to make individuals feel seen and heard was extremely rare at the time. Writing in the 1960s, Nina Maslova similarly emphasized Brother Ioann's "boundless" and "inclusive" love for all.[64] Over time, Kotiurova's relationships with members of the community deepened, taking on a character best described as *svoi*, in the sense of belonging to a greater "we" bonded through shared beliefs, perspectives, language, and emotions.[65] In this sense, Maria's testimony suggests continuity in the community's emotional practices long after Brother Ioann was gone.

Sober converts like Maria also had something in common with members of the hippie movement of the 1960s and 1970s. Although expressions of "sober" love and "hippiedom" were very different, both reflected a widely held desire for a community bonded by love as an antidote to "'normal' Soviet interpersonal relations," which, as Juliane Fürst has pointed out, tended to be cold, distant, and often alienating.[66] And indeed, the way that hippies recalled their movement bears a striking resemblance to Kotiurova's own memories of meeting a group of trezvenniki for the first time, with an emphasis on unconditional acceptance, belonging, and freedom from judgment: "when we met at other people's—everybody is a brother to you," one former hippie recalled. "Like a relative—that is understood. But even more—like a king. They put you the whole time on a pedestal . . . with this admiration, this warmth. I love you, as you are. . . . They warmed each other with their love."[67]

The long-term success of Kotiurova's conversion was not a given, however; on the contrary, her spiritual peace rested on her ability to bring her family into sobriety as well. This turned out to be difficult. When she first joined the movement, her husband Aleksei had given up drinking, smoking, and his habit of extreme swearing. But like many Soviet-era trezvenniki, he struggled to engage with family, friends, and colleagues who did not understand his sobriety. And when a colleague died in a car accident, he turned to smoking in order to cope with the loss.

Aleksei encountered an even bigger stress in his life when a medical exam revealed dark spots on his lungs, on his throat, his ear, and his nose—worrying signs for a smoker. The doctor recommended surgery, but on the advice of other trezvenniki, he decided to begin a strict fast instead. As they had in the past, Kotiurova and other members of the trezvennik community joined together in prayer and fasted on Aleksei's behalf, and before long, he was healed—without the operation. He soon embraced sobriety and prayed frequently to Brother Ioann out of gratitude, telling people, "By God's grace I am alive, otherwise I would have rotted a long time ago."

According to Kotiurova, her husband's sobriety changed him radically, both internally and externally. He became hardworking and kind—a quality she repeatedly notes when talking about fellow trezvenniki—and in his free time, he took up the task of writing. Lacking printed versions of Brother Ioann's besedy, trezvenniki would write them out in "beautiful longhand." Although fundamentally spiritual, the exercise was also therapeutic for former smokers like Aleksei who needed to keep their hands busy. Over time their marriage was strengthened as the couple attended meetings together, celebrated holidays soberly, hung icons, prayed, fasted, and discussed and meditated on the Gospels. "After those dirty feasts, scandals, fights, troubles ... God gave us peace, tranquility, prosperity, respect for each other! Even nature around us changed, it was as if [we] had woken up from a long hibernation of death." Their new life, Kotiurova reflected, was "beautiful."

Yet their faith continued to be tested. While the community of trezvenniki provided a safe and welcoming space, in the outside world where they lived much of the time, they continued to encounter a lot of doubt from relatives, friends, and coworkers. Most of all, Kotiurova worried about her son being sucked into the same morally unstable culture that had almost destroyed them. She had come to understand that the life choices confronting him were very different from the binary framework taught by atheists in school. Rather than the competition between communism or capitalism, the collective and the individual, or even science versus faith, the essential questions for a young person his age were whether to embrace sobriety over addiction, hope over despair, and life over death.

As Kotiurova tells it, Sasha had hated their life when he was a child, especially his parents' arguing. But he also struggled with their sobriety, especially at school where they taught—and convinced—him that there was no God. Although happy that his parents had found peace, as a teenager he became, in his mother's words, a "prodigal son." At age fifteen, he began to drink and smoke, and in 1972, he decided he didn't want to go to school anymore. Still "Soviet" enough to see his abandonment of his (secular) education as a problem, his parents bribed him to continue his studies by buying him an electric guitar—an interesting choice, given that it was a symbol of Western materialism and "rock and roll" and completely at odds with the trezvenniki's traditional disdain for all but religious music. In any case, the bribe did not work, and as school started in the fall, he and several of his friends disappeared to another town. One of the elders reassured a frantic Maria that her son would return safely in three days, but also warned her to accept him back with love, not anger. As predicted,

Sasha eventually returned to school, but his flirtation with drinking and smoking was far from over.

After his required military service ended in 1976, Sasha's life proceeded unremarkably: he returned home with an injured leg but found work operating a bulldozer; he met a young woman, fell in love, and got married; and by 1979 the couple welcomed a son. For all the apparent fullness of his life, however, Sasha suffered from a serious drinking problem that threatened to destroy everything. If alone in his misery at the time, he was far from alone in his addiction. A 1982 study by Vladimir Treml estimated a steady rise in annual alcohol consumption over Sasha's lifetime from 7.3 liters per person in 1955 to 15.2 in 1979.[68] When official statistics were finally released in the mid-1980s, they were even worse.[69]

As Maria and Aleksei watched Sasha's life deteriorate, they relied on other trezvenniki for prayers and advice, just as previous generations had relied on Brother Ioann in times of uncertainty and suffering. As an elder instructed, Kotiurova responded to her son's prodigal ways with love, not judgment, but she still wasn't able to reach him. In 1980, however, after many prayers and "bitter tears," a series of "miracles" began to happen. For the first time in his life Sasha reached for the Bible that his mother had given him years before and began to read it in search of God. Then, one night as he sat at home alone he decided to take a vow of absolute sobriety, with God as his only witness: "And the Lord freed him from all the base human mud." From that point on, Sasha began to attend besedy and to identify as a trezvennik.

According to Kotiurova's testimony, the sober community had been instrumental in saving her son, just as it had saved her. "Many of my brothers and sisters by faith worked for him," she observed, "and the Lord did not leave our prayers without attention." They were not just "her people," but people with an active sense of purpose and a moral obligation to support one another. Indeed, in Brother Ioann's absence, community members had stepped up to take on many of the roles that he had played in their lives—instructor, disciplinarian, counselor, and nurturer. Kotiurova even attributed the gift of prophecy to some of them, as when the elder predicted Sasha would return home. Most of all, she valued them for their prayers—the more, the better.

As important as the community was, however, another powerful relationship in Sasha's story is one that had animated the trezvennik movement all along: the love between mother and son, and between grandmother and child. After all, without his mother's relentless efforts and support, and without her role as a conduit connecting her son to the sober community, his life would likely have turned out very differently. As Sasha would later reflect, both his grandmother and mother had had an enormous influence on his spiritual development. While his grandmother had been reluctant to impose her own deep faith on her family, her piety and humility clearly impressed upon both her daughter and grandson, fostering shame in the former and an openness and warmth toward believers in the latter. And as we've seen, once his mother embraced faith herself, she remained determined to save her own family through sobriety, in spite of Soviet efforts to define the responsibilities of motherhood in distinctly secular and socialist ways. Eventually her persistence worked. "A mother's prayer will bring one back from the bottom of the sea," Sasha recalled.[70]

In an interesting twist of the trezvennik script, the love between a son and his parents was also instrumental in bringing about the final evolution of Kotiurova's own sober identity. In 1989, after almost a decade in the trezvennik community, Sasha decided to take his faith to a new level by testifying publicly. In a letter dated February 12, 1989, he published his conversion story in *Leningradskaia Pravda*, the same paper that had carried some of the most scathing critiques of Brother Ioann in the past. "My name is Sasha Zakharov. I became sober and a believer eight years ago. I am now thirty-two years old. I work a bulldozer. If it were not for the sober society of Brother Ioann Churikov, I think I would still be drunk and have lost everything human. Now I have a good family, [and] many friends [of the same faith]. At work, I am respected. [My] new life, I am convinced, began with faith. From this moment on, my conscience was awakened, [and in me] the need to live like a human being."[71] The following year, Sasha began studying at the Leningrad Theological Seminary; he was ordained by Metropolitan Ioann (Snychev) as a deacon in the Russian Orthodox Church in October 1991 and as a priest the following year, shortly after the formal dissolution of the Soviet Union. In 1990, after twenty-two years of sobriety, Maria and Aleksei also joined the Orthodox Church, and in 1999, they were married (*venchalis'*) in an Orthodox ceremony. Maria Kotiurova died in 2010, but her son, Father Aleksandr Zakharov, continues to serve his own parish in Sologubovka; today he is a highly respected author and temperance activist.

Shortly before her death in the 1960s, Brother Ioann's long-time sister Nina Maslova offered some reflections on faith and the Soviet people. As someone whose own experience of sobriety bridged the decades before and after 1917, the Stalinist repressions and the war, and the Thaw, Maslova had extraordinary range of perspective. Decades of living under official atheism had done little to convince her that people can live without God. On the contrary, "destroy faith in God," she observed, "and people will suffocate in a layer of their own evil."[72] Faith is essential not only for the individual but for all of society, since it serves as a necessary check on human nature, which is neither universally consistent nor inherently as good as the Soviet vision needed it to be.

At the same time, Maslova acknowledged the "complex make-up [stroenie]" of human beings, and found it only natural that people take many paths to God. Pushing back on the usefulness of official Soviet forms of enlightenment, she questioned any attempt to regulate people's thoughts and behaviors according to a single universalizing belief or ideology. Brother Ioann's goal had never been to impose beliefs on others, she observed, but rather to awaken individuals spiritually and bring them to self-awareness so that they could rise up on their own and change their lives—so as to attain not material comforts, but "peace of mind, peace and joy in life."[73] As even the most committed atheists would eventually acknowledge, Maslova was not wrong. Many people held on to their own version of God throughout the Soviet period, and by the 1970s alternative forms of God-seeking were matched by more secular forms of salvation on the larger map of mature socialism. "Disenchanted by officially sanctioned modes of believing and acting," Aleksei Yurchak has observed, members of the last Soviet generation regularly took emotional, intellectual, and spiritual refuge in non-Soviet spaces of their own choosing and design.[74]

As much as atheists worried that the fate of communism was linked to the defeat of religious belief, the Soviet system did not suffer—let alone fail—because the atheists failed, or because of the constellation of beliefs in the socialist universe. To be sure, as Juliane Fürst has argued, "with disengagement and disconnection becoming enduring features of 'normal' life, it was hard to create the sense of longevity and destiny that was so crucial to the socialist project."[75] Indeed, the way in which the trezvenniki's existence indicated a fragmentation of the abstract entity known as the "Soviet people" was one of the godless Iudin's biggest concerns.[76] Yet stories like Maria Kotiurova's suggest that the day-to-day stability of Soviet society depended in large part on the ability of people to find alternative ways to heal themselves and carry on in a system that did not meet their individual spiritual needs. In fact, it was precisely the support of families and local communities like the trezvenniki that helped to realize the Soviet promise of brotherhood, equality, and prosperity for many ordinary people.

The longevity of trezvennichestvo and other alternative communities of faith eventually led Soviet atheists to reassess their own assumptions, first in the 1960s as scholars like Aptekman began to embrace the "spiritual" as a meaningful category of experience, and then even in more official circles, with the decision to open up the religious sphere and to allow the Russian Orthodox Church to commemorate the millennial of the faith in 1988. Although largely a political move, the latter reflected an acceptance on the part of the Communist Party that faith of any kind—even a contradictory belief in both God and communism—was better than indifference.[77] To a certain extent, one might see in the party's decision a parallel with the Orthodox Church before the revolution; although the clergy aspired to make all lay people conform to church norms, they eventually had to acknowledge a spectrum of beliefs and behaviors, even among those who claimed to be "Orthodox." Although the official clergy was split between those who insisted on a perfect alignment between orthodoxy and orthopraxy, and those who were content to accept discipline or obedience in the absence of true faith, in the end it proved counterproductive to force everyone into a "pure" mold. In other words, both the tsarist Orthodox Church and the Soviet regime were pushed by religious believers on the margins to acknowledge weaknesses at their spiritual center and rethink their governance strategies.

While the threat of official sanctions against most believers lessoned considerably after the 1960s, the millennial celebration of the Russian people's conversion to Christianity in 1988 marked the opening up of a viable religious sphere for the first time since the 1920s. In July of that year, the trezvenniki took advantage of the relative freedom presented by glasnost and perestroika, and led by the elder of the Leningrad community, Vladimir Glinskii, petitioned the Soviet government to rehabilitate Brother Ioann; Maria and her family were among the seventy signatories on the petition.[78] As in the past, the trezvenniki testified to Brother Ioann's healings as evidence of his unique goodness and to their own "usefulness" as both sober workers and *Russian* citizens. The petition was also boldly religious in its claims to the still atheistic state. "Even if belatedly," it read, "let us absolve ourselves of some of the guilt before those who [like Ivan Alekseevich Churikov] lived not in their own name, but for the sake of the great spirit of God in man." Their plea was also strikingly nationalistic. Rather than turning to "foreign healers" to help "our people [who] suffer from drunkenness and lack of spirituality," the petition continued, it was time to recognize "the national history of the struggle for man," which included, first and foremost, leaders from the people like Brother Ioann.

For the first time in many decades the trezvenniki's petition to the Soviet state was successful, and the demand for Brother Ioann's rehabilitation granted. Soon the community in Vyritsa was able to take possession of the house the trezvenniki had built for him before the revolution, and to return freely to the sacred ground of Vyritsa.[79] In this sense, for trezvenniki 1988 was a liberation on the same scale as 1917, as well as an opportunity to begin reclaiming their history. As the Soviet project imploded over the coming years, bringing widespread impoverishment, uncertainty, poor health, and a spike in alcoholism, the trezvenniki in Leningrad-Petersburg began a new chapter of hope; although still deeply fragmented in terms of their beliefs, the movement for holy sobriety has since attracted many new members, long outliving another regime that had sought to silence it.

Epilogue
The Past Is Still Present

Holy sobriety found fertile ground in post-Soviet Russia. As the population struggled to survive the rapid increase in poverty, unemployment, and dangerously poor health conditions that accompanied the rapid transition from communism to capitalism, a new generation of trezvenniki emerged. Among them was a twenty-one-year old IV drug addict, Evgenii, who joined the sober community in Vyritsa in 2000 after living on the streets, landing in prison, and contracting HIV and hepatitis. "I was sick, I was dying, I was falling apart," he testified in a 2005 interview published in *Novyi Peterburg*, but "those who believe in the Word of God, the God of Dear Brother, will be healed of any disease."[1]

After pledging sobriety, Evgenii moved to Vyritsa permanently, where he became part of a modest but growing community of other former addicts. He worked "like an ox" for long hours, so as to distract himself from his addiction,[2] and in line with practices initiated by Brother Ioann, he observed a highly disciplined regimen of prayer and fasting—until 2:00 p.m. on Mondays and usually all day on Fridays. He also began studying Brother Ioann's written works and attending weekly besedy on Sundays at 2:00 p.m. in the very same room where Churikov preached until his arrest in 1929. Eventually he met a young woman in the community, and they got married.

To Evgenii, life in Vyritsa was "paradise." "God pulled me out of hell. I . . . do not want to go back there." Testifying to his healing brought him great joy, as it had many trezvenniki before him. Echoing Brother Ioann's besedy, Evgenii's testimony delivered a stunning critique of post-Soviet St. Petersburg, denouncing a contemporary preoccupation with money and the privileging of "debauchery, holidays, concerts, discos" while "everything that concerns human suffering is going down the drain." He acknowledged people's natural resistance to the idea that a better life might come through prayer and fasting: "It is fantastical to them," he observed, and "for a dying world, a sober person is like a thorn." Yet he also expressed faith that suffering would, eventually, bring them to God, just as it had for him and his wife. So he simply welcomed one and all to Vyritsa, to write a note to Brother Ioann and be healed. He even had a message for President Putin: "accept Sobriety and make Sobriety the official faith. Because without Sobriety . . . [and] without God . . . you cannot be successful in anything." "God will help everyone," he continued, no matter who they are, "the homeless, the president, the drug addict, the drunkard and the criminal. . . . Whoever he is, he is human. He is equal to all others before God."[3]

In many ways, Evgenii's beliefs and lifestyle are in line with generations of trezvenniki before him, but a closer look reveals two striking differences. First, Evgenii shares the belief with the sober community in Vyritsa that Brother Ioann was the Second Coming of Christ, who "came as God to heal all nations of drunkenness." Second, he believes in the divinity of the elder Aleksei Ivanovich Sinnikov, who served as head of the fraternal council of the Vyritsa community from 1994 until his death in 2007. As mentioned in chapter 9, in the late Soviet era Sinnikov gained a reputation for performing miraculous healings, expelling demons, and even "resurrecting the dead through his prayers," and this led some trezvenniki to see him as Brother Ioann's spiritual successor.[4] In fact, according to Maria Masagutova's recent ethnographic study of the community, some members go even further, claiming that Sinnikov is "the embodiment of Churikov, who returned, on a promise, fifty years later to finish what he did not have time to do"—in other words, he is seen as what one former member of the community called facetiously the "second part of the Second Coming."[5]

Sinnikov's identity continues to be a source of great controversy, and in the interest of protecting the Vyritsa community's image as unified and peaceful, the topic is rarely discussed in any public way. In the absence of new charismatic leaders to emerge since Sinnikov's death, Masagutova has argued, the community has now become more fully "textual"—that is, centered and bonded by a shared reverence for Brother Ioann's besedy and letters. While trezvenniki have long looked to his writings as a source of guidance and prophecy, some have come to see them as nothing less than the "fixed voice of the living God ready to communicate with his followers."[6] To them, his words are a channel of his divine grace. In fact, the reverence that the Vyritsa trezvenniki hold for Brother's words is such that no one is allowed to enter the hall during a reading. According to Masagutova, they even prioritize his besedy over Holy Scripture itself, seeing the relationship between the texts as similar to that between Brother Ioann and Christ, "as the same thing, but renewed."[7]

While not all trezvenniki in Vyritsa share the same views, belief in Brother Ioann's divinity—both his omnipotence and omnipresence—unites them, as does their belief that living according to the laws of sobriety will bring both spiritual salvation and earthly salvation, including good health and material well-being. Breaking one's sober vow or falling short of prescribed behaviors, conversely, will lead to punishment in the form of illness, misfortune, or poverty. To an extent, the association of sobriety with a prosperous life was manifested in Brother Ioann's colony, but the views of contemporary trezvenniki differ in at least two ways. They interpret the relative prosperity of sober people as a sign of the correctness of their faith, and they are on the whole less ascetic than earlier generations on the belief that whatever wealth they have is a gift from Brother Ioann. In this way, Masagutova has argued, their beliefs are consonant with prosperity theology popular among neo-Pentecostals.[8]

Today, the community of Brother Ioann's followers in Vyritsa is the largest in Russia. Although it is difficult to gauge the exact size, the journalist D. Sokolov-Mitrich estimated the sober population in Vyritsa at one thousand by 2008 and identified forty-seven additional communities scattered throughout Russia,[9] as well as cities in Belarus and Lithuania. Sunday meetings in Vyritsa regularly attract 100–150 people, and many more have registered on the website. The community's active presence on the Internet and social media, which included the livestreaming of weekly besedy during the 2020 pandemic, has increased its visibility. As in Brother Ioann's day, the community is welcoming to people of all backgrounds, including those from other faiths. Having fully detached from the Russian Orthodox tradition, the Vyritsa trezvenniki are even more convinced of the universality of holy sobriety, and they imagine Vyritsa as the epicenter of a global movement.

Aside from the attraction of sobriety as a way of life, the vitality of the community in Vyritsa reflects a widespread desire on the part of ordinary people to see God at work in the world, and to believe in miraculous possibilities and the imminence of the kingdom of God on earth. The community's belief in Brother Ioann's divinity remains highly controversial, but as this book has shown, it has run through the sober community since his lifetime in spite of attempts on the part of Brother Ioann, the Russian Orthodox Church, and other trezvenniki to weed it out of the sober garden. The belief gained greater traction after the "final judgment" of 1917 silenced many church authorities, and yet even more following Brother Ioann's death when, paradoxically, the state's strict controls over institutionalized religious life led to a flowering of alternative beliefs underground.

The Vyritsa community's beliefs would seem to suggest that the fears voiced by church authorities in the early twentieth century were justified—that is, that the degree of spiritual authority the trezvenniki attached to Brother Ioann was dangerously heretical and, if left unchecked, would erode rather than strengthen the Orthodox faith. And indeed, the Vyritsa community continues to shun the clergy, believing not only that the revolution was a form of divine justice on unrighteous tsars and crafty, exploitative priests, but also that the collapse of the USSR was a punishment for official atheism.[10]

The story of the Vyritsa trezvenniki is only one part of the movement's post-Soviet history, however. In 1990, the Society of Christian Trezvenniki was officially registered, but one year later the group split into two branches. The other major trezvennik community, which is centered in St. Petersburg and identifies as the Orthodox Society of Brother Ioann Churikov's Trezvenniki, adamantly denies Churikov's divinity and continues to revere him as a righteous individual and an Orthodox believer—saintlike, but not (yet) a saint. As their name suggests, they actively identify and practice as Orthodox believers, suggesting that the trezvenniki's marginalization from Orthodoxy after 1914 was not inevitable and that reconciliation with the Church and faith was and is possible.

As suggested by the case of Maria Kotiurova and her family in chapter 10, the process of reconciliation began in the late 1980s, with the decision of individual trezvenniki to become more involved with the Church, which was itself undergoing great changes as atheistic rule disintegrated. The road back to the fold of the Russian Orthodox Church was difficult; Brother Ioann's conflict with the Church, followed by decades of de facto alienation from the clergy, left the trezvenniki with a lot of questions. The first years of the 1990s were thus ones of religious searching and few clear answers.

When the society of Orthodox Christian followers of Brother Ioann registered in 1991, it met first in private apartments, then in the Palace of Culture of the First Five-Year Plan, and had no direct affiliation with any church. According to the group's leader at the time, Vladimir Glinskii, the next stage in the process of reconciling the trezvenniki with the institution of the Church was initiated by local clergy—especially Father Vladimir Sorokin, who reached out to some of Churikov's followers.[11] Aware of the community's active commitment to sobriety during a time of widespread alcoholism, Sorokin had read extensively about Brother Ioann and was willing to acknowledge his positive work among the morally and spiritually needy in Leningrad/St. Petersburg. Although only a few clergy were willing to praise Churikov at the time, Father Sorokin went so far as to denounce clerical efforts to silence him one hundred years earlier.

The next moment of reconciliation came in 1995, when Father Aleksandr Zakharov—Maria Kotiurova's son—helped to arrange a meeting between a small delegation of Petersburg trezvenniki and his mentor, Metropolitan Ioann (Snychev), shortly before his untimely death. In contrast to the emotional (and destructive) interactions between clergy and trezvenniki from 1910 to 1914, the meeting in 1995 was dominated by a new kind of hope and collaborative pragmatism, founded on the shared realization that reconciliation was a challenging yet worthwhile goal. As during the first decade of the twentieth century, the community's beliefs and activities fit nicely with the Church's developing mission in the early 1990s—that is, to expand its flock (both by cultivating piety and lessening the influence of foreign "sects") and to help curb alcoholism and drug addiction. Like Father Sorokin, the Petersburg metropolitan took time to become acquainted with Brother Ioann through the available documents (including his besedy and letters to his followers) and reached the conclusion that he was in fact a true Orthodox believer. While emphasizing how difficult it would be for the trezvenniki to reconcile with the Church after seventy years of being on the outside, he blessed them in their efforts.[12]

The metropolitan's willingness to validate the Petersburg trezvenniki's work helped to soften long-held negative attitudes within the community toward the Orthodox clergy. By studying Brother Ioann's works, which were being published and circulated more freely than ever before, and by working on reconstructing the history of the movement, they also came to a better understanding of the Church's concerns about his preaching; "slowly but steadily," Sergei Palamodov recalled, "we came to [realize] what [Brother Ioann] himself [had] said, that he was a man, and, being a man, could not avoid errors in the presentation and adherence to the truth kept in the Church." Assuming an attitude of humility, they decided to follow the path laid out by St. Augustine, "to live by Brother Ioann's example, but not by his mistakes."[13] To that end, they embraced the opportunity to learn from the Orthodox clergy about the faith, and to engage more fully in the Church's ritual life. Before long, remarked Glinskii (echoing the claims of trezvenniki one hundred years ago), the members of his community could claim to be just like other Orthodox believers, except that they do not drink wine while communicating or celebrating weddings or baptisms.[14]

Yet another stage of reconciliation came in 2001, when the Petersburg community received permission and Father Sorokin's blessing to hold its Sunday afternoon meetings in the Chapel of the New Martyrs and Confessors of Russia, next to the Feodorovsky Cathedral. Used as a dairy during the Soviet years, the once pungent and dilapidated church has since been beautifully renovated, and the chapel where the trezvenniki meet was built. Following tradition, they too gather on Sunday afternoons, usually after attending the Orthodox Liturgy in their own parishes throughout the city. As in Vyritsa, the primary purpose of the meetings is to hear sermons drawn from Holy Scripture and Churikov's besedy, preached by his followers, standing at a pulpit, in front of icons and a large portrait of Brother Ioann. In addition to collective prayer and the singing of hymns, individual trezvenniki present testimonials and, occasionally, speak on the history of the Church or offer contemplative thoughts drawn from their own experience or from the lives of the saints. Once day a month is set aside for new members to take an oath of sobriety and to celebrate those who have reached important milestones in their commitment to it. Typically, the meeting lasts for two to three hours, after which interested individuals can stay for tea, cakes and candy, and casual conversation. When the occasion rises, the community celebrates sober weddings, birthdays, and Angel days (the feast day of the saint after which one is named). The atmosphere is intimate but extraordinarily warm and welcoming even to newcomers.

Trezvenniki today stress the importance of showing up both for besedy and for each other; echoing generations before them, they emphasize that sobriety thrives best in the context of community.

According to Andrei Nechaev, a leading member of the Petersburg group who grew up in a sober family, "you have to live in the community" to model the hope of a sober life for others and to experience the support of other people who are sober in both a physical and spiritual sense.[15] After years of struggling with addiction and exploring different paths to sobriety, including Alcoholics Anonymous, the trezvennitsa Svetlana Semakina found the will to stay sober only after joining the Petersburg community. While taking comfort in the group's prayers, encouragement, and compassion, she also lives in fear of letting them down, and this sense of responsibility to others strengthens her resolve. Equally important to her sobriety is the community's positive messaging. Instead of seeing the addict as "sick" and perpetually "flawed" in an otherwise "healthy" world, the trezvenniki focus their attention less on "abstinence" than on living soberly for God's sake, as Brother Ioann instructed. This approach, in line with Churikov's insistence on each individual's "worthiness before God" (bogopodobie), makes them better able to see sober people as "healthy" and "on the right track." In this respect, Semakina points out, the trezvennik approach to sobriety differs meaningfully from that taken by AA.[16]

In addition to regular Sunday meetings, the Orthodox trezvenniki in St. Petersburg engage as a community in a range of activities and rituals throughout the year; these include holiday worship, cross processions, a prayer group, a youth Bible-study group, and a choir. They engage in outreach to the sick and dying, as well as those struggling with addiction, and make pilgrimages to monasteries and other Orthodox holy sites throughout the year. A highlight is the New Year's procession of Orthodox trezvenniki in the Holy Trinity Alexander Nevsky Lavra. Recently, the community has also begun to organize special group excursions, including a bus tour of St. Petersburg, highlighting sites important to the life and work of Brother Ioann, and a memorial service at the Levashovo memorial, commemorating "Brother Ioann Churikov and all teetotalers, who laid down their souls for the Faith of Christ and a sober life during the years of persecution."

In line with Brother Ioann's embrace of new technologies and his modern awareness of the need to self-fashion, the Orthodox trezvenniki have made the most of the contemporary media landscape to build community, to publicize holy sobriety, and to actualize an important component of their identity by testifying to their faith as sober Orthodox. As in Vyritsa, much of the Petersburg trezvenniki's outreach is conducted online, through a content-rich website.[17] Over the past decade, the community has also expanded its mission through radio, television, and social media; its connection with the Orthodox Church and its media resources (especially Radio Maria and the Orthodox station "Soiuz") has definitely helped in this respect. In 2014, the Petersburg trezvenniki also produced a documentary film of Churikov's life, *Apostle of Sobriety*, and in 2020 a full-length, high-quality documentary on their community, *And Sobriety Has Lasted More than a Century*.

For all the progress the Petersburg community has made in its efforts to (re)unite with the Orthodox Church, full reconciliation continues to be threatened by the visibility and popularity of the Vyritsa trezvenniki. To the Orthodox, of course, their belief in Brother Ioann's divinity is heretical, and thus the Petersburg trezvennniki are forced to disavow any connection to the Vyritsa group, as well as to prove—to both the Church and the public—that their devotion to Churikov and his teachings in no way contradicts their identity as Orthodox. The need to defend Brother Ioann to church authorities has long been a core part of trezvennik identity, and today the challenge is similar: "to tell the truth" about "the great religious ascetic of the Russian land," Brother Churikov, whose name has been "unfairly forgotten or unjustly linked with sectarianism."[18] At the same time, however, they are working to correct the distortion of his past and teachings that occurred during the Soviet period—a process involving both his (godless) critics and the self-appointed "brothers" who rewrote his besedy in the 1920s, claiming them as their own. In addition to extensive documentation of Brother Ioann's identity as both Orthodox and spiritually gifted on their website, the Petersburg community has sponsored academic conferences commemorating the anniversary of Brother Ioann's birth, including one in January 2016 at the Feodorovsky Cathedral, which was attended by clergy, historians, and ethnographers. Father Sorokin opened the 2016 conference with the hope that it would "enlighten" people about Brother Ioann and his good works, but Archbishop Maksim Pletnev expressed the more ambitious goal that "the conference will become a milestone in the unification of the temperance movement and the Church."[19] Time will tell, but it is fair to say that the Petersburg community is working very hard to bring Brother Ioann and his followers fully back into the church's fold.

Although the relationship between trezvenniki and the Orthodox Church remains an imperfect one today, many individuals have found a way to combine the two identities in ways that would have pleased both Brother Ioann and his clerical critics. Not least are those trezvenniki who, for the first time in history, made the decision to join the clergy. As noted in chapter 10, Father Aleksandr Zakharov was the first in a new generation of clerical trezvenniki, and he has been followed by others, including Sergei Palamodov and two members of the Khlynov family.[20] With three decades of clerical experience behind him already, Zakharov's path is of particular interest. While devoting himself to the Orthodox Church and faithfully serving the needs of his parishioners, most recently at Passion Bearers Cathedral in Sologubovka, Father Zakharov has continued to demonstrate an active commitment to sobriety by working with the patients of the Sologubovka Rehabilitation Center for drug addicts. Founded in 2012, the center takes a highly disciplined, multitherapeutic approach to rehabilitation; although the treatment plan uses modern approaches to mental health, it also involves structured Orthodox practices, including communion and confession, and highly disciplined labor practices—that is, practices that sound very similar to the daily routines pioneered by Brother Ioann on the colony in Vyritsa.[21]

The deep chasm that divides the two major trezvennik communities in Russia today remains a challenge for all. Although those who identify today as followers of Brother Ioann share a deep commitment to holy sobriety as a way of living in this world, they clearly differ with respect to their understanding of what is "holy." The views of the two communities are irreconcilable, and each serves as a serious check on the aspirations of the other—full reconciliation with Orthodoxy and the possibility of sainthood, on the one hand, and the spread of global sobriety, on the other. From a historical perspective, however, both branches of trezvenniki can claim to be the legitimate descendants of holy sobriety as a movement, since from the very beginning, Brother Ioann's identity has been disputed; while the Petersburg group's views are closer to Brother Ioann's own understanding of who he was and what he believed, the Vyritsa group equally reflects the beliefs of those trezvenniki who saw him as a divine figure who came to save the world. In short, today, just as in the past, Brother Ioann's identity has always been determined by his followers' needs and their faith, and these, it seems, continue to manifest along a spectrum of holiness.

Likewise, the persecution of the trezvenniki has historically served as a mirror on the broader social, religious, and political context. As we have seen, at both of Russia's revolutionary moments in the twentieth century—1917 and 1991—trezvenniki have argued that the respective regimes failed precisely because they did not want to embrace the truth of holy sobriety, and thus they faced divine justice for their sins. The promise of the contemporary historical moment is that even with their competing beliefs, both sober communities can exist and coexist openly. To be sure, there are some limits on sobriety even today, as in the case of the Zagoskin family mentioned at the start of this book. But more than any time in history, trezvenniki are able to reach out freely to people struggling with addiction and illness and offer them the peace, community, and hope of salvation that so many have found through holy sobriety.[22] As Brother Ioann argued, *trezvost'*—like any other faith or guiding truth—cannot be legislated or forced from above; it is something that each individual must come to and decide to embrace on their own, in their own time and in their own way. Thus, sobriety does best in a society that encourages individual choice and freedom in the broadest sense; and as every trezvennik would argue, the more sobriety, the better the society.

NOTES

Archival citations use the following abbreviations:

d. = delo, dela (file/s)
f. = fond (collection)
koll. = kollektsiia (collection)
l./ll. = list/y (sheet/s)
ob = oborot (versa)
op. = opis' (inventory)
t. = tom (volume)

Introduction

1. "Sektantka Sveta," *Zhurnal'nyi klub Intelros "Russkaia zhizn'*," no. 21, 2008, http://www.intelros.ru/readroom/rulife/21-38-5-nojabrja-2008-goda/3012-sektanktka-sveta.html.

2. "V sele Vologskoi oblasti idet spor, komu spasat' devochku," reported by Andrei Kuznetsov, October 20, 2008, https://www.1tv.ru/news/2008-10-20/184283-v_sele_vologodskoy_oblasti_idet_spor_komu_spasat_devochku_so_smertelnoy_opuholyu. See also Iuliia Lavrova, "Bez vmeshatel'stva sverkhu," *Rossiiskaia Gazeta*, no. 4778 (October 23, 2008), https://rg.ru/2008/10/23/sekta.html.

3. D. Sokolov-Mitrich, "Zagovor trezvykh," *Russkii reporter*, no. 26 (56) (July 11, 2008), https://expert.ru/russian_reporter/2008/26/trezvomolcy/.

4. Patricia Herlihy, *The Alcoholic Empire: Vodka and Politics in Late Imperial Russia* (Oxford: Oxford University Press, 2002).

5. N. Abramov, "Eshche o Churikove," *Petrogradskii listok*, no. 181 (July 2, 1916): 2.

6. In the tsarist period when the movement originated, the followers of Brother Ioann Churikov referred to themselves as *trezvenniki-pravoslavnye* (Orthodox teetotalers) to clarify the connection between their sobriety and their Orthodox identity. For more on terminology, see RGIA, f. 821, op. 133, d. 212, l. 286ob.

7. These are variations on Leonard Primiano's definition of "vernacular religion"—that is, religion as it was "encountered, understood, interpreted, and practiced." See "Vernacular Religion and the Search for Method in Religious Folklife," *Western Folklore* 53, no. 1 (January 1995): 44.

8. Jill Lepore, "Historians Who Love Too Much: Reflections on Microhistory and Biography," *Journal of American History* 88, no. 1 (June 2001): 133.

9. Tom Parfitt, "Putin Urged to Address 'Russia's Curse,'" *The Lancet* 367, no. 9506 (January 21, 2006): 197–98.

10. James Rodgers, "In the Putin Era, Alcohol Consumption Falls by 43%," *Forbes*, October 5, 2019, https://www.forbes.com/sites/jamesrodger seurope/2019/10/05/in-the-putin-era-alcohol-consumption-in-russia-falls-by-43/?sh=2b7be11b5153. See also, "Alcohol Consumption Falls 80% over 7 Years in Russia," *Orthodox Christianity*, January 16, 2018, http://orthochristian.com/109945.html.

11. Mark Lawrence Schrad, *Vodka Politics: Alcohol, Autocracy, and the Secret History of the Russian State* (Oxford: Oxford University Press, 2014), xi–xii.

12. In addition to Herlihy, *Alcoholic Empire* and Schrad, *Vodka Politics*, other works in English on Russia's drinking problem included David Christian, *Living Water: Vodka and Russian Society on the Eve of Emancipation* (Oxford: Clarendon Press, 1990); Laura L. Phillips, *Bolsheviks and the Bottle: Drink and Worker Culture in St. Petersburg, 1900–1929* (DeKalb: Northern Illinois University Press, 2000); Kate Transchel, *Under the Influence: Working-Class Drinking, Temperance, and Cultural Revolution in Russia, 1895–1932* (Pittsburgh: University of Pittsburgh Press, 2006); and Stephen White, *Russia Goes Dry: Alcohol, State, and Society* (Cambridge: Cambridge University Press, 1996). See also Daniel Beer, *Renovating Russia: The Human Sciences and the Fate of Liberal Modernity, 1880–1930* (Ithaca, NY: Cornell University Press, 2008), 73–75.

13. Helena Stone, "The Soviet Government and Moonshine: 1917–1929," *Cahiers du Monde russe et sovietique* 27, nos. 3/4 (July–December 1986): 359–79.

14. In an effort to conceal rather than draw attention to the nation's drinking problem, Soviet officials simply stopped recording consumption statistics in the early 1960s. White, *Russia Goes Dry*, 32.

15. See Katherine Keenan et al., "Social Factors Influencing Russian Male Alcohol Use over the Life Course: A Qualitative Study Investigating Age Based Social Norms, Masculinity, and Workplace Context." *PLoS ONE* 10 (11) (2015): e0142993, http://doi.org/10.1371/journal.pone.0142993.

16. Schrad, *Vodka Politics*, xi–xii.

17. Leon Neyfakh, "Why Russia's Drinkers Resist AA," *Boston Globe*, November 3, 2013, http://www.bostonglobe.com/ideas/2013/11/02/why-russia-drinkers-resist/6uJ7ugDd5H2Kko28ykXs9K/story.html.

18. A common approach is by means of "narcology," a combination of detox, drugs, and hypnosis. Interview with Eugene Raikhel by Heidi Brown, in "Drinking Games: Can Russia Admit It Has a Problem?" *World Policy Journal* 28, no. 2 (Summer 2011): 112. See also Eugene Raikhel, *Governing Habits: Treating Alcoholism in Post-Soviet Clinics* (Ithaca, NY: Cornell University Press, 2016).

19. Quoted in Neyfakh, "Why Russia's Drinkers Resist AA."

20. See, for example, Heather J. Coleman, *Russian Baptists and Spiritual Revolution, 1905–1929* (Bloomington: Indiana University Press, 2005); Laura Engelstein, *Castration and the Heavenly Kingdom: A Russian Folktale* (Ithaca, NY: Cornell University Press, 1999); Roy Robson, *Old Believers in Modern Russia* (Dekalb: Northern Illinois University Press, 1995).

21. Engelstein, *Castration and the Heavenly Kingdom*, xii.

22. Page Herrlinger, *Working Souls: Russian Orthodoxy and Factory Labor in St. Petersburg, 1880–1917* (Bloomington: Slavica, 2007).

23. Mark D. Steinberg, *Proletarian Imagination: Self, Modernity, & the Sacred in Russia, 1910–1925* (Ithaca, NY: Cornell University Press, 2002).

24. Aside from my own work, previous studies of Churikov in English have focused on the prerevolutionary period and include Herlihy, *Alcoholic Empire*, 79–81; W. Arthur McKee, "Sobering Up the People: The Politics of Popular Temperance in Late Imperial Russia," *Russian Review* 58, no. 2 (April 1999): 212–33; J. Eugene Clay, "Orthodox Missionaries and 'Orthodox Heretics' in Russia, 1886-1917," in *Of Religion and Empire*, ed. Robert Geraci and Michael Khodarkovsky (Ithaca, NY: Cornell University Press, 2001), 38–69; and Steinberg, *Proletarian Imagination*, 228–30.

25. The website trezvost.com is maintained by Brother Ioann's followers in Vyritsa, who identify as the Society of Brother Ioann Churikov's Spiritual Christian Trezvenniki (hereafter referred to as the Society of Spiritual Christian Trezvenniki). The websites trezvograd.3dn.ru and trezvograd.ru are maintained by trezvenniki in St. Petersburg, who identify as the Pravoslavnoe obshchestvo khristian trezvennikov Brattsa Ioanna Churikova (the Orthodox Society of Brother Ioann Churikov's Christian Trezvenniki) or alternatively, the Pravoslavnoe obshchestvo trezvennikov Brattsa Ioanna Churikova (the Orthodox Society of Brother Ioann Churikov's Trezvenniki); hereafter, the sites will be referred to in the notes as the Society of Spiritual Christian Trezvenniki and the Orthodox Society of Trezvenniki, respectively.

26. Monographs in English include Robert Greene, *Bodies Like Bright Stars: Saints and Relics in Orthodox Russia* (Dekalb: Northern Illinois University Press, 2010); James A. Kapalo, *Text, Context and Performance: Gagauz Folk Religion in Discourse and Practice* (New York: Brill, 2011); Nadieszda Kizenko, *A Prodigal Saint: Father Ioann of Kronstadt and the Russian People* (University Park: Pennsylvania State University Press, 2000); Irina Korovushkina Paert, *Spiritual Elders: Charisma and Tradition in Russian Orthodoxy* (Dekalb: Northern Illinois University Press, 2010); Vera Shevzov, *Russian Orthodoxy on the Eve of Revolution* (New York: Oxford University Press, 2007). Collected volumes in English include John-Paul Himka and Andriy Zayarnyuk, eds., *Letters from Heaven: Popular Religion in Russia and Ukraine* (Toronto: University of Toronto Press, 2006); Valerie Kivelson and Robert H. Greene, eds., *Orthodox Russia: Belief and Practice under the Tsars* (University Park: Pennsylvania State University Press, 2003); Mark D. Steinberg and Heather J. Coleman, eds., *Sacred Stories: Religion and Spirituality in Modern Russia* (Bloomington: Indiana University Press, 2007); Mark D. Steinberg and Catherine Wanner, eds., *Religion, Morality, and Community in Post-Soviet Societies* (Washington, DC: Woodrow Wilson Center Press; Bloomington: Indiana University Press, 2008); and Catherine Wanner, ed., *State Secularism and Lived Religion in Soviet Russia and Ukraine* (New York: Oxford University Press, 2012).

27. Paul Werth, "Lived Orthodoxy and Confessional Diversity: The Last Decade on Religion in Modern Russia," *Kritika: Explorations in Russian and Eurasian History* 12, no. 4 (Fall 2011): 849–65; Christine Worobec, "Lived Orthodoxy

in Imperial Russia," *Kritika: Explorations in Russian and Eurasian History* 7, no. 2 (Spring 2006): 329–50.

28. Primiano, "Vernacular Religion," 44.

29. Kivelson and Greene, *Orthodox Russia*, 5.

30. Vera Shevzov, "Letting the People into Church," in Kivelson and Greene, *Orthodox Russia*, 62.

31. K. E. Lindeman, ed., *Sbornik rechei o trezvennicheskom dvizhenii, proiznosennykh v sobraniiakh Tsentral'nago Komiteta Soiuza 17-go Oktiabria v Moskve i Peterburge 5, 6, 13, 14 maia 1913* (Moscow, 1913), 27–30.

32. In addition to Paert, *Spiritual Elders*, see V. A. Kuchumov, "Eldership in Russia: Some Consequences of the Petrine Reforms," *Russian Studies in History* 52, no. 1 (Summer 2013): 38–65; and Jeanne Kormina, "Russian Saint under Construction: Portraits and Icons of *Starets* Nikolay," *Archives de Sciences Sociales des Religions* 162 (April–June 2013): 95–119.

33. Gregory Freeze, "A Pious Folk? Religious Observance in Vladimir Diocese, 1900–1914," *Jahrbücher fur Geschichte Osteuropas*, n.s., 52, no. 3 (2004): 324.

34. Richard Stites, *Revolutionary Dreams: Utopian Vision and Experimental Life in the Russian Revolution* (Oxford: Oxford University Press, 1989), 10.

35. Sheila Fitzpatrick, *Stalin's Peasants: Resistance and Survival in the Russian Village after Collectivization* (New York: Oxford University Press, 1994); Lynne Viola, *Peasant Rebels under Stalin: Collectivization and the Culture of Peasant Resistance* (Oxford: Oxford University Press, 1996).

36. Miriam Dobson, "The Social Scientist Meets the 'Believer': Discussions of God, the Afterlife, and Communism in the Mid-1960s," *Slavic Review* 74, no. 1 (Spring 2015): 91, 103.

37. Wanner, *State Secularism and Lived Religion*, 2.

38. Tamara Dragadze, "The Domestication of Religion under Soviet Communism," in *Socialism: Ideals, Ideologies, and Local Practice*, ed. C. M. Hann (London: Routledge, 1993), 150–51.

39. For example, Oleg Kharkhordin, *The Collective and the Individual in Russia: A Study of Practices* (Berkeley: University of California Press, 1999).

40. Victoria Smolkin, *A Sacred Space Is Never Empty: A History of Soviet Atheism* (Princeton, NJ: Princeton University Press, 2018), especially chap. 7.

41. Juliane Fürst, "Where Did All the Normal People Go? Another Look at the Soviet 1970s," *Kritika: Explorations in Russian and Eurasian History*, n.s., 14, no. 3 (Summer 2013): 638–39.

42. Smolkin, *A Sacred Space Is Never Empty*, 216.

43. Aleksei Yurchak, *Everything Was Forever, until It Was No More: The Last Soviet Generation* (Princeton, NJ: Princeton University Press, 2006), 127–28.

1. Becoming "Brother Ioann"

1. For a version of this portrait taken about a decade later, see figure 8.

2. For a discussion of various definitions of the phenomenon of eldership (*starchestvo*), see Kormina, "Russian Saint under Construction," 95–96.

3. Paert, *Spiritual Elders*, 85.

4. "Zhizneopisanie osnovatelei obshchestva narodnykh trezvennikov," GMIR, f. 13. op. 1, d. 369, l. 16.

5. M. P. Komkov and V. V. Plotnikova, *Apostol trezvosti: Ioann Alekseevich Churikov* (St. Petersburg: Aleteiia, 2014), 12.

6. S. Zhivotovskii, "V Vyritskoi kolonii brattsa Ioanna Churikova," *Birzhevye vedomosti*, no. 14032 (March 2, 1914), back page of morning edition.

7. "Zhizneopisanie," GMIR, f. 13, op. 1, d. 369, l. 16.

8. Kizenko, *Prodigal Saint*, especially chaps. 1 and 2.

9. Komkov and Plotnikova, *Apostol trezvosti*, 73.

10. This is the position of contemporary trezvennik historian and Orthodox deacon Sergei Palamodov, as reported in January 2016 at a conference titled "The People's Trezvennik Movement: History, Modernity, Development Prospects," http://mitropolia.spb.ru/news/otdeli/?id=96843#ad-image-2.

11. Komkov and Plotnikova, *Apostol trezvosti*, 73–74. According to Brother Ioann's followers, the admiration was mutual. See Davydov and Frolov, *Dukhovnyi partizan protivu razvrata i p'ianstva (zashchitnik khristianstva): Bratets Ioann Alekseevich Churikov* (St. Petersburg, 1912), 9.

12. According to Steven Cassedy, the term "kenosis" was introduced into Russian discourse by the Orthodox theologian Mikhail Mikhailovich Tareev in 1892. See Steven Cassedy, *Dostoevsky's Religion* (Palo Alto: Stanford University Press, 2005), 11.

13. Engelstein, *Castration and the Heavenly Kingdom*, 17.

14. Sergei Maksimov, *Brodiachaia Rus' Khrista radi* (St. Petersburg, 1877), as cited in Pål Kolstø, "'For Here We Do Not Have an Enduring City': Tolstoy and the *Strannik* Tradition in Russian Culture," *Russian Review* 69, no. 1 (January 2010): 122.

15. Kolstø, "'For Here We Do Not Have an Enduring City,'" 121.

16. Quoted in Greene, *Bodies Like Bright Stars*, 27. On this point, see also Chris Chulos, "Russian Piety and Culture from Peter the Great to 1917," in *Cambridge History of Christianity: Eastern Christianity*, ed. Michael Angold (Cambridge: Cambridge University Press, 2006), 364.

17. As quoted in Greene, *Bodies Like Bright Stars*, 25.

18. *Pis'ma Brattsa Ioanna Samarskogo (Churikova)* (St. Petersburg: Glagol', 1995), 246. This extensive collection of Brother Ioann's letters is based on transcriptions first produced by the trezvennik Petr Terekhovich in 1971. Sergei Palamodov has since pointed out some inaccuracies in this collection, which he discovered through a careful comparison with the original letters now available in the archives. Sergei Iu. Palamodov, *Imia moe greshnoe pomyanite* [Remember My Sinful Name] (St. Petersburg: Aleteiia, 2011), 8–9.

19. *Pis'ma*, 215; See also Ivan Smolev, *Slovo k stoletiiu so dnia rozhdeniia Brattsa Ioanna Samarskogo 1861–1961 gg.* (Leningrad, 1961), 24.

20. According to Agrippina Smirnova's letter from February 17, 1898, Churikov was preaching his besedy on Ligovski prospect, Izmailovskii, Okhta, Za Nevskoi Zastavoi, Vasil'evskii Ostrov, Ekateringof, Ekaterninskii Kanal, Peterburgskaia storona, and the Fontanka. Evgenii Vasil'evich Kesarev, *Besednichestvo kak sekta* (Samara, 1905), 85–86.

21. *Pis'ma*, 224.

22. Smolev, *Slovo k stoletiiu*, 23.

23. Clay, "Orthodox Missionaries," 45; Komkov and Plotnikova, *Apostol trezvosti*, 11.

24. Mark D. Steinberg, *Petersburg, Fin-de-siecle* (New Haven, CT: Yale University Press, 2011), 122. The cholera outbreak in 1908-9 claimed 6,100 lives in St. Petersburg alone.

25. White, *Russia Goes Dry*, 10.

26. Herlihy, *Alcoholic Empire*, 114.

27. On clergy and temperance, see Jennifer Hedda, *His Kingdom Come: Orthodox Pastorship and Social Activism in Revolutionary Russia* (Dekalb: Northern Illinois University Press, 2008), chap. 5; Herlihy, *Alcoholic Empire*, chap. 5; and Herrlinger, *Working Souls*, chap. 1.

28. See Adele Lindenmeyr, "Building Civil Society One Brick at a Time: People's Houses and Worker Enlightenment in Late Imperial Russia," *Journal of Modern History* 84, no. 1 (March 2012): 1-39.

29. Steinberg, *Petersburg*, 134-36.

30. "Zhizneopisanie," GMIR, f. 13, op. 1, d. 369, l. 16.

31. *Pis'ma*, 191.

32. "Beseda 'Brattsa Ioanna,'" June 13, 1910, Orthodox Society of Trezvenniki, https://www.trezvograd.ru/-7. On Churikov's request, Tregubov began recording his besedy in 1909-10; he agreed because he wanted them to be more accessible to people, given their positive moral impact. Until May 1910, he published abridged versions in the newspaper *Novaia Rus'* and then complete versions in a collection entitled *Besedy Brattsa Ioanna Churikova* (1912).

33. A. S. Prugavin, *"Brattsy" i trezvenniki: Iz oblasti religioznykh iskanii* (Moscow: Kn-vo Zlatotsvet, 1912), 33.

34. Ekaterina Mel'nikova, *"Voobrazhaemaia kniga": Ocherki po istorii fol'klora o knigakh i chtenii v Rossii* (St. Petersburg: Izdatel'stvo Evropeiskogo Universiteta v Sankt-Peterburga, 2011), 128.

35. "Beseda 'Brattsa Ioanna' Churikova," March 25, 1912, 663. From Tregubov's collection at the Society of Spiritual Christian Trezvenniki website: http:www.trezvost.com.

36. "Beseda 'Brattsa Ioanna,'" May 22, 1911, Orthodox Society of Trezvenniki, https://www.trezvograd.ru/-54.

37. "Beseda 'Brattsa Ioanna,'" June 13, 1910, Orthodox Society of Trezvenniki, https://www.trezvograd.ru/-7.

38. S. I. Kondurushkin, "Bratets Ivanushka," *Rech*, no. 290 (October 22, 1910): 2.

39. "Zhizneopisanie," GMIR, f. 13, op. 1, d. 369, l. 16.

40. Their testimony was originally recorded by Ivan Tregubov in 1913, and then published as "Rasskaz Evlampiia Kuz'micha i Marii Vasil'evny Kuz'minykh," in Palamodov, *Imia moe greshnoe*, 188-90.

41. Palamodov, *Imia moe greshnoe*, 190.

42. Kesarev, *Besednichestvo*, 88.

43. TsGIA SPb, f. 680, op. 5, d. 13, ll. 2-8ob.

44. See, for example, the testimony of Kolobov. GMIR, f. 2, op. 17, d. 363, l. 9.

45. Palamodov, *Imia moe greshnoe*, 50.

46. *Pis'ma*, 223.

47. Prugavin, *"Brattsy" i trezvenniki*, 45.

48. Paul Valliere, "Modes of Social Action in Russian Orthodoxy: The Case of Father Petrov's *Zateinik*," *Russian History* 4, no. 2 (1977): 155-56.

49. This would include Rozhdestvenskii's successor as head of the Aleksandr Nevskii Society, Father Mirtov. S. Zhivotovskii, "V Vyritskoi kolonii brattsa Ioanna Churikova," *Birzhevye vedomosti*, no. 14026 (February 27, 1914), back page of morning edition.

50. Abramov, "Eshche o Churikove," 2.

51. *Pis'ma*, 317.

52. Kesarev, *Besednichestvo*, 95.

53. *Pis'ma*, 131-32.

54. Paert, *Spiritual Elders*, 142-43.

55. Mel'nikova, *"Voobrazhaemaia kniga,"* 137.

56. Coleman, *Russian Baptists*, chap. 1.

57. Kesarev, *Besednichestvo*, 78.

58. Kesarev, *Besednichestvo*, 78; Prugavin, *"Brattsy" i trezvenniki*, 36, 38.

59. Daniel Beer, "The Medicalization of Religious Deviance in the Russian Orthodox Church (1880-1905)," *Kritika: Explorations in Russian and Eurasian History*, n.s., 5, no. 3 (Summer 2004): 476-77.

60. GMIR, f. 2, op. 17, d. 362, l. 1; Palamodov, *Imia moe greshnoe*, 54.

61. *Pis'ma*, 131-32, 22.

62. I. M. Tregubov, *Otzyvy doktorov ob istseleniiakh, sovershaemykh "brattsem" Ioannom Churikovym* (St. Petersburg, 1912), 13.

63. Prugavin, *"Brattsy" i trezvenniki*, 39-40.

64. *Pis'ma*, 55.

65. Nadieszda Kizenko, "Written Confessions and the Construction of Sacred Narrative," in Steinberg and Coleman, *Sacred Stories*, 107.

66. Kesarev, *Besednichestvo*, 83.

67. Father Ioann of Kronstadt was also known for practicing scriptural exegesis regularly. Kizenko, *Prodigal Saint*, 16.

68. He was in the hospital from March to July 1898. According to Churikov, two doctors found him to show signs of insanity, but two others found him completely sane. Lindeman, *Sbornik*, 113.

69. "Poslanie ot Ioanna Peterburgskim Brat'iam," in *Pis'ma*, 68.

70. Kesarev, *Besednichestvo*, 82; Komkov and Plotnikova, *Apostol trezvosti*, 35.

71. *Pis'ma*, 68.

72. *Pis'ma*, 39.

73. *Pis'ma*, 72-73.

74. *Pis'ma*, 255.

75. *Pis'ma*, 72.

76. *Pis'ma*, 162.

77. Prugavin, *"Brattsy" i trezvenniki*, 45. From Churikov's *proshenie* to the Synod, April 1900.

78. *Pis'ma*, 37, 71.

79. *Pis'ma*, 69.

80. Kesarev, *Besednichestvo*, 91–92.

81. *Pis'ma*, 216.

82. TsGIA SPb, f. 680, op. 5, d. 8, ll. 17–18.

83. *Pis'ma*, 206.

84. According to Kesarev, Churikov initially wanted the approval of church authorities and wrote directly to the Synod, laying out his views on religious moral issues, along with a program of his preaching, but when the Synod did not respond, he mistakenly took silence as consent. Kesarev, *Besednichestvo*, 89–90.

85. *Pis'ma*, 223.

86. Prugavin, *"Brattsy" i trezvenniki*, 46–47.

87. Komkov and Plotnikova, *Apostol trezvosti*, 52.

88. TsGIA SPb, f. 680, op. 5, d. 8, ll. 8–12ob. For a copy of Churikov's own petition to the Synod, see *Pis'ma*, 224–25.

89. TsGIA SPb, f. 680, op. 5, d. 8, l. 13ob.

90. TsGIA SPb, f. 680, op. 5, d. 9, l. 4–4ob.

91. Kesarev, *Besednichestvo*, 91.

92. N. Abramov, "Churikov i missionery," *Petrogradskii listok*, no. 167 (June 20, 1916): 1.

93. Kesarev, *Besednichestvo*, 92.

94. N. Abramov, "'Bratets' Churikov i trezvenniki," *Petrogradskii listok*, no. 174 (June 27, 1916): 1.

95. TsGIA SPb, f. 680, op. 5, d. 13, ll. 2–8ob. There were several other officers as well as teachers. Many identified simply as "peasants."

96. TsGIA SPb, f. 680, op. 5, d. 18, l. 14–14ob.

97. TsGIA SPb, f. 680, op. 5, d. 18, ll. 15ob–16.

98. TsGIA SPb, f. 680, op. 5, d. 13, ll. 2–8ob.

99. Kesarev, *Besednichestvo*, 103.

100. A. T. Mikhailov, *Koloniia trezvennikov* (Petrograd, 1914), 24–25.

101. *Pis'ma*, 200.

102. Laurie Manchester, *Holy Fathers, Secular Sons: Clergy, Intelligentsia, and the Modern Self in Revolutionary Russia* (Dekalb: Northern Illinois University Press, 2008), 72, 76.

103. *Pis'ma*, 243.

2. An Extraordinary Man on a Sober Mission

1. Abramov, "'Bratets' Churikov i trezvenniki," 1–2.

2. Specifically, there was a large depiction of the "Krestnye stradanie" of Christ in the middle, flanked by the image "Molenie o Chash" and, on the right, the icon of the Holy Bogorodnitsa and St. Serafim of Sarov, who was canonized in 1903. RGIA, f. 821, op. 133, d. 212, ll. 278–79ob.

3. P. D. Dmitriev, *Povestvovanie o Ivane Grigor'evich, napisano dlia druzei, kotorym doroga pamiat' o nem* (Leningrad, 1966), 6.

4. Brother Ioann, as quoted by Ivan Tregubov in the foreword to his collection of Churikov's besedy, Orthodox Society of Trezvenniki, https://www.trezvograd.ru/predisl.

5. Prugavin, *"Brattsy" i trezvenniki*, 27.

6. Davydov and Frolov, *Dukhovnyi partizan*, 16.

7. GMIR, f. 2, op. 17, d. 363, l. 1.

8. Prugavin, *"Brattsy" i trezvenniki*, 32.

9. Since the authenticity of later versions has been disputed (Palamodov, *Imia moe greshnoe*, 10–22), for the sake of accuracy and consistency, I have relied whenever possible on the Tregubov texts, which are available on the website maintained by the community of Orthodox trezvenniki in St. Petersburg: https://www.trezvograd.ru/besedi.

10. V. F. Shishkin, *Tak sladyvalas' revoliutsionnaia moral': Istoricheskii ocherk* (Moscow, 1967), 223.

11. "Beseda 'Brattsa Ioanna,'" October 30, 1911, Orthodox Society of Trezvenniki, https://www.trezvograd.ru/-56.

12. *Peterburgskii listok*, no. 342 (December 17, 1902); a copy can be found in GMIR, f. 13, op. 1, d. 361, l. 16–16ob.

13. Lindeman, *Sbornik*, 34; Prugavin, *"Brattsy" i trezvenniki*, 17.

14. RGIA, f. 796, op. 442, d. 1632 (1896), l. 57.

15. S. G. Runkevich, *Studenty-propovedniki: Ocherki Peterburgskoi religiozno-prosvetitel'noi blagotvoritel'nosti* (St. Petersburg, 1892), 7.

16. Greene, *Bodies Like Bright Stars*, 51.

17. *Otchet o deiatel'nosti Obshchestva dlia rasprostraneniia religiozno-nravstvennago prosveshcheniia v dukhe Pravoslavnoi Tserkvi za 1906 i 1907 gg.* (St. Petersburg, 1908), 136.

18. Walter Brueggemann, *The Prophetic Imagination* (Minneapolis: Fortress Press, 2018).

19. Davydov and Frolov, *Dukhovnyi partizan*, 23.

20. "Beseda 'Brattsa Ioanna,'" December 11, 1911, Orthodox Society of Trezvenniki, https://www.trezvograd.ru/-63.

21. "The Priest at the Brother's Beseda," from Grigorii Petrov, *Zateinik* (St. Petersburg: St. Petersburg Publishing House, 1904), available at the website of the Society of Spiritual Christian Trezvenniki, http://www.trezvost.com/Articles/Petrov.htm.

22. Kizenko, *Prodigal Saint*, 155.

23. GMIR, f. 13, op. 1, d. 364, l. 14–14ob.

24. Paert, *Spiritual Elders*, 163–64.

25. Smolev, *Slovo k stoletiiu*, 98–99.

26. Yurchak, *Everything Was Forever, until It Was No More*, 148. See also Dale Pesmen, *Russia and Soul: An Exploration* (Ithaca, NY: Cornell University Press, 2000), especially 164–66.

27. GMIR, f. 2, op. 17, d. 363, ll. 4–5ob, Maria Grigor'eva, as cited in Palamodov, *Imia moe greshnoe*, 62.

28. For more details, see chapter 3.

29. For an interesting recent discussion of kenotic practice in the context of Orthodox pilgrimage, see Inna Naletova, "Pilgrimages as Kenotic Communities beyond the Walls of the Church," in *Eastern Christians in Anthropological Perspective*, ed. Chris Hann and Hermann Goltz (Berkeley: University of California Press, 2010), especially 262.

30. For examples, see Page Herrlinger, "Petitions to Brother Ioann Churikov," in *Orthodox Christianity in Imperial Russia: A Sourcebook on Lived Religion*, ed. Heather Coleman (Bloomington: Indiana University Press, 2014), 262–66.

31. GMIR, f. 13, op. 1, d. 354, ll. 178–79.

32. GMIR, f. 13, op. 1, d. 354, l. 179.

33. Lindeman, *Sbornik*, 118.

34. "Beseda 'Brattsa Ioanna,'" March 20, 1911, Orthodox Society of Trezvenniki, https://www.trezvograd.ru/-43.

35. *Pis'ma*, 145.

36. Leonid Heretz, *Russia on the Eve of Modernity: Popular Religion and Traditional Culture under the Last Tsars* (Cambridge: Cambridge University Press, 2008), 137.

37. *Pis'ma*, 145.

38. *Pis'ma*, 157.

39. *Petrogradskii spaso-preobrazhenskii koltovskii prikhod v 1915 godu* (Petrograd, 1916).

40. Quoted in Clay, "Orthodox Missionaries," 48. See also Kesarev, *Besednichestvo*, 113–14.

41. As Paert has observed, it was not uncommon for religious authorities to express suspicion about contact between an elder and female believers. Paert, *Spiritual Elders*, 155.

42. Kesarev, *Besednichestvo*, 83.

43. Iu. Beliaev, *Novoe Vremia* (October 24, 1900): 3–4, as cited in Prugavin, *"Brattsy" i trezvenniki*, 28–29.

44. Prugavin, *"Brattsy" i trezvenniki*, 25; *Pis'ma*, 252.

45. On the negative accounts, see Prugavin, *"Brattsy" i trezvenniki*, 25, and Liubomirov's articles in *Peterburgskii listok*, no. 346 (1903) and *Peterburgskii listok*, no. 342 (December 17, 1902); a copy of the latter can be found in GMIR, f. 13, op. 1, d. 361, l. 16–16ob. See also Kesarev, *Besednichestvo*, 75–113.

46. *Pis'ma*, 250–51.

47. *Pis'ma*, 354.

48. Komkov and Plotnikova, *Apostol trezvosti*, 68–69.

49. Roy Wallis, "The Social Construction of Charisma," *Social Compass* 29, no. 1 (1982): 25–39.

50. Greene, *Bodies Like Bright Stars*, 10.

51. Beer, *Renovating Russia*, 148–51.

52. *Pis'ma*, 318.

53. For the letters of E. V. Frolov, see GMIR, f. 13, op. 1, d. 361, ll. 16–34ob. For others, GMIR, f. 1, op. 13, d. 367, l. 3–3ob.

54. TsGIA SPb, f. 680, op. 5, d. 18, l. 12.

55. GMIR, f. 1, op. 13, d. 367, l. 3–3ob.

56. RGIA, f. 821, op. 133, d. 212, l. 207.

57. Komkov and Plotnikova, *Apostol trezvosti*, 69.

58. S. Zhivotovskii, "V Vyritskoi kolonii brattsa Ioanna Churikova," *Birzhevye vedomosti*, no. 14036 (March 5, 1914), back page of morning edition.

59. Some of his followers would interpret this as a form of prophecy, since he had helped so many avoid death on that day. GMIR, koll. I, op. 4, d. 61, l. 18; Smolev, *Slovo k stoletiiu*, 50.

60. "Beseda 'Brattsa Ioanna' (About the Prodigal Son)," February 6, 1911, Orthodox Society of Trezvenniki, https://www.trezvograd.ru/-37.

61. *Pis'mo sviashchennika Grigorii Petrova Mitropolitu Antoniiu* (St. Petersburg, 1905), 7.

62. Hedda, *His Kingdom Come*, 117–25.

63. Hedda, *His Kingdom Come*, 179–81.

64. RGIA, f. 821, op. 133, d. 212, l. 276–276ob.

65. Nina Maslova, *Povest'* (Leningrad, 196–), 35.

66. "Beseda 'Brattsa Ioanna' (About the Prodigal Son)," February 6, 1911, Orthodox Society of Trezvenniki, https://www.trezvograd.ru/-37.

67. A. S. Pankratov, *Ishchushchie Boga* (Moscow: A. A. Levenson, 1911), 68.

68. Mikhailov, *Koloniia trezvennikov*, 12.

69. "Beseda 'Brattsa Ioanna,'" November 27, 1911, Orthodox Society of Trezvenniki, https://www.trezvograd.ru/-60.

70. Mikhailov, *Koloniia trezvennikov*, 3.

71. Maslova, *Povest'*, 3–6.

72. GMIR, f. 13, op. 1, d. 277, l. 2.

73. Lindeman, *Sbornik*, 115.

74. Lindeman, *Sbornik*, 115.

75. Lindeman, *Sbornik*, 111.

76. Mikhailov, *Koloniia trezvennikov*, 19–21.

77. A. Iadrov, "'Bratets' Ivan Churikov," *Malen'kaia gazeta*, no. 79 (December 8, 1914): 3.

78. TsGIA SPb, f. 680, op. 5, d. 27, l. 6. Churikov paid ₽18,000 into the fund.

79. RGIA, f. 821, op. 133, d. 212, l. 287ob.

80. S. Zhivotovskii, "V Vyritskoi kolonii brattsa Ioanna Churikova," *Birzhevye vedomosti*, no. 14038 (March 6, 1914), back page of morning edition.

81. Mikhailov, *Koloniia trezvennikov*, 12.

82. Brother Ioann's office walls were plastered with scriptural quotations. They included John 3:27, John 12:40, Jeremiah 46:11, and Jacob/James 5:14–15.

83. Lindeman, *Sbornik*, 115.

84. Paert, *Spiritual Elders*, 116.

85. Mikhailov, *Koloniia trezvennikov*, 23.

86. In September 1917, over fifty people approved the decision to build the local volost' school (eight of whom appear to have been barely literate themselves). TsGA, f. 494, op. 2, d. 1, l. 19.

87. Mikhailov, *Koloniia trezvennikov*, 19.

88. Mikhailov, *Koloniia trezvennikov*, 17.

89. Komkov and Plotnikova, *Apostol trezvosti*, 142–43.

90. A. Iadrov, "'Bratets' Ivan Churikov," *Malen'kaia gazeta*, no. 99 (December 29, 1914): 3.

91. RGIA, f. 821, op. 133, d. 212, l. 291ob.

92. From an excerpt of an article published in *Rech'* in February 1912, in *Pis'ma*, 304.

93. Mikhailov, *Koloniia trezvennikov*, 29.

94. Palamodov, *Imia moe greshnoe*, 196.

95. Prugavin, *"Brattsy" i trezvenniki*, 71.

96. According to a secret police report in 1913, Churikov had accumulated a sizeable amount of wealth, including an estimated ₽80,000 in real estate. RGIA, f. 821, op. 133, d. 212, ll. 287ob–288.

97. Maslova, *Povest'*, 5.

98. RGIA, f. 821, op. 133, d. 212, ll. 287ob–288.

99. I. M. Tregubov, *Mir s zhivotnymi, provozglashennyi narodnymi trezvennikami* (St. Petersburg: A. S. Prokhanov, 1910), 10.

100. Tregubov, *Mir s zhivotnymi*, 3–4.

101. Tregubov, *Mir s zhivotnymi*, 5.

102. Tregubov, *Mir s zhivotnymi*, 9.

103. Tregubov, *Mir s zhivotnymi*, 16.

104. Lindeman, *Sbornik*, 4, 104.

105. Pankratov, *Ishchushchie Boga*, 57.

106. RGIA, f. 821, op. 133, d. 212, l. 280.

107. Steinberg, *Petersburg*, 200.

108. Mikhailov, *Koloniia trezvennikov*, 4–6.

109. Lindeman, *Sbornik*, 102.

110. Lindeman, *Sbornik*, 27–30.

111. S. Zhitovskii, "V Vyritskoi kolonii brattsa Ioanna Churikova," *Birzhevye vedomosti*, no. 14026 (February 27, 1914), back page of morning edition.

112. McKee, "Sobering Up the People," 229–30.

113. Palamodov, *Imia moe greshnoe*, 46.

3. Sober Brothers

1. Letters to the editor from E. V. Frolov, mostly from 1903, in response to Liubomirov's article in *Peterburgskii listok*, no. 346. GMIR, f. 13, op. 1, d. 361, ll. 34–35.

2. Davydov and Frolov, *Dukhovnyi partizan*, 37–40. This testimony was originally published in *Novaia Rus'* 209 (August 2, 1909).

3. Heather J. Coleman, "Becoming a Russian Baptist: Conversion Narratives and Social Experience," *Russian Review* 61, no. 1 (January 2002): 96. Steinberg, *Proletarian Imagination*, especially chap. 2.

4. "Beseda 'Brattsa Ioanna,'" November 21, 1910, Orthodox Society of Trezvenniki, https://www.trezvograd.ru/-30.

5. *Pis'ma*, 41.

6. The story of the "Prodigal Son," Dmitrii Danilovich Losev, was told by Ivan Smolev, in *S brattsem i bez brattsa* (Leningrad, 1969); a copy can be found in GMIR, koll. I, op. 4, d. 66, l. 8–9. Losev's letter was published in S. Zhivotovskii, "V Vyritskoi kolonii brattsa Ioanna Churikova," *Birzhevye vedomosti*, no. 14038 (March 6, 1914), back page of morning edition. For an example of a miracle story, see Greene, *Bodies Like Bright Stars*, 63.

7. As anthropologist Sonja Luehrmann observed, oral testifying presents unique interpretive challenges since it is "always the result of a complex exchange between a present self, a remembered past, and immediately present and imagined audiences." *Religion in Secular Archives: Soviet Atheism and Historical Knowledge* (New York: Oxford University Press, 2015), 74.

8. Tregubov, *Otzyvy doktorov*, 6.

9. Kizenko, "Written Confessions," 105.

10. Laura Engelstein and Stephanie Sandler, eds, *Self and Story in Russian History* (Ithaca, NY: Cornell University Press, 2000), 3.

11. Krylov's testimony, handwritten in dark ink, can be found in GMIR, f. 13, op. 1, d. 349, ll. 14–17ob. A published version appears in Palamodov, *Imia moe greshnoe*, 148–54.

12. Testimony of "Servant of God Mikhail [Cherniak]," GMIR, f. 13, op. 1, d. 349, l. 12–12ob.

13. Testimony of Aleksandr Grigor'ev Lobanov, GMIR, f. 13, op. 1, d. 349, ll. 18–20.

14. Quoted in Herlihy, *Alcoholic Empire*, 113–14.

15. Palamodov, *Imia moe greshnoe*, 149.

16. Palamodov, *Imia moe greshnoe*, 149.

17. Palamodov, *Imia moe greshnoe*, 150.

18. Palamodov, *Imia moe greshnoe*, 150.

19. Palamodov, *Imia moe greshnoe*, 151.

20. Palamodov, *Imia moe greshnoe*, 151.

21. Greene, *Bodies Like Bright Stars*, chap. 5; Christine D. Worobec, "Miraculous Healings," in Steinberg and Coleman, *Sacred Stories*, 22–43.

22. Mikhailov, *Koloniia trezvennikov*, 10.

23. Lindeman, *Sbornik*, 112.

24. Palamodov, *Imia moe greshnoe*, 199.

25. Palamodov, *Imia moe greshnoe*, 193–94.

26. Testimony of Klavdiia Vasil'evna Sedova (Karmishenskaia), from an interview on March 23, 1999, with Sergei Palamodov. Palamodov, *Imia moe greshnoe*, 202.

27. Prugavin, *"Brattsy" i trezvenniki*, 33.

28. Lindeman, *Sbornik*, 119.

29. Quoted in Smolev, *Slovo k stoletiiu*, 6.

30. Prugavin, *"Brattsy" i trezvenniki*, 40.

31. Paert, *Spiritual Elders*, 149.

32. Komkov and Plotnikova, *Apostol trezvosti*, 20.

33. Palamodov, *Imia moe greshnoe*, 192.

34. Palamodov, *Imia moe greshnoe*, 150.

35. Testimony of Aleksandr Grigor'ev Lobanov, GMIR, f. 13, op. 1, d. 349, l. 19ob.

36. Paert, *Spiritual Elders*, 128.

37. Palamodov, *Imia moe greshnoe*, 151.

38. Palamodov, *Imia moe greshnoe*, 192–94.

39. Testimony of V. Kolobov, GMIR, f. 2, op. 17, d. 363, l. 9.

40. Palamodov, *Imia moe greshnoe*, 150.

41. A.M., "V gostiakh u brattsa," *Malen'kaia Gazeta*, no. 13 (October 1913): 2.

42. Palamodov, *Imia moe greshnoe*, 152.

43. Tregubov, *Otzyvy doktorov*, 3.

44. Vasilii Petrovich Min'kov, *Moroshka* (Leningrad, 1986), 35.

45. Palamodov, *Imia moe greshnoe*, 151.

46. Palamodov, *Imia moe greshnoe*, 152.

47. GMIR, f. 13, op. 1, d. 364, l. 14ob.

48. Palamodov, *Imia moe greshnoe*, 153.

49. This framing was not unique to trezvenniki. See Daniel Winchester, "Converting to Continuity: Temporality and Self in Eastern Orthodox Conversion Narratives," *Journal for the Scientific Study of Religion* 54, no. 3 (September 2015): 439-60.

50. Mikhailov, *Koloniia trezvennikov*, 19-21.

51. Guliaev's testimony was recorded in multiple places, including in excerpted form by Kondurushkin, "Bratets Ivanushka," 2, and Prugavin, *"Bratsy" i trezvenniki*, 55-56, and in longer version by trezvenniki Ivan Smolev and Nina Maslova, both of whom knew him personally. GMIR, koll. I, op. 4, d. 62, ll. 64-66.

52. Keenan et al., "Social Factors," 10-11.

53. Kesarev, *Besednichestvo*, 80.

54. GMIR, f. 2, op. 17, d. 363, l. 1.

55. Palamodov, *Imia moe greshnoe*, 180.

56. Kondurushkin, "Bratets Ivanushka," 2.

57. Petr Gravrilovich Terekhovich, *Kratkii biograficheskii ocherk: Kak Ia poznal put' Gospoden' i sviatuiu trezvost' Brattsa Ioanna* (Leningrad, 1980), 34.

58. Mikhailov, *Koloniia trezvennikov*, 26.

59. Kizenko, *Prodigal Saint*, 106.

60. Following the Church's 1905 injunction that Brother Ioann preach in sync with the liturgy each Sunday, Luke 8 was necessarily a part of his rotation.

61. "Beseda 'Brattsa Ioanna,'" October 23, 1911, Orthodox Society of Trezvenniki, https://www.trezvograd.ru/-55.

62. Christine D. Worobec, *Possessed: Women, Witches, and Demons in Imperial Russia* (Dekalb: Northern Illinois University Press, 2001), 62.

63. GMIR, koll. I, op. 4, d. 62, ll. 57-72.

64. GMIR, koll. I, op. 4, d. 62, l. 67.

65. Stephen A. Smith, "Masculinity in Transition: Peasant Migrants in Late-Imperial St. Petersburg," in *Russian Masculinities in History and Culture*, ed. Barbara Evans Clements, Rebecca Friedman, and Dan Healey (New York: Palgrave, 2002), 99.

66. Kesarev, *Besednichestvo*, 104. See also Lindeman, *Sbornik*, 28-29.

67. Catherine Wanner, *Communities of the Converted: Ukrainians and Global Evangelism* (Ithaca, NY: Cornell University Press, 2009), 161.

68. Even today ROC officials do not agree on a single definition of *starchestvo*. See Kormina, "Russian Saint under Construction," 99.

69. Kuchumov, "Eldership in Russia," 50.

70. M. Vasil'ev, "Trezvenniki," *Bogorodskaia rech'*, no. 12 (March 17, 1913): 2-3.

71. Vasil'ev, "Trezvenniki," 3.

72. S. I. Kondurushkin, "Bratets Ivanushka," *Rech'*, no. 310 (November 11, 1910): 5.

73. Palamodov, *Imia moe greshnoe*, 192–94.

4. Sober Sisters

1. Petition (ca. 1905) to the tsar from Maria Spiridonova, Petrovskii Prospekt, dom 1. kv. 5, TsGIA SPb, f. 680, op. 5, d. 20, l. 14–14ob.

2. One desiatina = approx. 2.7 acres.

3. Herlihy, *Alcoholic Empire*, 95.

4. "The Story of Evdokiia Kuzminovna Ivanovskaia," GMIR, f. 13, op. 1, d. 349, ll. 28–29.

5. Kizenko, *Prodigal Saint*, 104–5.

6. On Ivanovskaia's diagnosis, see Tregubov, *Otzyvy doktorov*, 17.

7. Kizenko, "Written Confessions," 104–7.

8. GMIR, koll. I. op. 4, d. 19, ll. 193ob–194.

9. GMIR, koll. I, op. 4, d. 19, l. 171.

10. *Pis'ma*, 139. See also, Iu. Beliaev, "U Brattsa Ivanushki," *Novoe vremia*, no. 8858 (October 24, 1900): 4.

11. GMIR, f. 13, op. 1, d. 349, ll. 28–30ob.

12. GMIR, f. 13, op. 1, d. 349, l. 30–30ob.

13. Tregubov, *Otzyvy doktorov*, 3.

14. GMIR, f. 13, op. 1, d. 349, l. 30–30ob.

15. GMIR, f. 13, op. 1, d. 349, l. 30–30ob.

16. In fact, her story had much in common with that of a townswoman from Tambov by the name of Elizaveta Kononova Troshina. For an extended account of Troshina's case, see Worobec, "Miraculous Healings," 34–36.

17. TsGIA SPb, f. 680, op. 5, d. 8, l. 14. Davydov and Frolov, *Dukhovnyi partizan*, 6. This pamphlet has been recently republished on the website of the Orthodox Society of Christian Trezvenniki, accessed June 29, 2022, http://www.trezvograd.3dn.ru/partizan.htm.

18. GMIR, f. 13, op. 1, d. 349, l. 30–30ob.

19. Tregubov, *Otzyvy doktorov*, 14.

20. Tregubov, *Otzyvy doktorov*, 14.

21. A boy whose paralysis and epilepsy had been "cured" after he had a dream in which the Virgin Mary appeared and told him to pray at the chapel of All those who Suffer at the Stekliannoi factory.

22. Tregubov, *Otzyvy doktorov*, 6. He recalled how Father Ioann of Kronstadt's powers to perform miracles had begun to wane shortly before his death.

23. Tregubov, *Otzyvy doktorov*, 13.

24. Tregubov, *Otzyvy doktorov*, 6–7 and 13–14.

25. Dr. Nikitin also observed that the ability to induce suggestion in patients depended significantly on the individual's character, spiritual state, and intellectual development (or lack thereof). Tregubov, *Otzyvy doktorov*, 11.

26. V. M. Bekhterev, *Suggestion and Its Role in Social Life*, ed. Lloyd H. Strickland, trans. Tzvetanka Dobrev-Martinov (New Brunswick, NJ: Transaction Publishers, 1998), 36–37.

27. See, for example, the case of Mikhail Cherniak in GMIR, f. 13, op. 1, d. 349, l. 12.

28. Heretz, *Russia on the Eve of Modernity*, 138.

29. GMIR, koll. I, op. 4, d. 191, l. 211.

30. For examples, see Palamodov, *Imia moe greshnoe*, 17, 196–97.

31. Testimony of Vera Strazheva, GMIR, f. 2, op. 17, d. 363, ll. 17ob–18ob; Palamodov, *Imia moe greshnoe*, 56–57.

32. Kartasheva's account can be found in Palamodov, *Imia moe greshnoe*, 63–64.

33. Laurie Manchester, "Gender and Social Estate as National Identity: The Wives and Daughters of Orthodox Clergymen as Civilizing Agents in Imperial Russia," *Journal of Modern History* 83, no. 1 (March 2011): 64.

34. William R. Wagner, "Orthodox Domesticity: Creating a Social Role for Women," in Steinberg and Coleman, *Sacred Stories*, 127.

35. Wagner, "Orthodox Domesticity," 127.

36. Brenda Meehan-Waters, "To Save Oneself: Russian Peasant Women and the Development of Women's Religious Communities in Pre-Revolutionary Russia," in *Russian Peasant Women*, ed. Beatrice Farnsworth and Lynne Viola (Oxford: Oxford University Press, 1992), 123–24.

37. See, for example, the testimony of D. Sirotkina, GMIR, f. 2, op. 17, d. 363, l. 18ob.

38. See the case of Olga Bogdanova, discussed in chapter 7, GMIR, f. 2, op. 17, d. 363, l. 16–16ob.

39. Testimony of Z. G. Grigor'eva, GMIR, f. 2. op. 17, d. 363, ll. 7ob–8ob; Palamodov, *Imia moe greshnoe*, 65–66.

40. Palamodov, *Imia moe greshnoe*, 62.

41. See also the case of E. A. Ermolova, Palamodov, *Imia moe greshnoe*, 177.

42. Palamodov, *Imia moe greshnoe*, 63.

43. Palamodov, *Imia moe greshnoe*, 64.

44. Vera Shevzov, "The Struggle for the Sacred: Russian Orthodox Thinking about Miracles in a Modern Age," in *Thinking Orthodox in Modern Russia: Culture, History, Context*, ed. Patrick Lally Michelson and Judith Deutsch Kornblatt (Madison: University of Wisconsin Press, 2014), 142.

45. GMIR, f. 2, op. 17, d. 363, ll. 4–5ob.

46. *Bogu vse otkryto: Svidetel'stva trezvennikov o deianiiakh Brattsa Ioanna*, vol. 1 (St. Petersburg, 2004), 36.

47. TsGIA SPb, f. 680, op. 2, d. 47, l. 4.

48. *Bogu vse otkryto*, 28, 36.

49. *Bogu vse otkryto*, 9.

50. *Bogu vse otkryto*, 50.

51. "Peace-bringers" is what Brother Ioann called them: Kesarev, *Besednichestvo*, 83. *Pis'ma*, 276.

52. Paert, *Spiritual Elders*, 150–51.

53. Letter from Klavdiia Rogacheva, TsGIA SPb, f. 680, op. 5, d. 35, l. 3.

54. Christine D. Worobec, "Cross-Dressing in a Russian Orthodox Monastery: The Case of Maria Zakharova," *Journal of the History of Sexuality* 20, no. 2 (May 2011): 354; Paert, *Spiritual Elders*, 155.

55. Prugavin, *"Brattsy" i trezvenniki*, 71–73.

56. An increasingly sensationalistic press was eager to capitalize on any hint of religious scandal, as in the 1910 case of the Baltskii monastery, where the local prior Innokentii, was found to be forcing young female pilgrims to kiss his half-naked body. Worobec, "Cross-Dressing in a Russian Orthodox Monastery," 341.

57. *K voprosu o "Brattsakh": Spravedlivo li postupila Tserkov', otluchiv obshcheniia s soboiu "brattsev" Dm. Grigor'eva i Koloskova?* (Moscow, 1911), 39–40.

58. Vasil'ev, "Trezvenniki," 2–3.

59. TsGIA SPb, f. 680, op. 5, d. 55, ll. 1–2.

60. Komkov and Plotnikova, *Apostol trezvosti*, 26–27.

61. Pankratov, *Ishchushchie Boga*, 49.

62. Palamodov, *Imia moe greshnoe*, 59.

63. Isolde Thyrêt, "Women and the Orthodox Faith in Muscovite Russia: Spiritual Experience and Practice," in Kivelson and Greene, *Orthodox Russia*, 170–71.

64. Clay, "Orthodox Missionaries," 45.

65. *Bogu vse otkryto*, 45–46.

66. Father Ioann of Kronstadt attracted many letters from Orthodox women deeply invested in epistolary forms of spiritual advising. Kizenko, *Prodigal Saint*, 125–29.

67. Kizenko, *Prodigal Saint*, 111.

5. Not in Good Faith

1. D. Bogoliubov, "Bratets Ioann Churikov, kak religioznyi propovednik sredi petersburgskago prostonaroda," *Prikhodskii sviashchennik* (1911), nn. 14–15, 16, as cited in Prugavin, *"Brattsy" i trezvenniki*, 26–27. Also reprinted in I. Tregubov, *Besedy Bratsta Ioanna Churikova* (St. Petersburg, 1912), 5.

2. *Izvestiia po S.-Peterburgskoi eparkhii*, nos. 8/9 (1908): 46. Bogoliubov made a similar argument in the wake of the Church's case against the so-called Ioannity in 1909. Kizenko, *Prodigal Saint*, 227.

3. Quoted in Steinberg, *Petersburg*, 214.

4. Freeze, "A Pious Folk?," 324.

5. V. I. Iasevich-Borodaevskaia, *Bor'ba za veru* (St. Petersburg, 1912), 351.

6. Heather J. Coleman, "Defining Heresy: The Fourth Missionary Congress and the Problem of Cultural Power after 1905 in Russia," *Jahrbücher für Geschichte Osteuropas*, n.s., 52, no. 1 (2004): 72.

7. M.K. "The Need for struggle against sectarians," *Veche*, n. 87 (August 6, 1909): 2–3.

8. Kizenko, *Prodigal Saint*, 199.

9. Veniamin (Ieromonakh), *Podmena khristianstva* (St. Petersburg: V. M. Skvortsova, 1911), 1.

10. On this group, see Daniel Scarborough, "Missionaries of Official Orthodoxy: Agents of State Religion in Late Imperial Russia," in *Religious Freedom*

in Modern Russia, ed. Randall Poole and Paul Werth (Pittsburgh: University of Pittsburgh Press, 2018), 142–59.

11. According to one trezvennik, by 1913 Brother Ioann had been taken in for questioning fifty-five times. Lindeman, *Sbornik*, 113.

12. Paul Werth, *The Tsar's Foreign Faiths: Toleration and the Fate of Religious Freedom in Imperial Russia* (Oxford: Oxford University Press, 2014), 239.

13. For a brief introduction to the *khlysty*, see Engelstein, *Castration and the Heavenly Kingdom*, 14.

14. Lindeman, *Sbornik*, 87–91.

15. Coleman, "Defining Heresy," 88.

16. Misionerskii [sic] s"ezd, *Novoe vremia* (July 18, 1908): 4, as cited in Coleman, "Defining Heresy," 88.

17. Veniamin, *Podmena khristianstva*.

18. See Ivan Mikhailovich Tregubov, "Brattsy i ikh posledovateli," *Dukhovnyi khristianin* (July 1912): 55–76.

19. Prugavin, *"Brattsy" i trezvenniki*, 11.

20. Lindeman, *Sbornik*, 51.

21. Beliaev's testimony can be found in RGIA, f. 821, op. 133, d. 207, ll. 104–7ob.

22. The full text of the anathema can be found in Prugavin, *"Brattsy" i trezvenniki*, 87–89.

23. Pankratov, *Ishchushchie Boga*, 79.

24. The claims are from an editorial in *Kolokol*, as quoted in Prugavin, *"Brattsy" i trezvenniki*, 104, and from "Arest moskovskykh 'brattsev' i missii," *Kolokol*, no. 1501 (March 29, 1911): 11.

25. *Pis'ma*, 304. In May 1912, on the assumption of an on-going connection between Brother Ioann and the Moscow brattsy, the Ministry of Spiritual Affairs launched a secret investigation into Churikov's followers to find out whether or not they engaged in *khlyst*-like behavior, such as *radeniia* or "evenings of love." RGIA, f. 821, op. 133, d. 212, l. 55.

26. A copy of this letter can be found in TsGIA SPb, f. 680, op. 5, d. 32, ll. 7–8. It was republished in *Pis'ma*, 273–74.

27. *Pis'ma*, 273.

28. On this point, see John Strickland, *The Making of Holy Russia: The Orthodox Church and Russian Nationalism before the Revolution* (Jordanville, NY: Holy Trinity Publications, 2013).

29. *Pis'ma*, 274.

30. *Pis'ma*, 275–77.

31. *Pis'ma*, 277.

32. Aleksei Beglov, "Eschatological Expectations in Post-Soviet Russia," in *Orthodox Paradoxes: Heterogeneities and Complexities in Contemporary Russian Orthodoxy*, ed. Katja Tolstaja (Leiden: Brill, 2014), 111.

33. Veniamin, *Podmena khristianstva*, 2.

34. Veniamin, *Podmena khristianstva*, 3, 5.

35. Veniamin, *Podmena khristianstva*, 4–5.

36. Veniamin, *Podmena khristianstva*, 6.

37. Veniamin, *Podmena khristianstva*, 6–7.

38. Lindeman, *Sbornik*, 4–5.

39. Veniamin, *Podmena khristianstva*, 8.

40. The text of Churikov's beseda on October 10, 1910, was recorded and later published by Tregubov, available from the website of the Orthodox Society of Trezvenniki, https://www.trezvograd.ru/-24.

41. Veniamin, *Podmena khristianstva*, 16. For more on the *besedniki*, see chapter 1.

42. Greene, *Bodies Like Bright Stars*, 60.

43. Veniamin, *Podmena khristianstva*, 9.

44. Veniamin, *Podmena khristianstva*, 13.

45. Paert, *Spiritual Elders*, 128.

46. Shevzov, "The Struggle for the Sacred," 142.

47. Veniamin, *Podmena khristianstva*, 16. In this sense, they behaved much more like Baptists and the evangelical Christians known as Pashkovites (*pashkovtsy*) than the Orthodox they claimed to be.

48. Veniamin, *Podmena khristianstva*, 14–15.

49. Veniamin, *Podmena khristianstva*, 14.

50. Kapalo, *Text, Context and Performance*, 86–87.

51. Veniamin, *Podmena khristianstva*, 19.

52. Veniamin, *Podmena khristianstva*, 12.

53. Veniamin, *Podmena khristianstva*, 6.

54. Veniamin, *Podmena khristianstva*, 12–13.

55. Veniamin, *Podmena khristianstva*, 22.

56. Quoted in Kizenko, *Prodigal Saint*, 200.

57. Veniamin, *Podmena khristianstva*, 23.

58. A copy of Igumen Arsenii's November 1911 *Groza* article, "'O 'Brattse Ioann' Churikove," is reprinted in Davydov and Frolov, *Dukhovnyi partisan*, 47.

59. Igumen Arsenii, "'O 'Brattse Ioann' Churikove," *Groza*, no. 288 (December 13, 1911): 3.

60. Igumen Arsenii, "O novoiavlennom stolichnom lzhekhriste v litse imenuemago 'Br. Ioanna' Churikova," *Missionerskoe obozrenie*, no. 2 (February 1912): 449.

61. Arsenii, "O novoiavlennom stolichnom lzhekhriste," 451–52.

62. Lindeman, *Sbornik*, 95.

63. Arsenii, "O novoiavlennom stolichnom lzhekhriste," 449–50.

64. "Beseda 'Brattsa Ioanna,'" September 5, 1910, Orthodox Society of Trezvenniki, https://www.trezvograd.ru/-19.

65. For more on the Moscow case, see my article, "'Satan in the Form of an Angel'? The Russian Orthodox Church's Controversial Case against the Moscow *brattsy*, 1909 to 1913," *Religion, State and Society* 48 (June 2020): 196–212.

66. "Eparkhial'naia Khronika," *Izvestiia po Skt-Peterburgskoi eparkhii*, nos. 6/7 (1908): 54–57. See also Herrlinger, *Working Souls*, chap. 4.

67. Otets Mikhail Chel'tsov, "Churikovshchina," *Pribavlenie k tserkovnym vedomostiam*, nos. 51–52 (1912): 2088–2100.

68. For example, his assertion that although Churikov did not directly insult the clergy, he was lacking in respect for them and was therefore responsible

for undermining their influence among his followers (Chel'tsov, "Churikovsh-china," 2098).

69. Chel'tsov, "Churikovshchina," 2092.

70. Chel'tsov, "Churikovshchina," 2099.

71. Chel'tsov, "Churikovshchina," 2093–94.

72. Chel'tsov, "Churikovshchina," 2091, 2096–97.

73. Chel'tsov, "Churikovshchina," 2095.

74. Chel'tsov, "Churikovshchina," 2099.

75. Veniamin, *Podmena khristianstva*, 12.

6. An Unorthodox Conversation

1. Prugavin, *"Brattsy" i trezvenniki*, 117–18.

2. According to Prugavin, almost all of secular society was "on Brother's side." Prugavin, *"Brattsy" i trezvenniki*, 95–96.

3. Prugavin, *"Brattsy" i trezvenniki*, 119.

4. Laura Engelstein, "Personal Testimony and the Defense of Faith: Skoptsy Telling Tales," in Engelstein and Sandler, *Self and Story in Russian History*, 331.

5. "Beseda 'Brattsa Ioanna,'" November 21, 1910, Orthodox Society of Trezvenniki, https://www.trezvograd.ru/-30.

6. RGIA, f. 821, op. 133, d. 212, ll. 278–83ob.

7. Prugavin, *"Brattsy" i trezvenniki*, 103. GMIR, f. 13, op. 1, d. 338, l. 3.

8. Lindeman, *Sbornik*, 105–6.

9. Davydov and Frolov, *Dukhovnyi partizan*, "Predislovie," n.p.

10. They evidently did not have Brother Ioann's approval to publish the pamphlet, although it's unclear what he made of it. Smolev, *Slovo k stoletiiu*, 82.

11. See chapter 3 for Frolov's account.

12. Davydov and Frolov, *Dukhovnyi partizan*, 27.

13. Davydov and Frolov, *Dukhovnyi partizan*, 29.

14. Davydov and Frolov, *Dukhovnyi partizan*, 26.

15. "Beseda 'Brattsa Ioanna,'" June 13, 1910, Orthodox Society of Trezvenniki, https://www.trezvograd.ru/-7.

16. Davydov and Frolov, *Dukhovnyi partizan*, 26.

17. Davydov and Frolov, *Dukhovnyi partizan*, 26.

18. Curiously, the original printed version reads "We do not have the right . . .": "[My] **ne** imeem prava pretendovat' na Boga za Ego darovaniya," Davydov and Frolov, *Dukhovnyi Partizan*, 11. However, this makes little sense in either the specific or broader context, so subsequent versions have regarded it as a typo and thus omitted the "ne," so that the statement reads: "We have the right. . . ."

19. Davydov and Frolov, *Dukhovnyi partizan*, 39.

20. Davydov and Frolov, *Dukhovnyi partizan*, 15.

21. Davydov and Frolov, *Dukhovnyi partizan*, 16–17.

22. Davydov and Frolov, *Dukhovnyi partizan*, 10–11.

23. Davydov and Frolov, *Dukhovnyi partizan*, 15.

24. Kizenko, "Written Confessions," 105.
25. Davydov and Frolov, *Dukhovnyi partizan*, 23.
26. Davydov and Frolov, *Dukhovnyi partizan*, 24.
27. Davydov and Frolov, *Dukhovnyi partizan*, 15.
28. Davydov and Frolov, *Dukhovnyi partizan*, "Predislovie," n.p.
29. Veniamin, *Podmena khristianstva*, 12.
30. Veniamin, *Podmena khristianstva*, 15.
31. Davydov and Frolov, *Dukhovnyi partizan*, 9.
32. The reference was to Tregubov, the Free Christian. Excerpt from an article in *Rech'*, published on February 13, 1912, in *Pis'ma*, 305.
33. *Pis'ma*, 306.
34. "Beseda #76," March 25, 1912, recorded by "Trezvennik," in Tregubov, *Besedy*; see Tregubov's collection at the Society of Spiritual Christian Trezvenniki website: http:www.trezvost.com.
35. *Pis'ma*, 304.
36. RGIA, f. 821, op. 133, d. 212, l. 174–74ob.
37. See the unidentified article, "K izbieniiu Churikovtsev" (On the Churikovtsy beatings) found in RGIA, f. 821, op. 133, d. 212, l. 224.
38. RGIA, f. 821, op. 133, d. 212, ll. 108b, 175. Various accounts of the event differ only slightly with respect to this quote, but they differ more with respect to the size of the crowd, estimating from seven hundred to three thousand people.
39. See, for example, the accounts in *Kolokol*, on June 12, 13, 16, and 19, 1912.
40. RGIA, f. 821, op. 133, d. 212, ll. 103–4.
41. RGIA, f. 821, op. 133, d. 212, ll. 103ob–104.
42. RGIA, f. 821, op. 133, d. 212, l. 101ob.
43. Palamodov, *Imia moe greshnoe*, 195–96; Veniamin, *Podmena khristianstva*, 25.
44. N.S., "K Izbieniiu churikovtsev," *Pravda*, June 19, 1912, as quoted in D. M. Aptekman, "Kritika religiozno-eticheskikh vozzrenii i reaktsionnoi deiatel'nosti sekty trezvennikov" (PhD diss., Gosudarstvennyi Universitet imeni A.A. Zhdanova, 1965), 144–45.
45. TsGIA SPb, f. 680, op. 5, d. 41, ll. 5–6.
46. RGIA, f. 821, op. 133, d. 212, l. 156.
47. RGIA, f. 821, op. 133, d. 212, l. 156ob.
48. A copy of the published letter, along with other similar versions published in different (but unfortunately unidentified) newspapers, can be found in RGIA, f. 821, op. 133, d. 212, ll. 222–23.
49. The letter was signed by five individuals—Platon Semenov, Pavel Nikolaev, Adreian Bol'shakov, Vasilii Lomovtsev, and Georgii Igumanov—all of whom were among those who had petitioned secular and spiritual authorities as well.
50. RGIA, f. 821, op. 133, d. 212, l. 282.
51. N. G. Zarembo, "Dukhovnye vlasti Sankt-peterburga i narodnoe trezvennicheskove dvizhenie churikovtsev (1907–1914 gg.)," *Izvestiia Rossiiskogo gosudarstvennogo universiteta A.I. Gertsena*, no. 126 (2010): 34.

52. Recounted in *Rodnaia Gazeta*, no. 2 (1913) (so, January), allegedly written by Tregubov. Smolev, *Slovo k stoletiiu*, 105.

53. Smolev, *Slovo k stoletiiu*, 107.

54. Smolev, *Slovo k stoletiiu*, 108-9.

55. Lindeman, *Sbornik*, 9.

56. Lindeman, *Sbornik*, 105.

57. RGIA, f. 821, op. 133, d. 212, l. 331–31ob.

58. Komkov and Plotnikova, *Apostol trezvosti*, 147.

59. Zarembo, "Dukhovnye vlasti," 34. The appeal to the tsar and empress is RGIA, f. 821, op. 133, d. 212, ll. 139, 144.

60. The others were Protoierei Arkhangelov, a priest by the name of Krylov, priest-missionary Antsepetrov, and priest-missionary Chepurin. "Dopros Brattsa Ioanna," *Pis'ma*, 311.

61. *Pis'ma*, 312.

62. *Pis'ma*, 312-13.

63. *Pis'ma*, 314.

64. TsGIA SPb, f. 680, op. 5, d. 43, l. 3ob.

65. RGIA, f. 821, op. 133, d. 212, l. 329.

66. RGIA, f. 821, op. 133, d. 212, l. 315.

67. *Pis'ma*, 315.

68. *Pis'ma*, 316.

69. *Pis'ma*, 318.

70. Reported in a June issue of *Dym otechestva*, no. 17 (1914), quoted in Komkov and Plotnikova, *Apostol trezvosti*, 166.

71. Reported by Zhivotovskii in *Dym otechestva*, quoted in Komkov and Plotnikova, *Apostol trezvosti*, 146.

72. Komkov and Plotnikova, *Apostol trezvosti*, 166-67.

73. Churikov's most comprehensive response to the official August 13, 1914, charges against him, which detailed the nature of his "sectarianism," came in the form of his *proshenie* and *ob"iasnenie* to the Ministry of Internal Affairs, dated February 9, 1915, and located in *Pis'ma*, 321-31; and RGIA, f. 821, op. 133, d. 212, ll. 320-29. An earlier version (December 1914) can be found in GMIR, f. 13, op. 1, d. 351, ll. 21-31.

74. *Pis'ma*, 323.

75. *Pis'ma*, 324.

76. *Pis'ma*, 337.

77. In *Vsemirnaia panorama*, no. 257 (March 21, 1914): 4.

78. According to nonsober residents of Vyritsa (who may or may not have been hostile to the sober community), almost none of the trezvenniki living in the colony attended mass at the nearby church (Sv. Apostolov Petr i Pavla) after 1912, and very few were at annual confession/communion. RGIA, f. 821, op. 133, d. 212, l. 291ob.

79. RGIA, f. 821, op. 133, d. 212, l. 321.

80. *Dym otechestva*, no. 22, as quoted in Komkov and Plotnikova, *Apostol trezvosti*, 140-41.

81. RGIA, f. 821, op. 133, d. 212, ll. 274-75.

82. A.M., "U trezvennikov," *Malen'kaia gazeta*, no. 11 (1 October 1914): 3.

7. Revolutionary Sobriety

1. A.M., "U trezvennikov," 3. The full name was "Petrogradskoe vzaimo-vspominatel'noe obshchestvo trezvennikov v Rossii." "Torzhestvo churikovt-sev," *Petrogradskii listok*, no. 168 (June 2, 1916): 2. According to Soviet *bezbozhnik* journalist Pavel Petrov, a Petrograd trezvennik by the name of Nikolai Ivanovich Dumin founded a sober *obshchina* for workers in Reval/Tallinn around 1915. Pavel Petrov, *Sekt vyritskago poroka (trezvenniki-churikovtsy)* (Kostroma, 1929), 20.

2. Much in line with Orthodox authorities, Churikov rejected civil war but supported the war in Europe, because it is "a Christian duty" to fight against "brutalized enemies" who act against Christ's teachings, and "our duty and sacred responsibility" to defend the fatherland (*rodina*) and the Holy Church. Abramov, "Eshche o Churikove," 2.

3. GMIR, koll. I, op. 4, d. 61, l. 21.

4. Dmitriev, *Povestvovanie*, 10.

5. A. Khrapovitskii, "Dukhovnaia prelest'," *Ispoved'* (1919), available from the ABC of Faith website, https://azbyka.ru/otechnik/Antonij_Hrapovickij/ispoved/#0_10. I want to thank Nadia Kizenko and Eugene Clay for this reference.

6. GMIR, koll. I, op. 4, d. 27, ll. 1–3ob.

7. Its official title was "Obshchina narodnykh trezvennikov, posledovateli brattsa I. Churikova."

8. Quoted in Aptekman, "Kritika," 199.

9. GMIR, f. 13, op. 1, d. 141, l. 4. "Brother Ioann" Koloskov established a sober commune in the Moscow region around the same time and made similar arguments about the complementarity between sober and socialist principles. See O. V. Borisova and S. M. Shinkevich, eds., "Otkrytoe pis'mo I.N. Koloskova sledovateliu VChK I.A. Shpitsbergu," *Viestnik Sviato-Filaretovskogo instituta* 40 (2021), especially 211–12, 220. Many thanks to Eugene Clay for this reference as well.

10. GMIR, f. 13, op. 1, d. 278, l. 63ob.

11. Abramov, "Eshche o Churikove," 2.

12. M. Iu. Krapivin, A. Ia. Leikin, and A. G. Dalgatov, *Sud'by khristianskogo sek-tantstva v sovetskoi rossii (1917-konets 1930-kh godov)* (St. Petersburg: St. Petersburg University Press, 2003), 247.

13. Arkhiv UFSB, d. P-82319, t. 1, l. 290.

14. The communities in Omsk and Kostroma apparently maintained the closest relationship with Churikov. Krapivin, Leikin, and Dalgatov, *Sud'by*, 243.

15. Petrov, *Sekt vyritskago poroka*, 28, 20.

16. A. I. Klibanov, ed., *Konkretnye issledovaniia sovremennykh religioznykh verovanii (metodika, organizatsiia, rezul'taty)* (Moscow: Mysl', 1967), 82.

17. Klibanov, *Konkretnye issledovaniia*, 69.

18. Maslova, *Povest'*, 35–36.

19. Part of the problem stems from a lack of accurate sources. As trezven-nik Sergei Palamodov has stressed, besedy from the 1920s were often recorded with distortions; it was a time when "water [was] added to the milk of Brother's

sermons, so that it is impossible for a reader who does not know anything about [him] to separate one from the other." See "Posleslovie (Afterword)," Orthodox Society of Trezvenniki, accessed June 29, 2022, https://www.trezvo grad.ru/istoriy.

20. GMIR, f. 13, op. 1, d. 278, ll. 63–64.

21. GMIR, f. 13, op. 1, d. 141, l. 1.

22. On this point, see K. Rousselet, "Utopies socio-religieuses et révolution politique dans l'années 1920," *Revue des études slaves* 69, no. 1 (January 1, 1997): 258; see also Coleman, *Russian Baptists*, 139.

23. Although the provenance and accuracy of many of his besedy from the 1920s remains a matter of debate among his followers today, this single beseda was an exception; it was recorded by Nikolai Monashekov and published for distribution in three thousand copies with Brother Ioann's permission. Palamodov, *Imia moe greshnoe*, 19.

24. GMIR, f. 13, op. 1, d. 363, l. 24.

25. As quoted in Aptekman, "Kritika," 203.

26. GMIR, f. 13, op. 1, d. 363, l. 24.

27. Trezvennik, *Beseda brattsa "Ioanna Churikova": 16 aprelia 1922 g, Paskhal'naia nedelia* (Petrograd, 192-), 5–6.

28. Emma Feliksovna Liadova, *Vse otkryto*, 15–16, Society of Spiritual Christian Trezvenniki, accessed June 29, 2022, http://trezvost.com/Witnesses/All_Open_For_God_1_3.htm; for a similar testimony, see GMIR, koll. I, op. 4, d. 61, l. 68.

29. GMIR, f. 13, op. 1, d. 363, l. 24.

30. Edward E. Roslof, *Red Priests: Renovationism, Russian Orthodoxy, and Revolution, 1905–1946* (Bloomington: Indiana University Press, 2002), ix.

31. Aptekman, "Kritika," 198. The letter can be found in TsGIA SPb, f. 680, op. 1, d. 83, l. 15.

32. A description can be found in *Sobornyi razum*, nos. 1–2 (1923). On the growing popularity of general confessions in the 1920s, see Nadieszda Kizenko, "Sacramental Confession in Modern Russia and Ukraine," in Wanner, *State Secularism and Lived Religion*, 196.

33. Komkov and Plotnikova, *Apostol trezvosti*, 206.

34. On the Orthodox laity's response to the "Living Church," see Gregory Freeze, "Counter-Reformation in Russian Orthodoxy: Popular Response to Religious Innovation, 1922–25," *Slavic Review* 54, no. 2 (Summer, 1995): 305–6.

35. For examples, see GMIR, koll. I, op. 4, d. 60, ll. 2ob–3; Palamodov, *Imia moe greshnoe*, 63.

36. Sergei Palamodov, "Obshchestvo Khristian-Trezvennikov Brattsa Ioanna Churikova," Center for the Treatment of Alcoholism, "Revival," accessed December 12, 2022, http://narkolog.inkiev.net/index.cgi?action=main&lang=ru.

37. Irina Korovushkina Paert, "Mediators between Heaven and Earth: The Forms of Spiritual Guidance and Debate on the Elders in Present-Day Russian Orthodoxy," in Tolstaja, *Orthodox Paradoxes*, 141–42. See also Aleksei Beglov, *V poiskakh "bezgreshnykh katakomb": Tserkovnoe podpol'e v SSSR* (Moscow, 2008), 78–85.

38. V. Marovskii, "Bratets Churikov: 'Religioznyi durman,'" *Leningradskaia Pravda*, no. 224 (October 1, 1924): 6.

39. Balashov, who held Party card no. 5, became a trezvennik in the early 1920s.

40. N. B. Lebina, *Povsednevnaia zhizn' sovetskogo goroda 1920–30 gody* (St. Petersburg: "Letnyi Sad," 1999), 40.

41. Aptekman, "Kritika," 205.

42. For examples, see the case of Timofei Zaitsev, GMIR, f. 13, op. 1, d. 349, l. 27; Komkov and Plotnikova, *Apostol trezvosti*, 210; Min'kov, *Moroshka*; and Palamodov, *Imia moe greshnoe*.

43. Komkov and Plotnikova, *Apostol trezvosti*, 208.

44. Terekhovich tells an almost identical story about a young alcoholic musician who was cured of throat cancer, having turned to Brother on a similar logic, namely, "so many people went to him, how could they all be idiots?" Terekhovich, *Kratkii biograficheskii ocherk*, 54.

45. Quoted in White, *Russia Goes Dry*, 16.

46. White, *Russia Goes Dry*, 19.

47. GMIR, f. 2, op. 17, d. 363, l. 16–16 ob.

48. Anne Gorsuch, *Youth in Revolutionary Russia: Enthusiasts, Bohemians, Delinquents* (Bloomington: Indiana University Press, 2000), chap. 8.

49. Terekhovich, *Kratkii biograficheskii ocherk*, 10.

50. Terekhovich, *Kratkii biograficheskii ocherk*, 43.

51. See Dmitriev, *Povestvovanie*.

52. Terekhovich, *Kratkii biograficheskii ocherk*, 46.

53. Smolev, *Slovo k stoletiiu*, 149.

54. Dmitriev, *Povestvovanie*, 8–9, 12.

55. Dmitriev, *Povestvovanie*, 8–9.

56. From a Puchkov article in *Trezvyi Rassvet* (no date), TsGIA SPb, f. 680, op. 4, d. 7, l. 14, as cited in Aptekman, "Kritika," 208.

57. As quoted in Palamodov, *Imia moe greshnoe*, 18.

58. TsGA, f. 494, op. 2, d. 2, ll. 6–19.

59. TsGA, f. 494, op. 2, d. 2, l. 13.

60. The Moscow *bratets* Koloskov had already successfully registered his own commune, Trezvaia Zhizn', with the Soviet government in April of that year. Krapivin, Leikin, and Dalgatov, *Sud'by*, 243.

61. GMIR, f. 13, op. 1, d. 277, l. 2. The total amount of land in the commune's possession is difficult to determine. According to Maslova, at the time it was registered, the commune had thirty-seven desiatina (roughly one hundred acres) of (mostly) swampy land, and only three desiatina were cultivated. She also claims that it tried to get more from the state, but further subsidies did not materialize (Maslova, *Povest'*, 10–11). However, Tregubov reported that in 1923 the commune received an addition five hundred desiatina from the government, all but thirty-seven of which was forested (GMIR, f. 13, op. 1, d. 277, l. 3). In the fall of 1918, Churikov allegedly claimed that the trezvenniki possessed a total of five hundred desiatina (not all of which was necessarily located in Vyritsa), GMIR, f. 13, op. 1, d. 278, ll. 63–64.

62. Krapivin, Leikin, and Dalgatov, *Sud'by*, 245–46.

63. GMIR, f. 13, op. 1, d. 278, l. 63ob.

64. GMIR, f. 13, op. 1, d. 278, ll. 63–64ob.

65. GMIR, f. 13, op. 1, d. 367, l. 58ob.

66. Maslova, *Povest'*, 10–11.

67. TsGIA SPb, f. 680, op. 1, d. 68, ll. 2–3.

68. Stites, *Revolutionary Dreams*, 211.

69. Maslova, *Povest'*, 12.

70. According to a comprehensive investigation by local and state authorities, the commune's total population in the spring of 1928 stood at 239, including 62 adult males, 122 adult females, 18 teenagers, and 37 children. Of these, 52 men and 101 women were considered fit for work (*trudosposoby*), meaning that 10 men and 21 women were not. In terms of their regional origins, almost half of the population (106) came from Leningrad or Vyritsa, while the rest were migrants to the capital from around the northern and central provinces (with Pskov and Tver drawing the most). Five children had been born into the commune, and two adult men had arrived directly from the army. In terms of social origins, 31 were identified as workers (of these 5 were unskilled and 26 skilled), 164 were peasants, and 7 were office or white-collar workers (*sluzhashie*). TsGIA SPb, f. 680, op. 4, d. 6, l. 1–1ob.

71. Robert Wesson, *Soviet Communes* (New Brunswick, NJ: Rutgers University Press, 1963), 121.

72. GMIR, koll. I, op. 4, d. 27, l. 3.

73. GMIR, f. 13, op. 1, d. 278, ll. 74–77, contains copies of their "diplomas" for their agricultural achievements in 1923 and 1927 and 1928.

74. Maslova, *Povest'*, 2. By 1923, the commune counted eleven horses, forty-eight sheep, and seventy-five cattle. GMIR, f. 13, op. 1, d. 277, l. 3.

75. GMIR, f. 2, op. 17, d. 89, l. 2.

76. GMIR, f. 2, op. 17, d. 89, ll. 1–2ob: report from I. M. Tregubov to P. G. Smidovich, VTs Ispolkom, "Dokladnaia zapiska o sel'sko-khoziaistvennoi kommune imeni churikova v proshlom i nastoiashchem," dated May 25, 1930.

77. GMIR, koll. I, op. 4, d. 27, l. 3.

78. Testimony of kommunar Klavdiia Rogacheva, Palamodov, *Imia moe greshnoe*, 69–70.

79. Beglov, *V poiskakh*, 177–79 and 184–85. See also Stella Rock, "'They Burned the Pine, but the Place Remains All the Same': Pilgrimage in the Changing Landscape of Soviet Russia," in Wanner, *State Secularism and Lived Religion*, 164.

80. Maslova, *Povest'*, 37–38.

81. GMIR, f. 13, op. 1, d. 277, ll. 10–11.

82. A report filed by local state authorities in May 1928 offered a slightly different, but nonetheless, equally structured schedule of work, TsGIA SPb, f. 680, op. 4, d. 5, l. 3ob.

83. GMIR, koll. I, op. 4, d. 25, l. 1.

84. TsGIA SPb, f. 680, op. 4, d. 5, l. 3ob.

85. GMIR, f. 13, op. 1, d. 278, l. 44–44ob.

86. Maslova, *Povest'*, 41.
87. GMIR, koll. I, op. 4, d. 27, l. 1.
88. Testimony of Timofei Vasil'evich Zaitsev, January 21, 1929, GMIR, f. 13, op. 1, d. 349, l. 27.
89. See the case of V. Tikhomirova, GMIR, f. 2, op. 17, d. 363, l. 10–10ob, and in Palamodov, *Imia moe greshnoe*, 68–69; see also the case of P. Ivanovna, GMIR, f. 2, op. 17, d. 363, ll. 21ob–22.
90. Aptekman, "Kritika," 174.
91. A. Ivanovna, "Moia zhizn'," published in "Zhurnal Bich" (1926), in GMIR, f. 2, op. 17, d. 363, l. 13.
92. GMIR, f. 13, op. 1, d. 361, l. 98.
93. Maslova, *Povest'*, 48–49.
94. TsGIA SPb, f. 680, op. 4, d. 6, l. 2.
95. TsGIA SPb, f. 680, op. 4, d. 6. Although the Leningrad Circuit Court first found in favor of Brovina in May 1928, Churikov's *obshchina* appealed to a higher court, which overturned the first decision on the basis of inconclusive evidence.
96. "Obvinitel'noe zakluchenie," Arkhiv UFSB, d. P-82319, t.1, l. 284.
97. K. David Patterson, "Typhus and Its Control in Russia, 1870–1940," *Medical History* 37 (1993): 379.
98. Heather Coleman has estimated that there were approximately one hundred similar Evangelical communes, and twenty set up by the Baptists. *Russian Baptists*, 174–76.
99. William B. Edgarton, ed. and trans., *Memoirs of Peasant Tolstoyans in Russia* (Bloomington: Indiana University Press, 1993), 14.
100. Edgarton, *Memoirs of Peasant Tolstoyans*, 13.
101. Edgarton, *Memoirs of Peasant Tolstoyans*, 7.
102. Quoted by Andrej Walicki, *The Slavophile Controversy: History of a Conservative Utopia in Nineteenth-Century Russian Thought*, trans. Hilda Andrews-Rusiecka (Oxford: Clarendon Press, 1975), 257.
103. GMIR, koll. I, op. 4, d. 61, l. 28.
104. Letter from Klavdiia Rogacheva, TsGIA SPb, f. 680, op. 5, d. 35, l. 3.
105. Maslova, *Povest'*, 18–19.
106. From the memoirs of Mikhail Gorbunov-Posadov, Edgarton, *Memoirs of Peasant Tolstoyans*, 2.
107. GMIR, koll. I, op. 4, d. 67, l. 94.
108. Interview with E. A. Ermolova, Palamodov, *Imia moe greshnoe*, 183.
109. See, for example, I. Ia. Eliashevich, *Pravda of churikove i churikovtsakh* (Leningrad: Leningradskii Oblastlit, 1928).
110. GMIR, f. 13, op. 1, d. 278, l. 56.
111. Palamodov, *Imia moe greshnoe*, 184.
112. Greene, *Bodies Like Bright Stars*, 41.
113. GMIR, f. 13, op. 1, d. 349, l. 27.
114. GMIR, koll. I, op. 4, d. 61, l. 54.
115. GMIR, koll. I, op. 4, d. 27, l. 3. His comments were later published in *Krasnaia Gazeta*, the morning edition, on June 20, 1928 (no. 141), 5.

116. GMIR, f. 13, op. 1, d. 278, l. 55, letter dated August 1, 1929.
117. Stites, *Revolutionary Dreams*, 10.
118. TsGIA SPb, f. 680, op. 5, d. 43, l. 4ob.

8. The Soviet State's Campaign against the Trezvenniki, 1924–1933

1. On the far more troubled fate of Brother Ioann Koloskov and his follow-ers in Moscow in the early 1920s, see Borisova and Shinkevich, "Otkritoe pis'mo."
2. The press indicated that there was a sixfold increase in alcohol-related deaths in Leningrad between 1923 and 1927, and a sharp rise in the number of arrests for drunkenness, from 2000 in 1923, to 110,000 in 1927. See White, *Russia Goes Dry*, 19–22.
3. The commune's charter mandated observance of all state laws.
4. Following the 1924 party congress policy debates over sectarians, it was decided to continue being mindful about their relative usefulness and dan-ger to the state. The criteria for determining the degree of toleration accorded to sectarians included three categories: whether or not they paid their taxes, whether or not they served in the Red Army, and whether or not they main-tained good relations with kulaks. In all three ways, the trezvenniki behaved in ways acceptable to the state. On the 1924 decision, see Arto Luukkanen, *Party of Unbelief: The Religious Policy of the Bolshevik Party, 1917–1929* (Helsinki: Suomen Historiallinen Seura, 1994), 176.
5. Lebina, *Povsednevnaia*, 39.
6. Krapivin, Leikin, and Dalgatov, *Sud'by*, 242.
7. On this point, see Coleman, *Russian Baptists*, 136.
8. Ivan Smolev, *Slyshit: Povest' o Fevral'skom voskresenii 1928 goda v Vyritse* (Leningrad, 1958), 28.
9. Coleman, *Russian Baptists*, chap. 10; Scott Kenworthy, *The Heart of Russia: Trinity-Sergius, Monasticism, and Society after 1825* (New York: Oxford University Press; Washington, DC: Woodrow Wilson Center Press, 2010), chap. 9. Jennifer Jean Wynot, *Keeping the Faith: Russian Orthodox Monasticism in the Soviet Union, 1917–1939* (College Station: Texas A&M University, 2004); William R. Wagner, "Female Monasticism in Revolutionary Times: The Nizhnii Novogorod Con-vent of the Exaltation of the Cross, 1917–1935," *Church History* 89, no. 2 (June 2020): 350–89.
10. On this point, see Rousselet, "Utopies socio-religieuses et revolution politique," 270–71.
11. Stites, *Revolutionary Dreams*, 226.
12. Stites, *Revolutionary Dreams*, 241.
13. Copies of the "diplomas" the commune received for its agricultural achievements in 1923 and 1927 and 1928 can be found in GMIR, f. 13, op. 1, d. 278, ll. 74–77.
14. V. Marovskii, "Bratets Churikov: 'Religioznyi durman,'" *Leningradskaia Pravda*, no. 228 (October 5, 1924): 5.
15. On agit-plays, see Elizabeth Wood, *Performing Justice: Agitation Trials in Early Soviet Russia* (Ithaca, NY: Cornell University Press, 2005), especially chaps. 4 and 5.

16. Marovskii, "Bratets Churikov," 5.

17. Marovskii "Bratets Churikov," 5. See also Eliashevich, *Pravda*, 73.

18. V. Marovskii, "Bratets Churikov: 'Religioznyi durman,'" *Leningradskaia Pravda*, no. 287 (December 14, 1924): 6.

19. See chapter 5.

20. GMIR, f. 13, op. 1, d. 361, l. 100–100ob.

21. TsGIA SPb, f. 680, op. 1, d. 124, ll. 1–20ob.

22. See also Eliashevich, *Pravda*, 15.

23. Arkhiv UFSB, d. P-82319, t. 1, ll. 281–82. For additional excerpts, see l. 250.

24. Arkhiv UFSB, d. P-82319, t. 1, l. 292.

25. William B. Husband, *"Godless Communists": Atheism and Society in Soviet Russia, 1917–1932* (DeKalb: Northern Illinois University Press, 2000), 114.

26. Igor' Narskii, *Zhizn' v katastrofe: Budni naselenie Urala v 1917–1922 gg.* (Moscow: Rosspen, 2001), 416.

27. Arkhiv UFSB, d. P-82319, t. 1, l. 282.

28. Eliashevich, *Pravda*, 58–59.

29. Krapivin, Leikin, and Dalgatov, *Sud'by*, 248.

30. Arkhiv UFSB. d. P-66724, t. 1, l. 280.

31. "Prizyv," which appeared in *Trezvyi Rassvet* in 1926, as quoted in Palamodov, *Imia moe greshnoe*, 42.

32. Palamodov, *Imia moe greshnoe*, 42. Another new name reflecting Soviet influence and style was "the Great World Leader Brother Ioann."

33. Arkhiv UFSB, d. P-66724, t. 1, l. 280.

34. Arkhiv UFSB, d. P-66724, t. 1, l. 280.

35. Beglov, "Eschatological Expectations, 112–17; A. A. Panchenko, *Kristovshchina i skopchestvo: Fol'klor i traditsionnaia kul'tura russkikh misticheskikh sekt* (Moscow: Ob'edinennoe gumanitarnoe izdatel'stvo, 2002), 203–4.

36. Lynne Viola, "The Peasant Nightmare: Visions of Apocalypse in the Soviet Countryside," *Journal of Modern History* 62, no. 4 (December 1990): 748. See also Fitzpatrick, *Stalin's Peasants*, 45, 214.

37. Mel'nikova, *"Voobrazhaemaia kniga,"* chap. 4.

38. Arkhiv UFSB, d. P-66724, t. 1, l. 280.

39. Arkhiv UFSB, d. P-66724, t. 1, l. 281.

40. On the *Bapsomol*, see Coleman, *Russian Baptists*, 203–8; Terekhovich, *Kratkii biograficheskii ocherk*, 50.

41. Terekhovich, *Kratkii biograficheskii ocherk*, 57.

42. Arkhiv UFSB, d. P-82319, t. 1, l. 279.

43. Maslova, *Povest'*, 44.

44. Arkhiv UFSB, d. P-66724, t. 1, l. 294.

45. GMIR, f. 13, op. 1, d. 278, l. 37. Sestritsa Niusha would also be arrested in 1928.

46. Maslova called it a "ploy" to "disarm" Brother Ioann. Maslova, *Povest'*, 27.

47. GMIR, f. 13, op. 1, d. 278, l. 38ob. Similar arguments had been made during the forced closures of women's monastery communes in the early 1920s. Wynot, *Keeping the Faith*, 166.

48. GMIR, f. 13, op. 1, d. 278, l. 38ob.

49. Arkhiv UFSB, d. P-82319, t. 1, ll. 283, 286. Anna Grigor'evna was also accused of "systematically beating" her cook, Nastia.

50. Arkhiv UFSB, d. P-82319, t. 1, l. 287; Petrov, *Sekta vyritskago poroka*, 34. See also "Rabochii," "Pravda o brattse Churikove," *Krasnaia gazeta*, no. 141 (June 20, 1928): 5.

51. GMIR, f. 13, op. 1, d. 278, l. 38ob.

52. Arkhiv UFSB, d. P-82319, t. 1, ll. 277 and 284.

53. Eliashevich, *Pravda*, 60; Petrov, *Sekta vyritskago poroka*, 34.

54. Petition regarding the May 14, 1927, search of the commune and arrest of trezvenniki can be found in GMIR, f. 2, op. 17, d. 83, l. 1; another petition dated September 7, 1927, can be found in GMIR, f. 13, op. 1, d. 278, l. 86; and a third dated February 22, 1929, GMIR, f. 13, op. 1, d. 278, l. 37.

55. Letter from Klavdiia Rogacheva, TsGIA SPb, f. 680, op. 5, d. 35, l. 3.

56. Dmitriev, *Povestvovanie*, 27.

57. GMIR, f. 13, op. 17, d. 88, l. 3.

58. GMIR, f. 13, op. 1, d. 278, l. 23; also see ll. 46–48.

59. Exactly what prompted the visit is hard to say, but it was most likely part of a broader campaign (led mostly by the Komsomol) to go into the countryside in order to secure the flow of grain to the cities and factories in advance of the Five-Year Plan (revealed in October 1928 and officially adopted in April 1929). TsGIA SPb, f. 680, op. 4, d. 5, l. 4–4ob.

60. TsGIA SPb, f. 680, op. 4, d. 6, l. 4.

61. TsGIA SPb, f. 680, op. 4, d. 5, l. 4ob.

62. Eliashevich, *Pravda*. See also Petrov, *Sekta vyritskago poroka*.

63. Daniel Peris, *Storming the Heavens: The Soviet League of Militant Godless* (Ithaca, NY: Cornell University Press, 1998), 75.

64. Eliashevich, *Pravda*, 74.

65. Eliashevich, *Pravda*, 29–30.

66. Eliashevich, *Pravda*, 72.

67. Eliashevich, *Pravda*, 79.

68. Eliashevich, *Pravda*, 61.

69. Eliashevich, *Pravda*, 65.

70. GMIR, koll. I, op. 4, d. 27, ll. 1–3ob.

71. GMIR, koll. I, op. 4, d. 27, l. 1.

72. GMIR, koll. I, op. 4, d. 27, l. 3–3ob.

73. Petrov, *Sekta vyritskago poroka*, 29.

74. Petrov, *Sekta vyritskago poroka*, 16.

75. Petrov, *Sekta vyritskago poroka*, 35.

76. Kii, "V tenetakh religii: Churikovtsy," *Bezbozhnik u stanka*, no. 1 (1929): 6. For additional godless coverage of the trezvenniki, see A. Rostovtseva, "Kommuna 'BICh,'" *Bezbozhnik*, no. 18 (October 1928): 5; and Iu. Ardi, "Tam, gde orudoval Churikov," *Bezbozhnik*, no. 15 (August 1929): 13–14.

77. Maslova, *Povest'*, 43.

78. GMIR, f. 2, op. 17, d. 84, l. 4. The disenfranchised included P. F. Taptygin (chairman of commune); S. S. Dudykin; G. G. Mikhailov (Churikov's "right hand man"); Akulina Andreeva (secretary); V. I. Satrikov (treasurer); A. E. Andreev (chairman of the religious obshchina); V. D. Kolobov, G. K. Dmitriev,

and G. M. Kozharov (members of the executive organ of the religious obshchina); and Ivan Kovalenko (secretary of the obshchina).

79. For the text of the new law, see Mervyn Matthews, ed., *Soviet Government: A Selection of Official Documents on Internal Policies* (New York: Taplinger, 1974), 63–70.

80. Komkov and Plotnikova, *Apostol trezvosti*, 224.

81. Palamodov, *Imia moe greshnoe*, 98.

82. The details of Brother Ioann's death are still not fully known. See Palamodov, "Obshchestvo Khristian-Trezvennikov Brattsa Ioanna Churikova."

83. GMIR, f. 13, op. 1, d. 277, l. 12.

84. GMIR, f. 13, op. 1, d. 277, l. 12ob.

85. GMIR, f. 13, op. 1, d. 277, l. 13.

86. Maslova, *Povest'*, 66.

87. Zaitsev's draft petition, dated August 1, 1929, GMIR, f. 13, op. 1, d. 278, l. 55.

88. Petition from S. S. Dudykin and Timofei Vasil'evich Zaitsev on behalf of the now "Trezvyi put'" sel'sko-khoziaistvennaia kommuna, dated August 26, 1929, GMIR, f. 13, op. 1, d. 278, ll. 11–12ob.

89. Fitzpatrick, *Stalin's Peasants*, 67–69.

90. GMIR, f. 13, op. 1, d. 278, l. 12ob.

91. GMIR, f. 13, op. 1, d. 278, l. 12ob.

92. GMIR, f. 13, op. 1, d. 278, l. 12ob.

93. GMIR, f. 2, op. 17, d. 89, l. 3ob.

94. GMIR, f. 13, op. 1, d. 278, l. 12.

95. Report from Ivan Tregubov to P. G. Smidovich, dated May 25, 1930, GMIR, f. 2, op. 17, d. 89, l. 4.

96. GMIR, f. 2, op. 17, d. 89, l. 2–2ob.

97. Tricia Starks, *The Body Soviet: Propaganda, Hygiene, and the Soviet State* (Madison: University of Wisconsin Press, 2008), chap. 6.

98. Terekhovich, *Kratkii biograficheskii ocherk*, 61.

99. GMIR, koll. I, op. 4, d. 69, l. 1. The OGPU file includes a hand-drawn diagram outlining the relationships between Churikov and his closest followers (l. 2).

100. "Dvadtsat' 'Apostolov' ozhidaiut bozh'ego tsarstva," *Severnaia Pravda*, September 6, 1929, 4.

101. Golfo Alexopolous, "The Ritual Lament: A Narrative of Appeal in the 1920s and 1930s," *Russian History* 24, nos. 1/2 (Spring–Summer 1997): 119.

102. *Pis'ma*, 379.

103. GMIR, f. 13, op. 1, d. 278, ll. 37–38ob. For other petitions, see GMIR, f. 13, op. 1, d. 364, ll. 4–4ob, 13–14ob.

104. Trebugov's letter to the OGPU, dated May 15, 1929, GMIR, f. 13, op. 1, d. 364, l. 13ob.

105. Quoted in Lebina, *Povsednevnaia*, 40.

106. GMIR, f. 13, op. 17, d. 367, l. 50–50ob.

107. GMIR, f. 13, op. 17, d. 367, ll. 56–57.

108. GMIR, f. 13, op. 1, d. 363, l. 24ob.

109. Smolev, *Slyshit*, 23.

110. Arkhiv UFSB, d. P-75783, l. 387. The deceased was likely Ivan Aleksee-vich Nikitin, born in 1875 and a member of the BICh commune.

111. Terekhovich, *Kratkii biograficheskii ocherk*, 62, 103.

112. Coleman, *Russian Baptists*, 205.

113. Andrei Roshchin, *Kto takie sektanty?* (Moscow: Molodaia gvardia, 1930), 27, 31.

114. GMIR, f. 13, op. 1, d. 278, l. 56.

115. Terekhovich, *Kratkii biograficheskii ocherk*, 63. For Ivan Smolev's letters, see Dmitriev, *Povestvovanie*, 30–33. For believers' responses to Soviet repression, see Olena Panych, "A Time and Space of Suffering: Reflections of the Soviet Past in the Memoirs and Narratives of Evangelical Christians-Baptists," in Wanner, *State Secularism and Lived Religion*, 218–43.

116. TsGIA SPb, f. 680, op. 2, d. 49, l. 14.

117. Rogacheva letter, TsGIA SPb, f. 680, op. 5, d. 35, l. 3.

118. TsGIA SPb, f. 680, op. 2, d. 47, l. 18ob.

9. Promises of an Afterlife

1. Achmed Amba, *I Was Stalin's Bodyguard* (London: Frederick Muller, 1952).

2. Smolev, *Slovo k stoletiiu*, 121.

3. Paert, *Spiritual Elders*, 183.

4. Beglov, *V poiskakh*, 87.

5. Wallace Daniel, ed. and trans., *Women of the Catacombs: Memoirs of the Underground Orthodox Church in Stalin's Russia* (Ithaca, NY: Cornell University Press, 2021), 28.

6. Maslova, *Povest'*, 66.

7. Max Weber, *The Theory of Social and Economic Organization*, ed. Talcott Parsons (New York: Free Press, 1964), 364–68.

8. Dragadze, "Domestication of Religion."

9. Smolev, *Slovo k stoletiiu*, 16; N. I. Iudin, *Churikovshchina: Sekta "trezven-nikov"* (Leningrad: Znanie, 1963), 55.

10. Palamodov, *Imia moe greshnoe*, 56.

11. A letter from Grusha dated May 6, 1928, is one that describes Brother Ioann with saintlike qualities. TsGIA SPb, f. 680, op. 2, d. 47, l. 18ob.

12. Greene, *Bodies Like Bright Stars*, 163.

13. Petrov, *Sekta vyritskago poroka*, 34.

14. Terekhovich, *Kratkii biograficheskii ocherk*, 156.

15. "Stenogramma zasedaniia III Plenuma Leningradskoi oblasti Soveta Bezbozhnikov (March 1940)," TsGAIPD SPb, f. 27, op. 10, d. 539, l. 47ob.

16. Min'kov, *Moroshka*, 41.

17. Iudin, *Churikovshchina*, 50.

18. Iudin, *Churikovshchina*, 74–75.

19. GMIR, koll. I, op. 4, d. 60, ll. 1–4.

20. Lappo was officially rehabilitated on July 29, 1963. GMIR, koll. I, op. 4, d. 60, l. 5.

21. GMIR, koll. I, op. 4, d. 19, l. 215.

22. Dmitriev, *Povestvovanie*, 34.

23. Profile of A. V. Smirnova at "Pravoslavnye Trezvenniki Brattsa Ioanna Churikova," VKontakte, July 6, 2022, https://vk.com/club36765360.

24. Gijs Kessler, "The Passport System and State Control over Population Flows in the Soviet Union, 1932–1940," in "La police politique en Union soviétique, 1918–1953," special issue, *Cahiers du Monde russe* 42, nos. 2/4 (April–December 2001): 485.

25. Dmitriev, *Povestvovanie*, 34.

26. Plotnikov was amnestied after only six years. Testimony of Andrei Nechaev (Varfolomei Plotnikov's great-great-grandson), in "Trezvost' v samyi netrezvyi den'," Orthodox Society of Trezvenniki, accessed July 5, 2022, https://www.trezvograd.ru/01012018.

27. Dmitriev, *Povestvovanie*, 34.

28. William C. Fletcher, *Soviet Believers: The Religious Sector of the Population* (Lawrence: Regents Press of Kansas, 1981), 152–53.

29. For an example, see the testimony of Andrei Nechaev in "Trezvost' v samyi netrezvyi den'."

30. GMIR, koll. I, op. 4, d. 29, l. 41; see also V. Svetlova, "Mrakobesy," *Gatchinskaia Pravda*, May 29–30, 1963, 3.

31. Min'kov, *Moroshka*, 76; Beglov, *V poiskakh*, 177–79 and 184–85. See also Rock, "'They Burned the Pine, but the Place Remains All the Same,'" 164.

32. Jeanne Kormina, "'Avtobusniki': Russian Orthodox Pilgrims Longing for Authenticity," in *Eastern Christians in Anthropological Perspective*, ed. Chris Hann and Hermann Goltz (Berkeley: University of California Press, 2010), 275–76.

33. "Rasskaz Klavdii Vasil'evny Sedovoi," in Palamodov, *Imia moe greshnoe*, 207.

34. On the surge of elders during the Soviet period, see Paert, *Spiritual Elders*, 189–93.

35. Dmitriev, *Povestvovanie*, 7.

36. See Paert, *Spiritual Elders*, 150–51.

37. Aptekman, "Kritika," 239.

38. Panych, "A Time and Space of Suffering," 224.

39. According to recent fieldwork conducted by Maria Masagutova, trezvenniki in Vyritsa today continue to consider older members of the community—that is, especially those who survived persecution during the Soviet years—as "saints of the new religion." Maria M. Masagutova, "'Prekrasneishii trezvyi kovcheg': Blagopoluchie cherez samoogranichenie sredi posledovatelei Brattsa Ioanna Churikova" (MA thesis, European University of St. Petersburg, 2021), 103.

40. Dmitriev, *Povestvovanie*, 44.

41. Masagutova, "'Prekrasneishii trezvyi kovcheg,'" 8.

42. Memorial tributes to Vladimir Glinskii have been posted to the Petersburg community's website under "Ushel Podvizhnik trezvosti nashei dnei," accessed July 5, 2022, https://www.trezvograd.ru/single-post/%D1%83%D1%88%D0%B5%D0%BB-%D0%B2%D0%B5%D0%BB%D0%B8%D0%BA%D0%B8%D0%B9-%D1%87%D0%B5%D0%BB%D0%BE%D0%B2%D0%B5%D0%BA.

43. Masagutova, "'Prekrasneishii trezvyi kovcheg,'" 38. According to the Soviet researcher D. M. Aptekman, trezvenniki in the 1960s were already expressing belief in the possibility of reincarnation, or the transmigration at death of a soul from one person or animal into a new body. Aptekman, "Kritika," 237.

44. Komkov and Plotnikova, *Apostol trezvosti*, 208.

45. Smolev, *S brattsem i bez brattsa*; GMIR, koll. I, op. 4, d. 66.

46. After twenty-five years spent in a camp, Liadova returned to Leningrad and lived alone but remained an active participant in the trezvennik community until her death in 1978.

47. Nina Maslova's *Sbornik: Vospominaniia trezvennikov ob I.A. Churikova* (n.p., n.d.) can be found in GMIR, koll. I, op. 4, d. 62; Terekhovich's collection can be found in GMIR, koll. I, op. 4, d. 61; see also Min'kov, *Moroshka*.

48. The contents of these eight notebooks are available on the Vyritsa trezvenniki's website, accessed July 11, 2022, http://trezvost.com/Witnesses/All_Open_For_God_1_1.htm.

49. Palamodov, *Imia moe greshnoe*, 43–44.

50. Palamodov, *Imia moe greshnoe*, 44.

51. Ia. V. Plotnikov's testimony, from the website of the Orthodox Society of Christian Trezvenniki, accessed October 12, 2015, http://trezvograd.3dn.ru.

52. Min'kov, *Moroshka*, 76.

53. I. Voronov and B. Novikov, "Za zakrytnymi stavniami . . . pravda o churikove and churikovtsakh," *Gatchinskaia Pravda*, no. 136/6477 (July 12, 1959): 3–4.

54. Min'kov, *Moroshka*, 64.

55. Min'kov, *Moroshka*, 17. According to testimony in Liadova's collection, the tradition of burning notes dates back to the 1920s, when individuals petitioned Brother Ioann by note. For more on the meaning of this "tradition," see Masagutova, "'Prekrasneishii trezvyi kovcheg,'" 7–8.

56. V. Glinskii, "Emmochka," accessed January 2, 2013, http://slavache54.nichost.ru/ru/today/today-svidetel/po-vashim-stopam.che.

57. Kharkhordin, *The Collective and the Individual*, 313.

58. Aptekman, "Kritika," 223.

59. Masagutova, "'Prekrasneishii trezvyi kovcheg,'" 37.

60. When Ivan Smolev died, a photo of Brother Ioann was found around his neck, hidden evidently by his buttoned-up shirt. Dmitriev, *Povestvovanie*, 43.

61. Aptekman, "Kritika," 241.

62. Min'kov, *Moroshka*, 33.

63. "Vospominaniia Marii Iakovlevny," Orthodox Society of Christian Trezvenniki, accessed July 11, 2022, http://trezvograd.3dn.ru/publ/vospominanija_marii_jakovlevny/1-1-0-19.

64. "Svidetel'stva," in "Rasskazy o zhizni i deianykh I.A. Churikova," GMIR, koll. I, op. 4, d. 60, l. 34.

65. This was the case with Old Believers as well. Irina Korovushkina Paert, "Memory and Survival in Stalin's Russia: Old Believers in the Urals in the

1930s–50s," in *On Living through Soviet Russia*, ed. Daniel Bertaux, Anna Rotkirch, and Paul Thompson (New York: Taylor & Francis Group, 2003), 200–201.

66. Iudin, *Churikovshchina*, 50.

67. Kharkhordin, *The Collective and the Individual*, 317.

68. GMIR, koll. I, op. 4, d. 61, l. 31.

69. Maslova, *Povest'*, 25–26.

70. See, for example, E. A. Ermolova's testimony in Palamodov, *Imia moe greshnoe*, especially 180.

71. Maslova, *Povest'*, 53.

72. Aptekman, "Kritika," 244.

73. Aptekman, "Kritika," 243.

74. Aptekman, "Kritika," 244–45.

75. Aptekman, "Kritika," 246.

76. Aptekman, "Kritika," 248–50.

77. According to I. P. Tsamerian, writing in the 1960s, trezvenniki attended services "now and then" and received communion. Ivan Petrovich Tsamerian, *Stroitel'tsvo kommunizma i preodelenie religioznykh perezhitkov* (Moscow: Nauka, 1966), 103.

78. Min'kov, *Moroshka*, 78.

79. Min'kov, *Moroshka*, 79.

80. Aptekman, "Kritika," 233.

81. Quoted in Aptekman, "Kritika," 237.

82. A. Iu. Saperova, "Evoliutsiia obraza i obozhestvlenie osnovatelia obshchestva trezvosti Ioanna Churikova," *Religiovedenie*, no. 2 (2010): 58–64.

83. Dmitriev, *Povestvovanie*, 36–38.

84. "Bratets Ioann Samarskii (Ivan Alekseevich Churikov)," Orthodox Society of Trezvenniki, accessed July 5, 2022, https://www.trezvograd.ru/istoriy.

85. On this point, see the biographical insert on E. Liadova, in GMIR, koll. I, op. 4, d. 65.

86. Ivan Smolev, for example, received anonymous letters full of hate and calling him a sectarian. Dmitriev, *Povestvovanie*, 42.

87. Masagutova, "'Prekrasneishii trezvyi kovcheg,'" 60.

88. Autobiography of Pasha Angelina in Sheila Fitzpatrick and Yuri Slezkine, *In the Shadow of Revolution: Life Stories of Russian Women from 1917 to the Second World War* (Princeton, NJ: Princeton University Press, 2000), 307.

89. Emily Baran, "'I Saw the Light': Former Protestant Believer Testimonials in the Soviet Union, 1957–1987," *Cahiers du Monde russe* 52, no. 1 (January–March 2011), 171.

90. Terekhovich, *Kratkii biograficheskii ocherk*, 89.

91. Terekhovich, *Kratkii biograficheskii ocherk*, 68.

92. I. G. Smolev, "Nasha zadacha," September 30, 1964, published by Anatolii Obroskov, "Trezvennaia deiatel'nost' Brattsa Ioanna Churikova," Prosa.ru, accessed July 11, 2022, https://www.proza.ru/2009/10/13/693.

93. Maslova, *Povest'*, 67–68.

94. John 15:9, "As the Father has loved me, so have I loved you. Now remain in my love."

95. Smolev, *Slovo k stoletiiu*, 36. This included Brother Ioann's brush with death in 1923, addressed in Ivan Smolev, *Svoimi glazami: O bolezni Brattsa Ioanna* (Leningrad, 1961). For examples of his poetry, see Dmitriev, *Povestvovanie*, 27-28, and GMIR, f. 2, op. 17, d. 364, l. 5-5ob.

96. Smolev, *Slovo k stoletiiu*, 137-40.

97. Deborah A. Field, "The Moral Code of the Builder of Communism," Seventeen Moments in Soviet History, accessed July 5, 2022, http://soviethis tory.msu.edu/1961-2/moral-code-of-the-builder-of-communism/.

98. Smolev, *Slovo k stoletiiu*, 142.

99. Smolev, *Slovo k stoletiiu*, 67-68, 90.

100. Polly Jones, "Memories of Terror or Terrorizing Memories? Terror, Trauma, and Survival in Soviet Culture of the Thaw," *Slavonic and East European Review* 86, no. 2 (April 2008): 348-49.

101. After the arrest of some of the older sestritsy, she also served as the commune's secretary.

102. For example, her account includes the May 1924 report on the commune submitted by the local agricultural inspector, V. Shishkin (Maslova, *Povest'*, 37-39).

103. Maslova, *Povest'*, 21.

104. Maslova, *Povest'*, 17.

105. Maslova, *Povest'*, 21, 31.

106. Maslova, *Povest'*, 20.

107. Maslova, *Povest'*, 68.

108. Mark Edele, "More than Just Stalinists: The Political Sentiments of the Victors," in *Late Stalinist Russia: Society between Reconstruction and Reinvention*, ed. Juliane Furst (London: Routledge, 2006), 168.

109. Brueggemann, *The Prophetic Imagination*, 40.

110. Maslova, *Povest'*, 44.

111. Maslova, *Povest'*, 44-45.

112. Terekhovich, *Kratkii biograficheskii ocherk*, 139.

113. Terekhovich, *Kratkii biograficheskii ocherk*, 139.

114. Wanner, *State Secularism and Lived Religion*, 21.

115. Aptekman, "Kritika," 234-55, 340.

116. I. G. Smolev, "Nasha zadacha," September 30, 1964, published by Obroskov, "Trezvennaia deiatel'nost' Brattsa Ioanna Churikova."

10. Sober Truths during Late Socialism

1. Iudin, *Churikovshchina*, 3-4.

2. Dobson, "Social Scientist Meets the 'Believer,'" 81; Smolkin, *A Sacred Space Is Never Empty*, chap. 4.

3. N. Rusakov, "V religioznoi pautine," *Leningradskaia Pravda*, no. 204 (August 30, 1959): 2.

4. Fletcher, *Soviet Believers*, 3-4.

5. Smolkin, *A Sacred Space Is Never Empty*, 128.

6. Given his age, he was likely a veteran as well, although he does not mention this. Aptekman, "Kritika," 223.

7. Min'kov, *Moroshka*, 72–81.

8. Smolkin, *A Sacred Space Is Never Empty*, especially chap. 7 and the conclusion.

9. Voronov and Novikov, "Za zakrytnymi stavniami," 3–4.

10. Named trezvenniki included Dmitrii Egorovich Balashov, Gerasim Artem'evich Artem'ev, Evdokiia Garvilovna Komissarova, and Nadezhda Grigor'evna Miniaeva.

11. Voronov and Novikov, "Za zakrytnymi stavniami," 3–4.

12. Miriam Dobson, "Child Sacrifice in the Soviet Press: Sensationalism and the 'Sectarian' in the Post-Stalin Era," *Russian Review* 73, no. 2 (April 2014): 251.

13. Voronov and Novikov, "Za zakrytnymi stavniami," 3–4.

14. Dobson, "Child Sacrifice," 241–42.

15. See Benjamin M. Sutcliffe, "Introduction: Engendering *Byt* in Soviet Culture," in *The Prose of Life: Russian Women Writers from Khrushchev to Putin* (Madison: University of Wisconsin Press, 2009), especially 4–7.

16. Iudin, *Churikovshchina*, 4.

17. Iudin, *Churikovshchina*, 18, 26, 42.

18. Iudin, *Churikovshchina*, 12.

19. Iudin, *Churikovshchina*, 33.

20. Dobson, "Social Scientist Meets the 'Believer,'" 81–82. Baran, "'I Saw the Light,'" 172–73.

21. Iudin, *Churikovshchina*, 54.

22. Iudin, *Churikovshchina*, 52.

23. Iudin, *Churikovshchina*, 53.

24. Iudin, *Churikovshchina*, 54.

25. Iudin, *Churikovshchina*, 55.

26. While technically all members of the community could be held accountable, leaders were especially vulnerable. Fletcher, *Soviet Believers*, 3.

27. Iudin, *Churikovshchina*, 50–51.

28. Iudin, *Churikovshchina*, 59–60.

29. Iudin, *Churikovshchina*, 61–62.

30. Iudin, *Churikovshchina*, 61–63.

31. On the case of the public's reaction to the murder of a three-year-old by his Baptist mother, see Dobson, "Child Sacrifice," 252.

32. Dobson, "Child Sacrifice," 252.

33. Min'kov, *Moroshka*, 52. A similar observation would be made when the host of the popular television show *Vzglyad*, Sergei Bodrov, died young in an avalanche some years after calling trezvennichestvo a "sect." Masagutova, "'Prekrasneishii trezvyi kovcheg,'" 12.

34. "Otvet tomu, kto nazivaet sebia Tarasovym: eshche raz o Churikove i chuikovtsakh," *Gatchinskaia Pravda*, September 6, 1959, 3.

35. "Otvet tomu, kto nazivaet sebia Tarasovym," 3.

36. Svetlova, "Mrakobesy."

37. Svetlova, "Mrakobesy," 3.

38. Svetlova, "Mrakobesy," 3.

39. Svetlova, "Mrakobesy," 3.

40. Irina Korovushkina Paert, "Demystifying the Heavens: Women, Religion and Khrushchev's Anti-religious Campaign, 1954–1964," in *Women in the Khrushchev Era*, ed. Melanie Ilič, Susan Reid, and Lynne Attwood (Basingstoke: Palgrave Macmillan, 2004), 207.

41. Smolkin, *A Sacred Space Is Never Empty*, 153. See also Dragadze, "Domestication of Religion," 152.

42. Quoted in Deborah A. Field, "Mothers and Fathers and the Problem of Selfishness in the Khrushchev Period," in Ilič, Reid, and Attwood, *Women in the Khrushchev Era*, 103.

43. Quoted in Smolkin, *A Sacred Space Is Never Empty*, 147.

44. Fletcher, *Soviet Believers*, 13.

45. Smolkin, *A Sacred Space Is Never Empty*, 141.

46. Fletcher, *Soviet Believers*, 141.

47. Aptekman, "Kritika," iii. The research appeared first in a dissertation, and then in a shortened, published form in D. M. Aptekman, "K kharakteristike sovremmenogo sostoianiia religoznogo trezvennichestvo," in Klibanov, *Konkretnye issledovaniia*, 175–87.

48. Aptekman, "Kritika," xi.

49. Aptekman, "Kritika," 220–21.

50. Aptekman, "Kritika," 220.

51. Aptekman, "Kritika," 221.

52. Smolkin, *A Sacred Space Is Never Empty*, 130.

53. Dobson, "Social Scientist Meets the 'Believer,'" 88.

54. Aptekman, "Kritika," 241.

55. Aptekman, "Kritika," 253.

56. Aptekman, "Kritika," 222.

57. Dobson, "Child Sacrifice," 241–42.

58. Klibanov, *Konkretnye issledovaniia*, 82.

59. Klibanov, *Konkretnye issledovaniia*, 510–11.

60. Wanner, *State Secularism and Lived Religion*, 2.

61. Yurchak, *Everything Was Forever, until It Was No More*, 115.

62. Smolkin, *A Sacred Space Is Never Empty*, 134–35.

63. The testimony of Maria Iakovlevna Kotiurova can be found on the website of the Orthodox Society of Christian Trezvenniki, accessed July 5, 2022, http://trezvograd.3dn.ru/publ/vospominanija_marii_jakovlevny/1-1-0-19; all quotes and references are from this single text. Although it is not dated, she recorded her testimony between 1998 and 2010.

64. Maslova, *Povest'*, 60.

65. Yurchak, *Everything Was Forever, until It Was No More*, 131.

66. Juliane Fürst, "Love, Peace, and Rock 'n' Roll on Gorky Street: The 'Emotional Style' of the Soviet Hippie Community," *Contemporary European History* 23, no. 4 (2014): 565–87.

67. Fürst, "Love, Peace, and Rock 'n' Roll," 571.

68. Officials simply stopped recording consumption statistics in the early 1960s—that is, exactly at the same moment that they were incarcerating sober people. White, *Russia Goes Dry*, 32–33.

69. White, *Russia Goes Dry*, 41.

70. Elena Tupko, "Serdtsa poselka" [The Heart of the Village], *Ladoga plius*, September 4, 2015, https://ladoga-news.ru/news?id=10800.

71. Sasha's letter to the editor has been reproduced in its entirety as part of Kotiurova's testimony, published on the Petersburg community's website.

72. Maslova, *Sbornik*, GMIR, koll. I, op. 4, d. 62, l. 2–2ob.

73. GMIR, koll. I, op. 4, d. 62, ll. 2–2ob, 5.

74. Yurchak, *Everything Was Forever, until It Was No More*, 127–28.

75. Fürst, "Where Did All the Normal People Go?," 639.

76. Iudin, *Churikovshchina*, 62.

77. Smolkin, *A Sacred Space Is Never Empty*, 234.

78. Arkhiv UFSB, d. P-66724, t. 1, ll. 298–302.

79. Komkov and Plotnikova, *Apostol trezvosti*, 229.

Epilogue

1. Interview with "Evgenii," "Vera, pobezhdaiushchaia spid," recorded by K. Metodiev, *Novyi Peterburg*, no. 25 (June 16, 2005), Society of Spiritual Christian Trezvenniki, http://trezvost.com/Articles/Pray_winning_AIDS.htm.

2. Evgenii, aka "Zhenia," was profiled in another article by journalist Sokolov-Mitrich, "Zagovor trezvykh."

3. Interview with "Evgenii" (June 16, 2005).

4. Masagutova, "'Prekrasneishii trezvyi kovcheg,'" 44.

5. As quoted in Masagutova, "'Prekrasneishii trezvyi kovcheg,'" 48, n. 184.

6. Masagutova, "'Prekrasneishii trezvyi kovcheg,'" 38.

7. Masagutova, "'Prekrasneishii trezvyi kovcheg,'" 36.

8. Masagutova, "'Prekrasneishii trezvyi kovcheg,'" 110–11.

9. From an interview with Elena Rykovtseva, "Trezvye fanatiki: Ot Ioanna Churikova do Zaraba Tsereteli," Radio svoboda, August 7, 2008, https://www.svoboda.org/a/459733.html. The "Society" section of the Society of Spiritual Christian Trezvenniki website also claims that there are now communities in Vologda, Siamzha, Rybinsk, Cherepovets, Suzdal, Vyborg, Borovichi, as well as Krasnodar, Voronezh, Serdobsk, Zhitomir, and Kharkov; accessed July 11, 2022, http://www.trezvost.com.

10. Masagutova, "'Prekrasneishii trezvyi kovcheg,'" 123.

11. "Rossiia—Bermudskii treygol'nik," interview with Vladimir Nikolaevich Glinskii, Feodorovsky Cathedral, accessed October 19, 2012, http://www.feosobor.ru/db/459/.

12. "Vstrecha trezvennikov s Vladykoi Ioannom," Orthodox Society of Trezvenniki, accessed July 11, 2022, https://www.trezvograd.ru/mitropolit.

13. Sergei Palamodov, "Obshchestvo khristian-trezvennikov Brattsa Ioanna Churikova," Orthodox Society of Trezvenniki, accessed July 11, 2022, http://www.trezvograd.ru/.

14. "Rossiia—Bermudskii treygol'nik."

15. As quoted in Evgenii Perevalov, "Trezvost' na samyi netrezvyi den'," January 12, 1918, available on the website of the Orthodox Society of Trezvenniki, https://www.trezvograd.ru/01012018.

16. As quoted in Perevalov, "Trezvost'."

17. The Orthodox community's original website is trezvograd.3dn.ru, and the newer one is trezvograd.ru. There is considerable overlap between the two sites, but they are different in terms of both format and content.

18. From the main page of the Orthodox Society of Christian Trezvenniki, http://trezvograd.3dn.ru/.

19. "Sostoialas' konferentsiia 'Dvizhenie narodnykh trezvennikov,'" St. Petersburg Diocesan website, January 30, 2016, http://mitropolia.spb.ru/news/otdeli/?id=96843#ad-image-2.

20. Tamara Grigor'evna Khlynova converted to sobriety in 1968 and raised her three children as trezvenniki; today, both of her sons have joined the Orthodox clergy, and all three children have raised sober families, including seven grandchildren and four great-grandchildren. Khlynova's obituary was posted on July 19, 2021 on the social media site VKontakte, https://vk.com/club36765360; on Palamodov, see the St. Petersburg Metropolitan's website, accessed June 22, 2022, http://mitropolia.spb.ru/docs/sergey-yurevich-palamodov-rukopolozhen-vo-diakona.

21. Tupko, "Serdtsa poselka."

22. This includes workplace outreach. For example, Andrei Nechaev, who serves as the general director of the joint stock company Zavod ATI, a plastics and rubber manufacturer in St. Petersburg, began to introduce sober practices in his factory some twenty years ago and advises other companies who want to do the same. See his July 10, 2018, profile on the website Trezvaia zhizn', accessed December 18, 2022, http://trezvo.org/andrej-nechaev/.

BIBLIOGRAPHY

Archival Sources

Arkhiv UFSB: Arkhiv Upravleniia Federal'noi sluzhby bezopasnosti po Sankt-Peterburgu i Leningradskoi oblasti (Archive of the Administration of the Federal Security Service for St. Petersburg and Leningrad Oblast)

GMIR: Gosurdarstvennyi Musei Istorii Religii (State Museum of the History of Religion)

RGIA: Rossiiskii gosudarstvennyi istoricheskii arkhiv (Russian State Historical Archive)

TsGA: Tsentral'nyi gosudarstvennyi arkhiv Sankt-Peterburga (Central State Archive of St. Petersburg)

TsGAIPD SPb: Tsentral'nyi gosudarstvennyi arkhiv istoricheskikh politicheskikh dokumentov of St. Petersburg (Central State Archive of Historico-Political Documents of St. Petersburg)

TsGAKFFD SPb: Tsentral'nyi gosudarstvennyi arkhiv kinofotofono-dokumentov Sankt-Peterburga (Central State Archive of Documentary Films, Photographs, and Sound Recordings of St. Petersburg)

TsGIA SPb: Tsentral'nyi gosudarstvennyi istoricheskii arkhiv Sankt-Peterburga (Central State Historical Archive of St. Petersburg)

Primary Sources

Abramov, N. "'Bratets' Churikov i trezvenniki." *Petrogradskii listok*, no. 174 (June 27, 1916): 1–2.

——. "Churikov i missionery." *Petrogradskii listok*, no. 167 (June 20, 1916).

——. "Eshche o Churikove." *Petrogradskii listok*, no. 181 (July 2, 1916): 2.

Amba, Achmed. *I Was Stalin's Bodyguard*. London: Frederick Muller, 1952.

Ardi, Iu. "Tam, gde orudoval Churikov." *Bezbozhnik*, no. 15 (August 1929): 13–14.

"Arest moskovskykh 'brattsev' i missii." *Kolokol*, no. 1501 (March 29, 1911): 11.

Arsenii (Minin), Igumen. "'O 'Brattse Ioann' Churikove." *Groza*, no. 288 (December 13, 1911): 3.

——. "O novoiavlennom stolichnom lzhekhriste v litse imenuemago 'br. Ioanna' Churikova." *Missionerskoe obozrenie*, no. 2 (February 1912): 449–52.

Bekhterev, V. M. *Suggestion and Its Role in Social Life*. Edited by Lloyd H. Strickland. Translated by Tzvetanka Dobrev-Martinov. New Brunswick, NJ: Transaction Publishers, 1998.

"Beseda s I. Churikovym," *Dym otechestva*, no. 11 (March 13, 1914): 8–9.

Bonch-Bruevich, V. V. "Moskovskie trezvennniki." *Sovremennik*, no. 2 (1913): 299–315.

Chel'tsov, (Otets) Mikhail. "Churikovshchina." *Pribavlenie k tserkovnym vedomostiam*, nos. 51–52 (1912): 2088–2100.

Daniel, Wallace, ed. and trans. *Women of the Catacombs: Memoirs of the Underground Orthodox Church in Stalin's Russia*. Ithaca, NY: Cornell University Press, 2021.

Davydov and Frolov. *Dukhovnyi partizan protivu razvrata i p'ianstva (zashchitnik khristianstva): Bratets Ioann Alekseevich Churikov*. St. Petersburg, 1912.

Dmitriev, P. D. *Povestvovanie o Ivane Grigor'evich, napisano dlia druzei, kotorym doroga pamiat' o nem*. Leningrad, 1966.

Edgarton, William B., ed. and trans. *Memoirs of Peasant Tolstoyans in Russia*. Bloomington: Indiana University Press, 1993.

Eliashevich, I. Ia. *Pravda o churikove i churikovtsakh*. Leningrad: Leningradskii Oblastlit, 1928.

Iadrov, A. "'Bratets' Ivan Churikov," *Malen'kaia gazeta*, no. 79 (December 8, 1914): 3; no. 86 (December 15, 1914): 3; no. 93 (December 12, 1914): 3; no. 99 (December 29, 1914): 3.

Iasevich-Borodaevskaia, V. I. *Bor'ba za veru*. St. Petersburg, 1912.

Iudin, N. I. *Churikovshchina: Sekt "trezvennikov."* Leningrad: Znanie, 1963.

K voprosu o "Brattsakh": Spravedlivo li postupila Tserkov', otluchiv obshcheniia s soboiu "brattsev" Dm. Grigor'eva i Koloskova? Moscow, 1911.

Kesarev, Evgenii Vasil'evich. *Besednichestvo kak sekta*. Samara, 1905.

Klibanov, A. I., ed. *Konkretnye issledovaniia sovremennykh religioznykh verovanii (metodika, organizatsiia, rezul'taty)*. Moscow: Mysl', 1967.

Kondurushkin, S. I. "Bratets Ivanushka." *Rech'*, no. 290 (October 22, 1910): 2; no. 310 (November 11, 1910): 5.

Liadova, Emma Feliksovna. *Bogu vse otkryto*. Society of Spiritual Christian Trezvenniki. http://trezvost.com/Witnesses/All_Open_For_God_1_1.htm. Accessed July 11, 2022.

Lindeman, K. E., ed. *Sbornik rechei o trezvennicheskom dvizhenii, proiznosennykh v sobraniiakh Tsentral'nago Komiteta Soiuza 17-go Oktiabria v Moskve i Peterburge 5, 6, 13, 14 maia 1913*. Moscow, 1913.

Marovskii, V. "Bratets Churikov: 'Religioznyi durman.'" *Leningradskaia Pravda*, no. 224 (October 1, 1924); no. 228 (October 5, 1924); no. 287 (December 14, 1924).

Maslova, Nina. *Povest'*. Leningrad, 196–.

——. *Sbornik: Vospominaniia trezvennikov ob I.Ia Churikova*. N.p., n.d.

Mikhailov, A. T. *Koloniia trezvennikov*. Petrograd, 1914.

Min'kov, Vasilii Petrovich. *Moroshka*. Leningrad, 1986.

Moskovskye sektanty i moskovskie brattsy. Moscow, 1910.

Otchet o deiatel'nosti Obshchestva dlia rasprostraneniia religiozno-nravstvennago prosvesh-cheniia v dukhe Pravoslavnoi Tserkvi za 1906 i 1907 gg. St. Petersburg, 1908.

Pankratov, A. S. *Ishchushchie Boga.* Moscow: A. A. Levenson, 1911.

Petrogradskii spaso-preobrazhenskii koltovskii prikhod v 1915 godu. Petrograd, 1916.

Petrov, Pavel. *Sekt vyritskago poroka (trezvenniki-churikovtsy).* Kostroma, 1929.

Pis'ma Brattsa Ioanna Samarskogo (Churikova). St. Petersburg: Glagol', 1995.

Pis'mo sviashchennika Grigorii Petrova Mitropolitu Antoniiu. St. Petersburg, 1905.

Pozdniaev, M. "Vse nadezhda na 'brattsa': Fanatichno veruiushaia shkolnitsa otkazyvaetsia ot pomoshi vrachei." *Novye Izvestiia,* October 16, 2008.

Prugavin, A. S. *"Brattsy" i trezvenniki: Iz oblasti religioznykh iskanii.* Moscow: Kn-vo Zlatotsvet, 1912.

Roshchin, Andrei. *Kto takie sektanty?* Moscow: Molodaia gvardia, 1930.

"Rossiia—Bermudskii treygol'nik" (interview with Vladimir Nikolaevich Glinskii). Feodorovsky Cathedral. https://feosobor.ru/2006/07/vladimir-nikolaevich-glinskij-oni-pr-2/. Accessed December 2, 2022.

Runkevich, S. G. *Studenty-propovedniki: Ocherki Peterburgskoi religiozno-prosvetitel'noi blagotvoritel'nosti.* St. Petersburg, 1892.

Shishkin, V. F. *Tak sladyvalas' revoliutsionnaia moral': Istoricheskii ocherk.* Moscow, 1967.

Skvortsov, V. *Moskovskie sektanty i Moskovskie "brattsy."* Moscow, 1910.

Smolev, Ivan. *S brattsem i bez brattsa.* Leningrad, 1969.

——. *Slovo k stoletiiu so dnia rozhdeniia Brattsa Ioanna Samarskogo 1861–1961 gg.* Leningrad, 1961.

——. *Slyshit: Povest' o Fevral'skom voskresenii 1928 goda v Vyritse.* Leningrad, 1958.

——. *Svoimi glazami: O bolezni Brattsa Ioanna.* Leningrad, 1961.

Svetlova, V. "Mrakobesy." *Gatchinskaia pravda,* May 29–30, 1963, 3.

Terekhovich, Petr Gravrilovich. *Kratkii biograficheskii ocherk: Kak Ia poznal put' Gospoden' i sviatuiu trezvost' Brattsa Ioanna.* Leningrad, 1980.

Tregubov, I. M. *Mir s zhivotnymi, provozglashennyi narodnymi trezvennikami.* St. Petersburg: A. S. Prokhanov, 1910.

——. *Otzyvy doktorov ob istseleniiakh, sovershaemykh "bratstem" Ioannom Churikovym.* St. Petersburg, 1912.

Trezvograd.3dn.ru. Website of Pravoslavnoe obshchestvo khristian trezven-nikov Brattsa Ioanna Churikova (The Orthodox Society of Brother Ioann Churikov's Christian Trezvenniki).

Trezvograd.ru. Website of the Pravoslavnoe obshchestvo trezvennikov Brattsa Ioanna Churikova (The Orthodox Society of Brother Ioann Churikov's Trezvenniki).

Trezvost.com. Website of Obshchestvo dukhovnykh khristian trezvennikov Brattsa Ioanna Churikova (The Society of Brother Ioann Churikov's Spiritual Christian Trezvenniki).

Vasil'ev, M. "Trezvenniki." *Bogorodskaia rech',* no. 12 (March 17, 1913): 2–3.

Veniamin (Ieromonakh). *Podmena khristianstva.* St. Petersburg: V. M. Skvortsova, 1911.

Voronov, I., and B. Novikov. "Za zakrytnymi stavniami . . . pravda o churikove and churikovtsakh." *Gatchinskaia Pravda,* July 12, 1959, 3–4.

Zhivotovskii, S. "V Vyritskoi kolonii brattsa Ioanna Churikova," *Birzhevye vedomosti* n. 14036 (March 5, 1914).

Secondary Sources

Afanasyev, A. L. *Trezvennoe dvizhenie v Rossii v period mirnogo razvitiia. 1907–1914 gg: Opyt ozdorovleniia obshchestva.* Tomsk: TUSUR, 2007. http://www.litera tura.tvereza.info/01/Afanasiev/td1907-1914.html.

Alexopolous, Golfo. "The Ritual Lament: A Narrative of Appeal in the 1920s and 1930s." *Russian History* 24, nos. 1/2 (Spring–Summer 1997): 117–29.

Aptekman, D. M. "K kharakteristike sovremmenogo sostoianiia religioznogo trezvennichestvo." In *Konkretnye issledovaniia sovremennykh religioznykh verovanii (metodika, organizatsiia, rezul'taty)*, edited by A. I. Klibanov, 175–87. Moscow: Mysl', 1967.

——. "Kritika religiozno-eticheskikh vozzrenii i reaktsionnoi deiatel'nosti sekty trezvennikov." Doctoral dissertation, Gosudarstvennyi Universitet imeni A.A. Zhdanova, 1965.

——. "A Preliminary Characterization of the Contemporary Status of the Religious Temperance Movement." *Soviet Sociology* 8, nos. 3–4 (1970): 329–42.

Baran, Emily. "'I Saw the Light': Former Protestant Believer Testimonials in the Soviet Union, 1957–1987." *Cahiers du Monde russe* 52, no. 1 (January–March 2011): 163–184.

Beer, Daniel. "The Medicalization of Religious Deviance in the Russian Orthodox Church (1880–1905)." *Kritika: Explorations in Russian and Eurasian History*, n.s., 5, no. 3 (Summer 2004): 451–82. https://doi.org/10.1353/kri.2004.0035.

——. *Renovating Russia: The Human Sciences and the Fate of Liberal Modernity, 1880–1930.* Ithaca, NY: Cornell University Press, 2008.

Beglov, Aleksei. "Eschatological Expectations in Post-Soviet Russia." In *Orthodox Paradoxes: Heterogeneities and Complexities in Contemporary Russian Orthodoxy*, edited by Katja Tolstaja, 106–33. Leiden: Brill, 2014.

——. *V poiskakh "bezgreshnykh katakomb": Tserkovnoe podpol'e v SSSR.* Moscow, 2008.

Borisova, O. V., and S. M. Shinkevich, eds. "Otkrytoe pis'mo I.N. Koloskova sledovateliu VChK I.A. Shpitsbergu." *Viestnik Sviato-Filaretovskogo instituta* 40 (2021): 207–26. https://doi.org/10.25803/26587599_2021_40_207.

"Bratets Ioann Samarskii (Ivan Alekseevich Churikov)." Orthodox Society of Trezvenniki. https://www.trezvograd.ru/istoriy. Accessed July 5, 2022.

Brueggemann, Walter. *The Prophetic Imagination.* Minneapolis: Fortress Press, 2018.

Chulos, Chris. *Converging Worlds: Religion and Community in Peasant Russia, 1861–1917.* DeKalb: Northern Illinois University Press, 2003.

——. "Russian Piety and Culture from Peter the Great to 1917." In *Cambridge History of Christianity: Eastern Christianity*, edited by Michael Angold, 348–70. Cambridge: Cambridge University Press, 2006.

Clay, J. Eugene. "Orthodox Missionaries and 'Orthodox Heretics' in Russia, 1886–1917." In *Of Religion and Empire*, edited by Robert Geraci and Michael Khodarkovsky, 38–69. Ithaca, NY: Cornell University Press, 2001.

Coleman, Heather J. "Becoming a Russian Baptist: Conversion Narratives and Social Experience." *Russian Review* 61, no. 1 (January 2002): 94–112.

—. "Defining Heresy: The Fourth Missionary Congress and the Problem of Cultural Power after 1905 in Russia." *Jahrbücher für Geschichte Osteuropas*, n.s., 52, no. 1 (2004): 70–91.

—. *Russian Baptists and Spiritual Revolution, 1905–1929*. Bloomington: Indiana University Press, 2005.

Dixon, Simon. "The 'Mad Monk' Iliodor in Tsaritsyn." *Slavonic and East European Review* 88, nos. 1/2 (January/April 2010): 377–415.

—. "Superstition in Imperial Russia." *Past & Present*, no. 199, suppl. 3 (2008): 207–28.

Dobson, Miriam. "Child Sacrifice in the Soviet Press: Sensationalism and the 'Sectarian' in the Post-Stalin Era." *Russian Review* 73, no. 2 (April 2014): 237–59.

—. "The Social Scientist Meets the 'Believer': Discussions of God, the Afterlife, and Communism in the Mid-1960s." *Slavic Review* 74, no. 1 (Spring 2015): 79–103. https://doi.org.ezproxy.bowdoin.edu/10.5612/slavicreview.74.1.79.

Dragadze, Tamara. "The Domestication of Religion under Soviet Communism." In *Socialism: Ideals, Ideologies, and Local Practice*, edited by C. M. Hann, 148–56. London: Routledge, 1993.

Edele, Mark. "More than Just Stalinists: The Political Sentiments of the Victors." In *Late Stalinist Russia: Society between Reconstruction and Reinvention*, edited by Juliane Fürst. London: Routledge, 2006.

Engelstein, Laura. *Castration and the Heavenly Kingdom: A Russian Folktale*. Ithaca, NY: Cornell University Press, 1999.

—, "Personal Testimony and the Defense of Faith: Skoptsy Telling Tales." In *Self and Story in Russian History*, edited by Laura Engelstein and Stephanie Sandler, 330–50. Ithaca, NY: Cornell University Press, 2000.

Etkind, Aleksandr. *Khlyst: Sekty, literatura, i revoliutsiia*. Moscow: Novoe literaturnoe obozrenie, 1998.

Field, Deborah A. "The Moral Code of the Builder of Communism." *Seventeen Moments in Soviet History*. http://soviethistory.msu.edu/1961-2/moral-code-of-the-builder-of-communism/. Accessed July 5, 2022.

—. "Mothers and Fathers and the Problem of Selfishness in the Khrushchev Period." In *Women in the Khrushchev Era*, edited by Melanie Ilič, Susan Reid, and Lynne Attwood, 96–113. Basingstoke: Palgrave Macmillan, 2004.

Fitzpatrick, Sheila. *Stalin's Peasants: Resistance and Survival in the Russian Village after Collectivization*. New York: Oxford University Press, 1994.

Fitzpatrick, Sheila, and Yuri Slezkine. *In the Shadow of Revolution: Life Stories of Russian Women from 1917 to the Second World War*. Princeton, NJ: Princeton University Press, 2000.

Fletcher, William C. *Soviet Believers: The Religious Sector of the Population*. Lawrence: Regents Press of Kansas, 1981.

Freeze, Gregory. "Counter-Reformation in Russian Orthodoxy: Popular Response to Religious Innovation, 1922–25." *Slavic Review* 54, no. 2 (Summer 1995): 305–39.

——. "A Pious Folk? Religious Observance in Vladimir Diocese, 1900–1914." *Jahrbücher für Geschichte Osteuropas*, n.s., 52, no. 3 (2004): 323–40.

——. "Subversive Piety: Religion and the Political Crisis in Late Imperial Russia." *Journal of Modern History* 68, no. 2 (June 1996): 308–50.

Fürst, Juliane. "Love, Peace and Rock 'n' Roll on Gorky Street: The 'Emotional Style' of the Soviet Hippie Community." *Contemporary European History* 23, no. 4 (2014): 565–87. http://www.jstor.org/stable/43299691.

——. "Where Did All the Normal People Go? Another Look at the Soviet 1970s." *Kritika: Explorations in Russian and Eurasian History*, n.s., 14, no. 3 (Summer 2013): 621–40. https://doi.org/10.1353/kri.2013.0037.

Gorsuch, Anne. *Youth in Revolutionary Russia: Enthusiasts, Bohemians, Delinquents*. Bloomington: Indiana University Press, 2000.

Greene, Robert. *Bodies Like Bright Stars: Saints and Relics in Orthodox Russia*. Dekalb: Northern Illinois University Press, 2010.

Hann, Chris, and Hermann Goltz, eds. *Eastern Christians in Anthropological Perspective*. Berkeley: University of California Press, 2010.

Hedda, Jennifer. *His Kingdom Come: Orthodox Pastorship and Social Activism in Revolutionary Russia*. Dekalb: Northern Illinois University Press, 2008.

Heretz, Leonid. *Russia on the Eve of Modernity: Popular Religion and Traditional Culture under the Last Tsars*. Cambridge: Cambridge University Press, 2008.

Herlihy, Patricia. *The Alcoholic Empire: Vodka and Politics in Late Imperial Russia*. Oxford: Oxford University Press, 2002.

Herrlinger, Page. "Petitions to Brother Ioann Churikov." In *Orthodox Christianity in Imperial Russia: A Sourcebook on Lived Religion*, edited by Heather Coleman, 262–66. Bloomington: Indiana University Press, 2014.

——. "'Satan in the Form of an Angel'? The Russian Orthodox Church's Controversial Case against the Moscow *brattsy*, 1909 to 1913." *Religion, State and Society* 48 (June 2020): 196–212. https://doi.org/10.1080/09637494.2020.1765683.

——. "Trials of the Unorthodox Orthodox: The Followers of Brother Ioann Churikov and Their Critics in Modern Russia, 1894–1914." *Russian History* 40, no. 2 (2013): 244–63. http://www.jstor.org/stable/24667203.

——. *Working Souls: Russian Orthodoxy and Factory Labor in St. Petersburg, 1880–1917*. Bloomington: Slavica, 2007.

Himka, John-Paul, and Andriy Zayarnyuk, eds. *Letters from Heaven: Popular Religion in Russia and Ukraine*. Toronto: University of Toronto Press, 2006.

Husband, William B. *"Godless Communists": Atheism and Society in Soviet Russia, 1917–1932*. DeKalb: Northern Illinois University Press, 2000.

——. "Soviet Atheism and Russian Orthodox Strategies of Resistance, 1917–1932." *Journal of Modern History* 70, no. 1 (March 1998): 74–107.

Ilič, Melanie, Susan Reid, and Lynne Attwood, eds. *Women in the Khrushchev Era*. Basingstoke: Palgrave Macmillan, 2004.

Jones, Polly. "Memories of Terror or Terrorizing Memories? Terror, Trauma, and Survival in Soviet Culture of the Thaw." *Slavonic and East European Review* 86, no. 2 (April 2008): 346–71.

Kapalo, James A. *Text, Context and Performance: Gagauz Folk Religion in Discourse and Practice*. New York: Brill, 2011.

Kashevarov, A. N. *Pravoslavnaia Rossiiskaia Tserkov' i Sovietskoe Gosudarstvo (1917–1922)*. Moscow: Izdatel'stvo Krutitskogo Podvor'ia, 2005.

Keenan, Katherine, et al. "Social Factors Influencing Russian Male Alcohol Use over the Life Course: A Qualitative Study Investigating Age Based Social Norms, Masculinity, and Workplace Context." *PLoS ONE* 10(11) (2015): e0142993. http://doi.org/10.1371/journal.pone.0142993.

Kenworthy, Scott. *The Heart of Russia: Trinity-Sergius, Monasticism, and Society after 1825*. New York: Oxford University Press; Washington, DC: Woodrow Wilson Center Press, 2010.

Kessler, Gijs. "The Passport System and State Control over Population Flows in the Soviet Union, 1932–1940." In "La police politique en Union soviétique, 1918–1953," special issue, *Cahiers du Monde russe* 42, nos. 2/4 (April–December 2001): 477–503.

Kharkhordin, Oleg. *The Collective and the Individual in Russia: A Study of Practices*. Berkeley: University of California Press, 1999.

Kivelson, Valerie, and Robert H. Greene, eds. *Orthodox Russia: Belief and Practice under the Tsars*. University Park: Pennsylvania State University Press, 2003.

Kizenko, Nadieszda. *A Prodigal Saint: Father Ioann of Kronstadt and the Russian People*. University Park: Pennsylvania State University Press, 2000.

——. "Sacramental Confession in Modern Russia and Ukraine." In *State Secularism and Lived Religion in Soviet Russia and Ukraine*, edited by Catherine Wanner, 190–217. New York: Oxford University Press, 2012.

——. "Written Confessions and the Construction of Sacred Narrative." In *Sacred Stories: Religion and Spirituality in Modern Russia*, edited by Mark D. Steinberg and Heather J. Coleman, 93–118. Bloomington: Indiana University Press, 2007.

Knox, Zoe. *Russian Society and the Orthodox Church: Religion in Russia after Communism*. London: Routledge Curzon, 2005.

Kolstø, Pål. "The Demonized Double: The Image of Lev Tolstoi in Russian Orthodox Polemics." *Slavic Review* 65, no. 2 (Summer 2006): 304–24.

——. "'For Here We Do Not Have an Enduring City': Tolstoy and the *Strannik* Tradition in Russian Culture." *Russian Review* 69, no. 1 (January 2010): 119–34.

——. "A Mass for a Heretic? The Controversy over Lev Tolstoi's Burial." *Slavic Review* 60, no. 1 (Spring 2001): 75–95.

Komkov, M. P., and V. V. Plotnikova. *Apostol trezvosti: Ioann Alekseevich Churikov*. St. Petersburg: Aleteiia, 2014.

Kormina, Jeanne. "'Avtobusniki': Russian Orthodox Pilgrims Longing for Authenticity." In *Eastern Christians in Anthropological Perspective*, edited by Chris Hann and Hermann Goltz, 267–84. Berkeley: University of California Press, 2010.

——. "Russian Saint under Construction: Portraits and Icons of *Starets* Nikolay." *Archives de Sciences Sociales des Religions* 162 (April–June 2013): 95–119.

Krapivin, M. Iu, A. Ia. Leikin, and A. G. Dalgatov. *Sud'by khristianskogo sektantstva v sovetskoi rossii (1917-konets 1930-kh godov)*. St. Petersburg: St. Petersburg University Press, 2003.

Kuchumov, V. A. "Eldership in Russia: Some Consequences of the Petrine Reforms." *Russian Studies in History* 52, no. 1 (Summer 2013): 38-65.

Lebina, N. B. *Povsednevnaia zhizn' sovetskogo goroda 1920–30 gody*. St. Petersburg: "Letnyi Sad," 1999.

Lindenmeyr, Adele. "Building Civil Society One Brick at a Time: People's Houses and Worker Enlightenment in Late Imperial Russia." *Journal of Modern History* 84, no. 1 (March 2012): 1-39.

Luehrmann, Sonja, ed. *Praying with the Senses*. Bloomington: Indiana University Press, 2018.

——. *Religion in Secular Archives: Soviet Atheism and Historical Knowledge*. New York: Oxford University Press, 2015.

Luukkanen, Arto. *Party of Unbelief: The Religious Policy of the Bolshevik Party, 1917–1929*. Helsinki: Suomen Historiallinen Seura, 1994.

Manchester, Laurie. "Gender and Social Estate as National Identity: The Wives and Daughters of Orthodox Clergymen as Civilizing Agents in Imperial Russia." *Journal of Modern History* 83, no. 1 (March 2011): 48-77.

——. "Harbingers of Modernity, Bearers of Tradition: Popovichi as a Model Intelligentsia Self in Revolutionary Russia." *Jahrbücher für Geschichte Osteuropas*, n.s., 50, no. 3 (2002): 321-44.

——. *Holy Fathers, Secular Sons: Clergy, Intelligentsia, and the Modern Self in Revolutionary Russia*. Dekalb: Northern Illinois University Press, 2008.

Masagutova, Maria M. "'Prekrasneishii trezvyi kovcheg': Blagopoluchie cherez samoogranichenie sredi posledovatelei Brattsa Ioanna Churikova." MA thesis, European University of St. Petersburg, 2021.

McKee, W. Arthur, "Sobering Up the People: The Politics of Popular Temperance in Late Imperial Russia." *Russian Review* 58, no. 2 (April 1999): 212-33.

Meehan-Waters, Brenda. "To Save Oneself: Russian Peasant Women and the Development of Women's Religious Communities in Pre-Revolutionary Russia." In *Russian Peasant Women*, edited by Beatrice Farnsworth and Lynne Viola, 121-44. New York: Oxford University Press, 1992.

Mel'nikova, Ekaterina. *"Voobrazhaemaia kniga": Ocherki po istorii fol'klora o knigakh i chtenii v Rossii*. St. Petersburg: Izdatel'stvo Evropeiskogo Universiteta v Sankt-Peterburga, 2011.

Michelson, Patrick Lally, and Judith Deutsch Kornblatt, eds. *Thinking Orthodox in Modern Russia: Culture, History, Context*. Madison: University of Wisconsin Press, 2014.

Naletova, Inna. "Pilgrimages as Kenotic Communities beyond the Walls of the Church." In *Eastern Christians in Anthropological Perspective*, edited by Chris Hann and Hermann Goltz, 240-66. Berkeley: University of California Press, 2010.

Narskii, Igor'. *Zhizn' v katastrofe: Budni naselenie Urala v 1917–1922 gg*. Moscow: Rosspen, 2001.

Odintsov, Mikhail. *Russkaia Pravoslavnaia Tserkov' nakanune i v epokhu Stalinskogo sotsialisma 1917–1953gg*. Moscow: Rosspen, 2014.

Paert, Irina Korovushkina. "Demystifying the Heavens: Women, Religion and Khrushchev's Anti-religious Campaign, 1954-1964." In *Women in the Khrushchev Era*, edited by Melanie Ilič, Susan Reid, and Lynne Attwood, 203-21. Basingstoke: Palgrave Macmillan, 2004.

——. "Mediators between Heaven and Earth: The Forms of Spiritual Guidance and Debate on Spiritual Elders in Present-Day Russian Orthodoxy." In *Orthodox Paradoxes: Heterogeneities and Complexities in Contemporary Russian Orthodoxy*, edited by Katja Tolstaja, 134–53. Leiden: Brill, 2014.

——. "Memory and Survival in Stalin's Russia: Old Believers in the Urals in the 1930s–50s." In *On Living through Soviet Russia*, edited by Daniel Bertaux, Anna Rotkirch, and Paul Thompson, 192–211. New York: Taylor & Francis Group, 2003.

——. *Spiritual Elders: Charisma and Tradition in Russian Orthodoxy*. Dekalb: Northern Illinois University Press, 2010.

Palamodov, Sergei Iu. *Imia moe greshnoe pomyanite*. St. Petersburg: Aleteiia, 2011.

——. "Obshchestvo Khristian-Trezvennikov Brattsa Ioanna Churikova." Center for the Treatment of Alcoholism, "Revival." Accessed December 12, 2022. http://narkolog.inkiev.net/index.cgi?action=main&lang=ru.

Panchenko, A. A. *Khristovshchina i skopchestvo: Fol'klor i traditsionnaia kul'tura russkikh misticheskikh sekt*. Moscow: Ob'edinennoe gumanitarnoe izdatel'stvo, 2002.

Panych, Olena. "A Time and Space of Suffering: Reflections of the Soviet Past in the Memoirs and Narratives of Evangelical Christians-Baptists." In *State Secularism and Lived Religion in Soviet Russia and Ukraine*, edited by Catherine Wanner, 218–43. New York: Oxford University Press, 2012.

Patterson, K. David. "Typhus and Its Control in Russia, 1870–1940." *Medical History* 37 (1993): 361–81.

Peris, Daniel. *Storming the Heavens: The Soviet League of Militant Godless*. Ithaca, NY: Cornell University Press, 1998.

Pesmen, Dale. *Russia and Soul: An Exploration*. Ithaca, NY: Cornell University Press, 2000.

Primiano, Leonard. "Vernacular Religion and the Search for Method in Religious Folklife." *Western Folklore* 53, no. 1 (January 1995): 37–56.

Raikhel, Eugene. *Governing Habits: Treating Alcoholism in Post-Soviet Clinics*. Ithaca, NY: Cornell University Press, 2016.

Robson, Roy. *Old Believers in Modern Russia*. Dekalb: Northern Illinois University Press, 1995.

Roslof, Edward E. *Red Priests: Renovationism, Russian Orthodoxy, and Revolution, 1905–1946*. Bloomington: Indiana University Press, 2002.

Rousselet, K. "Utopies socio-religieuses et révolution politique dans l'années 1920." *Revue des études slaves* 69, no. 1 (January 1, 1997): 257–72.

Saperova, A. Iu. "Evoliutsiia obraza i obozhestvlenie osnovatelia obshchestva trezvosti Ioanna Churikova." *Religiovedenie*, no. 2 (2010): 58–64.

Scarborough, Daniel. "Missionaries of Official Orthodoxy: Agents of State Religion in Late Imperial Russia." In *Religious Freedom in Modern Russia*, edited by Randall Poole and Paul Werth, 142–59. Pittsburgh: University of Pittsburgh Press, 2018.

Shevzov, Vera. "Miracle-Working Icons, Laity, and Authority in the Russian Orthodox Church, 1861–1917." *Russian Review* 58, no. 1 (January 1999): 26–48.

——. *Russian Orthodoxy on the Eve of Revolution*. New York: Oxford University Press, 2007.

——. "The Struggle for the Sacred: Russian Orthodox Thinking about Miracles in a Modern Age." In *Thinking Orthodox in Modern Russia: Culture, History, Context*, edited by Patrick Lally Michelson and Judith Deutsch Kornblatt, 131–50. Madison: University of Wisconsin Press, 2014.

Smith, Stephen A. "Bones of Contention: Bolsheviks and the Struggle against Relics, 1918–1930." *Past & Present*, no. 204 (2009): 155–94.

——. "Masculinity in Transition: Peasant Migrants to Late-Imperial St. Petersburg." In *Russian Masculinities in History and Culture*, edited by Barbara Evans Clements, Rebecca Friedman, and Dan Healey, 94–112. New York: Palgrave, 2002.

Smolkin, Victoria. *A Sacred Space Is Never Empty: A History of Soviet Atheism*. Princeton, NJ: Princeton University Press, 2018.

Smolkin-Rothrock, Victoria. "Cosmic Enlightenment." In *Into the Cosmos: Space Exploration and Soviet Culture*, edited by James T. Andrews and Asif A. Siddiqi, 159–94. Pittsburgh: University of Pittsburgh Press, 2011.

——. "The Ticket to the Soviet Soul: Science, Religion, and the Spiritual Crisis of Late Soviet Atheism." *Russian Review* 73, no. 2 (April 2014): 171–97.

Sokolov-Mitrich, D. "Zagovor trezvykh." *Russkii reporter*, no. 26 (56) (July 11, 2008). https://expert.ru/russian_reporter/2008/26/trezvomolcy/.

Starks, Tricia. *The Body Soviet: Propaganda, Hygiene, and the Soviet State*. Madison: University of Wisconsin Press, 2008.

Steinberg, Mark D. *Petersburg, Fin-de-siecle*. New Haven, CT: Yale University Press, 2011.

——. *Proletarian Imagination: Self, Modernity, & the Sacred in Russia, 1910–1925*. Ithaca, NY: Cornell University Press, 2002.

Steinberg, Mark D., and Heather J. Coleman, eds. *Sacred Stories: Religion and Spirituality in Modern Russia*. Bloomington: Indiana University Press, 2007.

Steinberg, Mark D., and Catherine Wanner, eds. *Religion, Morality, and Community in Post-Soviet Societies*. Washington, DC: Woodrow Wilson Center Press; Bloomington: Indiana University Press, 2008.

Stites, Richard. *Revolutionary Dreams: Utopian Vision and Experimental Life in the Russian Revolution*. Oxford: Oxford University Press, 1989.

Stone, Andrew B. "'Overcoming Peasant Backwardness': The Khrushchev Antireligious Campaign." *Russian Review* 67, no. 2 (April 2008): 296–320.

Stone, Helena. "The Soviet Government and Moonshine: 1917–1929." *Cahiers du Monde russe et sovietique* 27, nos. 3/4 (July–December 1986): 359–79.

Strickland, John. *The Making of Holy Russia: The Orthodox Church and Russian Nationalism before the Revolution*. Jordanville, NY: Holy Trinity Publications, 2013.

Sutcliffe, Benjamin M. *The Prose of Life: Russian Women Writers from Khrushchev to Putin*. Madison: University of Wisconsin Press, 2009.

Tolstaja, Katja, ed. *Orthodox Paradoxes: Heterogeneities and Complexities in Contemporary Russian Orthodoxy*. Leiden: Brill, 2014.

Transchel, Kate. *Under the Influence: Working-Class Drinking, Temperance, and Cultural Revolution in Russia, 1895–1932.* Pittsburgh: University of Pittsburgh Press, 2006.

Tsamerian, Ivan Petrovich. *Stroitel'tsvo kommunizma i preodelenie religioznykh perezhitkov.* Moscow: Nauka, 1966.

Valliere, Paul. "Modes of Social Action in Russian Orthodoxy: The Case of Father Petrov's *Zateinik.*" *Russian History* 4, no. 2 (1977): 142–58.

Viola, Lynne. "The Peasant Nightmare: Visions of Apocalypse in the Soviet Countryside." *Journal of Modern History* 62, no. 4 (December 1990): 747–70.

——. *Peasant Rebels under Stalin: Collectivization and the Culture of Peasant Resistance.* Oxford: Oxford University Press, 1996.

Wagner, William R. "Female Monasticism in Revolutionary Times: The Nizhnii Novogorod Convent of the Exaltation of the Cross, 1917–1935." *Church History* 89, no. 2 (June 2020): 350–89.

——. "Orthodox Domesticity: Creating a Social Role for Women." In *Sacred Stories: Religion and Spirituality in Modern Russia,* edited by Mark D. Steinberg and Heather J. Coleman, 119–45. Bloomington: Indiana University Press, 2007.

Wallis, Roy. "The Social Construction of Charisma." *Social Compass* 29, no. 1 (1982): 25–39.

Wanner, Catherine. *Communities of the Converted: Ukrainians and Global Evangelism.* Ithaca, NY: Cornell University Press, 2009.

——, ed. *State Secularism and Lived Religion in Soviet Russia and Ukraine.* New York: Oxford University Press, 2012.

Werth, Paul. "Lived Orthodoxy and Confessional Diversity: The Last Decade on Religion in Modern Russia." *Kritika: Explorations in Russian and Eurasian History* 12, no. 4 (Fall 2011): 849–65. https://doi.org/10.1353/kri.2011.0044.

——. *The Tsar's Foreign Faiths: Toleration and the Fate of Religious Freedom in Imperial Russia.* Oxford: Oxford University Press, 2014.

Wesson, Robert. *Soviet Communes.* New Brunswick, NJ: Rutgers University Press, 1963.

White, Stephen. *Russia Goes Dry: Alcohol, State, and Society.* Cambridge: Cambridge University Press, 1996.

Winchester, Daniel. "Converting to Continuity: Temporality and Self in Eastern Orthodox Conversion Narratives." *Journal for the Scientific Study of Religion* 54, no. 3 (September 2015): 439–60.

Worobec, Christine D. "Cross-Dressing in a Russian Monastery: The Case of Mariia Zakharova." *Journal of the History of Sexuality* 20, no. 2 (May 2011): 336–57.

——. "Miraculous Healings." In *Sacred Stories: Religion and Spirituality in Modern Russia,* edited by Mark D. Steinberg and Heather J. Coleman, 22–43. Bloomington: Indiana University Press, 2007.

——. *Possessed: Women, Witches, and Demons in Imperial Russia.* Dekalb: Northern Illinois University Press, 2001.

Wynot, Jennifer Jean. *Keeping the Faith: Russian Orthodox Monasticism in the Soviet Union, 1917–1939*. College Station: Texas A&M University, 2004.

Young, Glennys. *Power and the Sacred in Revolutionary Russia: Religious Activists in the Village*. University Park: Pennsylvania State University Press, 1997.

Yurchak, Aleksei. *Everything Was Forever, until It Was No More: The Last Soviet Generation*. Princeton, NJ: Princeton University Press, 2006.

Zarembo, N. G. "Dukhovnye vlasti Sankt-peterburga i narodnoe trezven-nicheskove dvizhenie churikovtsev (1907–1914 gg.)." *Izvestiia Rossiiskogo gosudarstvennogo universiteta A.I. Gertsena*, no. 126 (2010): 30–35.

Zhuk, Sergei I. *Russia's Lost Reformation: Peasants, Millennialism, and Radical Sects in Southern Russia and Ukraine, 1830–1917*. Baltimore: Johns Hopkins University Press, 2004.

INDEX

Notes: Entries that include "Brother Ioann" refer to Churikov's deeds or thoughts in his capacity as a spiritual healer and preacher. Page numbers followed by "f" refer to figures.

CPSIA information can be obtained
at www.ICGtesting.com
Printed in the USA
LVHW040250230723
753116LV00027B/860/J